REA

ACPL ITEM
DISCARDED

D0789438

Contesting
Media Power

JUL 1 3 2004

Critical Media Studies
INSTITUTIONS, POLITICS, AND CULTURE

Series Editor
Andrew Calabrese, University of Colorado

Advisory Board

Patricia Aufderheide,
American University

Jean-Claude Burgelman,
Free University of Brussels

Simone Chambers,
University of Toronto

Nicholas Garnham,
University of Westminster

Hanno Hardt,
University of Iowa

Gay Hawkins,
The University of New South Wales

Maria Heller,
Eötvös Loránd University

Robert Horwitz,
University of California at San Diego

Douglas Kellner,
University of California at Los Angeles

Gary Marx,
Massachusetts Institute of Technology

Toby Miller,
New York University

Vincent Mosco,
Queen's University

Janice Peck,
University of Colorado

Manjunath Pendakur,
Southern Illinois University

Arvind Rajagopal,
New York University

Kevin Robins,
Goldsmiths College

Saskia Sassen,
University of Chicago

Colin Sparks,
University of Westminster

Slavko Splichal,
University of Ljubljana

Thomas Streeter,
University of Vermont

Liesbet van Zoonen,
University of Amsterdam

Janet Wasko,
University of Oregon

Recent Titles in the Series

Forthcoming in the Series

Contesting Media Power

Alternative Media in a Networked World

EDITED BY NICK COULDRY AND JAMES CURRAN

ROWMAN & LITTLEFIELD PUBLISHERS, INC.
Lanham • Boulder • New York • Toronto • Oxford

ROWMAN & LITTLEFIELD PUBLISHERS, INC.

Published in the United States of America
by Rowman & Littlefield Publishers, Inc.
A wholly owned subsidary of the Rowman & Littlefield Publishing Group
4501 Forbes Boulevard, Suite 200, Lanham, Maryland 20706
www.rowmanlittlefield.com

PO Box 317, Oxford OX2 9RU, United Kingdom

Copyright © 2003 by Rowman & Littlefield Publishers, Inc.

All rights reserved. No part of this publication may be reproduced, stored in a retrieval system, or transmitted in any form or by any means, electronic, mechanical, photocopying, recording, or otherwise, without the prior permission of the publisher.

British Library Cataloguing in Publication Information Available

Library of Congress Cataloging-in-Publication Data

Contesting media power : alternative media in a networked world / edited by Nick Couldry and James Curran.
    p. cm.—(Critical media studies)
Includes bibliographical references.
  ISBN 0-7425-2384-5 (cloth : alk. paper)—ISBN 0-7425-2385-3 (pbk. : alk. paper)
  1. Alternative mass media. 2. Mass media—Influence.   I. Couldry, Nick. II. Curran, James. III. Series.
  P96.A44 C66 2003
  302.23—dc21
                        2003004221

Printed in the United States of America

∞™ The paper used in this publication meets the minimum requirements of American National Standard for Information Sciences—Permanence of Paper for Printed Library Materials, ANSI/NISO Z39.48-1992.

Contents

PART IV: IN THE SHADOW OF CIVIL SOCIETY AND RELIGION

PART V: NEW MEDIA SPACES

Tables and Figures

Tables

Figures

Part I

INTRODUCTION AND THEORETICAL PERSPECTIVES

CHAPTER 1

The Paradox of Media Power

Nick Couldry and James Curran

To say that "the media are powerful" is a cliché, yet to ask in what media power consists is to open a riddle. Or so it seems. In the chapters that follow, we intensify this paradox by extending it to a global scale but also, through the rich comparative detail that is generated, aim to show that the paradox is more illusory than real.

One way of defining media power, if an unwieldy one, is as a label for the net result of organizing a society's resources so that the media sector has significant independent bargaining power over and against other key sectors (big business, political elites, cultural elites, and so on). This seems straightforward until one realizes that the media's bargaining power (for example, over the framing of a particular story) is of a curious sort: Media are unable to bargain over the basic rule of their existence, which is that they depend on "content" generated *by others*. (Or at least they did: One interpretation of the recent spread of celebrity stories and "reality" coverage in the press and television in the United States and Europe is that rising economic costs of news production have forced media to generate their own "contents" and treat them as if they were "external" reality.)

Here we come to the heart of the apparent paradox about media power, which derives from the fact that such power faces two ways. From one direction (the more common direction of analysis) "media power" is a term we use to point to how *other* powerful forces use the intermediate mechanism of media (press reports, television coverage, websites, and so on) to wage *their* battles (big business against labor, old professional and class elites against new cultural elites, and so on). From this direction, media power disappears; it is merely the door through which the contestants for power pass en route to battle. We find this approach, for example, in Manuel Castells's recent theory of the global "network society," in which he argues that in a space of accelerated information, people, and finance flows, the media portal is increasingly important for all social action, but the media themselves have no power as such (1997: 312–17). That this direction of analysis often has precedence is only to be expected; in studying the media's social role, our priority (whether as researchers or as social actors) may well be to analyze competing forces outside the media, whose conflict is waged in part through media coverage.

There is, however, another, equally valid direction of analysis from which media power does not disappear. This view holds that, contrary to the illusion that media only "mediate" what goes on in the rest of society, the media's representational power is one of society's main forces in its own right. From this perspective, media power (direct control over the means of media production) is an increasingly central dimension of power in contemporary societies (Melucci, 1996; Curran, 2002). It follows that, as with most forms of power, media power is not generally made explicit by those who benefit from it: the media. No wonder it is rarely the direct subject of public debate.

This second direction of analysis rejects the fallacy in traditional "fourth estate" conceptions of media and the liberal models based upon them. Far from media simply being there to guard us against the overweening influence of other forms of power (especially government), media power is itself part of what power watchers need to watch (see, for example, Curran and Seaton, 2003; Keane, 1991). On this view, even if we cannot imagine a society where media power is the *first* mover of social action (since without other forces, such as economic and political power, there would be nothing for media to represent), media power remains a very significant dimension of contemporary reality. In short, media power is *an emergent form of social power* in complex societies whose basic infrastructure depends increasingly on the fast circulation of information and images.

That, however, is not the end of the paradox. If we turn to the book's main subject—how power is contested under different but structurally comparable conditions across the world—it becomes obvious that media power is rarely the *explicit* subject of social conflict. This is not because media power isn't a "hard" type of power, like economic power, but rather because even "soft" forms of power (those relating to struggles over identity and respect, for example) involve conflicts whose main actors rarely fight for media power as such. Thus, for example, feminist struggles in the United States in the 1960s and 1970s sought to challenge patriarchy, thereby overriding any specific concerns about capturing media resources as a tool in that conflict.

This, however, is not the only possibility. As the reader will discover many times in this book, a conflict that appears initially to be about other forms of power turns out, in part, to be about relative control over society's representational resources (see, for example, the chapters by Gross, Lim, and Rodriguez). In some conflicts, parties may come to see their own relative lack of influence over how they are represented as being at stake in their struggle—or, at least, as Todd Gitlin (1980) described in his classic account of the 1960s U.S. student rebellions, as seeming crucial after the event. Contests over access to the means of media production are important, for example, in current antiglobalization battles.

The example of the global Independent Media Center movement and its role in antiglobalization struggles runs like a thread throughout this book (see especially the chapters by Bennett, Couldry, and Downing). Why does this example stand out? Perhaps because media power itself is an increasingly important *emergent theme of social conflict* in late modernity, as the mechanisms for representing social conflict themselves multiply. This is not the first time in history that media power has been explicitly contested; it was crucial to the French Revolution, to the slow social and cultural revolutions against Soviet rule in Eastern Europe in the 1970s and 1980s (Downing, 2001), and to the Iranian revolution of the 1970s (Sreberny-Mohammadi and Mohammadi,

1994). What was missing from those major conflicts was access by all sides to global means of self-representation, which could change the scale on which those conflicts were played out. The Internet, particularly through its linkages into traditional media, now gives any local actor the potential to reach global audiences (Hardt and Negri, 2000). As the scale-effects of media transform specific conflicts, it is possible that social actors may start to compete explicitly for influence over those scale-effects (that is, over media power). At the very least, a comparative look at how media power can be, explicitly or implicitly, contested in different places under different conditions is needed, as media studies attempt to globalize its discourse (Curran and Park, 2000).

Two Images

The shift between conceptions of media power that this book reproduces is captured through two contrasting images.

On the one hand, the media may be imagined as a waterfall whose intensity, size, and impact on the ground below (whose "power," in a word) depend almost entirely on the weight and direction of water collected on the land behind the waterfall; no one would say that the waterfall itself has "power," properly speaking, even though the particular configuration of rocks at the waterfall's edge would have a minor influence on the way water falls below. But that influence is infinitesimal compared with the mass and direction of water behind the waterfall. So too the term "media power" in traditional analysis is only a figure of speech for the media's role as a conduit for *other* forms of power, much larger than the media.

We, on the other hand, think of media power as more like a processing plant, built near the waterfall, and receiving all the diverted water and converting it into something quite different—first, energy and by-products of that energy, and, second, information on the amount of water farther upstream. Suppose that this water was the main energy source in our imaginary society; information about its pressure and volume would be vital for society as a whole. In this situation we *might* treat the processing plant as a "black box" and concentrate only on the flows across the plain, but this would be a great mistake. What about the efficiency of the processes that convert the water pressure into energy and the choices as to where that energy is sent, who controls it, and to what purpose? What if public readings of water flow are systematically inaccurate because the measuring instruments are incorrectly calibrated?

Here we see that the relationship between wider social forces (the flowing water) and media output (the energy and informational outputs of the processing plant) is not natural; it has nothing in common with a waterfall. So we must open up the "black box"—that is, enter the plant and study how decisions are made, who influences them and who doesn't, and analyze the consequences of those decisions (and exclusions) in the longer term. Once these questions are opened up, others follow; these are explored in the remaining chapters of part I (Bennett and Couldry).

This second image of media power invites us to think concretely about the *range of power sources* whose influence might be called upon to challenge the existing decision-making elite that runs our imaginary processing plant. Those wanting to challenge the processing plant's mechanism (which stands in, according to this image, for media power) might turn to *the state*. Part II of the book accordingly examines a range of perspectives on how the state directly or indirectly subsidizes challenges to existing configurations of media power. Another force, especially in countries dominated by market models of media provision (the majority of countries in the world), would be *the market*. Part III looks at how media markets of a certain complexity can generate, over time, alternatives to existing concentrations of media power. Yet another source of potential challenge would be the whole range of forces we call *civil society*, including various forms of religious organization and authority. Part IV looks at how particular elements of civil society have either become contestants for media power themselves or subsidized others to challenge media power.

Inevitably this scheme simplifies how different social forces compete explicitly or implicitly over the power represented by existing media institutions. Overlaps are crucial, of course, but we hope that the divisions around which the book is organized will highlight certain key comparisons.

Having considered the comparison between power sources on which challenges to media power might rely, we now need a different comparison relating to media technology. For our processing plant, we can imagine at least two different ways in which technological change might influence challenges to its media power: first, by enabling new types of processing plants, to be built as rivals, that divert water earlier or even extract energy in different ways and, second, by connecting the energy or information supply generated by the original processing plant to other processing plants across the world, thus perhaps linking the populations served by all those plants into a large-scale struggle. New media represent both types of change, affecting the local bases of media power and the scale on which it can effectively be contested. Part V considers various examples along these lines.

Before looking more closely at the detailed comparisons that emerge across the course of the book, we need to clarify one additional term: "alternative media."

Alternative Media: The Forgotten Land

The process we call "media" is the historic result of countless local battles over who has the power to represent the reality of others. Once such battles are won, they generally cease being remembered as battles. Who, for example, outside a small circle of media scholars, gives thought to the early days of dispersed radio production in the U.K. or France? The forward drive of media development not only foreshortens the past but obscures the present; yet in the shadow of even well-established concentrations of media power, contests continue to be fought for access to media resources or distributional opportunities. As social conflicts rise and subside, media power is frequently at least an incidental aspect of struggle; such was the case in the 1990s, when the broad front of popular protests against the long-standing conservative regime in Britain generated new press and video productions outside the mainstream (McKay, 1996). Yet media produced outside mainstream power concentrations have rarely received the attention of scholars; media studies has, for the most part, been content to treat the facts of media power as if they were necessities—indeed, natural features on the face of the media landscape.[1]

If media power itself is an increasingly significant theme of social conflict, then media studies should adjust its focus to include not only mainstream productions (major television and radio channels, film majors, the main Web portals, and so on) but also the wider terrain of media production, some of which seeks, explicitly or implicitly, to challenge central concentrations of media resources. This is what we mean by "alternative media" in this book: media production that challenges, at least implicitly, actual concentrations of media power, whatever form those concentrations may take in different locations.

This is not the only definition in use among researchers of nonmainstream media. The one that comes closest to our own is presented in Chris Atton's book *Alternative Media* (2002). John Downing (2001), the leading writer in this neglected field since the 1970s, prefers the term "radical media," as it highlights the role of nonmainstream media in contesting established power blocs with a view to wider social emancipation. A disadvantage of this second definition, however, is that it excludes from its understanding of "alternative media" any media on the right of the political spectrum, even those whose challenge to the concentration of media resources in central institutions is explicit and direct. Clemencia Rodriguez's (2001) concept of "citizens' media" develops Downing's notion of "radical media" in an interesting direction, by making explicit a link with forms of citizenship practice and empowerment, influenced in particular by Latin American theories of empowerment or "concientization" through education and more open communication (see also Rodriguez's chapter in this volume). Citizens' media, in Rodriguez's sense, is in effect a more politicized formulation of our own concept of alternative media; the two definitions are not incompatible. Nonetheless, for our purposes in this book, "alternative media" remains the more flexible *comparative* term, since it involves no judgments about the empowering effects of the media practices analyzed. What we bring together here may or may not be media practice that is politically radical or socially empowering; but in every case, whether indirectly or directly, media power is part of what is at stake.

"Media power" and "alternative media," then, are useful broad terms; they describe a vast range of media production activity, little of it familiar from media studies textbooks yet almost all closely embedded in everyday struggle by communities and individuals. In the final section of this introduction, then, let us explore what wider themes emerge from this complexity, whether as conclusions or as pointers to further research.

Media Power: A Landscape of Contestation

THEORIES AND CONTEXTS

The title of part I signals the more theoretical focus of the present chapter as well as chapters 2 and 3. In our use of "theoretical" here, however, we do not refer to the grand theory that "masters" all the empirical details of the later chapters; no such framework is possible yet, or perhaps ever. We mean only to signal that these opening chapters offer more generalized arguments that open up common questions across a range of local contests.

W. Lance Bennett's chapter on Internet-based global activism starts out from the paradox that corporate media power and concentration seem stronger than ever and the resources of global communication networks available to promote neoliberal discourse are larger than ever. How, then, can it also be true that new media (from mobile phones to digital radio to the Internet and the World Wide Web) are increasingly used by networks that aim to challenge the very same neoliberal discourse—often in spectacular fashion, as at the Seattle meetings of the World Trade Organization? To understand this, we must, Bennett argues, move beyond technological determinism in our accounts of new media and look to the "social, psychological, political, and media contexts" that give new media forms their elective affinity with new forms of protest. Without minimizing the Web's purely technical changes that allow protest groups to replicate across national borders with unprecedented speed, sometimes occupying the very same branded communication space that they are attacking (as with the campaigns against Coca-Cola and Starbucks that Bennett discusses), there must be more involved than technology. The answer, Bennett argues, lies in the cultural dimensions of globalization itself, particularly the globalization of markets and labor: the increasing fluidity and mobility of political identities, within and across national borders; a greater awareness of and engagement with the global scale of problems raised by corporate neoliberalism; and the increasing permeability of media distribution channels themselves to alternative, viral flows that spread countermessages at a speed deriving from the global reach of the very discourses they attack. This cultural and media "subpolitics" of globalization, as Ulrich Beck (2001) calls it, offers a particularly good fit with Internet-enhanced communication space.

In the subsequent chapter, Nick Couldry also seeks to uncover some contextual factors underlying possible new challenges to the concentration of media power. But Couldry is less interested in the successes of certain recent global mediated protests than in practices that contest media power as such. He scans the contemporary scene for signs of a new orientation to media and communication that challenges the traditional idea that these should be concentrated in a narrow sector of society. Here, like Bennett, Couldry foregrounds not technological change in isolation but broader cultural changes in people's thinking about media, specifically challenging the assumption that media production is an activity fundamentally separate from media consumption. Couldry develops two examples: the media philosophy of Matthew Arnison, who was crucial in developing the software on which the global Indymedia news website network relies, and the contrasting market-based philosophy of Paul Eedle, the co-founder of the Web news service "Out There News." Deciding which innovations will have long-range significance, he argues, is not the main issue at this stage; more important is identifying the factors likely to be crucial in any alternative media practice taking root over the long term.

THE FRAGILITY OF STATE SUBSIDY

The three chapters in part II pursue this question in relation to an obvious, but also problematic, source of encouragement for challenges to media power: the state. Each chapter concentrates on a country whose media history has been dominated by state-subsidized media: the U.K., Australia, and Sweden.

Chris Atton offers a sobering assessment of the long-term impact of the U.K. "infoshop" movement, which grew out of earlier state provision for the unemployed but sought to develop a base for political and social activism. Drawing on a rich range of social and political theory (from Alberto Melucci on "new social movements" to public-sphere analysis), Atton analyzes the trajectory of the Autonomous Centre of Edinburgh (ACE) in Scotland, which grew out of the Edinburgh Unemployed Workers' Centre. This originally state-sponsored centre was closed down in the 1990s, and its offshoot had to acquire premises in a poorer district, losing its previous links to local networks. While the new ACE's marginality removed it from direct state surveillance, its lack of resources—other than the "self-exploited" labor of a small group of activists and the proceeds of a small trade in punk music—constrained it from growing. Over the longer term the Centre has been unable to develop into a base for social resistance, neither expanding its membership nor developing a vision that could be communicated to a wider community. Atton's chapter indicates the long-term price that derives not so much from state subsidy itself as from the state's wider influences over socialization and cultural definition.

Christine Morris and Michael Meadows's chapter suggests a much more positive account of state subsidies to media operations among indigenous communities in Australia. But it is a story that offers little encouragement either to traditional top-down models of state media provision or to well-meaning but vacuous market-based notions of the "knowledge economy." Starting out by acknowledging the importance of communication (in Raymond Williams's sense) as "a central organizing element of Indigenous society," Morris and Meadows critique earlier ideas of how the state might encourage Indigenous media. Whereas earlier centralized schemes involved little consultation about local needs, the more successful recent developments these authors discuss (often very remote from conurbations) involve networks with a strong community impetus. Such networks respect traditional participatory forms of community management, with "intellectual property" based not on individual possession but on "responsibility and reciprocity." Underlying these is a new non-market-based concept of "knowledge management" that respects all community members' status as "knowledge workers" and their right to participate in decisions about how a communications infrastructure can be built. This is a positive answer to Bennett's question about the cultural contexts in which information and media technologies connect with social change.

Lennart Weibull's chapter examines one of the most potentially promising sites for state subsidy of the dispersal of media power. In Sweden since the late 1960s, the state has acted to redress what it saw as inherent market pressures toward press concentration. With a weak national press and Social Democratic newspapers particularly prone to market pressures, the Social Democratic government, after much public debate, began subsidizing newspaper delivery and production costs. In the longer term, however, that subsidy system appears not to have worked, failing to prevent the erosion of smaller newspapers because it was not pitched at a high enough level to outweigh market pressures exerted by other newspapers, advertising markets, and the increasing importance of other media as news and entertainment sources. The result, Weibull concludes, has been the limited long-term impact of an apparently laudable state attempt to mitigate the antidemocratic impacts of a newspaper free market.

Indeed, the implication of all the chapters in part II is that subsidies have only a limited effect in redressing the concentration of media power unless they are linked to community structures and practice.

THE AMBIGUOUS MARKET

If the Swedish state seems, on the face of it, a promising source of effective subsidy for a more even distribution of media power, the Californian marketplace would seem the opposite. However, as Rodney Benson shows, in the first chapter of part III, California's weekly press challenges assumptions that market pressures always work against alternative and politically contentious voices. The circumstances of the four San Francisco and Los Angeles weekly papers that Benson examines in his meticulous study vary of course, with only one (the *San Francisco Bay Examiner*) being financially independent from corporate influence. The radicalness of their contents also varies. While some give consistent attention to social activism and radicalism, others are positioned slightly to the right of the political spectrum, although they still give more prominence to socially focused news than does the commercial national press. What emerges, however, is evidence that under certain circumstances large media marketplaces may generate alternative voices quite effectively: The key factors here, Benson argues, are the social and cultural dynamics of the local journalistic field, the diffusion of radical politics among the wider readership, and the strength and diversity of the advertising market and its target audience. While affluent California offers a particularly favorable case, this account provides an important corrective to overly simple readings of the market's relation to media radicalism.

Andrea Press and Tamar Liebes take this argument into potentially even more hostile territory in discussing the fate of feminist discourse in Hollywood films of the 1990s. Yet the outcome is ambiguous. Even when we consider the particular constraints of the film industry, which, after all, must generate products that persuade people to leave the security of their homes, the visible influence of feminist ideas at the end of the century is disappointingly limited. Excluding film genres that are predefined as exclusively male (pure action or martial arts films), only a few notable advances have occurred. These, argue Press and Liebes, are significant but concentrated in areas such as police and legal dramas; an example is *The Silence of the Lambs*, in which, exceptionally, a desexualized role is available to the heroine. By contrast, in areas such as the stereotypically female genre of "romance," storylines represent a significant regression from the feminist films of the 1970s. At the same time, no exclusively "female" genre has emerged as a counterweight to the all-male genres.

While the first two chapters of part III consider difficult cases for alternative media subsidy and reach contrasting conclusions, Terhi Rantanen and Elena Vartanova's study of current developments in Russian media highlights an important national case where the dividing lines between state and market influences are less clear. Rantanen and Vartanova show that, in the semi-chaotic aftermath of the collapse of the Soviet

Union, a different organizational order is important—especially in terms of generating pressures in favor of, or away from, a weakened federal center. The consequence has been a very particular mix of global, national, and local influences, worked out across different media. The Russian press faced the dramatic collapse of state infrastructure, including the state printing industry, resulting in a sharp fall of circulation for national publications and the emergence of many local newspapers; this is a centrifugal force that the new Putin regime has only partly reversed. In broadcasting, by contrast, while regional television outlets are increasing, the continued structural link between state ownership and private funding remains crucial, with even market pressures (competing for advertising sources) reinforcing centripetal trends. It is too early to say whether the Internet will offer any alternative to these developments, since its emergence in Russia remains extremely uneven and metropolitan-focused. Russia thus emerges as the limit case for crude typologies of how support for alternative media emerges, since in locations where state and market infrastructure is itself underdeveloped or crumbling, a more complex picture must be studied in its local specificity.

THE CENTRALITY OF CIVIL SOCIETY

Part IV analyzes another source of alternative media subsidy: civil society. We understand civil society to include the whole range of social forces, whether secular or religious, in which alternative forms of authority and cultural influence can develop beyond the pull of state or corporate power.

Chin-Chuan Lee's chapter traces the successive stages whereby media liberalization emerged in Taiwan since the 1970s without resulting in a full political liberalization or a broad-based public sphere. The political magazines of this decade had close links with local civil society, unlike the Chiang Kai-Shek Kuomintang (KMT) regime they opposed, which represented a defeated mainland elite; ultimately, however, market forces dominated in this sector over political engagement. The history of television's expansion was also entangled in the last stages of resistance to the KMT regime, including the lightning spread of unauthorized cable television operations, albeit accompanied by the increasing penetration in Taiwan of Rupert Murdoch's Hong Kong–based Star TV. From 1992 on, however, underground radio offered a new focus of opposition coinciding with further splits in Taiwan's political parties. Though an exciting development that seemingly promised to challenge the inequalities of media power, the actual result, Lee argues, was to inflame ethnic antagonism. Looking back on Taiwan's intense relationship between media innovation and political conflict, Lee concludes that market and political pressures have led not to a genuine broadening of representation but to an increasingly fractured media space offering few prospects of further democratic change.

Clemencia Rodriguez's chapter presents a sharply contrasting account of media proliferation in a particular region, the Chiloé archipelago off the southwest coast of Chile. Despite Chile's exceptionally bloody national politics, this poor isolated region has seen a remarkable growth of community-based media; operating outside state and market forces, they rely instead on the cultural and social subsidy of the radical liberationist wing of the Catholic church. In Latin America, the Catholic church's authority as a social reformer derives from a combination of religious teaching and the secular educational philosophy of Paulo Freire's work on concientization (empowerment through community-based communication). And the Chiloé area in particular, where modern media came late, has benefited from the presence of an inspirational leader, Bishop Juan Luis Ysern. The result of Ysern's strategy has been not only a significant network of community radio stations but also a much more broad-based community-managed practice of media production and local self-education. By focusing on this specific issue, Rodriguez highlights an important general point: the necessity to ground the analysis of alternative media in the study of how media are used in actual community practice, so as to put into context the abstract audience ratings that dominate most accounts of which media matter.

Keyan Tomaselli and Ruth Teer-Tomaselli's account of the controversial history of the Catholic newspaper *New Nation* in apartheid and postapartheid South Africa offers a very different perspective on the Catholic church's global media politics. For while *New Nation* itself was influenced by liberation theology aimed at social change, it faced virulent opposition from Tradition, Family, and Property (TFP), a conservative overseas arm of the Brazilian Catholic church. TFP, in a temporary but initially powerful alliance with the threatened apartheid regime in the late 1980s, tried to eradicate *New Nation* in the context of the regime's wider battle to discredit the radical South African churches. *New Nation* itself drew on state subsidies, but from outside South Africa (that is, from the European Union and elsewhere); it also sought support from Freirean philosophies of communication. The long-term consequences of the end of apartheid for alternative media in South Africa remain uncertain, as external subsidies for *New Nation* were withdrawn, leading to its closure in 1997, and no new forms of subsidy for alternative media within South Africa have emerged.

The People's Republic of China, in turn, offers a different version of how battles for social and media power may be waged both within and across national borders. As Yuezhi Zhao's vivid study brings out, the spiritual movement Falun Gong, which in the 1990s became the leading voice against Chinese state authority, is no radical voice. On the contrary, after the movement had emerged from an intra-elite struggle over the direction of modernization, its increasing opposition to state power in the late 1990s was geared to social ends that are profoundly conservative. Falun Gong's media presence initially developed through a mixture of state and market subsidy, with a strong range of underground media outlets as well. But as Falun Gong was outlawed in China, it turned to the very different media resources of the Chinese diaspora in exile, waging a battle across U.S. media (cable television, books, press, websites) and increasingly, like left-wing movements, using the organizational potential of the Web to develop a media activism that has included hacking into Chinese state television. As Zhao's chapter makes clear, globally resourced media activism, while of major local political importance, need have no radical political potential.

NEW MEDIA: A SPACE OF HOPE?

Part V steps back from the sectoral question—From where in society is subsidy to alternative media likely to come?—to concentrate on the cultural and organizational possibilities of new media forms themselves. Of course, as many have pointed out, new media are not themselves radical, and it is particularly important here in this new terrain to look closely at a range of local developments.

In his chapter on the history of the Web-based current affairs site "openDemocracy," James Curran examines the specific potential of the Internet to open up new spaces of democratic engagement. Whereas economic and other factors have previously held back alternative media, the Internet lowers entry costs and lessens the importance of certain kinds of restricted managerial expertise. The question remains, however, whether the Internet's influence is emancipatory or not, to which Curran's answer is a qualified yes. In the aftermath of September 11, openDemocracy—initially a modest, relatively insular British pilot project—was transformed into a flourishing, international magazine, specifically because the Internet allowed for the speedy building of a global audience. However, the nature of this audience is problematic: If it is true that a global civil society is emerging on the Web, it is one that is segmented by interest and structured by inequality.

John Downing's chapter looks in detail at the dynamics of the Independent Media Center (IMC) movement, which many have regarded as one of the most significant alternative media developments at the end of the twentieth century. Without in any way discounting the technological importance of robust interactive software for the IMC movement's success in spreading beyond North America, Downing argues that this success needs to be understood in terms of its roots in the socialist anarchist tradition prevalent throughout the twentieth century, on the one hand, and its continued utopian promise, on the other. He traces the survival of such notions as community and self-organization, against very great odds, as well as the notion of "prefigurative" politics, which offers a further perspective on the community-based communication philosophies discussed in the chapters by Morris and Meadows and by Rodriguez. What gives the IMC story its special significance is its protagonists' increasing awareness of the importance and potential of developing globally based resistance and media participation outside the mainstream. The result, Downing argues, is a vision (with of course both potential and achieved reality) of media activism that is strategically astute as well as politically effective.

Larry Gross's analysis of the explosion of spaces for gay self-expression and communication on the Internet also insists on the positive potential of the vast new communication spaces that the Internet has opened up. The change is not confined, as Gross shows, to single countries in the West with privileged Internet access, but represents a truly international development covering gay virtual communities in much of the developing world (including India and China). Lacking social spaces around them where they can be open about their sexuality, countless gay men have found support in websites opened up by market pressures and the Internet's resistance to explicit censorship. Gross, however, refuses to see in these important developments an automatically positive outcome, since it is quite possible that the strands of social and indeed media activism in gay self-representation will recede as commercial and corporate pressures on the Internet play out. We return here to the ambiguity of media power as a submerged theme within social activism waged—sometimes necessarily, as here—through media forms.

The last two chapters shift our focus to mediated struggles in mainstream politics. Merlyna Lim explores a situation in which new media focused opposition at a time of political turmoil: the overthrow of Indonesia's President Suharto in 1998. Here, the influence of state media censorship was paramount. Lim's analysis centers on the basis of new media's influence in civil society (rather than on political parties, as in the subsequent chapter). What is striking about the campaign to topple Suharto, Lim argues, was its roots in new civil spaces that emerged very quickly around the *warnet*, the Internet-enabled version of the traditional Indonesian *warung* or street-side eating-house. Independently owned, small, and closely linked to neighborhood communication networks, *warnets* helped spread Web-based news and scandal among the whole urban population, including millions who themselves had no direct access to new media. Lim's analysis once again confirms the importance of looking, as Bennett advises, at the cultural and social underpinnings of particular challenges to media power. For in the region under discussion, this challenge operated only at the margins of media power's operations. It could not prevent subsequent corporate investment in the *warnet* sector, and Indonesia's new corporate-owned chains of Internet cafes are less closely linked to civil society.

Finally, Sharon Ling examines the intra-elite conflict within the Malaysian government over the succession to Prime Minister Mahathir Mohamad that led to the sacking of his deputy Anwar Ibrahim in 1999. This major political event was picked up in the heretofore weak alternative press, which, as in Taiwan, is closely linked to opposition parties that lack proper representation in the state-sponsored media. As Ling points out, whereas the Malaysian alternative press failed to articulate any genuine alternative political vision, partly because of the state censorship under which the press operates, Internet sites offered more resistance, often drawing on foreign news sources. The prospects for an alternative Internet sector in Malaysia remain highly uncertain, however, as state action targets the Internet as well.

Conclusion

This book presents, we suggest, a picture, inevitably tentative, of a contested global media landscape of immense breadth and complexity, far wider than usually allowed onto media studies' small screen. From *warnet* cafes in Indonesia to local educational media in Chile and Australia and community information centers in Scotland, to critical strands of fiction or news practice in the South African press, U.S. West Coast weeklies and Hollywood, to the ambiguous space of post–Soviet Russia's expanding media, we see a landscape of many battles through and over media power involving many social forces: global corporations, local entrepreneurs, local churches, even networks at street level.

Firm conclusions would be premature, although the inadequacy of analyzing state, market, or religious subsidies in isolation from broader changes (and potential subsidies) within civil society is already clear. We need, no doubt, further detailed work on the specific factors that enable or constrain challenges to media power in specific local conditions within the increasingly global frame of Internet-enhanced communication space. At the very least, we hope, this book will encourage others to continue that work.[2]

Notes

1. Media history is the one subarea of media studies where this is not true. The "Alternative Media" special issue of *Media History* (vol. 7, no. 2, 2001) provides a useful entry point to the fairly extensive historical literature on this topic.

2. We wish to record here our thanks to Richard Smith for his vital editorial assistance in the final stages of editing this book. Many thanks also to Brenda Hadenfeldt and Andrew Calabrese for their enthusiastic support of this book project, and to Alden Perkins for calmly guiding us through the production process.

References

Atton, Chris (2002). *Alternative Media*. London: Sage.

Beck, Ulrich (2001). *World Risk Society*. Cambridge, U.K.: Polity.

Castells, Manuel (1997). *The Power of Identity*. Oxford: Blackwell.

Curran, James (2002). *Media and Power*. London: Routledge.

Curran, James, and Park, Myung-Jin (eds.) (2000). *De-Westernising Media Studies*. London: Routledge.

Curran, James, and Seaton, Jean (2003). *Power without Responsibility,* 6th ed. London: Routledge.

Downing, John (2001). *Radical Media,* 2nd ed. Thousand Oaks, Calif.: Sage.

Gitlin, Todd (1980). *The Whole World Is Watching*. Berkeley: University of California Press.

Hardt, Michael, and Negri, Antonio (2000). *Empire*. Cambridge, Mass.: Harvard University Press.

Keane, John (1991). *The Media and Democracy*. Cambridge, U.K.: Polity.

McKay, George (1996). *Senseless Acts of Beauty*. London: Verso.

Melucci, Alberto (1996). *Challenging Codes*. Cambridge, U.K.: Cambridge University Press.

Rodriguez, Clemencia (2001). *Fissures in the Mediascape*. Hampton Press.

Sreberny-Mohammadi, Annabelle, and Mohammadi, Ali (1994). *Small Media, Big Revolution.* Minneapolis: University of Minnesota Press.

CHAPTER 2

New Media Power

THE INTERNET AND GLOBAL ACTIVISM

W. Lance Bennett

Prospects for contesting media power may appear to be smaller today than ever. Observers note a combination of global media trends that have diminished the quantity, quality, and diversity of political content in the mass media. These trends include growing media monopolies, government deregulation, the rise of commercialized news and information systems, and corporate norms shunning social responsibility beyond profits for shareholders (Bagdikian, 2000; McChesney, 1999; Herman and Chomsky, 1988). In the United States, the quest to deliver consumers to advertisers with low-cost content has dramatically shrunk the space for even mainstream news about politics, government, and policy (Bennett, 2003a; Patterson, 1993, 2000). The political space that remains is increasingly filled by news formulas based on scandal, mayhem, and personality profiles (Bennett, 2003a). These conditions are clearly less severe in systems with dominant public-service commitments, but even the venerable British news system has undergone substantial upheaval as commercial pressures have reduced news programming on private channels (Semetko, 2000) and the formidable BBC has entered a period of reinvention.

The unanswered question is: *Have these changes in media systems limited the capacities of groups contesting established power arrangements to communicate both among themselves and to larger publics?* Since political content space has been sacrificed to more commercially viable programming, it might be easy to conclude that political activists and minorities are even farther removed from the mass media picture. If this is the case, the political viability of new movements might be in doubt. As German political scientist Joachim Raschke put it, in starkly describing the importance of mass media for movements: "A movement that does not make it into the media is non-existent" (quoted in Rucht, forthcoming). Despite the hyperbole in this claim, there are notable cases in which media logic has undermined the viability and even changed the organizational coherence of movements (Gitlin, 1980).

D. Rucht (forthcoming) argues that stark generalizations about media and movements are difficult to support, as different protest eras have been characterized by different media patterns. William Gamson (2001) observes that media coverage of collective action movements even varies considerably from issue to issue. And, finally, media access varies with the public communication strategies and organization models adopted by cause movements, as indicated in a comparative analysis of abortion discourse in Germany and the United States (Feree, Gamson, Gerhards, and Rucht, 2002).

Adding to the theoretical challenge of generalizing about patterns of media power is the core question of just what we mean by "media" these days. With the fragmentation of mass media channels and audiences, and the proliferation of new digital communication formats, it is difficult to draw sharp boundaries around discrete media spheres. As various media become interactively connected, information flows more easily across technological, social, and geographical boundaries. Hence the subject of this chapter: the rise of global protest networks aimed at bringing social justice to the neoliberal world economic regime. These activist networks have used new digital media to coordinate activities, plan protests, and publicize often high-quality information about their causes. Considerable evidence suggests that global activists have figured out not only how to communicate with each other under the mass media radar but also how to get their messages into mass media channels (Bennett, forthcoming).

Many activists are sharply critical of mass media coverage, charging that the press and officials have criminalized their protest behaviors. However, it is also clear that global activists have been neither isolated nor destroyed by mass media filtering. The dense information networks of the Web offer ample evidence of internal communication. Large numbers of mass actions around the world have received extensive, if generally negative, media coverage. At the least, such coverage signals the presence of a movement that is demanding a say in world economic policies and their social and environmental implications. Moreover, numerous campaigns against corporate business practices, trade, and development policies have received favorable coverage in leading media outlets (Bennett 2003b, forthcoming). There is little evidence that global media have marginalized global protest. George Monbiot proclaimed in *The Guardian* that "the people's movements being deployed against corporate power are perhaps the biggest, most widespread popular risings ever seen" (quoted in Redden, 2001, n.p.).

In this chapter I explore the rise of global activist networks that have challenged mass media power. My analysis does not ignore the fact that many conventional media power relations still apply to the representation of the radicals and their causes. As noted above, news coverage of demonstrations, in both Europe and the United States, is often filled with images of violence and hooliganism. Most of that coverage makes little effort to describe the diversity of issues and demands in the movement—opting, instead, to lump them all together under the largely journalistic construction "antiglobalization." Nor have activists networked and communicated so effectively that they have somehow put global capitalism on the run. As Saskia Sassen (1998) points out, the preeminent uses of global communications networks remain the efforts of corporations and governments to strengthen the neoliberal economic regime that dominates life on the planet today.

All of this said, impressive numbers of activists have followed the trail of world power into relatively uncharted international arenas and found creative ways to communicate their concerns and to contest the power of corporations and transnational economic arrangements. In the process, many specific messages about corporate abuses, sweatshop labor, genetically modified organisms, rainforest destruction, and the rise of small resistance movements, from East Timor to southern Mexico, have made it into the mass media on their own terms (Bennett, forthcoming). Moreover, in developing direct power relations with global corporations, activists have exploited the vulnerability of carefully developed brand images by tagging them with politically unpleasant associations. The threat of holding brands hostage in the media spotlight has become an important power tactic in the fight for greater corporate responsibility (Bennett, 2003b).

This analysis is concerned with identifying *what conditions enable activists to use so-called new media—mobile phones, the Internet, streaming technologies, wireless networks, and the high-quality publishing and information-sharing capacities of the World Wide Web—to communicate the messages of their protest networks across both geographical and media boundaries.* The phrasing of this question is important to reiterate. I have talked elsewhere about *how* activists are using new media to promote their causes (Bennett, 2003b, forthcoming). But what is missing from my account thus far, and from many others as well, is an understanding of the social, psychological, political, and media contexts that make new media particularly conducive to enhancing the power of this global activist movement. To put the issue starkly: The Internet is just another communication medium. Admittedly, the Net has a number of distinctive design features and capabilities, but these differences do not inherently or necessarily change who we are or what we do together. However, personal digital media offer capacities for change if people are motivated by various conditions in their environments to exploit those capacities. In short, the question of whether we go shopping or make revolution on the Internet—and of how the shopping trip or the revolution compares with its less virtual counterparts—is more the result of the human contexts in which the communication occurs than the result of the communication media themselves (Agre, 2002). Accordingly, the remainder of this chapter addresses the interactions between new media and the social conditions that have enabled their uses for often impressive political ends.

Assessing the Political Significance of the Internet

Much of the attention to the Internet and politics has been directed where the least significant change is likely to occur: in the realm of conventional politics. Established organizations and institutions such as unions, political parties, governments, and election campaigns are likely to adapt new communication technologies to their existing missions and agendas. Thus, it becomes hard to see transformative effects beyond reducing the speed or cost of existing communication routines. However, in areas where new patterns of human association are emerging in response to new issues—and new forms of political action are developing as well—new communication options have the potential to transform both political organization and political power relations. (For a review of various political applications and effects of the Internet, see Graber, Bimber, Bennett, Davis, and Norris, forthcoming.)

As noted above, the recent period has been marked by impressive levels of global activism, including mass demonstrations, sustained publicity campaigns against corporations and world development agencies, and the rise of innovative public accountability systems for corporate and governmental conduct. All of these activities seem to be associated in various ways with the Internet. In some cases, the simple exchanges of information involved could also be accomplished by mail, phone, or fax. In these cases, the Internet simply enhances the speed and lowers the costs of basic communication—at least for those who have crossed the digital divide. In other cases, however, the Internet and other technologies, such as cellular phones and digital video, enable people to organize politics in ways that overcome limits of time, space, identity, and ideology, resulting in the expansion and coordination of activities that would not likely occur by other means. Even for those still on the other side, the digital divide can be crossed—in some cases, with the assistance of groups dedicated to transferring technology. For example, Greenpeace has made efforts to empower continuing victims of the Bhopal disaster.

Communication in distributed networks becomes potentially transformative when networks spill outside the control of established organizations. Networks that are not limited to the agendas of any of their members may, under the right conditions, become sustainable, growing democratic organizations. They may exhibit high-volume, simultaneous, interactive communication, complete with Web-based organizing and planning as well as hyperlinked public access to large volumes of politically diverse information.

When networks are not decisively controlled by particular organizational centers, they embody the Internet's potential as a relatively open public sphere in which the ideas and plans of protest can be exchanged with relative ease, speed, and global scope—all without having to depend on mass media channels for information or (at least, to some extent) for recognition. Moreover, the coordination of activities over networks with many nodes and numerous connecting points, or hubs, enables network organization to be maintained even if particular nodes and hubs die, change their mission, or move out of the network. Indeed, the potential of networked communication to facilitate leaderless and virtually anonymous social communication heightens the challenge involved in censoring or subverting broadly distributed communication even when it is closely monitored. These points are elaborated by Redden:

> The fact that it is a decentralised, distributed network currently makes it hard for any elite to control online activities. It allows fast one-to-one, one-to-many and even many-to-many communication in web and conferencing forums. Together, the technological and economic aspects of the Net allow for cheap self-publication without mediation by corporate publishing. . . . Of course, cheap is a relative term. The Net is cheap, not in absolute terms, but relative to the efficiency of message distribution. It is clearly not a panacea that guarantees freedom of speech for all. But while it is not accessible to everyone who has something to say, it *does* dramatically increase the numbers of people who can afford the time and money to distribute information translocally to large numbers of other people. In short, it allows individuals and community groups to reduce the influence gap between themselves and wealthier organizations. (2001, n.p.)

The capacity to transform time, space, costs, and the very roles of information producers and consumers also enables the rapid adaptation and transformation of political organizations, and the creation of new sorts of power relationships (Bennett, forthcoming). For example, a short but creative partnership between Adbusters (www.adbusters.org) and Greenpeace (www.greenpeace.org) created a counterimage campaign for Coca-Cola. One of the *subvertisements* featured Coke's polar bear icons— a mother and her cubs—huddled together on a melting arctic ice flow as Coke's fantasy consumer world suddenly merged with the harsh environmental effects of the gases (HFCs) employed by Coke in its cooling and bottling processes. As part of this power struggle, a rogue version of the company's actual website was created, and Coke's carefully crafted consumer icons were replaced with politically disturbing images, including the cowering bears. The threat of hijacking and subverting the company's branded environment during its biggest commercial event, the Olympics, led the company to make a quick business calculation and commit to changing the chemicals used in its manufacturing process. One can get a sense of the communication politics of this campaign by visiting the rogue site at www.cokespotlight.org. For a look at the Climate Change bears, click on *action* and then on *print a poster*.

What Kinds of Organizations Are Global Activist Networks?

The theoretical vocabularies used to describe hierarchical Weberian organizations or brokered political coalitions (e.g., McAdam, Tarrow, and Tilly, 2001) capture only part of the shifting social formations of vast, linked networks of individuals and organizations operating loosely but persistently to expand the public accountability of corporations, trade and development regimes, and governments. Yet it is not altogether clear how to characterize these networks. Even network theorists recognize that network structures are as varied as their social memberships and purposes (Wellman et al., 1996).

Some observers wax dramatic about the potential of vast Internet movements to organize and react rapidly to threats against human rights or planetary survival anywhere on the globe. For example, Richard Hunter has coined the term "Network army," which he describes as "a collection of communities and individuals who are united on the basis of ideology, not geography. They are held together by public communications, the Internet being a prime example. . . . Network armies don't have a formal leadership structure. They have influencers, not bosses who give orders" (quoted in Holstein, 2002, n.p.). The military metaphor is also employed by J. Arquilla and D. Ronfeldt (2001), who use the term "netwar" to describe the swarming behaviors of terrorists, criminal networks, and high-tech political militants. Another allusion to the distributed organizational impact of networked communication comes from technology popularizer Howard Rheingold, who has coined the term "smart mobs" to refer to people acting in concert on the basis of digital personal communication. He cites diverse examples of smart mob behavior that include the overthrow of Philippine President Estrada in 2001 with a series of demonstrations coordinated through cellphone messaging, the instant strategy and publicity by activists at the

World Trade Organization demonstrations in Seattle in 1999, and the planning of the September 11 terrorist attacks on New York and Washington (Rheingold, 2002; Schwartz, 2002).

Terms such as "network armies," "netwars," and "smart mobs" dramatize the transforming potential of new communication technologies, yet they seem inadequate to describe the emergence of loosely organized (segmented and independent, yet connected), geographically dispersed, and locally engaged collections of activists. The mob and army metaphors break down in part because they do not capture the daily activities of activists; at best, they (inadequately) refer to episodic collective outbursts. Beyond the occasional mass demonstration, activist networks are more likely to be found working on public information campaigns, negotiating standards agreements with the managers of companies, sharing information with other members of their networks, and finding ways to build local communities around social justice issues both at home and elsewhere.

Moreover, unlike armies, most global activist networks do not display a hierarchical command organization. And unlike mobs, they have considerably more refined communication and deliberative capacities. Perhaps the best account of the type of movement organization that enables vast networks to pursue diverse social justice goals on a global level is the SPIN model proposed by L. P. Gerlach and V. H. Hines (1968) and updated by Gerlach (2001). SPIN refers to movement organization types that are segmented, polycentric, integrated networks. *Segmentation* involves the fluid boundaries that distinguish formal organizations, informal groups, and single activists that may join and separate over different actions, yet remain available to future coordination. *Polycentric* refers to the presence of multiple hubs or centers of coordination in a network of segmented organizations. In their earlier formulation, Gerlach and Hine (1968) referred more explicitly to leadership, and used the term "polycephalous," referring to many heads. In recent years, Gerlach (2001) has noted an avoidance of formal leadership, as well as a preference for personal ties among activists that enable each to speak for the organization and to hold multiple organizational affiliations—hence, the shift to the term "polycentric." The *integration* principle has also evolved to reflect the horizontal structure of distributed activism. Ideologies figured more prominently in earlier movement accounts, in terms of both integrating and dividing groups (creating new segments). The requirement for ideological coherence seems far weaker in global activist circles today. The integrative function is provided by personal ties, recognition of common threats, pragmatism about achieving goals, and the ease of finding associations and information through the Internet. Inclusiveness has become a strong meta-ideological theme.

The resulting *networks* characterized by this segmented, polycentric, and integrated organizational form are not centrally or hierarchically limited in their growth or in their capacities to recombine around different threats or internal disruptions. Since the social network linkages are nonhierarchical, information exchange is relatively open. And the redundancy of links in segmented polycentric networks enables them to continue to function even when important organizations leave or change their roles. This is how Gerlach described the emergence of SPIN organization in global activism:

> Since at least the 1990s, an increasingly broad array of environmental rights, social justice, farm, and labor activists, as well as anticapitalist anarchists,

have worked in various ways to define multinational corporations and international banking, trade, and economic-development organizations as threats to human welfare and environmental health, because of their pursuit of global economic integration and growth. These activists promulgate their ideas about these global threats through personal contact, print media, and, especially, the Internet. Thus informed, the activists use major worldwide meetings of officials of the international community as forums to gather in protest and publicly communicate the threats they perceive. Their often militant demonstrations force responses from police and local governments, which then provide new opposition against which they can converge. One noted example took place in Seattle, Washington from late November to early December at a meeting of the World Trade Organization. (Gerlach, 2001: 300–301)

Limits on Definitions of Global Activism as a Movement

In a useful attempt to distinguish global activism from many other types of transnational political action, Sydney Tarrow (2002) offers an inventory of other patterns of activism on the world scene that are often mistakenly linked to globalization. In the process, he issues a warning about too-casual uses of globalization as an explanatory factor:

> Many forms of transnational activism—such as human rights, humanitarian aid, and justice against genocide and torturers—have little or nothing to do with globalization and much more to do with dictatorship, democracy, and the abridgement of human rights. By placing such movements under the global umbrella we risk obscuring their distinct origins and dynamics. I prefer to limit the term "globalization" to major increases in the interdependence of economic relations—a trend that has occurred several times in history (Tilly, 2002) and is by no means unilinear. What is perhaps distinct about it in our era is that it is accompanied by a partially-independent process, the creation of a web of international institutions and organizations. By reducing the causal chain of transnational politics to a by-product of globalization, analysts both risk ignoring a great deal of transnational activism that has nothing to do with globalization and ignoring the significant independent role of both state and international institutions in bringing people together across national boundaries. (Tarrow, 2002: 16–17)

These points are well taken. However, beyond their confines lies a protest movement that is uniquely engaged with the "partially independent process" at the root of national and international power shifts associated with economic globalization. Not only is this movement engaged with new sites of global economic power, but the activists associate in ways that reflect new globalization-related aspects of identity and resistance. Because of these patterns of association (some identified by Gerlach, above), these global activists have developed models for empowering uses of digital communication media that have not been employed by many of the groups that Tarrow rightly rules out of the globalization protest movement. Why some activists are pursuing more empowering applications of new communication technology, and others are not, is a question that involves their being rooted in very different (e.g., globalization versus state centered) social and political contexts. These contextual factors are developed theoretically in the next section.

Internet Empowerment:
Some Theoretical Generalizations

An obvious generalization is that networks of diverse groups could not be sustained without the presence of digital communication channels (e-mail, lists, organization and campaign websites, mobile phones) that facilitate information exchange, coordinate action, and establish electronic records of common cause. A related generalization is that the scale of protest on a global level seems impossible without the global communication and coordination capabilities of the Internet. A third generalization building on the first two is that the Internet enables both the diversity and the global scale of protest at greatly reduced costs of brokerage that are ordinarily attributed to the expansion of movement coalitions (McAdam, Tarrow, and Tilly, 2001).

Even more important for explaining the flexibility, diversity, and scale of this activism is the way in which the preferences for leaderless and inclusive networks is suited to the distributed and multidirectional capabilities of Internet communication. Communication within many of the organizations in these networks also reflects a similar decentralized, distributed model. An interesting example is the Indymedia (www.indymedia.org) activist information system analyzed by Downing in this volume. This system has grown from a single collective that produced live information during the "Battle in Seattle" in 1999, to nearly 100 affiliates around the world. While there is some hierarchical editing and writing of stories, Indymedia is remarkably true to its open-publishing commitment, which enables virtually anyone to become a reporter. This commitment to democratize the media is promoted in efforts to create open-source, automated systems for posting, archiving, editing, and syndicating networked information.

Another case involves the French organization ATTAC (www.attac.org), the Association for the Taxation of Financial Transactions for the Aid of Citizens. Founded in Paris in 1998, ATTAC has produced various national counterparts in Sweden, Germany, and elsewhere—counterparts whose agendas and political tactics all seem different. Even ATTAC's network in France has grown in ways that resist direction from central leadership in Paris, while the peripheral committees have elevated a variety of their own issues to the common agenda. Although a leadership group in Paris still takes actions in the name of the organization, the agenda of the organization reflects the churn of local initiatives and virtual deliberations. One result is that ATTAC has moved away from its initial chartering mission of securing a "Tobin" tax on world financial transactions to be returned to aid impoverished localities (Le Grignou and Patou, forthcoming).

Understanding Global Activism as a Product of Globalization

What the above examples suggest is that the rise of global activism—as reflected primarily in the coordination of issue campaigns and far-flung demonstrations—should not be attributed solely to the reduced communication costs of the Internet. A stronger theoretical proposition involves specifying what the activists bring to their digital interactions. I propose that the underlying social and political dynamics of protest have changed significantly due to the ways in which economic globalization has refigured politics, social institutions, and identity formation within societies. In particular, we should not take for granted the multi-issue linkages, the choice of transnational targets, the facelessness, the inclusiveness, or the global scale of this activism. These features of the global social justice movement may reflect the underlying social and psychological contexts in which both the activists and their Internet applications are embedded. In other words, digital personal media enable the fine linkages that connect people across time, space, and issues; but what opens growing numbers of activists to see so few temporal, spatial, political, or issue barriers in the first place? *What features of contemporary society motivate activists to form networks that are at once fluid, collective, and individualistic?*

Showing how domestic restructuring shapes the political outlooks and the communication styles of activists is a key element of our story, but there is more. Global communication infrastructures have also changed in important ways, enabling (1) the production of high-quality content by ordinary people, (2) the creation of large-scale interactive networks engaged by that content, (3) the transmission of that content across borders and continents, and (4) the convergence of media systems so that personal (micro media) content has more pathways through which to enter mass media channels. In these ways, the global change movement is empowered by the dual capacity of the Internet for internal and external communication. For example, the Internet attracts growing numbers of ordinary media consumers who may encounter activist information on the Net itself and in the growing interfaces between the Net and the mass media. This audience-building capacity of the Internet seems to differ from earlier activist internal communication (niche newspapers, mimeographed pamphlets, underground radio) by reaching audiences that frequently extend far beyond activist circles. One question that emerges here is: *What properties of digital media systems enable information to flow through the information layers of the Web until it reaches both consumers and producers of the mass media?*

Based on these considerations, the power of the Internet in global protest (and in many other political settings as well) can be traced to at least three important elements of its human context—the first two of which derive from the economic effects of globalization, and the third from the globalization of communication infrastructures:

1. the willingness of activists to share, merge, and tolerate diverse political identities;
2. the perception on the part of many activists that vast and complex problems have escaped the regulatory grasp of governments and nations, and that these problems require the scaling of protest activities across great reaches of time and space; and
3. the growing permeability of all media—mass and niche, old technology and new—to cross-cutting communication that enables viral messages to travel the newly configured bounds of cyber-time and -space (see point 2) and to reach large publics with identities that are open to the diverse experiences that global change has visited on many inhabitants of the planet (see point 1).

Why are these elements the most important contextual factors shaping the power of personal digital media in global activism? They happen to be, in my view, the three most important noneconomic correlates of globalization itself: the freeing of identity from the conforming dictates of modern organizations; the refiguring of time, distance, and place; and the construction of ever more sophisticated and interlinked communication networks that both drive and harmonize the first two factors. (For development of these ideas, see Giddens, 1991; Beck, 1999, 2001; and Castells, 1996, 1997.)

Putting Internet Politics in Context

Thus far, I have contended that the Internet is not inherently transformative of either human communication or social and political relations. Rather, it is the interaction between the Internet and its users—and their interactions, in turn, in material social contexts—that constitute the matrix within which we can locate the power of the new media to create new spaces for discourse and coordinated action. Our exploration of new media power thus entails a theoretical exploration of the three primary social, spatial, and communicational contexts in which the Internet is used.

GLOBALIZATION OF RESISTANCE: THE IDENTITY SHIFT

There is a burgeoning literature on how global economic change has affected the basic institutions of society (family, church, school, job, community) in ways that produce profound effects on individual identity. Anthony Giddens (1991) was among the first to recognize that these changes were both negative (producing stress, insecurity, complex life management issues, and personal responsibility-taking for structural problems) and positive (expanding personal freedoms to choose and change identities). What seems most important is that as identity bonds weaken from groups, people have less reason to create and maintain their identities through conventional (partisan, national, and ideological) forms of social conflict and exclusion.

The important (and not to be underestimated) exceptions, of course, are threatened traditional and conservative groups (Christian and Islamic fundamentalists, ethnic nationalists, etc.) in fragmenting modern societies. While reactionary groups struggle to hold the line on change, often by trying to impose threatened moral values on the rest of society, those who are more adaptive to the transformation of society often engage in remarkable explorations of self and identity: forming new types of families and new spiritual movements, exchanging world art and music, exploring new jobs and careers, attributing less importance to nation and government, and forming cosmopolitan ties with others in distant parts of the world.

As Tarrow (2002) notes, cosmopolitanism is not a new phenomenon. (The Silk Road and the Hansa League come to mind as examples from the past.) However, there does appear to be something of what he and his colleagues term a *scale shift* in recent times, implying both an increase in numbers of those with identifications and activities in transnational localities, and the emergence of a class of ordinary citizens who increasingly see the sites of their political action as ranging from local to global without necessarily passing through national institutions on the way. Tarrow characterizes global social justice activists as constituting a movement in contrast to other cosmopolitans who have long worked in international arenas to deliver disaster relief aid, to assess the conditions of immigrant populations, or to target specific states for human rights abuses: "I will, however, use the term *global justice movement* to apply to that coalition of environmental, human rights, developmental and protectionist groups and individuals who came together around the turn of the century against the injustices of the international financial system and its leading member, the United States" (Tarrow, 2002: 21).

R. Inglehart (1997) identifies those most likely to shift their identifications and interests away from conventional national politics as younger, more educated generations who have come into adult life during the advanced stages of globalization. I have discussed the ways in which these identity changes have resulted in a shift toward a *lifestyle politics* in which ideology, party loyalties, and elections are replaced with issue networks that offer more personal and often activist solutions for problems (Bennett, 1998). As identities become more fluid, and less rooted in geographical place (e.g., nation) and political time (e.g., the election calendar), individuals are both freer and under greater pressure to invent themselves and their politics.

It is important to recognize the structural roots of these broad identity changes. Ulrich Beck (2001) makes a distinction between the late-modern condition that he terms *individualization* and the older ideological concept of *individualism*. Individualization reflects the breakdown of one set of social welfare structures and their replacement by more direct market experiences with work, heath care, and other basic social needs. This restructuring of the individual experience makes the state less protective or useful, while at the same time freeing individuals to explore cosmopolitan, transnational political arrangements that may better address the problems in their current condition (Beck, 2001).

Old (modernist) labor and ideological activism continue in the present transitional phase of global change, yet the institutional foundations of such collective consciousness are eroding. This means that the social and identity principles underlying resistance itself need to be refigured as new generations of activists emerge. For example, Antonio Gramsci's classic assessment of the social foundations of political identity seem to poorly describe the ranks of the Direct Action Network, the Ruckus Society, Indymedia, and the many neo-anarchists joining protest networks today:

> In acquiring one's conception of the world, one always belongs to a particular grouping which is that of all the social elements which share the same mode of thinking and acting. We are all conformists of some conformism or other. . . . The starting point of critical-elaboration is the consciousness of what one really is, and is "knowing thyself" as a product of the historical process to date which has deposited in you an infinity of traces, without leaving an inventory. (Gramsci, 1971: 324)

J. H. Mittleman (2000) and many others (for example, Beck, 1999, 2001; Giddens, 1991) argue that globalization has transformed this process of group-based identity formation and resistance by altering the conditions of group life not just in the servant states of the global economy but in the dominant postindustrial democracies as well. As individuals experience social fragmentation, the ironic result is that the unexamined traces of group memberships become replaced with far more examined identity processes. People are more likely to discover the self as an active project involving reinvention, therapy, self-improvement, personal and planetary renewal, and spiritual quests. As collective identities expressed in ideologies become less useful in mediating and linking movement networks, individual activists are more able to identify with the experiences of "other" classes, causes, cultures, and places (Mittleman, 2000: 169).

The ease of identifying with distant and diverse partners in problem definition, solution, and cosmopolitan community is the engine that drives the process of individualization into new collective forms. The Internet happens to be a medium well suited for easily linking (and staying connected) to others in search of new collective actions that do not challenge individual identities. Hence global activist networks often become collectivities capable of directed action while respecting diverse identities. This diversity may create various problems for maintaining thematic coherence in networks (see Bennett, forthcoming) and for ensuring the capacity of outsiders—particularly those still embedded within modernist political contexts—to grasp the core concerns of the activists. Despite such vulnerabilities of networks, the power of the Internet is thus inextricably bound to the transformation of identity itself (Castells, 1997). This echoes the earlier claim that communication technologies cannot be understood without reference to the identities and symbolic interfaces of the people using them.

Despite the chaotic potential of SPIN-type networks, the diversity permitted by loosely linked communication nodes makes them both enduring and adaptive. Ideological motivation may still drive participants in their own spheres of action, but their coordinated activities need not be based on shared ideological understandings, or even on common goals. Moreover, unlike old-style coalitions of convenience, virtual activists need not be located in the same place or even threatened by the same root problem.

COFFEE ACTIVISM

An interesting example here is the North American Fair Trade coffee network, a broad collection of activists dedicated to creating a fairly priced market for coffee grown by small producers in various parts of the world. According to the activists, small farmers are rapidly being driven off their farms by price systems that favor large industrial growers who, not incidentally for our story, also tend to replace shaded coffee plantations with larger acreages of cleared land. For agribusiness interests, cutting the shade canopy means growing more robust beans that can be tended with more mechanized farming. For environmentalists and conservationists, this means killing species of songbirds that migrate from southern forests to North America each year.

The North American Fair Trade coffee network is currently led by a coalition of three organizations that have little in common ideologically. Yet they have developed a campaign to pressure American coffee retailers to subscribe to fair trade business standards and to promote fair trade coffee in their advertising and marketing. The following capsule account of this network follows an analysis by David Iozzi (2002), a student who has studied the network in detail. The three hubs of the coffee network are Global Exchange, a world development and social justice organization based in San Francisco; the Audubon Society, a national bird watchers and conservation organization with a staff person in the Seattle office dedicated to the campaign; and the Organic Consumers Association, an organic and health-food association based in Minnesota.

Global Exchange has developed a set of business standards suitable for North American coffee companies and, to secure compliance, has designed a campaign that threatens corporate brand images. This *logo campaign* (Klein, 1999) recognizes that complex political and economic arguments are hard to communicate across the identity boundaries of ordinary people who are most concerned with the quality of their immediate lifestyles. Enter the Audubon Society, which provides a "lifestyle symbol" for the campaign: birds. The Audubon Society is a credible information source for the claim that cutting the shade canopy to plant hardier, more economical Robusta beans destroys songbird habitat, thus reducing the numbers of songbirds migrating to the backyards of North America. Here we have a symbol that easily connects an aspect of many North American lifestyles (pleasant singing visitors in millions of parks and backyards) with corporate images of coffee as an integral part of a satisfying consumer lifestyle.

How were songbirds connected to a corporate logo? The initial target of this campaign was Starbucks, a Seattle-based international company that successfully marketed its coffee as an upscale lifestyle brand. Not just a hot caffeinated beverage (which would be difficult to sell at premium prices in far-reaching markets), a cup of Starbucks is worth far more when understood as a lifestyle experience. Entering a Starbucks puts one in a quiet world with quality product, surrounded by quality people, soothed by demographically chosen music (which can be purchased for home listening), and tempted by kitchen coffee gadgets to recreate the Starbucks lifestyle experience on mornings when one has the luxury of staying in.

Killing the songbirds that chirp in the backyard on that special Starbucks morning is not an image that the company wanted to have associated with its lifestyle brand.

It did not take the company long to do the math. Today, Starbucks has extended its brand to include the fair trade logo that appears on some of its coffees. It even displays humanitarian posters in some (test-marketed) locations, explaining the company's dedication to paying a fair price to the small growers who produce the high-quality beans on which the company's quality product depends. Thus, a political message that might not have penetrated the personal-symbol world of average consumers was attached successfully to a common consumer experience and, eventually, embraced by one of the chief corporate purveyors of that experience.

Typical of many protest networks, the organization and communication activities of the campaign were accomplished mostly through the Internet. This is where the Organic Consumers Association (OCA) comes in. The OCA powers the website through which protest activities are scheduled, organized, and scaled worldwide. For example, OCA labor makes it possible for Starbucks customers (both actual and potential) to find the campaign and to e-mail their indignation directly to Howard Schultz, founder and major shareholder of Starbucks, along with other company executives. What is the OGA's problem with Starbucks? Not the disruption of small farm economies. Not the threat to bird populations. Rather, Starbucks has been using genetically altered soybeans in its vegan lattés, and milk with bovine growth hormone in its cappuccinos. The OGA was able to attach its political messages to the fair trade and songbird discourses as people were brought through its website in the process of getting information, registering a virtual protest, or finding out about actual demonstrations.

As Starbucks expanded its locations around the world, the protest network followed with demonstrations. The OCA website announced that the Global Week of Action against Starbucks (February 23–March 2, 2002) led by the Organic Consumers Association was a success, with demonstrations held at over 400 Starbucks locations worldwide. OCA described it as the largest simultaneous global protest event of its kind in history. The demonstrations attracted activists motivated by one or more of the network causes. Despite the ideologically inchoate network, the collective negative focus on the company image (reinforced by a number of news reports linking the demise of songbirds to the coffee business) was enough to convince Starbucks management that its precious brand image was better served by embracing the activists' demands than by resisting them. In this fashion, network actions travel through time and space, following global targets while accommodating activists' diverse political identities and local community ties.

Redefining Political Time and Space: New Venues for Contesting Power

For many global activists, the boundaries of the personal world—social, political, and geographical—are fluid. Global problems can be found in virtually any locality—from the life conditions in export processing zones created in Mexico or Indonesia by distant corporations, governments, and trade regimes, to the loss of migrating songbirds in American and Canadian backyards. Beck (2001) has argued that both the arenas and forms of politics have been dispersed as economic restructuring has given business unusual degrees of power over domestic labor, environmental, tax, and social welfare policies. Threats to move elsewhere, close plants, and shift capital markets have been legitimized by world trade agreements, creating a sphere of what Beck calls "subpolitics," in which important issues are removed from national institutional agendas. As a result, national election and legislative calendars may be less important for activists to follow than the schedule of World Trade Organization or G-7 meetings.

New communication technologies enable this resistance to occur in new temporal and spatial terms. Part of what made the "Battle in Seattle" during the 1999 meetings of the World Trade Organization such a signal event was the simultaneous staging of dozens of other demonstrations around the world. M. I. Lichbach and P. Almeida (2001) document demonstrations concurrent with Seattle in at least eighty-two other cities, including twenty-seven locations in the United States, forty in other "northern" locations including Seoul, London, Paris, Prague, Brisbane, and Tel Aviv, and fifteen in "southern" locations such as New Delhi, Manila, and Mexico City.

The Internet was important not just in the organization of simultaneous protest; it contributed to the global imaging of those events. Demonstrations were linked by streamed Indymedia reports by activists themselves—reports that tied the activists together in a virtual political space. Mass media reports of the various local demonstrations put them in the context of the global event that shut down the WTO meetings in Seattle. Thus local actions were re-imaged in global network terms both for the activists and for the various global publics who witnessed them.

The capacity for simultaneous membership in local and global community again implies that old Gramscian notions of class and group foundations of consciousness and resistance must be refigured. Mittleman describes the technological refiguring of space, time, and social identification in communication terms:

> Contemporary social movements simultaneously occupy local, national, transnational, and global space as a result of innovations in, and applications of, technologies . . . which produce instantaneous communication across traditional frontiers. . . . The Gramscian framework of resistance thus must be stretched to encompass new actors and spaces from which counterhegemonic consciousness is expressed. (Mittleman, 2000: 169)

At least three distinctive aspects of this cosmopolitan consciousness are associated with the global contention of power. First, and most obvious, this resistance is less distinctively nationalistic than global in character—what Mittleman (2000: 169) terms "collective resistance transcending national borders." Second, the collectivism of this movement is less rooted in ascribed (Gramscian) social group memberships than in individual choices of social networks. Finally, this "collective individualism" is facilitated in part by discourses conceived less in ideological terms than in broad categories of threat, harm, and justice.

Deemphasizing ideological discourse also enables communication with broader "lifestyle publics" (Bennett, 2003b). The public political vocabulary of this movement is laden with *memes*—easily imitated and transmitted images that cross social networks because they resonate with common experiences, from enjoying the beauties of nature to personally identifying with branded products (Dawkins, 1989: 192; Lasn, 1999). "Starbucks protects songbirds/Starbucks harms songbirds" are good political memes (Bennett, 2003b, forthcoming). Whereas ideological communication restricts the flow of ideas to particular places (nations), groups (parties, unions, classes), times (elections), and spaces (party meetings, union halls), memes travel across the more fluid time and space possibilities of social networks and the Internet. An interesting example of this is the experience of a "culture jammer" named Jonah Peretti who visited the Nike Corporation shopping site and pushed the limits of its promised freedom to customize his personal Nikes by requesting that they send him shoes branded with the term "sweatshop." Suddenly, Nike's promise of personal freedom was merged with the image of exploited workers in distant factories of Asia.

Peretti sent an e-mail containing the amusing exchanges with Nike representatives (who repeatedly denied his requests) to a dozen friends, who forwarded the message to others. This "viral" communication spread exponentially until it was estimated to reach somewhere between several hundred thousand and fifteen million people around the globe (Peretti, 2001: 4). Culture jamming spreads ideas by playfully subverting the familiar ideas captured by popular cultural and commercial memes. Ideologies also rely on memes (for example, immaculate conception is a prime Christian meme), but ideology contextualizes memes to promote common understandings. When people in ideological movements differ in their interpretations of the core memes, the result is often factional segmenting or splitting. This contrast between culture jamming and more conventional ideology was evident in the reactions of some ideologues who received the Nike e-mail and contacted Peretti as its originator. He explains the source of ideological discomfort with culture jamming as follows:

> Culture Jamming is a strategy that turns corporate power against itself by co-opting, hacking, mocking, and re-contextualizing meanings. For people accustomed to traditional politics, Culture Jamming can seem confusing or even counter-productive. The following email is representative of the type of message I received from people who were uncomfortable with Culture Jamming: "Why do you want to support Nike and their immoral production of shoes and condemn them at the same time? I found your little dialogue immature and morally irresponsible. If you really think that sweatshop labor is wrong, then don't buy Nike shoes." (Peretti, 2001: 2)

Liberation from ideology creates the potential for crossing many social, cultural, and geographical boundaries because there is less need for the education, indoctrination, or physical force that often accompanies the spread of ideologies. Culture jamming memes compress the time of communication because they require little repackaging before they are communicated again. The memes that run through global activism networks also travel well because they ride on cross-culture carriers produced by globalization itself: brands, movies, music, celebrities. Thus, Monsanto was universally pilloried when a small Canadian activist organization dubbed its genetically modified line of sterile seeds "The Terminator." Such message packages require little elaboration. If someone asks how Starbucks harms birds, the answer is deforestation. The

Nike story can be reduced to a company branding itself around personal freedom, yet exploiting its own (contract factory) workers.

The transmission model for "viral" or "swarm" communication is not the old two-step flow from elites to group members but, rather, a networked, distributed flow in which the communication format (the meme), the communication technology (personal digital media), and the social contact (network) travel in chaotic yet patterned ways. This, I think, is what Manuel Castells (1996) means when he talks about the flow of spaces and the space of flows. Time and geography have been refigured by the introduction of new technologies and by the changing social boundaries that enable people to construct diverse social networks with those technologies. Following Richard Dawkins' (1989) formulation of memes, Peretti explained the global reach of his viral communication:

> Dawkins explains that some memes have "high survival value" and "infective power" while other memes die out quickly. In the context of emails, this means that some messages get erased while others get forwarded. The Nike Sweatshop meme had success because it appealed to several different demographics, including Culture Jammers, union organizers, teachers, parents, anti-globalization protesters, human rights advocates, religious groups, and people who simply enjoy a humorous prank. The Nike Sweatshop email thrived because it had access to such a wide range of different *social networks*. (Peretti, 2001: 3; original emphasis)

Network Communication and Media Flows

Peretti's Nike adventure shows how radical messages can leap from the seemingly remote spheres of micro media (e-mail, lists, personal weblogs) to mass media (newspapers, TV talk shows). Examples of micro-to-mass media crossover can be found in various antisweatshop campaigns against world brands such as The Gap and Nike. In one of those campaigns, the global activist organization Global Exchange used the Internet to coordinate demonstrations that featured a speech by an Indonesian factory worker in front of Nike stores across the United States. Global Exchange then applied good old-fashioned publicity strategies to induce the press to cover and frame those demonstrations in terms consistent with the activists' own preferred messages. The result was that Nike's image in the American mass media shifted from a glowing success model for corporate globalization to a sinister company with a dirty little labor secret (Bullert, 2000). Between 1996 and 1998, coverage of Nike in the leading American papers changed overwhelmingly from positive to negative. The company was virtually rebranded with the term "sweatshop" (Bennett, 2003b). In 1998, Nike CEO Phil Knight admitted that "the Nike Product has become synonymous with slave wages, forced overtime, and arbitrary abuse" (Herbert, 1998).

The digital public sphere for contesting media power would be far less important if it were sealed off from other communication channels in society. However, as noted above, the various media spheres are becoming increasingly porous. Researchers are beginning to pay attention to the pathways from micro-to-middle media that bring important messages in contact with mass media gatekeepers. The distributed property of the Web makes it difficult for news organizations to close the gates on provocative stories that competitors will be tempted to report if they don't. The rise of 24/7 cable news operations makes the demand for novel information high.

Jonah Peretti described the travels of his Nike e-mail exchange as it crossed from micro to middle to mass media. When reporters called him for interviews, he, in turn, interviewed them about their discovery of the story. They generally found it via e-mail from trusted friends, or on weblogs or webzines that they frequented for entertainment and new ideas. Such news material represents a novel break from the journalistic routine of reporting news manufactured from the inputs of government press offices, corporate public relations firms, and newsroom formulas. Peretti described the enthusiasm of the journalists who contacted him:

> Many journalists find themselves covering carefully scripted press conferences, or worse, converting corporate press releases into news stories. The Internet provides these disgruntled journalists with an opportunity to discover authentic stories. Reporter after reporter "discovered" the Nike Sweatshop meme, either as an email forward or on a site like Plastic.com, and it was clear from the tone of their voices that they were excited by this process of discovery. (Peretti, 2001: 8)

Conclusion

People who have long been on the receiving end of one-way mass communication are now increasingly likely to become producers and transmitters. With the advent of interactive communication and information systems, from Indymedia to the future BBC, the distinction between information producers and consumers will become increasingly difficult to draw. Moreover, people who have experienced what Beck (2001) termed the structural individuation of globalization are finding new ways of organizing collectively. As experiments with global citizenship go forward, the empowerment offered by distributed, networked digital communication may become shared more widely, warranting an important adjustment to media hegemony theories.

This theoretical adjustment does not contradict the perspective held by those who see globalization and deregulation of media content as direct threats to communicating diverse political messages to large audiences (McChesney, 1999). Indeed, the idea of media democracy is an increasingly important theme in global activist circles. Kalle Lasn (1999) of the culture jamming, anticommercial agency Adbusters (www.adbusters.org) has articulated the notion of *media carta* as one of five "meta-memes" for promoting planetary social justice. Lasn has encountered obstacles to running his *subvertisements* on commercial channels because broadcasters regard them as introducing dissonance into media environments that are carefully cultivated to support advertising (Lasn, 2002). Yet his organization's creative culture jams often make it into the mass media in other forms, akin to Peretti's Nike adventure above. These political openings are worth noting for what they reveal about the structure of media systems and their permeability.

The long-term picture of new media/mass media information flows is hard to project with much precision. Mass media news outlets are struggling mightily with changing gatekeeping standards due to demands for interactive content produced by audiences themselves. As consumer-driven content progresses beyond chats and click polls, new possibilities arise for high-quality political information governed by more democratic and less elite editorial standards. Technologically savvy activists are writing software that enables automated and democratic publishing and editing. Ordinary people are empowered to report on their political experiences while being held to high standards of information quality and community values. In the long run, these trends (see, for example, www.indymedia.org and www.slashdot.org) may be the most revolutionary aspects of the new media environment.

The Internet and other personal digital media have been a large part of the story related in this chapter. But the importance of these new media in contesting power involves more than just their sheer existence as new communication tools. The political impacts of emerging technologies reflect the changing social, psychological, and economic conditions experienced by citizens who use them.

References

Agre, P. (2002). "Real-Time Politics: The Internet and the Political Process," *The Information Society* 18(5): 311–331.

Arquilla, J., and Ronfeldt, D. (2001). "The Advent of Netwar (Revisited)," in J. Arquilla and D. Ronfeldt (eds.), *Networks and Netwars: The Future of Terror, Crime, and Militancy,* pp. 1–25. Santa Monica, Calif.: Rand.

Bagdikian, B. (2000). *The Media Monopoly,* 6th ed. Boston: Beacon Press.

Beck, U. (1999). *What Is Globalization?* Cambridge, U.K.: Polity.

——— (2001). *World Risk Society,* Cambridge, U.K.: Blackwell.

Bennett, W. L. (1998). "The Uncivic Culture: Communication, Identity, and the Rise of Lifestyle Politics," *PS: Political Science and Politics* 31(4): 741–61.

——— (2003a). *News: The Politics of Illusion,* 5th ed. New York: Longman.

——— (2003b). "Branded Political Communication: Lifestyle Politics, Logo Campaigns, and the Rise of Global Citizenship," in M. Micheletti, A. Follesdal, and D. Stolle (eds.), *The Politics Behind Products.* New Brunswick, N.J.: Transaction Books. Available online at www.engagedcitizen. org (under "Publications"). Last accessed on 1 April 2003.

——— (forthcoming). "Communicating Global Activism: Some Strengths and Vulnerabilities of Networked Politics," in W. van de Donk, B. D. Loader, P. G. Nixon, and D. Rucht (eds.), *Cyberprotest: New Media, Citizens and Social Movement.* London, Routledge. Available online at www.engagedcitizen.org (under "Publications"). Last accessed on 1 April 2003.

Braunstein, E. (2001). "From Sweatshops to Shopping Malls," *Shopping Center World,* September. Available online at http://shoppingcenterworld.com/ar/retail_hot_topic_sweatshops. Last accessed on 1 April 2003.

Bullert, B. J. (2000). "Strategic Public Relations, Sweatshops, and the Making of a Global Movement," Joan Shorenstein Center on the Press, Politics, and Public Policy, Harvard University, working paper no. 2000-12. Available online at www.engagedcitizen.org (under "Issue Campaigns, Nike"). Last accessed on 1 April 2003.

Castells, M. (1996). *The Rise of the Network Society.* Oxford: Blackwell.

——— (1997). *The Power of Identity.* Oxford: Blackwell.

Cleaver, H. M. (1998). "The Zapatista Effect: The Internet and the Rise of an Alternative Political Fabric," *Journal of International Affairs* 51(2): 621–40.

Dawkins, R. (1989). *The Selfish Gene.* Oxford: Oxford University Press.

Feree, M. M., Gamson, W. A., Gerhards, J., and Rucht, D. (2002). *Shaping Abortion Discourse: Democracy and the Public Sphere in Germany and the United States.* New York: Cambridge University Press.

Gamson, W. A. (2001). "Promoting Political Engagement," in W. L. Bennett and R. M. Entman (eds.), *Mediated Politics: Communication in the Future of Democracy*, pp. 56–74. New York: Cambridge University Press.

Gerlach, L. P. (2001). "The Structure of Social Movements: Environmental Activism and Its Opponents," in J. Arquilla and D. Ronfeldt (eds.), *Networks and Netwars: The Future of Terror, Crime, and Militancy* (pp. 289–309). Santa Monica, Calif.: Rand.

Gerlach, L. P., and Hines, V. H. (1968). "Five Factors Crucial to the Growth and Spread of a Modern Religious Movement," *Journal for the Scientific Study of Religion* 7(23): 23–39.

Giddens, A. (1991). *Modernity and Self Identity: Self and Society in the Late Modern Age.* Stanford: Stanford University Press.

Gitlin, T. (1980). *The Whole World Is Watching.* Berkeley: University of California Press.

Global Citizen Project (n.d.). Available online at www.globalcitizenproject.org. Last accessed on 1 April 2003.

Graber, D. A., Bimber, B., Bennett, W. L., Davis, R., and Norris, P. (forthcoming). "The Internet and Politics: Emerging Perspectives," in M. Price and H. Nissenbaum (eds.), *The Internet and the Academy.* New York: Peter Lang Publishing.

Gramsci, A. (1971). *Selections from the Prison Notebooks,* translated and edited by Q. Hoare and G. N. Smith. London: Lawrence and Wishart.

Herbert, B. (1998). "Nike Blinks," *New York Times*, May 28 (and nationally syndicated). Available online at www.globalexchange.org (search the Nike campaign archive). Last accessed on 1 April 2003.

Herman, E. S., and Chomsky, N. (1988). *Manufacturing Consent: The Political Economy of the Mass Media.* New York: Pantheon.

Holstein, W. J. (2002). "Online, the Armies Have No Borders." *New York Times*, April 28. Available online at www.NYT.com. Last accessed on 1 April 2003.

Inglehart, R. (1997). *Modernization and Postmodernization: Cultural, Economic, and Political Change in 43 Societies.* Princeton: Princeton University Press.

Iozzi, D. (2002). Case Materials and Analysis of the North American Fair Trade Coffee Campaign. Available online at www.engagedcitizen.org (click on "Undergraduate Research"). Last accessed on 1 April 2003.

Klein, N. (1999). *No Logo: Taking Aim at the Brand Bullies.* New York: St. Martins/Picador.

Lasn, K. (1999). *Culture Jam: The Uncooling of America.* New York: William Morrow.

——— (2002). Interview. Center for Communication and Civic Engagement. Available online at www.engagedcitizen.org (click on "Culture Jamming"). Last accessed on 1 April 2003.

Le Grignou, B., and Patou, C. (forthcoming). "The Expert Always Knows Best? ATTAC Uses of the Internet," in W. van de Donk, B. D. Loader, P. G. Nixon, and D. Rucht (eds.), *Cyberprotest: New Media, Citizens and Social Movement.* London: Routledge.

Lichbach, M. I., and Almeida, P. (2001). "Global Order and Local Resistance: The Neoliberal Institutional Trilemma and the Battle of Seattle." Unpublished manuscript, University of California Riverside Center for Global Order and Resistance.

McAdam, D., Tarrow, S., and Tilly, C. (2001). *Dynamics of Contention*. New York: Cambridge University Press.

McChesney, R. W. (1999). *Rich Media, Poor Democracy: Communication Politics in Dubious Times*. Urbana: University of Illinois Press.

Mittleman, J. H. (2000). *The Globalization Syndrome: Transformation and Resistance*. Princeton: Princeton University Press.

Organic Consumers Association. (n.d.). Available online at www.organicconsumers.org. Last accessed on 1 April 2003.

Patterson, T. E. (1993). *Out of Order*. New York: Knopf.

——— (2000). "Doing Well and Doing Good: How Soft News and Critical Journalism Are Shrinking the News Audience and Weakening Democracy—and What New Outlets Can Do About It," Cambridge, Mass.: Harvard University, Joan Shorenstein Center on Press, Politics, and Public Policy, Kennedy School of Government.

Peretti, J. (2001). "Culture Jamming, Memes, Social Networks, and the Emerging Media Ecology," Center for Communication and Civic Engagement, University of Washington. Available online at www.engagedcitizen.org (indexed in the section on "Culture Jamming"). Last accessed on 1 April 2003.

Redden, G. (2001). "Networking Dissent: The Internet and the Anti-Globalization Movement," *MotsPluriels*, no 18, August. Available online at www.arts.uwa.edu.au/MotsPluriels/MP1801gr.html. Last accessed on 1 April 2003.

Rheingold, H. (2002). *Smart Mobs: The Next Social Revolution*. New York: Perseus.

Rucht, D. (Forthcoming). "Media Strategies of Protest Movements Since the 1960s," in W. van de Donk, B. D. Loader, P. G. Nixon, and D. Rucht (eds.), *Cyberprotest: New Media, Citizens and Social Movements*. London, Routledge.

Sassen, S. (1998). *Globalization and Its Discontents*. New York: New Press.

Schwartz, J. (2002). "Motivating the Masses, Wirelessly." *New York Times*, July 22. Available online at www.NYT.com. Last accessed on 1 April 2003.

Semetko, H. (2000). "Great Britain: The End of News at Ten, and the Changing News Environment," in R. Gunther and A. Mughan (eds.), *Democracy and the Media: A Comparative Perspective*, pp. 343–74. Cambridge: Cambridge University Press.

Tarrow, S. (1998). "Fishnets, Internets, and Catnets: Globalization and Transnational Collective Action," in M. P. Hanagan, L. P. Moch, and W. Brake (eds.)., *Challenging Authority: The Historical Study of Contentious Politics*. Minneapolis, University of Minnesota Press.

——— (2002). *Rooted Cosmopolitans: Transnational Activists in a World of States*, unpublished manuscript (chapter 1).

Tilly, C. (2003). "Past, Present, and Future Globalizations," draft chapter for Gita Steiner-Khamsi (ed.), *Lessons from Elsewhere: The Politics of Educational Borrowing and Lending*. New York: Teachers College Press.

Wellman, B., Salaff, J., Dimitrova, D., Garton, L., Gulia, M., and Haythornthwaite, C. (1996). "Computer Networks as Social Networks," *Annual Review of Sociology* 22: 213–38.

CHAPTER 3

Beyond the Hall of Mirrors?

SOME THEORETICAL REFLECTIONS ON THE GLOBAL CONTESTATION OF MEDIA POWER

Nick Couldry

> There is no alternative communication without a social practice which determines and ratifies it.
>
> —Fernando Reyes Matta (quoted in Lozade and Kincar, 2000: 8)

This chapter asks: Can we model theoretically the possibilities for contesting media power around the world? The question is a controversial starting point because it isolates "media power" as a separate dimension of social conflict, and thus goes against the trend of most social and media theory. Yet this move is important if the full comparative significance of much alternative media is to be grasped.

What is "media power"? Media institutions and media productions constantly register the influences of many forces outside themselves (state and corporate influences, to name only two). But you might ask: Can "media" possess a power that is contestable separately from the state or corporate sector's representations of itself through media? Certainly there are overlaps between the contestation of media power and other forms of power, but this is not to say that distinctive social issues don't arise about "media power"—that is, the overwhelming concentration of most, if not all, societies' symbolic resources in the separate institutional sphere we call "the media." Rather, the point is that those issues often seem more remote than others. This is one result of the distinctive features of symbolic power in general.

"Symbolic power" is perhaps the least understood of the fundamental types of power (economic, political, military, symbolic). For while "symbolic power," at its most basic level, is easily understood as "the capacity to intervene in the course of events, to influence the actions of others and indeed to create events, by means of the production and transmission of symbolic forms" (Thompson, 1995: 17), we have to grasp something wider: the effect of the overwhelming *concentration* of symbolic power in particular places, especially the media. In this concentrated form, symbolic power (including media power) is better defined as a "power of constructing reality" (Bourdieu, 1991: 166)— that is, social reality. To contest media power is to contest the way social reality itself is defined or named (cf. Carey, 1989; Melucci, 1996). This is no easy thing, since it involves contesting the prevailing definitions of what is socially contest*able*; in particular, it means contesting media institutions' preeminent position as our frame onto the "realities" of the social world (Silverstone, 1988; Couldry, 2000: ch. 1). Much more than contesting specific media representations is involved.

Given these complexities, there is value in giving theoretical order to the divergent forms that media power's contestation might take—and, indeed, this is the purpose of the chapter. An image may help bring home what is distinctive about this approach. If, for a moment, we imagine contemporary power as a large, sprawling palace, economic, military, and political power would occupy the central rooms with their own dedicated rear exits—sites where instructions are given, orders planned, and priorities decided. Today's main forms of symbolic power, including media power, would be located in the entrance rooms to the palace, the mirrored halls where actors enter, wait, and publicly exit. This image—of a palace complex of separate rooms and divided powers—is of course an illusion, since the pervasive transnational reach of today's power relations and their complex interconnections make any architectural image of power unsustainable. In a notable rethinking of global power, Michael Hardt and Antonio Negri (2000: xii) characterize "Empire" as "a decentered and deterritorializing apparatus of rule that progressively incorporates the entire global realm within its open, expanding frontiers." All the more striking, then, that even these authors, when thinking about resistance to Empire, retain a nostalgia for the mirrored space of global media events into which local acts of resistance to capitalism are sometimes transformed. "Perhaps," they write, "the more capital extends its global networks of production and control, the more powerful any singular point of revolt can be" (2000: 58). "Any" singular point, whatever its conditions and location? Following the protests against global corporate values at Seattle and elsewhere, one finds seductive the idea that, as global capitalism's functioning relies increasingly on global media, its vulnerability to local contestation increases exponentially. But whatever temporary subsidy is provided by global media to the spread of resistant images, the result is rarely a redistribution of media power. The longer-term importance of Seattle lay not only in the media attention it generated, or its challenges to corporate values and global governance, but also in its new and still continuing challenge to the infrastructure of global media power: the Indymedia movement (see Downing's chapter in this volume). Now I turn from the comings and goings in global media's hall of mirrors to the conflicts over symbolic resources being waged in countless specific locations. It is on this distinctive thread within today's forms of global social conflict that I want to concentrate.

The concentration of symbolic power in specific institutional spheres is not, in itself, new. Medieval and early modern Western Europe was characterized by an intense concentration of symbolic power, and symbolic production, in the Catholic church, a concentration that the emergence of the printed book helped to undermine (Curran, 2002: ch. 2). From the late seventeenth century onward, the modern state emerged not just as a concentration of economic and military power but, increasingly, as a rival concentration of symbolic and definitional power—controlling, by the late nineteenth century, the terms on which all corporations and individuals operated and even existed. (For a developed theory of the French state in particular, see Bourdieu, 1996.) The contemporary interrelations between the state's and the media's symbolic powers remain, however, largely uncharted.[1] In some late-modern states, media power has come into conflict not so much with the state's symbolic power as with that of religious institutions—as occurred, for example, in Iran during the 1970s and 1980s (Moham-madi and Sreberny-Mohammadi, 1994). Profound concentrations of, and contesta-tions for, symbolic power are not therefore new; yet in many accounts by sociologists and political scientists, the concept of media power (the latest form of such concen-trations) is either absent or collapsed into its supposed determinants in economic or state power. It is crucial to keep this concept distinct, if we are to grasp how corporate and state actors, as well as individuals, communities, NGOs, and transnational net-works, contest the local and global structures of media power. (Again, I emphasize that we must not rule out the possibility, indeed the likelihood, that those actions will over-lap with contests over other forms of power and specific media representations.)

The insistence on the analytic separation of media power has implications for wider debates about media's social impacts. Contrary to one narrow version of the po-litical economy thesis, media power is only partly about the ownership structure of me-dia corporations and the infrastructure of media distribution. This (very real) political economy has a "cultural" dimension: the universe of beliefs, myths, and practices that allows a highly unequal media system to seem legitimate (cf. Couldry, 2000). This is why, in considering possible sites of resistance to media power, we must look not only at the distribution of economic and organizational resources and at contests over spe-cific media representations of reality, but also at the sites from which alternative gen-eral frames for understanding social reality are offered. Beliefs in the media's central place in social life can be effectively challenged only by *alternative* frames. This follows from the special nature of symbolic power as both practical resource (in the hands of particular people and institutions) and long-term influence over people's beliefs about social reality. Put another way, as in the quotation by Matta at the start of the chapter, any lasting challenge to media power requires a different social practice. Contesting media power thus ultimately means developing new forms of communication—that is, new ways "in which people come to possess things in common" (John Dewey, quoted in Carey, 1989: 22).

I will first tentatively review the possibilities for, and constraints upon, the con-testation of media power, in a way, I hope, that stimulates comparative perspectives. Second, and less abstractly, I will look at two specific visions of how media power might shift: one that is market-based (drawing on an interview with the founder of the online news platform "Out There News"), and the other, community-based (drawing on documents recently circulated within the global Indymedia network).

Contesting Media Power: Where to Start?

In a sense, the answer is simple: "Just do things differently," echoing the phrase coined by the 1960s U.S. activists known as the Yippies and, more recently, adapted both by Nike's global strategists and by alternative videomakers (Rubin, 1970; O'Connor, 1995). In other words, the answer lies in practice. But *why* and *how* exactly should everyday practice be reconfigured, if sustainable challenges to media power are to emerge?

Contesting media power, in that sporting metaphor loved by management gurus, means thinking "outside the box." The box in question is what the anthropologist Maurice Godelier referred to as the little-understood "black box of those mechanisms which govern the distribution of the same representations among social groups with partially or profoundly opposed interests" (Godelier, 1986: 14)—in other words, the black box of "the media." The media are part of contemporary society's "habitus," or (in Pierre Bourdieu's general sense of that term) its "history turned into nature" (Bourdieu, 1977: 78). Challenging the social order that passes for "nature" means, at the very least, thinking differently about our own orientation to media. Consider the following words from Australian media and software activist Matthew Arnison:

> Old media technology creates a natural hierarchy between the storytellers and the audience. The storyteller has access to some piece of technology, such as a TV transmitter or a printing press. The audience don't. . . . Somewhere along the way, this has been justified by assuming that most people aren't that creative, that having only a handful of people to tell stories in a city of millions is a natural way of doing things. But is it? (Arnison, 2002a: 1)

Beneath the fable-like phrase "somewhere along the way" lies a whole (infamous) history of how, as part of a wider process of centralization and government (cf. Mattelart, 1994), modern populations became accustomed to the idea that society's principal stories and images should be told from one place, "the media," and that this "place," while of public importance, is such that access to its everyday operations is strictly controlled.

This concentration of symbolic resources (or "media power," as I call it for short) could not work if its operations were transparent, or if accepting it were a matter of explicit belief. *Why believe* that certain institutions have a special status in narrating the social world, privileged above individuals' accounts of living in that world? Media institutions depend on a silent division, reproduced across social space, between those who make stories and those who consume them. You can call this division a "division of labor," but that risks naturalizing it as an irreducible economic "fact." Most of us have our work cut out for us, holding down a job (or jobs), looking after our bodily needs, and leading a social life; and consuming media is an activity that takes place in most of our lives. But producing media is generally someone else's job. Most of us don't have the time or the resources to challenge the division between society's story-tellers and story-consumers.[2] Or, rather, for the lucky ones among us who still have some choice, it does not seem sensible to spend our limited "free" time in contesting the large-scale inequalities underlying how and by whom society's stories are told. Except, perhaps, when we feel individually wronged by one of those stories; in earlier research, I foregrounded the accounts of people who, though not previously much exercised by media power, experienced the everyday asymmetry of media operations on the ground (Couldry, 2000, pt. 3). But precisely because the media process is so selective, such disruptive encounters are not most people's experience. As acknowledged earlier, then, not only are contests over the generality of media power often difficult to distinguish from other social contests channeled through media, but the *very idea* of contesting media power is difficult to articulate, because that power is not profoundly naturalized.

So how are we to think about the possibilities for contesting media power in the general run of social life?

Symbolic power requires prior organizational and economic resources (to buy cameras, own radio frequencies, produce news stories); but, if accumulated on a sufficient scale, it results over the long term in something qualitatively different: influence over people's beliefs, in particular those beliefs (barely articulated) through which we frame the social world.[3] It follows that contesting media power is possible only if there exists a well-resourced social site outside media institutions from which a rival narrative authority over the social world can plausibly be enunciated. Where might such alternative concentrations of symbolic power be? Let's begin by considering corporations, followed by the state and/or military and religious institutions.

Corporations are not a promising source for alternatives to media power, precisely because the business of selling is intimately bound up with the maintenance of market access, which in turn, in all contemporary societies, depends on the reach of media institutions. Occasionally, an embattled corporation's own myth-making is at odds with the media's working assumptions (for example, when employees of Arthur Andersen used photo opportunities to project their loyalty to that firm's "values," as the company faced scandal for its role in the Enron collapse), but such cases will always be exceptional.

States are, prima facie, more promising, at least as a source of subsidy to those who want to build alternatives to media power. One reason is that states have their own well-established symbolic resources (to regulate state boundaries and definitions of citizenship, to control the terms on which business can and cannot operate, and goods and images can circulate). Another reason is that specific states may believe that their interests are at odds with the agendas of media institutions. The occasions when states have contested media power (with or without the military, which we can avoid considering separately since they generally lack symbolic resources of their own) are hardly to be celebrated (recall Chile in the 1970s). On the other hand, twentieth-century media history offers examples of how the modern state's close interest in the rhetorical reach of emerging media (such as the BBC in Britain) subsidized institutional alternatives to complete media centralization (examples include BBC's regional programming and the "access" television movement of the 1960s and '70s). Without such state subsidies, the relatively balanced "media ecology" (Born and Prosser, 2001: 63) could not have emerged in countries, such as Britain, with a public-service tradition. However, as its ability to influence global market structures declines, the state becomes an increasingly precarious rival to media power, especially when state power, like corporate power, is increasingly dependent on media access to markets (usually called "electorates").[4]

What of religious institutions, acting within or outside the ambit of the state? On the face of it, this scenario is promising. In most societies, religious institutions promulgate their own framing narratives of the social world, and indeed the cosmos, that are not directly reliant on media reference points. The role of religious belief, as a site of challenges to the media "frame," is one of the most neglected topics in media studies,[5] although after September 11, 2001, its neglect has been hard to defend. The importance of the Catholic church in the development of alternative, especially community-based, media in Latin America is discussed elsewhere in this volume (Rodriguez), but note the contribution of Paulo Freire's (1972) secular concept of "conscientization" to that history.

Religious institutions are, of course, not the only source of large-scale framing narratives: Until 1989, state socialism, rightly or wrongly, was an obvious alternative, and both socialism and anarchism live on in different forms (again, see Downing's chapter), sometimes intersecting with media practice. In various fragmented ways, utopian and/or religious visions are traceable in the current work of national and global NGOs, although NGOs do not generally engage in direct contestations of media power, since they, like corporate and state forces, depend on the existing reach of media institutions. Perhaps the most powerful alternative frame in current global politics is the World Social Forum's principle that "another world is possible,"[6] but as yet this has not been specifically applied to a critique of media power.

The foregoing analysis is admittedly schematic. Power does not flow in straight lines, nor are institutions the only source of power or its contestation. *Actual* contestations of power are usually the result of multiple forces. Such is the systemic complexity of media markets, say, that they may sometimes, against corporate interests, generate alternative symbolic resources; a similar case can be made for state-subsidized media systems. In such cases, the only partly institutionalized force of civil society is crucial (Keane, 1998).

Rather than pursue this institutional complexity any further, maybe we should ask a different question: What potential contributions to long-term shifts in media power will be made by changes in what individuals do with media? There are a number of dimensions along which we could look:

1. *new ways of consuming media*, which explicitly contest the social legitimacy of media power;
2. *new infrastructures of production*, which have an effect on who can produce media and in what circumstances;
3. new infrastructures of distribution, which change the scale and terms on which symbolic production in one place can reach other places.

The first dimension—consumption—has been strikingly absent from most accounts of alternative media until now (Downing, 2003), and almost as little is known about how people select from, or adjust for, the inadequacies of mainstream media.[7] Media consumption takes place largely in private, in what Sartre called "serial absence" (quoted in Lodziak, 1987: 175), such that the cumulative impact of individuals' private media consumption becomes obscure. At what point, for example, will our habit of getting news from a changing variety of localized Web sources (including semipublic networks and private testimonies) turn into skepticism about the truth-claims of large-scale news institutions? How significant, indeed, are these new habits, compared with Web use, for more convenient access to newspaper and television news? Clearly we can only speculate on such questions at present, although it is worth insisting that individual practice cannot change independently of *social assumptions* about the trustworthiness of media and other institutions, which are linked to shifts in the infrastructures of knowledge production and distribution (cf. Silverstone, 1994).

This brings us to the second and third dimensions, production and distribution—dimensions that are less familiar, since infrastructural changes are always difficult to isolate. The Internet has dramatically heightened our interest in media infrastructure:

first, because it has increased the ease with which any digitalized material can be distributed across national, organizational, and social boundaries; second, because new forms of open-source software are increasing the speed with which innovations in digital production can spread, at least among those with considerable computer literacy. The long-term impacts of these changes on media consumption, and on people's beliefs about the media's social status, remain uncertain; but it is, I suggest, to new hybrid forms of media *consumption-production* that we should look for change, since they would challenge precisely the entrenched division of labor (producer of stories versus consumer of stories) that is the essence of media power.

I am thinking, for example, of the Indymedia movement, with its local websites that combine specialized production with an open invitation for nonspecialists to contribute largely unedited news material. As a result, every Indymedia consumer is encouraged to be a producer as well, and vice versa (every Indymedia producer must become a consumer of the media productions not just of fellow specialists but also of the wider audience). Thus an explicit aim of the original Indymedia website at Seattle is "to empower individuals to become independent and civic journalists by providing a direct, unmoderated form for presenting media . . . to the public via the Internet" (Seattle IMC, 2002: 2). Once again, however, these emergent forms of consumption-production are not isolated individual choices. They occur in certain places and under certain material conditions that perhaps are, and will always be, exceptional (small community networks whose maintenance depends on hidden subsidies?). We need to know much more about the possibilities for *sustaining* such hybrid practices within, or at least alongside, increasingly "flexible" labor markets.[8] And even if such hybrid practices prove sustainable for some, who else outside Indymedia's limited circle of consumer-producers knows about, and can be influenced by, these new practices? I return to such questions shortly.

Here the contestation of media power merges into the wider question of how social change is possible, and from where—very much an open question, as older forms of citizenship, community, and politics undergo intense scrutiny.[9] As we saw earlier, such overlaps are to be expected, but this is not the end of the story. If, as Paul Clarke argues (1996: 125), "to be a deep citizen is to determine *for oneself* that an action is political," then perhaps the concept of media is in equal need of redefinition. In short, who do we expect to participate in the process of mediation, and from where? This is a good point for the generalities of theory to make way for more specific and personal narratives.

Two Narratives of Change

I want to pursue two different visions of change: the first from Matthew Arnison, one of the Australian developers of the open-source software on which the Indymedia websites across the world rely; and the second from Paul Eedle, the U.K. founder of the website www.megastories.com, which from the mid-1990s until early 2002, under the title "Out There News," gathered a huge range of individual stories about global news events from across the world, as well as valuable information archives on major news stories.[10] The first was developed within local community politics in Sydney and the global open-source software movement (Himanen, 2001); the second had ties to the mainstream news market (Eedle is a former Reuters journalist). I hope to show, however, that these differences are outweighed by the complementarity of the understanding of the underlying dynamics of media power implicit in each.

"OPEN PUBLISHING" AND ITS LIMITATIONS

Let's begin with Arnison's definition of "open publishing," which he believes the Web enables and the Indymedia movement embodies:

> Open publishing means that the process of creating news is transparent to the readers. They can contribute a story and see it instantly appear in the pool of stories publicly available. Those stories are filtered as little as possible to help the readers find the stories they want. Readers can see editorial decisions being made by others. They can see how to get involved and help make editorial decisions. If they can think of a better way for the software to help shape editorial decisions, they can copy the software because it is free and change it and start their own site. If they want to redistribute the news, they can, preferably on an open publishing site. (Arnison, 2002b: 1)

Arnison suggests that a real shift in media power must involve all dimensions of the media process (production, distribution, consumption, and the infrastructure that links them). This new way of consuming information (via visibly edited online texts) may encourage people to participate in production; indeed, the technical possibility of such participation depends on the formats made available through new, easily transferable open-source software, creating an open field of media production/consumption replicable on further linked sites.

   This concept of open publishing, far from being an abstraction, is linked to Arnison's vision of a new form of community media.[11] Arnison is a key producer of the Active Sydney website[12] (part of an Australian network of community information sites that encourage individual postings). Active Sydney's aim is "to tailor electronic communication to the needs of the community, rather than corporate or government interests" (Active Sydney, 2002). In his document on open publishing (Arnison, 2002b), Arnison takes this notion of community media even further:

> The most successful internet sites rely on the creativity of their users, not on professional producers as was the tradition with earlier electronic media. . . . On the old one-way systems, community media was the exception. On the net, community media is very much part of the mainstream. (Arnison, 2002b: 6)

While the concept of "community" remains a difficult one, it at least puts on the table issues of public use and public purpose. Interestingly, the Seattle Independent media Center's editorial group states that one of its aims is "to maintain the [Indymedia] newswire and website as a community space" (Seattle IMC, 2002: 1).[13]

   Still unanswered is one question regarding Arnison's and Indymedia's vision of participatory media: How broad is the social cross-section from which their producer/ audiences[14] are drawn? Inasmuch as "open publishing is overwhelmingly done by volunteers" (Arnison, 2002b: 3) rather than paid workers, and given the principle of "copyleft," which Arnison has adopted from Richard Stallman (all material is freely copiable, provided that when copied the original source is always transparent to the reader), it follows that Indymedia production is necessarily done in people's spare time. This restricts participation to those whose resources allow them to give up "free" time in this way: people who must work two or three jobs to make ends meet are automatically excluded. There are other bases of exclusion as well, the most obvious, apart from literacy, being the computer skills necessary to convert material into the format required for use on Indymedia and similar sites.

Equally, we can ask about the nonproducing audience for this new, more open media form. Indymedia U.K.'s Web statement is striking for its insistence that what it offers is not journalistic "objectivity": "Indymedia U.K. clearly states its subjectivity" (Indymedia U.K., 2002; cf. Harding, 1997: 22–23). The directness is refreshing, but it leaves unclear the nature of Indymedia U.K.'s consumers. Are they postmodern readers who happily accept that all truth is "relative"? Or are they committed to the rightness of a certain view of the world and its inequities? If the former, then the Indymedia news philosophy is less interesting than it seems; but if the latter, what degree of accountability to its audience does it accept?

The answer, I suggest, lies in a different vision of how news production and consumption are interrelated—a vision articulated by Matthew Arnison through his notion of "open editing" (Arnison 2002a): In contrast to behind-the-scenes editing, open editing permits *any reader* to post an edited version of a text back onto the site where it was published, but with the editing and the name of the author displayed in another file directly accessible on the site. This is an engaging idea, although there remains an important question regarding the social conditions under which sufficient reader/producers would be available.

RETHINKING THE MAINSTREAM NEWS AUDIENCE

As noted, the other (equally radical) vision of change in media power is that of Paul Eedle, founder of www.megastories.com. For several years, this news site featured minimally edited first-person stories about world events, either sent in by readers of the site or encouraged by its team of usually part-time "stringers" around the world. The site attracted mainstream media attention for its personal stories after the terrorist attacks on September 11, 2001, collected not just from the United States but also from Pakistan, Palestine, and elsewhere in the Middle East.

The importance given to personal narratives and reader discussion was an aspect of the news site's original philosophy. As Eedle explained when I interviewed him in his London home:

> John West and I started Out There News because we thought that the online medium had a lot of potential that wasn't being exploited by mainstream organisations. We saw the potential, particularly in two areas. One was to provide in-depth news, news that you could explore context and background

> to current events. . . . We saw the potential with on-line to separate breaking news and the context and background. . . . The idea was to produce explorable depth, using the multimedia nature of the medium, using audio, using images, using graphics and using different sorts of writing. . . . The second direction, where we thought the medium was not being used by the mainstream, was contributed journalism, [where the idea was] to use the readers of the website as the sources. And there I think the mainstream still is being very conservative. We felt that on-line changed the relationship between journalists and the audience. It's not just a two-way relationship where readers can comment on what you put out but it . . . puts journalists or puts the audience on the same level as the journalist. And the journalist has to . . . earn the right to communicate by having something to say. And equally the audience may well know as much about the subject as the journalist and . . . if you're prepared to put that at the centre of the site, then I think you can produce radically new views of the world. (Interview with author, 11 July 2002)

The aim was to expand the potential of mainstream news production, not to offer a direct alternative. This affected the audience targeted (Eedle "never really wanted to address a niche alternative audience. . . . I have no interest in preaching to the converted") as well as readers' expected routes to the site (most of the site's financing came from contracts requiring the site to provide content via links to the Web portal AOL and the NTL cable interface).

Out There News's editorial policy was quite different from Indymedia's avoidance of editorial intervention, combining normal principles of journalistic "objectivity" (for example, in its use of information archives for particular "megastories" and in its concern that a totally open policy would risk overwhelming the site "with rubbish") with the belief that editorial intervention should nonetheless be kept to a minimum. It exercised editorial judgment by highlighting certain major themes for contributions and facilitating particular narrators (for example, Abdul Malouk, a Pashtun living in a refugee camp on the Pakistan/Afghanistan border, who spoke no English and obviously had no computer access); but much of the material it obtained (interviews, diaries, and message-boards linked to diary entries) was relayed largely unedited. We should not allow Out There News's mainstream context to blind us to the radicalness of its editorial philosophy. In effect, this was an experiment with journalistic control. Unlike other largely dishonest attempts at media "democratization" (such as *Big Brother*), Out There News gave its diarists regular chances to update their diaries on their own terms and to respond at leisure to comments from readers. The journalists became, for some purposes, not reporters but *moderators*—yet without the ritualistic boundary-setting role common in, say, television talk shows (cf. Couldry, 2002, ch. 7).

Underlying this shift in the journalist's role was a distinctive assessment of the "ordinary" news consumer:

> It was built on some assumptions about how people consume information on-line. . . . We believed that people . . . came to the web in two modes. One was browsing mode to see what's there, you know, show me the latest.

And the other was actively seeking information, a mode of actually seeking information. . . . That's why we set up Mega-Stories because we thought that people would actively seek information and that people would set their own agenda. (Interview with author, 11 July 2002)

This assumed "active reader" was also understood by Eedle to be a potential producer:

I mean everybody quickly cottoned on to having message boards and doing live chat and so on. . . . Although we were early doing that, we were also perhaps different in the importance we attached to it in saying that this wasn't a kind of comment on the site, *this was the site* in some cases. (Interview with author, 11 July 2002; emphasis added)

Whereas Arnison's "open publishing" philosophy imagined a producer-consumer building production resources outside mainstream media institutions, Eedle imagined a consumer-producer emerging from the mainstream news audience. Out There News, however, faced significant constraints. First, as already mentioned, its funding derived from the early period of AOL's and NTL's development, when each had a clear interest in acquiring links to a range of content sources; funding was not renewed, leading to the eventual closure of new writing on the site in early 2002. Second, the site needed to exercise a degree of editorial control (given the funding arrangements, there was no option). As this control was not transparent, Out There News would not have qualified as "open publishing" in Arnison's (2002b) definition; nor would it have wanted to. Nonetheless, Eedle's long-term vision for a future multimedia information and news platform is democratic in its ambitions:

We would have a whole range of different levels of contributor from professional filmmakers with a broadcast background for whom this would be an interesting way to finance projects that wouldn't otherwise see air, down to activists and students and other people who are gaining multimedia literacy, video literacy, as equipment gets cheaper and skills spread. And of course there'd still be room for people without any media skills at all to contribute by us sending a crew to work with somebody to tell a story through their eyes. (Interview with author, 11 July 2002)

On the other hand, Eedle is less sanguine than Arnison about the underlying skill constraints on opening up production:

I don't think that we should underestimate the level of skill that's needed to produce watchable—you know, compelling—television. . . . It is a wider range of skills and, in fact, normally really a team effort compared to writing a readable textural contribution. (Interview with author, 11 July 2002)

Even so, Eedle believes that the balance of power might shift: "There are going to be an awful lot more people who can tell a story in video in the future than would ever get an airing on conventional television channels" (Interview with author, 11 July 2002).

While more limited and cautious than Arnison's, Eedle's vision of an enlarged media mainstream is valuable for its clear grasp of the effective separation of most media consumption from activist practice:

> I think that the value of a platform like Out There News is to encourage people who wouldn't otherwise contribute to contribute. And an activist will always find a way, but it's encouraging [and] stimulating people *who wouldn't imagine that their voice was worth hearing.* Encouraging them to contribute is I think . . . an interesting ambition. (Interview with author, 11 July 2002; emphasis added)

Behind this observation lies Eedle's sense that the power of both media and political institutions is changing through the dispersal of information sources:

> Media become less relevant because people now have multiple information sources which are not controlled by gatekeepers. Anybody can communicate anything and that means that people can find out whatever they need to find out for their particular issue . . . So there is a very large irrevocable shift of power away from hierarchical bureaucracies whose hey-day was in a nineteenth-century and early-twentieth-century industrial state, a huge spread of power away from bureaucracies to individuals which . . . has effects on every aspect of public life and politicians will need to catch up with it.

Whether right or wrong, Eedle's vision of the links between media power and social change is hardly trivial.

In Place of a Conclusion

Having followed in some detail two different visions of how the landscape of media power may be changing—the first developed on the margins of institutional media production and the second developed near its center, but each illuminating the axes of change within the media sphere (production, distribution, consumption) and the sphere of "the political"[15]—we now arrive back at the question of framing, which was central to the earlier, more theoretical section of this chapter. As we look toward future challenges to the structures of media power, the question of framing can be put more specifically: What are the social purposes for which we use and make media, and are they changing? Instead of providing a neat resolution to that question, I want, finally, to address a further unanswered question about long-term changes in media's place in social and political life.

In this connection, consider an earlier period in which changes in communication technology contributed to fundamental long-term changes in the organization of social and political life: the spread of book printing during the early-modern era in Western Europe. In *Communities of Discourse,* Robert Wuthnow (1987) characterizes this development, and the new information networks it made possible, as essential to major ideological shifts such as the Reformation and the birth of modern democratic politics. What is so useful about Wuthnow's analysis is that it encompasses the social contexts that came into being as a result of book printing: the new or altered networks (among churches, schools, and political parties, say) in which the technology of the book was central; the many paths that allowed those networks to connect with other spaces, such as formal political arenas; the new circuits for the distribution of ideas that emerged in printed form (such as journals and newspapers); and, above all, the social hierarchies that arose in the course of those changes, including the literary public sphere and the social exclusions on which it was based (the coffeehouse versus the market square). Without addressing new media (Wuthnow was writing in 1987), he helps us imagine not only the social architecture through which communication technologies become socially established but also the ways in which new power relations inhere within them.

Few would doubt the potential significance of computer-based communication interfaces for the future of media power, but the Internet's first prophets were blind to questions like those posed by Wuthnow. In the spirit of such questions, we can ask some new ones. Regardless of current hopes to the contrary, will the Internet come to be seen primarily as a quasi-private space (just as casual conversations on the street are almost never thought of as publicly significant, inasmuch as they occur in a private subzone of public space)? Or will the Internet become a genuine supplement to or replacement for existing mediated public space? What hierarchies will develop between the Internet and other public or private spaces, or between certain Internet spaces and others? Will those hierarchies prove as socially entrenched as those associated with the twentieth century's main electronic media? If so, will the result be to undermine, or further entrench, media power?[16]

There is one key paradox that may prove crucial in all this—a paradox experienced by most of us daily, although less often articulated. By this I mean the shift that has occurred over the past 150 years from a world with insufficient information flows (leading to the mid-nineteenth-century "crisis of control" that James Beniger [1986] saw as the driving force behind both modern communications and the birth of "scientific" management and accounting) to a world with too much information (many times over)—in effect, a reverse "crisis of control," whereby the highest premium applies not to information production but to information selection. Media are part of that information excess; but insofar as media involve leisure activities rather than compulsory ones, they are especially vulnerable to drastic shifts in how people select from the information and image environment.[17] Perhaps we are entering an era in which many of us will want to look more closely at where *and to what end* we obtain news about the world.

A virtue of producers outside mainstream media channels—those concerned, at least in part, with contesting media power itself—is that they refuse to take for granted either the question of what social ends media serve or the connection between those ends and that hard-pressed ideal we call "democracy." If so, there is reason to believe that their voices will be heard more clearly in this century's expanding media universe than they were in the last.

Notes

Many thanks to Paul Eedle for giving up his time to be interviewed, and to Alan O' Connor for permission to quote from his unpublished translation of Lozade and Kincar (2000).

1. See Couldry (2003) for further discussion of this point.

2. For the best explanation of how this division and its ideological consequences are embedded in the organization of production, see Lodziak (1987).

3. Here I am drawing on and generalizing the concept of frame that originated in Goffman's (1975) sociology but has been most actively used in the analysis of social and political movements (see, for example, Snow and Benford, 1992; Keck and Sikkink, 1998).

4. See Meyer (2002) on the long-term consequences of media dependence on the political process.

5. For rare exceptions, see Zimmerman Umble (1992) and Hoover (forthcoming).

6. See paragraph 2 of the Charter of Principles, available via www.forumsocialmundial.org.br.

7. For a pioneering study, see Lembo (2000).

8. There is a great deal to be learned from earlier studies of spare-time fan-producers (Jenkins, 1992; Bacon-Smith, 1992).

9. On citizenship, see Clarke (1996) and Rodriguez (2001). And for a fresh look at the significance of the "community" dimension to community and alternative media, see Rennie (2002), which discusses in particular the practice of the "Active.org" community media websites in Australia that Matthew Arnison and others have pioneered.

10. This site remains a useful source, but since spring 2002 it has served as an archive only.

11. I have learned a great deal on this point from Ellie Rennie's recent paper. (See Rennie, 2002.)

12. The address is www.active.org.au/Sydney/.

13. It is perhaps significant that the word "community" is not used in the Web statement of Indymedia U.K., since Britain is a country where this word has been particularly abused by various Conservative and Labour governments (Indymedia U.K., 2002).

14. Assuming they are largely separate, which may not be the case.

15. I stress "the political" rather than the narrow sphere of formal "politics" (cf. Wolin, 1995).

16. For a fundamental exploration of such issues in relation to Internet infrastructure, see Lessig (1999).

17. For an interesting and unusual consideration of the implications of information excess on alternative media, see the interview with John Sellers (2001: especially 83–84), director of the Ruckus Society that was active in the Seattle antiglobalization protests.

References

Active Sydney (2002). "What Are the Aims of Active-Sydney?" Available online at www.active.org.au/sydney/about. Last accessed on 4 September 2002.

Arnison, Matthew (2002a). "Crazy Ideas for Webcasting." Available online at cat.org.au/cat/webacast.html. Last accessed on 4 September 2002.

——— (2002b). "Open Publishing Document." Available online at cat.org.au/maffew/cat/openpub.html. Last accessed on 4 September 2002.

Bacon-Smith, Camille (1992). *Enterprising Women*. Philadelphia: University of Pennsylvania Press.

Beniger, James (1986). *The Control Revolution: Technological and Economic Origins of the Information Society*. Cambridge, Mass.: Harvard University Press.

Born, Georgina, and Prosser, Tony (2001). "Culture and Consumerism: Citizenship, Public Service Broadcasting and the BBC's Fair Trading Obligations," *Modern Law Review* 64(5): 657–87.

Bourdieu, Pierre (1977). *Outline of a Theory of Practice*. Cambridge, U.K.: Cambridge University Press.

—— (1991). *Language and Symbolic Power*. Cambridge, U.K.: Polity Press.

—— (1996). *The State Nobility*. Cambridge, U.K.: Polity Press.

Carey, James (1989). *Communication as Culture*. Boston: Unwin Hyman.

Clarke, Paul (1996). *Deep Citizenship*. London: Pluto.

Couldry, Nick (2000). *The Place of Media Power*. London: Routledge.

—— (2002). *Media Rituals: A Critical Approach*. London: Routledge.

—— (2003). "Media, Symbolic Power and the Limits of Bourdieu's Field Theory," Media@lse Electronic Working Papers series, http://www.lse.ac.uk/depts/media.

Curran, James (2002). *Media and Power*. London: Routledge.

Downing, John (forthcoming, 2003). "Audiences and Readers of Alternative Media: The Absent Lure of the Virtually Unknown," *Media Culture & Society* .

Freire, Paulo (1972). *Pedagogy of the Oppressed*. Harmondsworth, U.K.: Penguin.

Godelier, Maurice (1986). *The Mental and the Material*. Cambridge, U.K.: Cambridge University Press.

Goffman, Erving (1975). *Frame Analysis*. Harmondsworth, U.K.: Penguin.

Harding, Thomas (1997). *The Video Activists' Handbook*. London: Pluto.

Hardt, Michael, and Negri, Antonio (2000). *Empire*. Cambridge, Mass.: Harvard University Press.

Himanen, Pekka (2001). *The Hacker Ethic and the Spirit of the Information Age*. New York: Random House.

Hoover, Stewart (forthcoming). *Religion in the Media Age*. London: Routledge.

Indymedia U.K. (2002). "Mission Statement vs. 0.9 17.05.02." Available online at uk.undymedia. org/ms.php3. Last accessed on 4 September 2002.

Jenkins, Henry (1992). *Textual Poachers*. New York: Routledge.

Keane, John (1998). *Civil Society: Old Images, New Visions*. Cambridge, U.K.: Polity.

Keck, Margaret, and Sikkink, Kathryn (1998). *Activists Beyond Borders*. Ithaca, N.Y.: Cornell University Press.

Lembo, Ron (2000). *Thinking Through Television*. Cambridge, U.K.: Cambridge University Press.

Lessig, Lawrence (1999). *Code and Other Laws of Cyberspace*. New York: Basic Books.

Lodziak, Conrad (1987). *The Power of Television*. London: Frances Pinter.

Lozade, Fernando, and Kincar, Gridvia (2000). "The Miners' Radios of Bolivia: An Historic Experience of Self-Managed Communication," unpublished translation by Alan O'Connor of a chapter from F. R. Matta (ed.), *Comunicacion Alternativa y Busquedas Democraticas*. Santiago, Chile: ILET/ Friedrich Ebert Stiftung, 1983.

Martin-Barbero, Jesus (1993). *Communication, Culture and Hegemony*. London: Sage.

Mattelart, Armand (1994). *The Invention of Communication*. Minneapolis: Minnesota University Press.

Melucci, Alberto (1996). *Challenging Codes*. Cambridge, U.K.: Cambridge University Press.

Meyer, Thomas (2002). *Media Democracy*. Cambridge, U.K.: Polity.

Mohammadi, Ali, and Sreberny-Mohammadi, Annabelle (1994). *Small Media, Big Revolution*. Minneapolis: Minnesota University Press.

O'Connor, Paul (1995). "Talking Turkey with Television," in booklet accompanying *Undercurrents* [video magazine], Vol. 4. Oxford: Undercurrents Productions.

Rennie, Ellie (2002). "Community Media: Fenced Off or Walled Out? Finding a Space of Community in the New Media Environment," paper presented at IAMCR conference, Barcelona, July 2002.

Rodriguez, Clemencia (2001). *Fissures in the Mediascape*. Creskill, N.J.: Hampton Press.

Rubin, Jerry (1970). *Do It!* New York: Simon and Schuster.

Seattle IMC (2002). "Editorial Collective Statement." Available online at seattle.indymedia. org/policy. Last accessed on 4 September 2002.

Sellers, John (2001). "Raising a Ruckus," *New Left Review* 10: 71–85.

Silverstone, Roger (1988). "Television Myth and Culture," in J. Carey (ed.), *Media, Myths and Narratives*. Newbury Park: Sage.

——— (1994). *Television and Everyday Life*. London: Routledge.

Snow, David, and Benford, Robert. (1992). "Master Frames and the Cycle of Protest," in A. Morris and C. Mueller (eds.), *Frontiers in Social Movement Theory*. New Haven: Yale University Press.

Thompson, John (1995). *The Media and Modernity*. Cambridge, U.K.: Polity.

Wolin, Sheldon (1995). "Fugitive Democracy," in S. Benhabib (ed.), *Democracy and Differences*. Princeton: Princeton University Press.

Wuthnow, Robert (1987). *Communities of Discourse*. Cambridge, Mass.: Harvard University Press.

Zimmerman Umble, Diane (1992). "The Amish and the Telephone Line: Resistance and Reconstruction," in R. Silverstone and E. Hirsch (eds.), *Consuming Technologies*. London: Routledge.

Part II

IN THE SHADOW
OF THE STATE

CHAPTER 4

Infoshops in the Shadow of the State

Chris Atton

The 1990s saw the development of the phenomenon of the "infoshop," intimately related to the "free information networks" (FINs) that grew up in the wake of the latter-day free festival movement along with cooperatively run alternative libraries and reading rooms (Atton, 1996: 142–47; Atton, 2002: 47–48). The infoshop movement saw the development of a loose network of infoshops concentrated in North America and Europe (for an overview of the infoshop movement in the United States, see Dodge, 1998; Sigal, undated). These were often homes not only to debate and discussion but also to alternative media.

The British model of the infoshop grew out of the squatted anarchist centers of the 1980s, such as the 121 Centre in Brixton, London. As the term suggests, central to the function of an infoshop is the dissemination of information. To this end it provides information—for example, by acting as an alternative Citizens' Advice Bureau to claimants and squatters. It might offer a reading room of alternative publications, perhaps even a small library. It can act as a distribution point for free publications and as a retail outlet for priced publications. It often provides cheap do-it-yourself design and reprographic services to alternative publishers (at their most basic, these may constitute a table and a photocopier, although some infoshops have professional desktop-publishing facilities). Here, the media and the forum are intimately connected, perhaps in a much stronger way than in previous decades of alternative media in Britain. This is confirmed by Teal Triggs's (1995) survey of British zines, where she echoes John Downing's (1984) assessment of the alternative press, seeing it as a home for "'alternative critical spaces' unconstrained by the rules and conventions of mainstream publishing."

In Gramscian terms, the infoshop "movement" appears as counter-hegemonic strategy—as a series of attempts to establish pockets of resistance—to demarcate "free spaces" within which anarchist-revolutionary aims and strategies may be formulated and enacted, and tactics developed to act as mechanisms for struggles against capitalism. From a Habermasian perspective, the infoshop is at the center of a counter public sphere, within which revolutionary political discourse is nurtured, consequently to be taken into the "dominant" public sphere in the form of intellectual arguments and physical protests. To what extent, though, does the infoshop movement represent an autonomous public sphere of revolutionary activity? Do the activities of the infoshop live up to expectations? In short, how successful has the infoshop movement been in (1) creating "free spaces" independent of the state and its agents/agencies and (2) enabling aims and strategies to be developed within those spaces?

These are important questions to ask, and not only in relation to the centrality of the infoshop movement in European and North American anarchist praxis—and, thus, of its significance to the global anticapitalist movement, part of which has roots in anarchist philosophy and protest. Such questions also affect the production and dissemination of alternative media. One of the infoshop's key functions is as a repository and distributor of alternative media (mostly, though not exclusively, anarchist media), and it appears to function as a hybrid form of information resource, acting as library, archive, distributor, and sales outlet. It can also be a site for the production of such media, often produced by the same collective that runs the infoshop itself (Atton, 2002; Dodge, 1998). The success of the infoshop as a node of "free space" within a diffuse, antihierarchical network then assumes further significance as the armature of alternative media.

Let us now examine the assumptions underlying the significance of the infoshop for the anarchist movement. We shall do this first by addressing the notions of free space and counter public sphere. Having established what these terms suggest for the political and cultural desiderata of the infoshop, we shall then turn to the praxis of the infoshop, critically examining the notion of its enabling a counter-hegemonic discourse through an analysis of infoshop "experiences" in Europe and the United States.

The Infoshop as a Free Space

Alberto Melucci has proposed a definition of collective action based on

> a network of active relationships between actors who interact, communicate, influence each other, negotiate, and make decisions. Forms of organization and models of leadership, communicative channels and technologies of communication are constitutive parts of this network of relationships. (Melucci, 1996: 75)

In this reading of social movements the role of the network and that of communication—of media as activators of that network—assume key positions. Melucci defines the network as comprising "active relationships" at the heart of collective action. Autonomy fostered by solidarity through networks is activated among groups of individuals as a means to self-education, self-reliance, and creativity. In these contexts, as Laurence Cox argues, autonomy in collective action is employed for "the creation of new social forms for self-determined purposes" (Cox, 1997). This entails autonomy as a reflexive practice and "demands an active reflexivity, in the sense of the creation of meanings and practices which defend the 'free space' necessary for the project."

Ron Eyerman and Andrew Jamison (1991) consider such a space to be the product of a coming together of groups; for them a social movement is a "cognitive territory" through which the various groups and organizations are able to come together to "carve out an actual societal space" (p. 55) and "create for a time a space of social activity, a public space for interest articulation" (p. 60). This free space is characterized by reflexive practice, creativity, and challenge. In turn, Melucci (1995) stresses the necessary independence of such spaces from government, the state, and other dominant political institutions and practices—an independence that allows for their maintenance as experimental zones within which alternative means of "sociation" may be developed. Cox (undated) similarly defines free spaces as "situations of a relative weakening of determination by the logics of power and economics" and Bookchin considers the affinity group as the "free space" *par excellence*, "in which revolutionaries can make themselves, individually, and also as social beings" (Bookchin, 1986: 243). Such theorizations bear upon the characteristics and values we have found in the practices of alternative media; they center on autonomy, solidarity, and the development of reflexivity in the creative processes of democratic media production (Atton, 2002: 156).

We also might consider this free space as a form of alternative public sphere. In her influential critique of Jürgen Habermas's (1962/1989) original bourgeois formulation of the public sphere, Nancy Fraser (1992) posited a multiplicity of public spheres, each of which acts as a forum for the articulation of a particular social, cultural, or class section. The key word here is empowerment—empowerment of the disenfranchised and marginalized whose discourse remains outside the dominant public sphere. These groups Fraser refers to as "subaltern counterpublics," developing the notion from Gayatri Spivak's work on the repressed colonial voice of the Other (notably Spivak, 1988). Members of such groups are able to engage in these "parallel discursive arenas" in order "to invent and circulate counterdiscourses to formulate oppositional interpretations of their identities, interests, and needs" (Fraser, 1992: 123).

Rather than attempt to homogenize or "accommodate contestation" within a single public sphere, Fraser argues for "a plurality of competing publics [that] better promote the ideal of participatory parity themselves than does a single, comprehensive overarching public" (p. 122). Her argument here is that the acknowledgment of a diversity of discursive spaces in which members of particular groups are able to produce their own discourses, rather than have them constructed on their behalf (or, at worst, have them not considered worthy of construction at all), will best represent those groups.

We can identify three key elements of infoshop praxis from the above: first, that it should be independent from oppressive relations of power (whether understood as the power of dominant institutions, or as ideologies based on class, race, or gender); second, that it needs to be relatively underdetermined by economics; third, that it should foster "autonomy," to be realized through the practice of self-reliance and self-reflexivity. These elements suggest a free space that will encourage the performance of highly experimental approaches to organization, power-sharing, finance, social interaction, and personal growth. Modeled in this way the infoshop may be seen as autonomous and nonhierarchical, as a radical space connected by complex, though informal, communications networks, playing a key role in the creative processes of activist politics. As such, the free space model has much in common with the celebratory and resistant readings in many recent studies of youth and working-class culture (such as those critiqued in Atton, 2001). Rather than celebrate these free spaces uncritically, as if the identification alone of such an impressive aim provides unproblematic evidence of "radical democracy" in action, what follows will explore this aim through the elements that comprise it to essay a sociopolitical analysis of the bureaucratic structures and social formations that shape the actual, lived "autonomous" political activity/experience of the infoshop. It will do so primarily through a focus on one infoshop, the Autonomous Centre of Edinburgh (ACE), in Scotland.[1] The history of this intervention, beginning with its attempted transformation from a council-run center for the unemployed into an "autonomous" site for radical political activity, offers a complex picture of an infoshop founded on revolutionary anarchist praxis. The analysis will be presented "top down"; that is, it will begin with an examination of the determinations of state power and its agents on the infoshop. It will then consider the extent to which the infoshop is economically "free" before concluding by addressing key aspects of social organization and the impact these have on the ability of the free space of the infoshop to enable "reflexive practice, creativity, and challenge" among its participants.

The Determinations of State Power

The uneasy relationship between the infoshop and the state is vividly illustrated by the history of the Autonomous Centre of Edinburgh. The roots of ACE can be traced to the setting up of the Edinburgh Unemployed Worker's Centre in the 1990s. This was funded by and housed in premises owned by Lothian Regional Council but run by volunteering unemployed workers. It appears that a small group of these volunteers, radicalized in the face of what they saw as repressive measures to curb the freedoms of the unemployed (the Jobseekers' Allowance, the "New Deal" for the unemployed), moved to transform the Centre from a nonpolitical advice and community resource. The aim was to go beyond the provision of advice on state benefits and tax issues (specifically, the emerging problems around the recently instituted council, or "poll," tax in the U.K.) as well as to establish "a base for social struggles, such as claimants' resistance and opposition to the M77 [a motorway being built in the West of Scotland and the focus for Scottish antiroad building protests]" ("Evicted," 1995). In its heyday, the Centre offered "a thriving café, and busy crèche, well-used meeting spaces, a darkroom, a reading room, community arts space, music workshops, claimants' resistance and benefits advice, frequent socials and so on" ("Defend the Occupation!" 1994). It was these radical political activities, as evinced by "claimants' resistance"—rather than the less controversial, and more "inclusive," functions of the Centre (café, crèche, darkroom)—that prompted the council to move against it.

The council moved swiftly to counter what its officers perceived as a threat to the normal running of the Centre and its takeover by an unrepresentative minority. June 1994 saw the Centre occupied by its radical members in an effort to defy the council's calls for its closure. In September 1994 a "move to eject" decree was served on the premises, requiring its volunteer staff to relinquish control and leave the building. However, it was not until December 1994 that the six-month occupation was ended by police and council officials, resulting in the arrest of twenty-one people. The revolutionary anarchist news sheet *Counter Information* claims that "80 people resisted the surprise eviction for 8 hours," though how many of these were active members of the Centre and how many were supporters are not clear. The council appeared to have succeeded in what *Counter Information* described as its attempt to "destroy an autonomous space which has long been a base for direct action and grass-roots struggles" ("Defend the Occupation!" 1994).

The experiences of 1994 demonstrate the repressive regulation the state landlord was prepared to undertake to prevent the Centre from being hijacked by volunteers whose political aims were clearly at variance with those of the council. The council was also acting on a principle of access. Council officers felt that the radicalization of the Centre would only lead to the exclusion of a majority of "ordinary" unemployed. In this case we see the wholehearted support of a Labour-controlled council toward a center for the unemployed, but whose support was sorely tested (along with its apparent liberalism) when activities at the Centre began to engage with wider social and political issues and events. While the relevance to the Centre's aims of an engagement in the M77 protests by a minority of the Centre's members is questionable, it was the attempts to radicalize the unemployed through meetings and protests that finally brought the state's repressive apparatuses to bear.

Yet the radicals' claim that what the council had worked to "destroy" was "an autonomous space" requires attention. Given the ownership of the premises and the funding of resources by the council, the space was curtailed in its autonomy from the outset. Attempts by the volunteers to weaken these determinations were met with powerful and successful resistance from regional government. This failed first attempt at autonomy "in the shadow of the state" was followed by a second intervention by the volunteers, who, after their eviction, found a temporary home in the basement of a local community center. They emerged only partially from that shadow into an organization that was itself partly funded by the regional government. Despite its more limited access to resources (relying on those borrowed from the community center), the small core group of the former Centre established the activist group known as Edinburgh Claimants and produced an occasional newsletter (*Dole Harassment Exposed!*) detailing the group's protests against benefit cuts and compulsory "workfare" schemes. The core group also continued its involvement in the production of the revolutionary anarchist news sheet *Counter Information*. Despite its apparent isolation and marginalization in the public life of Edinburgh, the group developed and maintained contacts with like-minded groups across the U.K. Edinburgh Claimants became part of a U.K.-wide network of unemployed activists, known as Groundswell. (For an overview of this network see Shore, 1997.) *Counter Information*, as it had before the eviction, continued to be produced by three collectives, based respectively in Edinburgh, Glasgow, and Leeds. Sustaining their part in these networks would prove valuable when the core group finally found its own premises and moved into its final phase of autonomy. Here too, though, the attempt at autonomy was significantly curtailed—on this occasion, by economics.

"Free" Economics and the Infoshop

The economic survival of the infoshop, whether in Europe or the United States, has depended heavily, if not exclusively, on "self-exploited" labor and access to cheap, often borrowed or donated resources such as second-hand photocopiers, computers, and furniture. In this respect, the financing of these projects bears a close similarity to the anarchist media that are often produced in such locations. Not all alternative media have had to endure such a precarious existence. In the United States, publications as diverse as the monthly magazine *Mother Jones* and the *Earth First!* newspaper have been able to sustain themselves in part through the economy of scale resulting from being based in a vast, English-speaking country. By contrast, attempts at establishing nationally distributed, alternative media in small countries such as the U.K. have foundered, largely due to a smaller base of potential readers. The generalist, nonparty and non–special interest "progressive" perspective of a magazine such as *Mother Jones* has also proved appealing to specialist advertisers such as trade unions, pressure groups, NGOs, and independent book publishers. *Earth First!* has survived without the need to take advertising, instead relying largely on its large nationwide subscription base to sustain it. Economies of scale are not available to the specialized, anarchist media in the U.K.; neither are these publications attractive to advertisers, assuming that such media wish to seek advertising at all. Many radical publications refuse to accept advertising on ideological grounds, fearing that it "could interfere with their freedom as a result of advertisers seeking to dictate the content of the rest of the publication" (Atton, 2002: 37). As the British radical newspaper *Squall* told its readers in 1996, it did not carry advertising for "multinationals or cultural hijackers" (cited in Atton, 2002). Taken together, these two limits on finance perpetuate such media as small-scale interventions, virtually invisible to all but their immediate, self-selected audiences (many of whom are involved in their production).

Any future development of the former Edinburgh Unemployed Worker's Centre depended acutely on finance. It not only had a stake in the continuance of two publications but also hoped to replicate, with no visible means of support, its status as a physical center for radical political activity in Edinburgh. Its earlier premises, however jeopardized they turned out to be, were at least located on a busy thoroughfare in a prominent "bohemian" area of the city. This opened up the possibility that the Centre would attract (or at least "advertise" itself to) a wider public than the already-committed radicals responsible for its birth.

While self-exploited labor would enable the group to refurbish and run any new premises, funding had to be sought to rent such a property (buying was out of the question). The bulk of this money came from donations and benefit concerts, replicating precisely the primary subsidies that have been at the heart of alternative media production and counter-cultural activity at least since the 1960s (Fountain, 1988). More than two years after the closure of the original Centre, enough money had been raised to rent a small shopfront on a quiet, unfashionable street in the north of Edinburgh. An area known for its cheap housing, this new location had none of the visibility or bohemianism of the Centre's previous homes. The area was rather more working class, an aspect that might well have appealed to a group whose primary aim as revolutionary anarchists was to support class struggle. Nevertheless, the combination of bureaucratic intervention and economic limits immediately forced the group to establish its center in an area where, as a physical presence, it would probably be largely passed by. This made the group's task of establishing and promoting the Centre that much harder.

The new establishment—which, as noted, is named the Autonomous Centre of Edinburgh (ACE)—opened in February 1997. As noted in the following list taken from a flyer distributed by ACE (styled exactly as in the original), it promises an impressive array of services, functions, and resources:

- Advice and solidarity against dole harassment
- A meeting place for community-political groups
- Radical books, zines, and information
- A low-cost vegan cafe and drop-in centre
- Local arts and crafts
- Underground records, demos, t-shirts, badges
- People's food co-operative
- Socializing in an *anti*-sexist, -racist, or -homophobic environment
- An epicenter of alternative/DIY [do-it-yourself] kulture

The items on this list are common to the offerings of many infoshops, thus demonstrating how many of them understand the realization of a "free space." In short, the intent is to be more than just a repository for information; it is to offer information with advice (from a specific political standpoint, one of revolutionary anarchism)—thus producing a radical Citizens' Advice Bureau, if you will. The Centre is also seen as a space for dialogue, for the sharing and development of ideas. (The promotion of dialogical praxis within anarchism had emerged in the 1990s, inspired by the Zapatista struggle in the Chiapas region of Mexico. As John Jordan has argued: "Zapatismo is a living example of how we can open the space, prepare the soil, and, through direct democratic dialogue, witness the radical roots going deep" [Jordan, 2001: 21].) Alongside these desires to establish an environment for "socializing" that is free of the social and cultural restraints that anarchism tends to see as products of capitalism (sexism, racism, homophobia), there appears to be a cultural narrowing of ACE's cultural sights. The types of subcultural production it hopes to encourage are specialist (if not minority) interests.

The "underground records" offered for sale by ACE are almost exclusively Punk, acknowledging the contemporary youth anarchist movement's debt (at least in Europe and the United States) to that musical movement in popularizing anarchist philosophy and praxis through the work of bands such as Crass. (For a convincing assessment of Crass's contribution to anarchist politics and to British political life in general, see McKay, 1996: ch. 3.) ACE's program demonstrates its concern with welfare, intending to offer low-cost food and cooperative means of supplying and distributing that food. We should note, though, that the emphasis on a minority dietary philosophy (veganism) somewhat skews the Centre's general aim to be "a base for social struggles," as it had previously claimed. This aim is to "[provide] resources and solidarity so that people can take control of their own struggles and define their own priorities" (as quoted in its leaflet titled "The Autonomous Centre of Edinburgh: What Is It and What Does It Do?"). As with the emphasis on Punk music, ACE appears to be catering to a specialist group of already-committed activists. While it clearly supports and "tries to develop links to other [working-class] groups, such as . . . the Gartocher residents in Glasgow who are trying to stop a landfill site being built in their residential area," its immediate audience appears to be a small, politically active fraction of the Left who might be persuaded—if they are not already—to support revolutionary anarchism as the means of waging class struggle. This looked-for political commitment from ACE's audience is expected to be accompanied by a similar commitment to specific cultural forms of protest (veganism, Punk music). ACE's "wish list," despite its wide range, does appear rather more limited in its appeal than the facilities provided at the former Edinburgh Unemployed Worker's Centre.

Notwithstanding the apparently "closed" aspects of the community ACE was attempting to establish in its new premises, the list of promised facilities and functions is impressive. To achieve them all would require significant resources (labor, capital, and equipment). As recently as 2002, volunteers from ACE argued that all have been achieved save for the café and the food cooperative. Visiting the Centre, one finds significant collections of alternative media, recorded music, and related cultural artifacts. The Centre remains the only source of advice on "dole harassment," and its continuing role as a home for the Edinburgh collective of *Counter Information* provides some evidence that it is indeed "an epicenter for alternative/DIY Kulture." Attendance at its many meetings, even a perusal of its e-mail bulletins, suggests that ACE also functions as a meeting place; but the extent to which it is open or available to a range of "community-political groups" needs to be examined. Doing so would require an analysis of the organizational methods of the Centre and how these might determine ACE's activities at the social level.

Social Organization

Previous studies of organizational strategies in alternative media, in counter-cultural activities, and in new social movements have identified a collective approach to policy formation and decision making. This emphasis on the collective springs from a notion of "equality . . . interpreted and evaluated in terms of *sharing*" (Landry et al., 1985: 7; original emphasis). In this instance, "sharing" emphasizes collective organization without any reference to the size of the collective, or to whether it is possible to work collectively regardless of the numbers involved. Furthermore, such sharing rejects the formal, bureaucratic, and hierarchical methods of doing business. The research group Comedia (1984) has argued that such nonhierarchical, collective methods can only disadvantage the alternative media, because they are always adopted for political ends, never for economic ones. This argument is not a new one in radical milieus. Jo Freeman's (1972) classic critique of structurelessness in the women's movement makes much the same point in the wider context of political organizing. Andrea Baker's

(1982) study of lesbian-feminist organizations and Amy Farrell's (1994) case study of the feminist magazine *Ms.* confirm Freeman's argument.

A radical approach to the collective often rejects entirely the importance of business and, with it, the value of individuals taking responsibility, acquiring specific skills, and exercising authority (which are seen as autocratic features of despotic hierarchy). The abandonment of business practices as capitalist and reactionary produces, according to Landry and his colleagues, an organization where the quest to be "maximally democratic" is achieved at the expense of the organization's "economic imperatives" (1985, p. 31). As we have seen in the case of ACE, this leads to financial stringency, to a reliance on self-exploited, voluntary labor, cheap materials, and even squatted office space—in short, to what these authors term "barefoot economics" (1985, p. 24). By contrast, more hierarchical and centralized forms of alternative media (such as the *Big Issue* in the U.K., an alternative "advocacy" publication) have succeeded.

To what extent have the volunteers at ACE learned from the past in their choice of organizational model? To what extent have their chosen methods of organization encouraged the diversity of voices and groups to be heard within their free space? ACE currently employs a full collective approach to its organization, based on consensus decision-making. Its "business" meetings are open to all and everyone; long-standing participants or newcomers have the same right to make proposals. That this open method of collective organizing does not produce the kind of democratic paralysis found, for example, in the British radical community papers of the 1970s (Minority Press Group, 1980) is due to another common feature of radical organizing: the small number of activists committed enough to attend meetings on a regular basis. This small base of regular volunteers inevitably has an effect on the facilities that ACE is able to offer. The Centre is currently open only twice a week (Tuesday and Sunday afternoons), for a total of seven hours per week, for general access to its resources (although it does open at other times for specific events such as film screenings and political meetings). This restriction significantly curtails its ability to function as a "drop-in center" and as a location for "socializing." We should also note that, despite the diversity of activities based at ACE, many of them are undertaken or organized by a single set of volunteers. For example, one small group (a core of around five people) is responsible for the production of *Counter Information,* and a smaller number taken from this group organize not only the Edinburgh Claimants activities but also most of the discussion meetings held at ACE in the evening.

While this small group makes collective decision-making efficient, it is far from inclusive and calls into doubt some of ACE's grander statements about developing an environment free from racism, sexism, and homophobia. Such an aim is much easier to achieve when those making up the bulk of that environment are small in number and already committed to those practices. This is not a deliberate strategy, resulting as it does from a reluctance to establish an elite organizing collective, but its effect is debilitating. The small, closed group—it can appear closed to "outsiders" at least—restricts the development of the infoshop. In particular, it conflicts with ACE's desire to assist in a range of working-class struggles and with its claims to provide a nonhierarchical free space. Though the latter might not be foreclosed, the organizational methods of ACE strongly suggest that this free space is an ideal at best.

Assessing Failure

Earlier we explored the free space of the infoshop in terms of its potential as an alternative public sphere. This potential implies a space for the radical performance of citizenship practices. Practices of cultural democratization can then be encouraged within what Nick Couldry has termed "a community of *incomplete, uncertain* selves, working through dialogue to transform one another—a community without closure" (Couldry, 2000: 140; original emphasis). Central to such a community is dialogue; independent control over symbolic resources is crucial to enable the "exchange [of] representations of such 'reality' as we share" (Couldry, 2002). This is not to say that there is no potential for creating such a dialogical, democratized space out of the narrower space that is ACE. Skepticism appears appropriate, however. Since its establishment in 1997 as a space whose autonomy from state determination was seen as an indicator of its future strength, the Centre has shown few signs of expanding either its core organizing collective or its audience. It remains a specialist space, of significance in the main to that small number directly responsible for its maintenance.

This situation is hardly unique in the infoshop movement. Brad Sigal (undated) has remarked on the failure of anarchist and radical communities to sustain infoshops. He notes this even in the case of the Beehive Infoshop in Washington, D.C., a city with a general population far greater than that of Edinburgh. At least ACE has avoided the in-fighting and schisms Sigal has found in all his examples of American infoshop organizing, though ACE has achieved this end only through the permanence of a small core group. ACE's situation bears out the criticisms of Landry and his colleagues against collective decision-making. It shows that a small group with clear responsibilities tends to work better than large diffused groups and that activities based on small groups tend to last longer. Such small groups are not incompatible with more inclusive methods of discussion and decision-making, but in the present case these seem not to have occurred.

Perhaps this outcome is due in some part to the lack of communicable vision and strategy of the infoshop. Its politics are far from popular, and even among a significant section of its potential audience (activists working on broad national and international campaigns such as genetically modified crops, road-building, and anticapitalism), its ideology of revolutionary anarchism is neither generally understood nor especially well communicated by ACE's core group. Sigal (undated) has argued that one of the two "missing links" in the success of the infoshop movement is a "unifying vision" (the other is internal group dynamics). Without the formulation of clear goals and strategy it becomes very difficult to judge the efficacy of activities within the infoshop. Neither is it straightforward to explain the purpose of those activities to outsiders, save in very general terms (contributing to class struggle, for instance). This more or less abstract vision Segal terms "the unstated (dis)ideology of infoshops," highlighting the tension between an infoshop's internalized, yet unexpressed, vision and the lack of communication to a wider public of that vision.

Sigal's second missing link, that of internal group dynamics, we have already examined. For him, though, the problem stems from internal conflict within the group, whether to do with race, class, gender, or what color to the paint the meeting room. Sigal suggests "revolutionary pluralism" as a way out of these impasses. That is, rather than becoming the established center from which all radical activity is developed, the infoshop need be only one node in a network of autonomous activities. ACE has succeeded in avoiding internal conflict if only by virtue of its small organizing group, but its members continue to hold by the notion of the infoshop as the center from which all anarchist revolutionary activity should proceed. As an empowering strategy this does not seem to have been successful; as a means of encouraging a diversity of voices it is extremely limited; the possibilities for experiments with autonomy become the preserve of a few. In terms of objectives, however, much is apparently achieved by ACE: publications, meetings, discussion groups, video presentations, organization of protests. Yet these are achieved by a perpetually small group that seems to engage only marginally with a wider public, even with the wider counter public spheres of protest and dissent within which ACE must be located.

Conclusion

Melucci (1996) holds that for an "antagonist movement . . . what is at stake is the possibility of giving a different form to, and profoundly reorganizing, the structure and goals of the appropriation of social resources" (p. 38). In the case of ACE, there is clear evidence that developing different forms and reorganizing structures have met with some success, but the vagueness of its goals—resulting in the exclusiveness of its membership—appears to have prevented it from developing more than a very limited "public space of representation" (p. 220). This space, which Melucci characterizes as one "distinct from the institutions of government, from the party system, and from the state apparatuses" (p. 220), has been only partially achieved by ACE, and at some cost. Ironically, it was more successful when more visible, both to a wider public (the unemployed) and to the apparatuses of the state and government. Yet, as we have seen, it was at that stage in the career of the infoshop that the state intervened in its activities and severely curtailed them. Melucci's argument about state repression— that it tends to make itself felt towards "the organization and political participation of interests that call [the] limits [of institutional confines] into question" (p. 247)— seems most powerful here. Further, as Melucci reminds us, the state works "not only at the purely repressive level but also by exercising control over the socialization and cultural apparatuses" (p. 249). In the shadow of the state ACE lost not only its economic base but also much of its burgeoning social and cultural impetus. In effect, it was forced underground, returned to a condition that for most similar projects is prototypical. As the Unemployed Workers' Centre the infoshop was becoming established as a living political force in an environment where it was both visible and increasingly recognized as a center for radical activity. Indirectly, though undoubtedly, the economic and "environmental" impact of its closure, while enabling a purer form of autonomy, resulted in its regression to a ghetto-like state of marginality. The status of ACE as an autonomous space is thus called into question. Just as Greg Martin notes in the case of New Age travelers, the members of ACE find themselves in a "predicament" that is "a direct consequence of government policies" (2002: 84). To this extent, the strategy of the state has been successful; in seeking to return the Unemployed Workers' Centre to a condition of beneficent harmlessness, it coincidentally ensured that the future of radical politics in Edinburgh would be forced back to the margins. The present and continuing state of ACE makes it an unlikely future target for the predations of the state, to which it appears largely irrelevant.

Note

1. The information on ACE was collected through a combination of participant observation, interviews with participants, and examination of the many publications and e-mail bulletins produced at ACE. Chief among these is the news sheet *Counter Information*.

References

Atton, Chris (1996). *Alternative Literature: A Practical Guide for Librarians*. Aldershot, U.K.: Gower.

——— (2001). "The Mundane and Its Reproduction in Alternative Media," *Journal of Mundane Behavior* 2(1): 122–137. Available online at www.mundanebehavior.org/index.htm. Last accessed on 21 March 2002.

——— (2002). *Alternative Media*. London: Sage.

Baker, Andrea J. (1982). "The Problem of Authority in Radical Movement Groups: A Case Study of Lesbian-Feminist Organization," *Journal of Applied Behavioral Science* 18(3): 323–41.

Bookchin, Murray (1986). "A Note on Affinity Groups," in Murray Bookchin, *Post-scarcity Anarchism*, 2nd. ed., pp. 243–44. Montreal: Black Rose.

Comedia (1984). "The Alternative Press: The Development of Underdevelopment," *Media, Culture and Society* 6: 95–102.

Couldry, Nick (2000). *Inside Culture*. London: Sage.

——— (2002). "Alternative Media and Mediated Community." Paper presented at the International Association for Media and Communication Research, Barcelona, 23 July.

Cox, Laurence (1997). "Reflexivity, Social Transformation and Counter Culture," in Colin Barker and Mike Tyldesley (eds.), *Third International Conference on Alternative Futures and Popular Protest: A Selection of Papers from the Conference, 24–26 March 1997*, Vol. I. Manchester, U.K.: Manchester Metropolitan University, Faculty of Humanities and Social Science, Department of Sociology and Interdisciplinary Studies.

——— (undated). "Towards a Sociology of Counter Cultures?" Unpublished manuscript (copy in author's possession).

"Defend the Occupation!" (1994). *Counter Information*, issue 41 (October–December).

Dodge, Chris (1998). "Taking Libraries to the Street: Infoshops and Alternative Reading Rooms," *American Libraries* (May): 62–64.

Downing, John (1984). *Radical Media: The Political Experience of Alternative Communication*. Boston: South End Press.

——— (2001). *Radical Media: Rebellious Communication and Social Movements*. Thousand Oaks, Calif.: Sage.

"Evicted—But the Centre Lives On!" *Counter Information,* issue no. 42 (March–May).

Eyerman, Ron, and Jamison, Andrew (1991). *Social Movements: A Cognitive Approach.* Cambridge, U.K.: Polity Press.

Farrell, Amy Erdman (1994). "A Social Experiment in Publishing: *Ms.* Magazine, 1972–1989," *Human Relations* 47(6): 707–30.

Fountain, Nigel (1988). *Underground: The London Alternative Press, 1966–74.* London: Comedia/Routledge.

Fraser, Nancy (1992). "Rethinking the Public Sphere—A Contribution to the Critique of Actually Existing Democracy," in Craig Calhoun (ed.), *Habermas and the Public Sphere*, pp. 109–42. Cambridge, Mass./London: MIT Press.

Freeman, Jo (1972). "The Tyranny of Structurelessness," *Berkeley Journal of Sociology* 17: 151–64.

Habermas, Jürgen (1962/1989). *The Structural Transformation of the Public Sphere: An Inquiry into a Category of Bourgeois Society.* Translated by Thomas Burger with the assistance of Frederick Lawrence. Cambridge, U.K.: Polity Press.

Jordan, John (2001). "Zapatismo and the Invisible Icons of Anti-Capitalism," *Red Pepper* (September): 19–21.

Landry, Charles, et al. (1985). *What a Way to Run a Railroad: An Analysis of Radical Failure.* London: Comedia.

Martin, Greg (2002). "Conceptualizing Cultural Politics in Subcultural and Social Movement Studies," *Social Movement Studies* 1(1): 73–88.

McKay, George (1996). *Senseless Acts of Beauty: Cultures of Resistance since the Sixties.* London: Verso.

Melucci, Alberto (1995). "The New Social Movements Revisited: Reflections on a Sociological Misunderstanding," in Louis Maheu (ed.), *Social Movements and Social Classes: The Future of Collective Action*, pp. 107–19. London: Sage.

——— (1996). *Challenging Codes: Collective Action in the Information Age.* Cambridge, U.K.: Cambridge University Press.

Minority Press Group (1980). *Here Is the Other News: Challenges to the Local Commercial Press* (Minority Press Group Series No. 1). London: Minority Press Group.

Shore, Albert (1997). "Managing the Unemployed: Recent Patterns of Resistance to the Government Manipulation of the Jobless," *The Raven* 9(4) (Autumn): 314–17.

Sigal, Brad (undated). "The Demise of the Beehive Collective: Lessons for the Infoshop Movement in North America." Reprinted from *Love and Rage* 6(4) (August/September 1995), where it appeared under the title "Demise of the Beehive Collective: Infoshops Ain't the Revolution."

Spivak, Gayatri Chakravorty (1988). "Can the Subaltern Speak?" in Cary Nelson and Lawrence Grossberg (eds.), *Marxism and the Interpretation of Culture*, pp. 271–313. Basingstoke, U.K.: Macmillan.

Triggs, Teal (1995). "Alphabet Soup: Reading British Fanzines," *Visible Language* 29(1): 72–87.

CHAPTER 5

Framing the Future
INDIGENOUS COMMUNICATION IN AUSTRALIA

Christine Morris and Michael Meadows

Technology has had and is having a great effect on our culture and traditions. This effect can be negative for our culture and traditions (as it mostly is at the moment), or we can devise ways to utilise technology to maintain and perpetuate our traditional knowledge. It is likely that the long-term survival of our traditional knowledge will depend upon our ability to exploit the new information and communication technology. For us to continue to rely upon our oral traditions is unsustainable. The new information technology has the real potential to help our people maintain our traditions—we need to grapple with it and devise strategies for exploring its potential.

—Noel Pearson (2000a: 64)

This observation by Indigenous lawyer Noel Pearson highlights some of the challenges facing Indigenous communication in the new millennium. There are many Indigenous people like Pearson who continue to work within their communities, searching for ways of ensuring survival in a world where information has become a commodity of global significance. And for many of these visionaries, the future they see is not one where survival alone is their aim. They seek access to a world where Indigenous intellectual property is highly valued. For Indigenous communities, it is less a matter of learning new skills than one of rediscovering the frameworks that have enabled them to survive into the new millennium. Communications technology, in many and varied forms, has always played a central role in this process.

Supported by a grant from the Australian Research Council in the late 1990s, we set out to make sense of communication by looking at existing Indigenous social structures. Instead of thinking of Indigenous communication as something separated from the processes of everyday life, we began to explore the idea that it needs to be seen as *a central organizing element* of Indigenous society. We identified a set of key ideas as a framework on which concepts of Indigenous communication could be based—intellectual property, the traditional economy, and knowledge management. We chose these because all are already part of the agenda in Indigenous communities. They have a direct impact on the Indigenous communication process because they are all connected. Our study investigated how these ideas could help to manage information technology and telecommunications *as tools* for sustaining Indigenous culture. In this way, communication technologies can be seen as important community cultural resources.

Indigenous communication systems on the Australian continent existed for millennia before the European invasion in 1788. At that time, between 200 and 250 distinct Aboriginal languages (nations) existed. In 1788, there were perhaps 500 different Indigenous dialects used by as few as 100 people, or by as many as 1,500. At the turn of the new millennium, it is estimated that 50 of these 200 languages are now extinct, about 100 have very small speech communities, and 50 remain in a situation in which they are likely to survive into the next century (Blake, 1981; Schmidt, 1993). Australia can be seen through Indigenous eyes as a multicultural, multilingual continent of Indigenous sovereign nations coping with different levels of invasion while maintaining their languages (Morris, 2002: 10). The threat to languages and cultures has become one of the primary driving forces behind the movement of Indigenous people globally to appropriate communication technologies—where possible, on their own terms.

Aboriginal social organization is bound up in the notion of "the Dreaming," which might be interpreted as referring to the law and a relationship to time and space in which ancestral beings' journeys across the landscape shaped natural features and described Dreaming tracks (Michaels, 1987: 28–30). Such tracks might be considered as "information conduits" or media, along which people travel, carrying goods for exchange and moving to ceremonial sites (Michaels, 1986: 508). Another view is put forward by the Anangu. Following the return of their ancestral lands in 1985, the Anangu (Pitjantjatjara) now co-manage the Uluru–Kata Tjuta National Park (Ayers Rock–Mount Olga) in central Australia. They use the term *Tjukurpa* to help explain their religious heritage and the relationship between people, plants, animals, and physical features in the landscape. They explain that while this represents the law and rules of everyday behavior, it is also about the past, the present, and the future. The Anangu remind us, "The *Tjukurpa* is not a dream; it is real" (Australian National Parks and Wildlife Service and Mutitjulu Community, 1990). A senior lawman of the Kimberley region of northwestern Australia, Mowaljarlai, talks about it in terms of a "Sharing system":

> I want to show you something. I want to show you how all Aboriginal people in Australia are connected in the *Wunnan* system. The squares are the areas where the communities are represented, and their symbols and the languages of the different tribes in this country from long, long time ago. The lines are the way the history stories travelled along these trade routes. They are all connected: it's the pattern of the Sharing system. (1993: 190)

This notion of the ways in which traditional societies see themselves connected to each other and the land is important in understanding the notion of Indigenous information transfer. During his years living with the Warlpiri in central Australia, Michaels concluded that the maintenance of what he termed "communication tracks" (Dreaming tracks) was critical for the maintenance of identity:

> The mass media pose an enormous challenge to the maintenance of the traditional communication system. New media can move information instan-

taneously via electronic transmission or reasonably quickly with air-delivered videotapes. Where it is traditional Aboriginal material that is so transported between communities that would otherwise be linked (or segregated) by Dreaming tracks, not only may the authority to display be ignored but intermediary exchange processes may be overridden. (Michaels, 1986: 508)

Using this framework, Michaels argued that traditional Aboriginal social organizations might be considered "information societies" where access to knowledge is of particular social and economic consequence (Michaels, 1985: 69): "Aboriginal society, as I have come to understand it, makes explicit distinctions between the right to know, the right to speak, and the right to speak for, or repeat. In societies without print, where the word is inseparable from the author of the word, information can take on special values" (Michaels, 1983: 52). The objective, according to Michaels, is the maintenance of language and culture. And it is this which is perceived as being threatened by the European satellite television invasion of remote communities from the mid-1980s—and by the very nature of mass communication itself. Mary Graham (1992) identifies "the two great axioms of Aboriginal thinking"—the land as the law and the principle that Aboriginal people are not alone in the world. She explains that identity for every Aboriginal group means autonomy: Everybody is equal, which explains the absence of leaders in Aboriginal society. The media's constant reference to "Aboriginal leaders" is thus a source of great annoyance to many. A place in the world through kinship and a relationship to the land dominate notions of Aboriginal identity, as Mary Graham (1992) explains:

> For Aboriginal people you can't get a meaning of life from a great personage, a great figure like a great teacher because in the end, they're just human beings too, with all the vulnerability of humans. All they can ever be is to be great exemplars. The only solid thing you can get meaning out of is land because it's the only thing that exists besides us.

Within these ideas of identity, then, how have Indigenous people managed their interactions with communication technologies? Indigenous media represent Australia's fastest-growing communication sector. It has emerged as a result of two important social forces: discontent with mainstream media misrepresentation of Indigenous affairs and the desire to appropriate communication technologies as a first level of service for communities. Access to communication technology has always been a struggle—little has ever been given to Indigenous people, despite the rhetoric, which has become almost commonplace in sections of Australian politics. Indigenous communities have survived in an environment that is often racist and discriminatory. At the same time, there have been some significant collaborations with non-Indigenous people that have made a contribution to the prospect of real reconciliation between Indigenous and non-Indigenous Australia.

The Indigenous media sector has emerged despite some of these obstacles and as a response to others. While its existence and significance have only recently been acknowledged by Australian policy-makers (Productivity Commission, 2000), policy, as in so many other spheres, often trails behind the reality of on-the-ground experience. The next step may be the most difficult: to break away from a constraining non-Indigenous framework within which the media sector has emerged, and to consider an Indigenous way of doing things. Some communities, like those that are part of the Cape York Digital Network (CYDN) and those in the Torres Strait, have already adopted this approach and are moving ahead as a result. For other communities, this will be more challenging because they lack access to the necessary expertise (both human and financial). But regardless of which direction Indigenous communities decide to go, they must be allowed to do it their way. Our brief history suggests that anything else is destined to fail.

A Brief History of Indigenous Media in Australia

PRINT

The earliest identified publication produced by an Aboriginal organization was published under two names: *The Aboriginal* and *Flinders Island Chronicle*. It was first published in 1836. On many others, few details exist until the 1950s. The number of publications increased dramatically during the land rights protests of the late 1960s and 1970s and have continued since. News sheets appeared in the early 1980s in response to talk of launching Australia's own satellite and of the possible effects that broadcasting would have on remote communities (Langton and Kirkpatrick, 1979). The monthly newspaper *Land Rights News*, based in the Northern Territory, began publishing in 1976 as a roneoed newsletter by the Northern Land Council in Darwin. It turned tabloid in 1980 and continues today as the major, regular national Aboriginal newspaper. A more recent addition is the Lismore-based *Koori Mail*, a monthly that began publishing in mid-1991 (Rose, 1996). Other regular publications include *Land Rights Queensland*, published by the FAIRA Corporation since 1994 in Brisbane.

BROADCASTING

From humble beginnings in 1974 to its present level of more than 200 stations throughout Australia, community radio has been at the forefront of Indigenous broadcasting and continues to provide a means for access to new technologies. By the turn of the new millennium, there were more than 100 licensed Indigenous radio stations in Australia broadcasting more than 1,000 hours of Indigenous content weekly. The Central Australian Aboriginal Media Association (CAAMA) in Alice Springs was the first station for which the Indigenous Special Interest community radio license was granted, in 1985. The first capital city Indigenous Special Interest community radio license, 4 AAA, was awarded to the Brisbane Indigenous Media Association (BIMA) in 1993. There are now at least 12 licensed community stations run by Indigenous media groups. On 25 January 1996 the National Indigenous Radio Service (NIRS) was launched, and early in 2001 a National Indigenous News Service started. The NIRS links around 20 Indigenous radio stations by satellite and landline and can broadcast to a further 170 community-based stations, giving it a potential reach second only to the Australian Broadcasting Corporation (ABC). The ABC supports programming produced by Indigenous media associations through "resource broadcasting"—a combination of regional and community stations using ABC transmitters. The corporation has also supported Indigenous radio programs such as *Awaye* and Indigenous television programs such as *Speaking Out, Blackout, Kum Yan,* and *Songlines* (Molnar and Meadows, 2001).

REMOTE COMMUNITY RADIO, TELEVISION, AND NEW MEDIA

Since 1987, the Broadcasting for Remote Aboriginal Communities Scheme (BRACS) has delivered satellite radio and television to 28,000 remote Indigenous Australians. Eighty-three Aboriginal and Torres Strait Islander communities were initially provided with equipment that enabled them to receive available radio and television services. Three remote commercial television services are available via satellite, with communities making the decision about which of them to accept. BRACS also provides basic facilities for communities to produce and broadcast their own community radio and television programs, including those in their own languages, should they so desire. Almost all communities claim there was little or no consultation before the BRACS equipment was installed. Another key complaint from communities is that there has been little backup funding for training and maintenance of the equipment. For all its faults, however, BRACS at least has encouraged the development of regional communication associations. It is estimated that

Figure 5.1.   Radio Torres Strait: Vinitta Keane (left) and Ina Gebaldi (right) in the Radio Torres Strait studio on Thursday Island.
Source: Photo by Michael Meadows.

Figure 5.2.   Torres Strait BRACS: The BRACS unit on Saibai Island in the Torres Strait, a few kilometers from Papua New Guinea.
Source: Photo by Michael Meadows.

more than 200 Aboriginal and Torres Strait Islander women and men are involved with BRACS broadcasting alone, with a great many more in voluntary roles throughout the sector. In 1997, BRACS units were reclassified as Community Stations.

In the early 1990s, four communities in the Tanami Desert pioneered communication links using compressed videoconferencing and satellite technologies. Called the Tanami Network, the system links the centers—Yuendumu, Kintore, Lajamanu, and Willowra—with Alice Springs, Darwin, and the rest of the world. The scheme began to return a small operating profit in 1993–1994. Since its launch, the Tanami Network has enabled a disparate array of links permitting (1) communication between families and imprisoned relatives, (2) the sale of art internationally, (3) discussions with the Sioux, (4) delivery of education and health programs, (5) and the organization of local ceremonial business. As with every other structure in traditional Indigenous communities, the operation of the network is governed by cultural rules (Molnar and Meadows, 2001).

THE POLICY ENVIRONMENT

The ad hoc policy environment in which Indigenous communication has emerged is indicative of the relationship that exists between communities and mainstream governance. A lack of communication between government agencies concerned with the Indigenous communication sector was one of the main findings of a comprehensive review of the sector (ATSIC, 1999). Some communication concerns have been met by initiatives under a scheme called Networking the Nation, in which money from the partial sale of Australia's telecommunications utility, Telstra, was earmarked to improve regional and remote telecommunications.[1] The wider pattern, however, is reflective of a lack of focus in thinking about Indigenous communication, which has been a hallmark of the policy-making process. Apart from studies dealing specifically with the communication sector, research had largely ignored the potential of communication technology for Indigenous people. When it has been considered, Indigenous communication has never been seen as an integral part of the Indigenous world; rather, it is perceived as being on the fringe. The belated recognition in 2000 by the Productivity Commission that an Indigenous communication sector *actually exists* is evidence for this (Molnar and Meadows, 2001; Meadows, 2000; Productivity Commission, 2000). As we suggest here, communication should be seen as a major organizing element of Indigenous society—a framework for the past, the present, and the future.

We will now consider what we have identified as key factors in defining the nature of Indigenous communication: intellectual property rights, the traditional economy, and knowledge management.

Intellectual Property Rights

The concept of intellectual property rights for Indigenous people determines identity and each person's place in society in relation to the law. Intellectual property rights operate through sophisticated management systems that have survived for millennia. As an example, Mer (Murray Islands) Chairman Ron Day addresses the question of how different concepts of culture must be understood to grasp the full meaning of Indigenous intellectual property rights. He explains that Torres Strait Islanders see a cultural object—such as a stone implement created by ancestors—as having spiritual value. Others, he argues, might look at the artifact and merely see a piece of rock:

> Let me put it this way. When we address international or national forums with respect to culture, people usually give it out from the top of their minds. I question that all the time. Anybody can talk about culture but not everyone practises it. So when you talk about culture you have to talk about it from your own being and not from a text book. So when you approach objects like that (the artefact), its power naturally becomes part of you. (quoted in TSIMA, 1999a)

Day's observation suggests that an important starting point for thinking about Indigenous intellectual property rights is to consider culture as a dynamic, lived experience. This is in accord with concepts of culture as "a constitutive social process" (Williams, 1977: 19) that incorporates both "lived practices" and "practical ideologies" to enable societies to make sense of their lives (Hall, 1982: 77). Within this definition, the media and communication emerge as important cultural resources in the process of manufacturing and winning consent—or managing society (Meadows, 2000: 12–13).

Intellectual property rights have been described as the "rights asserted in the products of the mind" (Simons, 2000: 412), thus placing traditional knowledge and cultural products—such as media—in a realm where they have commercial value (da Costa e Silva, 1995). There is an international debate over how to manage intellectual property rights in the face of increasing changes in technology and social demands. The implication is that traditional, moral, and ethical issues can no longer be separated from such issues as how communication technology is managed, who owns innovative ideas and products, and what business procedures are conducted (Ganguli, 2000: 44). Indigenous societies have an advantage here in that suitable laws governing cultural processes and products already exist—Indigenous cultural products "come out of a Law and are managed and protected by that Law" (Morris, 1999). Henry Garnia, chairman of the Hammond Island Community Council, uses the analogy of Torres Strait Islanders' use of boats to explain how the law is practiced:

> The sea is our highway to the next island. . . . Out of common respect to owners of those boats you have to ask permission before you can use a boat. Otherwise you haven't got self-respect in doing that. You think that you're above the law by just going and taking what you want to use without actually first talking with the owners. First of all you must have respect for yourself and learn to respect others. (TSIMA, 1999b)

TRADITIONAL MANAGEMENT STRUCTURES

When an Indigenous community produces CDs containing a traditional song or a story broadcast by the BBC World Service, who owns these products? Who will benefit from any commercial gain that accrues from their sale? One solution is for Indigenous communities to look to the *traditional* processes that determine ownership of their cultural products. These crucial questions have been dealt with for generations by Indigenous people who traded with each other under the terms of traditional Law. Many communities still use this framework as a way of determining ownership of knowledge. In the new communication environment, this legal framework must be extended to include all cultural products, including media. But how can this be done within a Western-dominated legal system?

The question of managing intellectual property rights has been taken up directly in the Torres Strait, where Islanders are now using traditional management systems to mediate disputes over ownership of land. The Murray Islands, or Mer, are perched at the northern end of the Great Barrier Reef, about 200 kilometers northeast of Cape York in far-north Queensland. They were at the center of the historic 1992 *Mabo* High Court decision on Native Title, which overturned the "legal fiction" of the notion of Australia being *terra nullius* (an empty land) at the time of British settlement (Brennan, 1991; ATSIC, 1997).[2] The islands' traditional owners are considering using their existing local Native Titleholders' Court system as a way of resolving questions of ownership of Mer intellectual property. The Native Titleholders' Court is made up of representatives from each of Mer's clans. Although the court sits to determine ownership under non-Indigenous federal law—the Native Title Act—it has adopted a resolution process based on traditional approaches. Most of the members of the Native Title-holders' Court are elders of the community representing the eight tribes on Mer, independent of the elected Mer Island Council. Any issues concerned with the land or the culture now come through the tribunal. The system used on Mer has moved toward recognizing the existence of two laws—traditional Law and Western common law. Using a similar process, disputes over ownership of cultural property—whether a song, a dance, or a story—could be discussed at this forum or another based on this framework. Resolutions would be reached via consensus. The same knowledge management system might be applied, for example, to managing non-Indigenous filmmakers' access to island locations (TSIMA, 1999b).

In October 2000, the Torres Strait Regional Authority (TSRA) agreed to view this model as one that might be implemented throughout the Torres Strait. It is an example of how one community is moving to set up an alternative framework for determining how intellectual property rights issues could be handled using traditional approaches.

THE POWER OF PUBLIC POLICY

Public policy is crucial in shaping the way in which information—including traditional information—is legally and socially defined. The way in which the Australian government favors non-Indigenous structures of ownership is a result of the public policy process and it is a global trend, as Shalini Venturelli (2000: 34) suggests: "The forms of public policy chosen by the state and their tendencies to favour certain structures of ownership are becoming central to determining which social groups benefit or are vastly enriched by proprietary control over advanced information technologies, intelligent networks and the content they will carry."

Recent developments such as WIPOnet—a worldwide electronic information network for intellectual property matters—might be useful for Indigenous people as a way of trading their intellectual property rights across national borders. It offers "significant opportunities to promote the use, protection of, and trade in IPR across the globe" (Idris, 2000: 66). International developments such as these cannot be ignored by the Indigenous communication sector. They are as much a part of the communication environment as the technology itself.

Our main points thus far are these:

- Indigenous people, through their communities and representative bodies, must work to introduce policies that recognize existing traditional structures of ownership of cultural property, including media.
- Communities need to set up processes to determine ownership of cultural products and management structures based on traditional lines. As the Torres Strait experience suggests, perhaps the best place for this process to start is at the clan level.
- Indigenous communities and their representative communication organizations should be aware of current intellectual property debates and be active in the policy-making process to ensure that Indigenous perspectives are represented.

The Traditional Economy and Knowledge Management

> Of course racism, dispossession and trauma are the ultimate explanations for our precarious situation as a people. But the point is: they do not explain our recent, rapid and almost total social breakdown. . . . Our current social dysfunction is caused by the artificial economy of our communities and by the corrupting nature of passive welfare. (Pearson, 2000a: 38)

COMMUNICATION AND THE TRADITIONAL ECONOMY

Mer Chairman Ron Day (2000) describes how, for many generations, people from his own island community—Stephens Island and Darnley Island (85 and 55 kilometers from the mainland, respectively) have traditionally joined for festivals. With no modern communication systems like telephones, they "knew" when it was time to celebrate. He concludes: "I don't know how, maybe it was telepathy." Like many others, he acknowledges that communication was, and remains, a central part of the traditional economy:

> The main thing is the sharing of the concept of spirituality. I think that was the main thing because people have to be in contact with other people and the only way you can do that is through something spiritual like [with] Darnley and Stephens, for example, and I'm sure they had some sort of contact. In my tribal area we had what we call a communication point where people go to get information from other islands, including Kaurareg [Thursday Island]. (Day, 2000)

The difficulty for people in the Torres Strait is that missionaries imposed a new spirituality on people and Islanders now need to rediscover "the old ways." Day sees these contradictions, but he also acknowledges that prior to the arrival of the London Missionary Society in the Torres Strait in 1871,[3] the traditional economy had established an order:

> Today we're finding it hard to get it [the traditional structure] back because most of the young people won't cooperate. They just feel they are not part of it. So we have to sit down and get this small community to understand from where they came to exist; what was in place before. There was an order of something that made them to be what they are now. (Day 2000)

Indigenous thinkers like Ron Day and Noel Pearson are in no doubt about the value of traditional structures as a framework for modern Indigenous society—and communication. As Pearson (2000a: 20) writes: "Central to the recovery and empowerment of Aboriginal society will be the restoration of Aboriginal values and Aboriginal relationships which have their roots in our traditional society." He acknowledges that despite all of the losses Indigenous people have experienced, what has survived are traditional relationships, values, and attitudes that gave (and continue to give) structure and strength to families and communities (Pearson 2000a: 23).

As Michaels (1986: 508) reminded us earlier, the "Dreaming tracks" that crisscross the continent are "information conduits," or media, along which people travel, carrying goods for exchange and moving to ceremonial sites. This system is an important part of how traditional economies are managed and should be seen as an important framework for shaping modern communication technologies. But the traditional or subsistence economy has given way, in most parts of Australia, to a cash economy or an artificial economy based on what Pearson calls "passive welfare" (Pearson, 2000a: 5). If communication continues to develop on this basis, it threatens the effectiveness and power of traditional management models. Pearson stresses the importance of seeking out traditional structures of governance for Indigenous societies—regional, community, and clan-based (2000a: 68). The processes of traditional subsistence economies—with their built-in systems of responsibility and reciprocity—may offer a model for Indigenous communication. Unless communication processes are part of this traditional economy, their chances of success seem minimal. This could be one reason why most of BRACS's production centers across Cape York have failed to reach their potential (Harris, 2000).

THE CAPE YORK DIGITAL NETWORK

A small group of Indigenous communities on Cape York Peninsula has established a network that relies on the innovative use of communication technology based on a framework drawn from the local traditional economy—particularly the key aspects of responsibility and reciprocity. Called the Cape York Digital Network (CYDN), the project aims to provide a wide range of electronic communications to communities across Cape York and to create a framework that supports local economic development (Balkanu Cape York Development Corporation, 2002). The network has learned from BRACS's mistakes and sees it as essential to "get management priorities right so that they reflect the wishes of people on the ground so members of the community get their voices heard" (Grainger, 2000). The traditional economy may be a basis on which the network is being developed, but this is not to say that technology can't play a key role. Grainger stresses that every decision made regarding how technology might be used is based on its functionality:

> We want to be functionally focussed. Too much thought has been given to the technical side. We've only got so much capacity and effort. We've got to concentrate it at the right place. We're community servicing. We're not technologically researching and developing and all that type of stuff. If the unis want to walk in and see what we do—come and assist us in developing these technologies. But ours will be a business arrangement and the only way this is going to survive is through business. And we've got to get the business right; so we've got to treat our mob right. (Grainger, 2000)

The organization ran a series of workshops across Cape York communities to train young people, in particular, in computer use. As Grainger suggests, these workshops revealed a strong desire and ability by young Indigenous people to apply the new technologies:

> The kids picked it up quickly. Now I don't know why they picked it up quickly but they picked up websites and hyperlink stuff. It must be intuitive because the kids knew what was happening. They knew what to check— troubleshooting, checking connections, etc. Kids are smart. I was very impressed by that. (Grainger, 2000)

It is worth noting here that "trust" has been identified as one of the key elements of successful e-commerce in intellectual property (Bock, 1999: 237). As such, it resonates strongly with the very basis of the values of a traditional Indigenous economy— responsibility and reciprocity. It would seem to place Indigenous people in a good position to develop such opportunities. And as one of the present authors argues (Morris, 2000), Indigenous people have been involved in trading intellectual property since well before the arrival of the first non-Indigenous explorers. They, perhaps more than the European invaders, "understood the importance of goodwill and interaction with their neighbours" (p. 297).

KNOWLEDGE MANAGEMENT

> All knowledge is political, that is, it is constructed by relationships of power—of domination and subordination—and is inseparable from these. Power is, therefore, productive of knowledge. (Wong, 1997: 103)

Western management theory recognizes some of the questions that are central in understanding why Indigenous management styles should be different. Among these questions are the following, which, according to L. Wong (1997: 103), lead to the construction of "official knowledge" in management:

- "What counts as knowledge?"
- "How is knowledge organized?"
- "Who is empowered to teach it?"
- "What counts as an appropriate display of having learned it?"
- "Who is allowed to ask and answer all these questions?"

Hence there is a need for a greater understanding of "other" ways of doing things, as Paulson (1996: 82) argues: "Not only does Western society differ from Indigenous people in terms of cosmology, ideology and worldview but in all of the universal values. . . . [A] discussion of the universal values and the difference between Western and Indigenous experiences of them clearly shows the tensions between the two social systems."

The Central Australian Aboriginal Media Association (CAAMA)—the first licensed Indigenous broadcasting organization in Australia—is an example of how Indigenous concepts of intellectual property rights and cultural frameworks are applied in everyday communication management practice. Indigenous people have a different sense of intellectual property rights than do non-Indigenous people; for example, Indigenous management must vet the use of Indigenous knowledge before it can be placed in the public domain. When Indigenous and non-Indigenous people work together, there is a "sharing of knowledge" that can create tensions (Morris, 1997: 9). Merv Franey (1998) argues that researchers wrongly assume that because they have researched a people, or collaborated in the research, they are entitled to go out on their own and do as they see fit with the intellectual property from that research. The current laws of copyright allow people to do this as long as there is acknowledgment and it is in the public domain. However, non-Indigenous law does not include values such as reciprocity, which is central to the operation of Indigenous law. As G. Paulson (1996: 85) points out: "We are a relational-type society. Our whole system is held together by relationships, the relationship between individuals in our society is more important than the simple performance of task." So when Indigenous people enter a community, they must first ask themselves "What is it that they [members of the community] require of me?" rather than "What can I do for them?" (Franey, 1998).

For CAAMA, all cultural products must benefit the community, as most of the organization's staff members are answerable in some way to the local community. This is contrary to normal business practice whereby holding the copyright over a product is more desirable. In this way, trust emerges out of what an individual brings to the organization. Instead of a tangible asset or skill it may be a network with another organization or a particular community group. CAAMA appears to operate in a constant state of cultural accountability, facilitating a continuing dynamic interaction between the organization and the community. Ceremonial obligations are part of Indigenous cultural life, and they inevitably take precedence over business activities in a mainstream sense. For Indigenous people, of course, this *is* business.

KNOWLEDGE WORKERS

Knowledge is fast becoming a key factor determining the strength and prosperity of nations. In an environment increasingly influenced by international and global factors, Australia is making a major transition from an economy based on the wealth of its physical resources and commodities to an information or knowledge economy in which its competitive advantage increasingly relies on the skills and creativity of its people. The success of that transition will profoundly influence the quality of life for all people—including Indigenous people.

We suggest that the future of Indigenous people lies in their participating in the global village as knowledge workers, but it is hard to imagine them doing so effectively in the current political climate. Observations by Noel Pearson (2000a) present a dismal view of the present, but solutions are being put forward to tap into the capacity of the people to compete internationally. Pearson's views in *Our Culture: Our Future—A Report on Australian Indigenous Cultural and Intellectual Property Rights* (ATSIC, 1996) suggest that Indigenous people fall into a downward spiral of exploitation when they try to enter the knowledge market. But these are early days. New media developments such as the Cape York Digital Network, the Outback Digital Network (ODN),[4] and the Tanami Network, along with some BRACS units, have resulted from creative thinking by Indigenous people. Their ideas have involved the use of existing technologies in innovative and culturally appropriate ways. We have suggested that these ideas are likely to succeed only if they are (1) developed within Indigenous frameworks for managing knowledge, (2) designed in keeping with community functionality, and (3) managed with a high level of cultural accountability. These are not impossible expectations. As Grainger (2000) reminds us, Indigenous people can do anything: "We're into law, art, media—they're as hard as technology." Pearson (2000b) stressed this point, too, during the recent launch of an Indigenous art exhibition in Cairns, when he acknowledged how Indigenous artists have "soared internationally"—so why not "recognise and celebrate Indigenous genius" and those working on the "cutting edge of creativity." Why not indeed?

The main points emerging from this section of the chapter are these:

- The processes of the traditional economy—specifically, responsibility and reciprocity—offer a framework upon which Indigenous communication should be based.
- The communication technologies adopted must relate to their functionality.
- Traditional structures of governance seem best suited to managing Indigenous intellectual property.
- When working in and/or with Indigenous communities, we must remain aware of (a) cultural laws, (b) the idea of Indigenous people as knowledge workers, (c) the notion that ideas are likely to become functional if they are developed within Indigenous frameworks by organizations with a high level of cultural accountability, and (d) the importance of thinking about the possibility of trading the intellectual property rights of innovative ideas internationally.

Conclusion

We have stressed that the solutions to many of the issues facing the Indigenous communication sector lie in applying traditional frameworks to present-day issues. Indigenous peoples for millennia have developed and applied systems for managing their everyday affairs. Communication in its varied forms has played a central functional and symbolic role in this process. Through trade/gift exchange, social relations are established and reaffirmed. Intellectual property was traded along with pearl shells, canoes, and ochre, for example. The "communication hub" identified by Ron Day on Mer acted like a traditional telecommunications network in which information about the movement of people and property through the Torres Strait could be monitored. Similarly, trading routes—or "Dreaming tracks"—across the continent linked up with sea routes, all of which were communication corridors. We have argued here, like Rodriguez (2002), for consideration of Indigenous communication in ways that do not rely on what it is not—namely, a form described variously as "alternative" or even as "citizens' media." The symbolic role of communication in many Indigenous communities around the world suggests something more profound. As the Productivity Commission acknowledged in 2000, Indigenous media in Australia were providing "a first level of service" to its communities as well as acting as a "cultural bridge" between Indigenous and non-Indigenous people (Productivity Commission, 2000: 3). And drawing from Native Canadian experiences, Lorna Roth and Gail Valaskakis argue persuasively that the most interesting broadcasting developments in Canada are taking place regionally and locally in Native communities, contributing to the distinctiveness and democratization of Canadian broadcasting (1989: 230). We suggest that a similar pattern has emerged in particular places in Australia. Morris reminds us of the term "conceptual boundary rider," coined by Anangu lawman Yami Lester (1995), who used the expression to describe ways in which Indigenous park rangers working with biologists keep stretching and challenging the boundaries of interpretation. Morris argues (2002: 15) that this kind of Indigenous intellectualizing is exactly why developments coming out of the remote regions of Australia are the most provocative.

These flow from the community's desire, rather than from an economically dictated objective that some well-meaning bureaucrat believes is in the Indigenous people's democratic right to possess. Therefore, liberation is not dependent on technology but complementary to it.

We must remember that in many cases, we are talking about communities where cultural survival remains a central objective. The role of communication technologies in this process is beginning to be realized, as some of the examples we have alluded to here suggest. Radical, emancipatory communication projects are taking place in Indigenous communities around the world, enabling the *possibility* of a kind of media that is different from the mainstream in form, content, goals, and effects (Kellner, 1989). Social relations within communities are the very forces that shape this kind of cultural production (Kulchyski, 1989). Without this level of cultural accountability, the media cease to be Indigenous. Traditional economies are about building relationships and kinship systems between clans—the main commodity being intellectual property. This is the basis for then establishing international relationships. Indigenous people were involved in international relations with the people of modern nations such as Indonesia, Papua New Guinea, and the Pacific Island countries for generations before the arrival of the first non-Indigenous explorers.

We must recognize the existence of Indigenous intellect and innovation, which flow from millennia of experience. When technological "solutions" are offered, they must be scrutinized carefully: Are they enhancing or inhibiting traditional frameworks? Are they dominated by Western criteria of intelligence and moral behavior? Do they impose a foreign set of ethics? Based on our continuing interaction with Indigenous communities across Australia and throughout the world, our focus in this chapter has been on *ways of doing things*. We offer this framework as an option for communities, organizations, funding agencies, and policy-makers to consider as a way of enhancing the development of an appropriate kind of Indigenous communication that acknowledges its central role as a community cultural resource. Ultimately, of course, it must be the Indigenous people who decide.

Notes

This chapter has been drawn from research funded jointly by the Australian Research Council and the Aboriginal and Torres Strait Islander Commission (ATSIC), and supported by the former National Indigenous Media Association of Australia (NIMAA) through the work of Research Fellow Brian Arley. Christine Morris worked on the project as a Research Fellow.

1. Networking the Nation is a federal government initiative, funded by the part sale of Telstra. A five-year program (1999–2004), it provides support for regional and remote communities to improve service, access, and cost of telecommunications through a $250 million Regional Telecommunications Infrastructure Fund.

2. This High Court decision was named after one of five plaintiffs from Mer, Eddie Mabo. The legal battle began ten years earlier in the Queensland courts, prior to the High Court decision handed down on 2 June 1992. Tragically, Eddie Mabo died of cancer a few months before.

3. The arrival of representatives of the London Missionary Society in 1871 is celebrated on July 1 each year in the Torres Strait as the Coming of Civilization or the Coming of the Light. Christianity has had a profound effect on Torres Strait Island people: Every single inhabited island has a monument commemorating the event; no aspect of life in the Torres Strait is unchanged by the coming of religion (Schnukal, 1987).

4. The Outback Digital Network was formed by the coming together of five Indigenous community-based organizations from regions stretching from the Cape York of Queensland, through the Tanami Desert, Tennant Creek, and Top End communities of Northern Territory, out to Western Australia's Pilbara and Kimberley Regions. See www.odn.net.au/index1.html.

References

ATSIC (1993). *Aboriginal and Torres Strait Islander Broadcasting Policy: Review Report and Draft Policy Statement* (January). Canberra: ATSIC Infrastructure Branch.
——— (1996). *Our Culture: Our Future—A Report on Australian Indigenous Cultural and Intellectual Property Rights*. Canberra: ATSIC.
——— (1997). *National Aboriginal and Torres Strait Islander Cultural Industry Strategy* (September). Canberra: ATSIC.
——— (1999). *Digital Dreaming: A National Review of Indigenous Media and Communications*, Executive Summary. Canberra: ATSIC.
Australian National Parks and Wildlife Service and the Mutitjulu Community (1990). *An Insight into Uluru: The Mala Walk and the Mutitjulu Walk*. Tourist booklet.
Balkanu Cape York Development Corporation (2002). "Cape York Digital Network." Available online at www.balkanu.com.au/projects/telecommunications/digital.htm. Last accessed on 26 August 2002.
Blake, Barry J. (1981). *Australian Aboriginal Languages*. London: Angus and Robertson.
Bock, Christian (1999). "The Need for Trust in Electronic Commerce in Intellectual Property," *World Patent Information* 21: 237–39.
Brennan, Frank (1991). *Sharing the Country: The Case for an Agreement between Black and White Australians*. Ringwood: Penguin.
da Costa e Silva, E (1995). "The Protection of Intellectual Property for Local and Indigenous Communities," *European Intellectual Property Review* 11(17): 546–49.

Day, Ron (2000). Chairman of Murray Island, interview in Cairns, 10 July.

Franey, Merv (1998). Deputy General Manager of CAAMA, personal communication, February and April.

Ganguli, Prabuddha (2000). "Intellectual Property Rights: Mothering Innovations to Markets," *World Patent Information* 22: 43–52.

Graham, Mary (1992). Interview with Carolyn Jones, *The Search for Meaning*, ABC Radio National, 15 November.

Grainger, Daniel (2000). Project Manager of the Cape York Digital Network, interview in Cairns, 11 July.

Hall, Stuart (1982). "The Rediscovery of 'Ideology': Return of the Repressed in Media Studies," in M. Gurevitch, T. Bennett, J. Curran, and J. Woollacott (eds.), *Culture, Society and the Media*. London: Methuen.

Harris, Alastair (2000). Project Officer, Apunipima Cape York Health Council, interview in Cairns, 11 July.

Idris, K. (2000). "WIPOnet Charts Course for IP Information Exchange in the Digital Age," *World Patent Information* 22: 63–66.

Kellner, Douglas (1989). "Resurrecting McLuhan? Jean Baudrillard and the Academy of Postmodernism," in Marc Raboy and Peter A. Bruck (eds.), *Communication for and against Democracy*. Montreal: Black Rose Books.

Knights, D., and Morgan, G. (1991). "Corporate Strategy, Organisations and Subjectivity: A Critique," *Organisation Studies* 12: 251–73.

Kulchyski, Peter (1989). "The Postmodern and the Paleolithic: Notes on Technology and Native Community in the Far North," *Canadian Journal of Political and Social Theory* 8(3): 49–62.

Langton, Marcia, and Kirkpatrick, Brownlee (1979). "A Listing of Aboriginal Publications," *Aboriginal History* 3(2): 120–27.

Lester, Yami (1995). *Learning from the Land*. Alice Springs: Institute for Aboriginal Development.

Meadows, Michael (2000). "Silent Talking: Indigenous Media Policy and the Productivity Commission," *Media International Australia* 95: 29–48.

Michaels, Eric (1983). "Aboriginal Air Rights," *Media Information Australia* 34: 51–61.

——— (1985). "New Technologies in the Outback and Their Implications," *Media Information Australia* 38: 69–72.

——— (1986). *Aboriginal Invention of Television Central Australia 1982–1985*. Canberra: Australian Institute of Aboriginal Studies.

——— (1987). *For a Cultural Future: Francis Jupurrurla Makes TV at Yuendumu*. Melbourne: Manic Exposeur.

Molnar, Helen, and Meadows, Michael (2001). *Songlines to Satellites: Indigenous Communication in Australia, the South Pacific and Canada*. Leichhardt: Pluto Press.

Morris, Christine (1997). "Indigenous Intellectual Property Rights: The Responsibilities of Maintaining the Oldest Continuous Culture in the World," *Indigenous Law Bulletin* 4(2): 9–10.

——— (1999). *Cultural Policy, Law and Communication: Indigenous Film Makers and Their Perspectives*. Background Paper. Brisbane: Griffith University, Australian Key Centre for Cultural and Media Policy, November.

——— (2000). "Constitutional Dreaming," in C. Samford and T. Round (eds.), *Beyond the Republic: Meeting the Global Challenges to Constitutionalism*. Sydney: Federation Press.

——— (2002). "Developing Methodologies, Techniques and Protocols for Indigenous Audience Research in Australia and New Zealand," unpublished research report. Brisbane: Griffith University, Australian Key Centre for Cultural and Media Policy. Hamilton: Waikato University, Department of Screen and Media.

Mowaljarlai, D. M. J. (1993). *Yorro Yorro*. Broome: Magabala Books.

Paulson, G. (1996). "The Value of Aboriginal Culture," in A. Pattel-Gray (ed.), *Aboriginal Spirituality: Past, Present and Future*. Sydney: HarperCollins Religious.

Pearson, Noel (2000a). *Our Right to Take Responsibility*. Cairns: Noel Pearson and Associates.

——— (2000b). Speech launching the Lockhart River Art Gang collection at the Cairns Regional Art Gallery, 10 June.

Productivity Commission (2000). *Broadcasting: Inquiry Report*. Report No. 11, 3 March. Canberra: Ausinfo. Available online at www.pc.gov.au/inquiry/broadcst/index.html. Last accessed on 1 April 2003.

Rodriguez, Clemencia (2002). "Citizens' Media and the Voice of the Angel/Poet," *Media International Australia* 103: 78–87.

Rose, Michael (1996). *For the Record: 160 years of Aboriginal Print Journalism*. Sydney: Allen and Unwin.

Roth, Lorna, and Gail Valaskakis (1989). "Aboriginal Broadcasting in Canada: A Case Study in Democratisation," in Marc Raboy and Peter A. Bruck (eds.), *Communication for and against Democracy*. Montreal: Black Rose Books.

Schmidt, Annette (1993). *The Loss of Australia's Aboriginal Language Heritage*. Canberra: Aboriginal Studies Press.

Schnukal, Anna (1987). "Torres Strait Creole: Historical Perspectives and New Directions," unpublished conference notes, University of Queensland.

Simons, Michael S. (2000). "Aboriginal Heritage Art and Moral Rights," *Annals of Tourism Research* 27(2): 412–31.

TSIMA (Torres Strait Islanders' Media Association) (1999a). *You'll Find Out When You Make That Call*, Film Protocols in the Torres Strait, videotape. Brisbane: Griffith University, Australian Key Centre for Cultural and Media Policy.

——— (1999b). *It's Our Law and Culture So Let's Protect It!* IPR and copyright in the Torres Strait, videotape. Brisbane: Griffith University, Australian Key Centre for Cultural and Media Policy.

Venturelli, Shalini (2000). "Ownership of Cultural Expression: Speech and Culture in the New Intellectual Property Rights Regime of the European Union," *Telematics and Infomatics* 17: 9–37.

Williams, Raymond (1977). *Marxism and Literature*. London: Oxford University Press.

Wong, L. (1997). *Management Theory Meets the "Other,"* ANZAM (Australian and New Zealand Academy of Management). Melbourne: Monash University.

CHAPTER 6

The Press Subsidy System in Sweden

A CRITICAL APPROACH

Lennart Weibull

When first introduced in the late 1960s, the Swedish system of direct subsidies to the press was regarded in many other Western countries as a dangerous government intrusion into the free press. An oft-asked question was how a democratic country like Sweden could introduce a system in which government was given a chance to manipulate public opinion. In Sweden itself, the subsidy system at first created an intense controversy, but despite continuous criticism on the grounds of principle, the system as such was gradually accepted as a means to maintain pluralism in the newspaper market.

The direct newspaper support in Sweden is regarded as one main factor behind the internationally strong position of the Swedish press. The problem, however, is that despite the fact that the subsidies still play an important role, pluralism in the Swedish press is rapidly declining both by closures and by mergers. How can this be understood? Did the subsidy system mean so little, even with all the controversy? The aim of this chapter is to look into the premises of the Swedish system of press support.

The Setting: The Swedish Newspaper Tradition

As in most other European countries, the first newspapers were either political pamphlets or trade papers. Local papers were established in some main trade towns in the early eighteenth century, but an important change came with the introduction of the Freedom of the Press Act in 1766. It was a constitutional law guarding press freedom, regarded as the first in the world of this kind. Censorship was abolished, and the right to disseminate information was protected (cf. Axberger, 1984). The Freedom of Press Act played an important role for the establishment of an independent press (Hadenius and Weibull, 2002).

THE RISE OF THE PARTY PRESS

Newspaper history in Sweden is in many ways very similar to that of other European countries, but its special feature has been the strength of the countryside newspapers

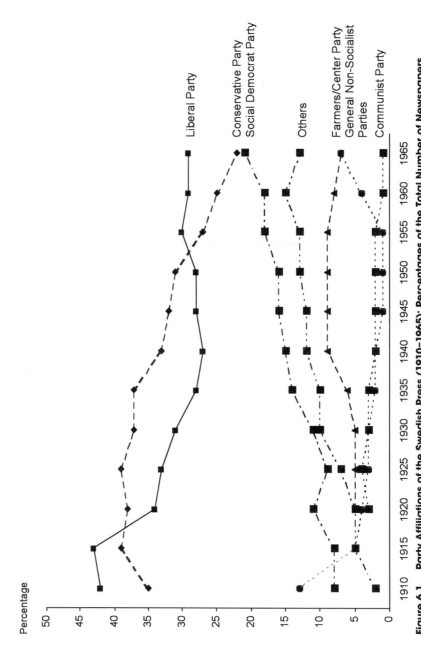

Percentage

Liberal Party

Conservative Party
Social Democrat Party

Others

Farmers/Center Party
General Non-Socialist Parties
Communist Party

1910 1915 1920 1925 1930 1935 1940 1945 1950 1955 1960 1965

Figure 6.1.   Party Affiliations of the Swedish Press (1910–1965): Percentages of the Total Number of Newspapers.

Source: Author.

and the relative weakness of the national press (cf. Gustafsson and Weibull, 1997). Another characteristic pattern in Swedish press development has been the rise of a strong social democratic countryside press, competing with the local nonsocialist press (Hadenius, Seveborg, and Weibull, 1968, 1969, 1970). Decades later, the Farmers Party and the Communist Party started publishing local newspapers, such that in most Swedish towns of some size there were now often three or four newspapers (even more in the bigger cities), representing different party political affiliations (see figure 6.1).

Normally, party affiliation was seen not only on the editorial page but also in terms of the selection and presentation of news. The social democratic press, especially, often focused on comments (Hadenius, Seveborg, and Weibull, 1970). But there were differences between party papers. The liberal press had been established by private initiative and had formally loose ties to the very weak Liberal Party. But for the Social Democratic Party (which had a strong party organization), the Farmers Party (later the Center Party), and the Communist Party (established as the Left Socialists in 1917), the situation was the opposite: These parties largely influenced their press development.

The Social Democrats on the national level had a clear press strategy, stating that there must be at least one social democratic paper covering each electoral area or region. The Central Party level was also prepared to subsidize such papers, if they could not survive by local means (Hadenius, Seveborg and Weibull, 1970). Thus, the markets for the social democratic papers were politically determined, whereas the liberal press was based on local commercial markets. The conservative press was in between; it was often connected with the Conservative Party (later the Moderate Party), but its market base was similar to that of the liberal press.

THE DECLINE OF THE NEWSPAPER MARKET

One important consequence of political involvement was that all political parties were in favor of a strong press, although for different reasons. Most people also believed that a party political press was important for a well-functioning democracy. But in the postwar era the threat against the party press came from the newspaper market itself.

In 1948 there were 201 newspapers published at least twice a week; in 1965 there were only 134. The decline of the newspaper market affected the party press differently. The conservative and liberal presses were the main losers, decreasing in number of newspapers, respectively, from 66 to 28 and from 53 to 35. The social democratic press, however, had mainly kept its position, declining from 31 to 28 papers between 1948 and 1964 (SOU [Government Commission Report], 1965, no. 22). But even with the reduced number of conservative papers, its total circulation was higher in 1964 that it had been in 1948. The liberal press, because of its geographical distribution, also reached more households in 1964 than in 1948. The same was true of the social democratic press, though its subscriptions were significantly fewer (37 percent of households) than those of the liberal press (68 percent). The development of the latter was also influenced by the growth of the first two really national papers, *Expressen* and *Aftonbladet;* both were of tabloid character, but one was liberal and the other social democratic in party affiliation. In contrast to the rest of the press, both were also single-copy sale papers and not as dependent on advertising as other newspapers (Weibull, 1995).

What took place during these years was actually a structural rationalization of the Swedish press. The number of communities with two or more newspapers decreased from 51 in 1950 to 23 in 1965, whereas monopoly communities increased from 42 to 59. Most social democratic papers were in local competition; they had a weak market position as well as economic problems and had received subsidies from the party or the trade unions to keep them on the market. Between 1948 and 1963 the social democratic press was subsidized with more than 80 million Swedish crowns, compared with less than 10 million for the liberal press. The conservative press also received relatively high subsidies, but in 1957 the foundations close to the party reduced the subsidies dramatically, and from 1962 on they were totally stopped, forcing a large number of papers to close down.[1]

The consequence was that most surviving liberal and conservative presses occupied leading market positions, whereas many social democratic papers were kept alive by subsidies; some of the latter were successful, however. During the political debate of the 1950s and 1960s, as well as in research about the press, the decline of the press per se was not the main issue. Rather, the focus was on the problem of what happened to readers who lost "a paper of their own" and had to read a paper with a content colored by another party's outlook (cf. Westerståhl and Janson, 1958; Westerståhl, 1964). What consequences might this have for Swedish public opinion? Here the conditions varied across sympathizers of different parties, depending on the strength and distribution of the papers (Weibull, 1982, 1983a). Studies of how readers chose their newspapers clearly show that sympathizers of the Liberal and the Conservative parties had the best position, whereas sympathizers of the Farmers Party had the worst.

Our purpose here is not to discuss whether party affiliation was really the determining factor behind the choice of paper but, rather, to note that equal access to party political papers was a most important issue in the 1960s. Thus, for example, the 1963 closure of the biggest newspaper thus far, *Ny Tid*, a social democratic paper in Göteborg with 45,000 copies in paid circulation, caused a strong political reaction. Within two weeks after this occurrence, the first government press commission in Sweden was initiated. Its task was to describe the situation and to propose ways to maintain pluralism in the newspaper market.

Newspaper Subsidies as a Political Issue

The 1963 government commission was the first in a long series of press commissions. Its task formulation specified that "free and independent press is of decisive importance for the freedom of public opinion and, hence, for our democracy" and that this was guaranteed by the Freedom of the Press Act. But, it added, the development of the press in the last few decades created serious consequences for application of freedom of the press legislation. Also the current problem of the newspaper industry makes it a general social concern (SOU, 1965, no. 22: 7). The formulation thus pointed to the very issue that soon became the focus of controversy: the relation between the Freedom of the Press Act and the desire for a pluralistic press.

The 1963 commission made a detailed study of newspaper development and its economic conditions, using leading experts from both the academic field and the industry. Its conclusion was that although the newspaper industry per se was not in a state of general crisis, the threat of discontinuation loomed over a group of newspapers called "secondary papers." These were second or third in circulation in the publication area, in contrast to "primary papers," which were bigger and better financed because of their dominant position on the advertising market; indeed, advertising was the dominant source of income for most papers, accounting for about 65 percent of newspaper revenues (SOU 1965, no. 22; Gustafsson and Hadenius, 1977: 77–78). The practical conclusion was that state subsidies needed to be extended only to the "secondary papers."

The idea of newspaper support created immediate controversy. The criticism was based not only in fears for the independence of the papers but also in the fact that a majority of the so-called secondary papers had Social Democratic Party affiliation, even though the category also contained some conservative and Center Party papers. To make the proposal politically acceptable it was formulated not as a direct newspaper subsidy but as a grant to the political parties, calculated in relation to their election results, and to be used for their newspapers. This was said to be "natural already for the reason that 85 percent of the Swedish newspapers has a party political affiliation." The commission stated that such a model was in accordance with the Swedish idea of a strong press, fulfilling the need of a democratic society to have a pluralistic public opinion: "Thus, the political parties—together with the society and the newspaper consumers—represent the main interests in the newspaper field" (SOU, 1965, no. 22: 119).

The commission reporting in 1965 was not unanimous. The conservative and the liberal commission members formulated a reservation "on principle and practical grounds," whereas the representative of the Center Party accepted the model but wanted a broader party subsidy system. Thus, the Social Democrats and the Center Party joined forces, creating a political alliance that since has dominated Swedish media politics.

The debate that followed was intense. The liberal and conservative presses argued that the proposal was not in accordance with the constitutional law of freedom of the press, since it meant that the state intrusion also harmed the big papers by changing the condition of competition. The government accepted a lot of the criticism and changed the proposal to include general party subsidies. The party subsidies were mainly thought of as a contribution to opinion-generating work, given in proportion to the number of seats in parliament. Even though the subsidies were not explicitly devoted to newspapers, they could be used for that purpose, and it is known that the Social Democratic Party used most of them to subsidize its press (cf. Borden, 1995: 106–108).

THE SECOND PRESS COMMISSION

Since the economic analysis of the newspaper market made by the first press commission was correct and the party subsidies were too small to be able to bring about substantial changes, it was not surprising that the secondary papers' problems continued. In 1966 the biggest social democratic paper, *Stockholms-Tidningen*, with a circulation of more than 150,000 paid copies, had to close down, meaning a substantial loss for

Table 6.1. Shares of Newspaper Circulation by Political Affiliation, in Sweden (in percentages)

Political Affiliation	1945	1950	1955	1960	1965	1967
Conservative	22.4	21.2	21.9	21.4	22.6	18.3
Liberal	50.6	49.5	51.0	46.3	48.0	49.2
Center	4.8	4.3	3.8	3.5	3.1	2.7
Social Democrat	14.8	17.9	16.5	23.3	22.1	20.2
Others (incl. independents)	7.4	7.1	6.8	5.5	4.2	9.7

Source: SOU 1968, no. 48: 54

the Social Democrats (see table 6.1). There was a strong feeling of crisis, and in 1967 a new government press commission was initiated. Its task was to find, within a year, "such measures that will bring about a significant stimulus for economically weak businesses" (SOU, 1968, no. 48: 7–8).

The new commission confirmed all the observations made by the first one, but instead of party politically motivated subsidies aiming at the weaker papers, it proposed a general support to all newspapers. The political logic behind the model was that it was regarded as the only way to transfer state money to the press, given the existing opinion. Accordingly, it proposed a special grant to stimulate a joint-subscription home-delivery system in the local markets. This move was especially important for the secondary papers, which had a more expensive delivery system, even though the model meant that the primary papers received more money because of their bigger circulation. Further, the state was to set up a loan fund to help weaker newspapers become more competitive.

The commission reporting in 1968 *was* unanimous. The government bill, based on the commission proposal, created the expected parliamentary debate; but this was less intense than it had been in 1965, and even the conservatives could accept financial assistance if it was available to all papers (Borden, 1995: 112–113). The success of the second commission can partly be explained by the fact that there was now a strong feeling of general crisis for the newspaper industry. A second factor, however, was probably the increasing importance of television—a topic addressed in one chapter of the commission's report.

THE DECISION ON THE SELECTIVE PRESS SUBSIDIES

Even if the general support brought help to the weakest papers, the secondary papers were under almost the same pressure as before. The social democratic government regarded the situation as very serious and wanted selective measures taken. However, as the government had no parliamentary majority it decided to make a coalition with the Center Party. Thus, a government bill, without a foregoing press commission, was presented in 1971. The bill followed the lines of the 1963 commission. For production, subsidies were estimated at 33 million Swedish crowns annually, compared with 10 million crowns for the joint-delivery subsidy and 25 million crowns for the loan fund.

The proposal was met with strong criticism among conservative and liberal newspapers, as well as among politicians from those parties (Borden, 1995: 120–122). But

Table 6.2. Subsidy Distributions Based on Party Affiliation, in Sweden (1971)

A Party Affiliation	B Number of Newspapers	C Entitled to How Many Grants	D C as % of B[a]	E C as % of Entitled Newspapers	F Grants in 1000s of Crowns	G F as % of Total Grants
Moderate	21	2	9.5	3.8	3,700.0	10.3
Liberal	34	2	5.9	3.8	3,971.2	11.0
Center	19.5[b]	15.5[b]	79.5	29.8	6,624.3	18.4
Social Dem.	20.5[b]	16.5[b]	80.5	31.7	16,588.5	46.1
Communist	2	2	100.0	3.8	400.0	1.1
Christian Dem.	1	1	100.0	1.9	290.0	0.8
Syndicalist	1	1	100.0	1.9	200.0	0.6
Bourg/Indep. Lib.[c]	14	2	14.3	3.8	1,626.0	4.5
Independent	32	10	38.5	19.2	2,594.0	7.2
Total	145	52	35.9	99.7	35,994.0	100.1

[a] The columns are rounded off to the nearest tenth of a percent. The format for this table is the same one used by the Moderates in their party bill (1971: 1281).

[b] The subsidy of Gotlands Tidningar is equally divided between Gotlands Folkblad (Social Democratic) and Gotländningen. The latter is 2/3 owned by Center Party members and 1/3 owned by Liberal Party members, which does not qualify Liberals for significant ownership. However, their share of the grant money is counted (451,000/2 = 225,500/3 = 75,166). Their minority interest entitled them to express at least some editorial views. For production grant purposes, Gotlands Tidningar is counted as one newspaper since Gotländningen and Gotlands Folkblad have substantially the same content, although two newspapers were separately sold with different first and editorial pages.

[c] Bourgeois and Independent Liberal newspapers supported views to the right of the Social Democratic Party. One cannot predict which, if any, of the bourgeois parties will be supported in the national elections.

Source: Borden (1995: 139).

this time the debate concerned not press subsidies per se but their selective character. The new model was rejected on principle by the conservatives, meaning that there was no need for more subsidies, but accepted to some extent by the liberals—though only if financed in a way other than through a tax on the newspaper industry. In the debate the obvious interests of the two parties behind the bill were also at stake, especially the extension of the subsidies to weekly papers "of newspaper character," which mainly had a Center Party affiliation. Critics called it a tailored proposal, but the Center Party leader argued that the state had an obligation to guarantee weak political groups a voice in the interests of pluralistic public opinion (Borden, 1995: 112–113).

Backed by two parties, which had a clear majority, the government bill won the parliamentary vote. With this decision the most important press subsidy model, by far, had been introduced. Of 52 papers entitled to subsidies, 32 had either a social democratic or Center Party affiliation, but also conservative (among others the leading conservative daily *Svenska Dagbladet*), liberal, and independent papers were entitled to support (see table 6.2).

Even though it concerned selective subsidies, the parliamentary debate demonstrated a consensus on the importance of the press for political democracy, and on general state grants for newspapers (Borden, 1995). Similarly, nobody argued that the government should use the selective subsidies for intrusions into individual papers, or that a paper should adapt to government policy because it had received subsidies.

REFINING THE SYSTEM: THE THIRD PRESS COMMISSION

The decision to introduce the selective press subsidies included a decision on a third government press commission, initiated in 1972. Its task was to refine the subsidy system in terms of goals and formal rules on the basis of an evaluation of existing measures, but also, if necessary, to propose complementary measures (SOU, 1975, no. 79). The commission engaged academic experts to make extensive studies, both theoretical analyses of media and democracy and empirical research on newspaper structure, contents, and readership. The results were presented in three public reports, on which the final report was based.

The commission concluded that the existing subsidy system, with its combination of general and selective measures, functioned well to preserve pluralism in the press. State money was a way to compensate papers in a weak market position, measured by household penetration, for their inability to attract advertising. The commission also specified four functions of the press in the democratic process to ideologically found the subsidy system: *Information* on current events in society, *comments* on the events of the day, *surveillance* of the political power, and mediator of *group communication* (SOU, 1975, no. 79: 292; Gustafsson and Hadenius, 1977: 55–57). The four functions were later regarded as general functions of journalism and, hence, were used both as a point of departure for Swedish radio and television policy and as guidelines in textbooks on journalism (e.g., Furhoff, 1986).

In the proposal, only small refinements of the existing system were made; for example, subsidies were calculated based not on circulation but on household coverage in the local market. Further, a special development aid model was introduced for primary newspapers in temporary difficulties. The commission pointed out the risk of a system focusing only on preserving the existing press structure, and thus proposed a special support to stimulate the establishment of new, complementary papers—in this case, weeklies "of a newspaper character." The commission also made available a new type of subsidy designed to stimulate cooperation between newspapers. Such cooperation would occur on the local level and concern only administration or advertising. According to the commission, economic cooperation, even a merger, was the only way to keep a pluralistic content in the long run. The new model is similar to the American "Joint Operation Agreement" (JOA) model (Borden, 1995: 145–184).

The new extended press subsidy system proposed by the 1972 press commission was accepted primarily as a platform for the Swedish press policy, but was also accepted by the liberal press. It was made a government bill and in 1976 was decided by parliament, creating relatively little debate. The principles laid down through this decision are still those guiding subsidies to Swedish newspapers.

The Subsidy System in Practice

So far we have focused on the introduction of direct subsidies, but before going further we should note that the support system is broader than that. If we make the simplified distinction between direct and indirect subsidies, on the one hand, and between general and selective subsidies, on the other, we can distinguish four different approaches to press subsidies, which can be used individually or together: general-indirect, general-direct, selective-indirect, and selective-direct. The direct subsidies must also be placed in the context of different types of indirect press support.

INDIRECT SUBSIDIES

General-indirect press subsidies have a long tradition in most countries. Most often they concern reductions of post and transport rates or exemptions from or reductions in value-added tax. Indirect support to the press is generally regarded as legitimate, considering the importance of newspapers in public opinion.

In Sweden there have been indirect subsidies of the press (e.g., a reduction on the value-added tax—until 1996, a full exemption). The principle of broad public advertising, introduced in 1971, was also regarded as an indirect subsidy. Over the years, however, the indirect subsidies have declined in importance. Earlier, postal rates were reduced for newspapers; but when the post office was turned into a public company and had to deliver profits, market principles took over. The same has happened to public advertising, such that efficiency rather than a preselected carrier guides government information activities.

It is generally hard to estimate the value of indirect subsidies. The value might be different for different papers, although the subsidies are general. In Sweden it has been demonstrated that newspapers in less densely populated areas gained more from the reductions in postal rates than did home-delivered papers in big cities. Thus, indirect subsidies in Sweden have been regarded as somewhat problematic, despite their general acceptability as a measure to support the press.[2]

DIRECT SUBSIDIES: DEVELOPMENT

The Swedish press subsidy system is based on direct newspaper support, and the selective subsidies constituted the lion's share (about 85 percent) from the beginning; indeed, they still do. However, the amount granted for subsidies, which strongly increased during the system's first years in existence (see below), has gradually declined since the early 1980s. This was due in part to the booming economy in the late 1980s, which caused advertising to spill over onto the weaker papers, and in part to the fact that some of the weakest papers, in spite of the subsidies, had to close down (see figure 6.2).

GENERAL SUPPORT: JOINT HOME DELIVERY SUBSIDIES

The most stable government subsidy form has been the joint home delivery system, which was established in 1969. Here the state subsidies were general in character, but they played a more important role for newspapers in weak market positions. Under this system, the state subsidizes each newspaper copy with a small amount if the newspaper distributions are carried out not by the companies themselves but by special delivering companies, such that all newspapers in the same area have the same distribution price per copy. Although small newspapers, whose distribution area is the same size as that of big papers, benefit from such cooperation, the bigger papers get more of a subsidy because of their bigger circulation. The network is also open for papers in other areas if they can meet time conditions.

Soon, almost all local newspapers in Sweden had joined the co-distribution system, even though some of them had to change their publication time from evening to morning. This model is still the predominant one for home delivery, but the state cost for it has not increased as much as for the selective subsidies, probably because the model is regarded as economically effective by all groups.

It is remarkable that the joint delivery model was immediately accepted, especially given that critics often had focused on state intrusion in the market competition. Looking closely at the joint delivery model, we can see why there would eventually be no competition between Swedish morning papers, since the dominating papers have lost their advantage in distribution—for example, in terms of relatively lower costs and unilateral decisions on distribution time. This issue came up for discussion again in the 1990s, when some strong regional papers challenged the system. In this case, the reason was not to get an advantage over weak papers in the same region but to block the regional distribution network for national papers, which put the network under pressure because of their volume. However, those challenges have thus far been resolved through internal negotiations within the newspaper industry.

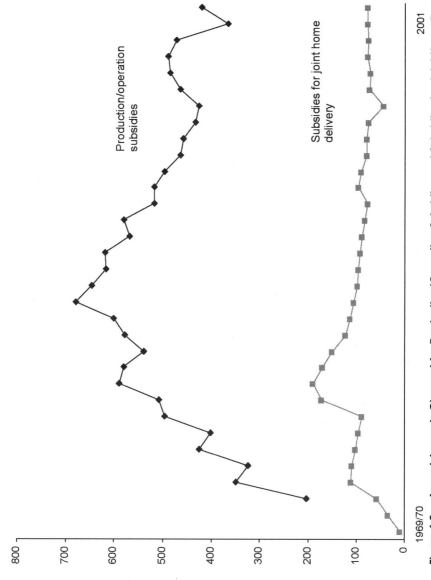

800
700
600
500
400
300
200
100
0

1969/70

2001

Production/operation
subsidies

Subsidies for joint home
delivery

**Figure 6.2. Annual Amounts Charged for Production/Operation Subsidies and Subsidies for Joint Home De-
livery, in Sweden (1969–2001) (in millions of Swedish crowns at 2001 value).**

Source: Council for Press Support and Nordicom.

SELECTIVE SUBSIDIES

Whereas the amount granted in general subsidies stayed fairly stable, the selective support, especially the production subsidies to so-called secondary papers, increased dramatically during the system's first years of existence. In 1971 it totalled 36 million Swedish crowns; in 1972, 65.5 million; in 1974, 96.5 million; and in 1976, 138.5 million. But since it was an expansive period for the press in general, the subsidies did not exceed 5 percent of the revenues of the Swedish newspaper industry. After the mid-1980s the support declined in value, because it was less compensated for inflation.

The rules guiding the selective subsidies or production support (termed operation support from 1990 on) have generally been the same over the years. They are detailed, but the main principles are relatively simple. First, the support can be given only to newspapers of "newspaper character, published at least once a week, being mainly subscribed, and having at least 2000 subscribers." There are two levels of support (originally three), based on both publication frequency and circulation. For each level there is a maximum support available. The support is dependent on household coverage in the main local market, where the coverage may not exceed 40 percent. The maximum support is significantly higher for newspapers in the three metropolitan areas (in 1998, it amounted to 54.3 million Swedish crowns) than for other high frequency papers (12.7 million Swedish crowns). Since 1990 the actual amount has been calculated on the basis of the total circulation of the paper.

There are additional rules making it possible for newspapers that publish some portion in another language (such as Finnish) to have a special subsidy for that. However, the principle stated by the 1972 press commission is that the subsidies should be based on "automatic rules," with no special concern for individual papers. On the other hand, it is obvious that rules sometimes have been changed to include, or exclude, specific papers, though always by parliamentary decision. In the same way, the support for the papers in the three metropolitan areas has increased considerably more than that for the countryside papers.

If we look at data from the late 1990s, we find that of 125 newspapers in Sweden, defined in terms of the subsidy rules, 51 received selective subsidies and 74 did not. Of the total amount available, almost half (45 percent) went to the three metropolitan papers: *Arbetet* in Malmö and Göteborg (two editions, with a social democratic affiliation), *Skånska Dagbladet* in Malmö (with a Center Party affiliation), and *Svenska Dagbladet* in Stockholm (with a conservative affiliation), whereas the 13 high-frequency countryside papers had to share 35 percent of the total 452 million. The average subsidy for the metropolitan papers was 50 million Swedish crowns; for the countryside high-frequency papers, 12 million Swedish crowns; and for the low-frequency newspapers, 0.5 million Swedish crowns.

A study from 1994 shows that the main receivers, in terms of party affiliation, were the social democratic and Center Party papers. They received 72 percent of the total 413 million Swedish crowns that year (see table 6.3), whereas the conservative and party politically independent press received a little more than 10 percent each. In comparison with the situation in the early 1970s (see table 6.4), the social democratic and conservative presses experienced a small increase in their share, mainly because of the higher

Table 6.3. Operating Grants Based on Party Affiliation, in Sweden (1994)

A Party Affiliation	B Number of Newspapers[a]	C Entitled to How Many Grants	D C as % of B[b]	E C as % of Entitled Newspapers	F Grants in 1000s of Crowns	G F as % of Total Grants[b]
Moderate	23	3	13.0	3.8	51,003	12.3
Liberal	29	2	6.3	2.6	4,071	1.0
Center	32	21	65.6	32.1	76,737	18.6
Social Dem.[c]	31	25	80.6	28.8	220,807	53.4
Socialist[d]	4	4	100.0	5.1	5,976	1.4
Christian Dem.	1	1	100.0	1.3	2,667	0.6
Environmental	1	1	100.0	1.3	1,494	0.4
Syndicalist	1	1	100.0	1.3	1,494	0.4
Bourgeois and Indep./Lib. Indep.	16	1	6.3	1.3	1,494	0.4
Independent[e]	41	19	46.3	24.4	47,404	11.5
Total	179	78	43.6	102.0	413,147	100.0

[a] Newspaper editions are included here. For example, the Press Support Board counts *Arbetet* and its zoned edition, *Arbetet Väst*, as two different newspapers; thus each is entitled to a grant. Also, *3 Dagar* and *Gotlands Tidningar* are owned by both social democrats and centrists. One newspaper is counted for each party. The latter newspaper is only 1/6 owned by liberals. Therefore, it is not counted as a liberal newspaper, but 1/6 of the grant is credited to the liberals. *3 Dagar* folded in August 1994 and was replaced by a weekly, *Växjöbladet-Kronobergaren*, which retained *3 Dagar's* political affiliation.

[b] To the nearest tenth percent.

[c] Includes three independent social democratic newspapers: *Länstidningen Östersund, Örebro Kuriren,* and *Nya Östgöten.*

[d] Includes newspapers that label themselves communist, independent socialist, and opposition. None of these newspapers is a spokesman for the Leftist Party. The editor-in-chief of M-L Proletären told this writer that the Left Party was an enemy.

[e] Includes thirteen different labels such as politically free, provincial, and politically neutral.

Source: Borden (1995: 228).

Table 6.4.   Direct Newspaper Subsidies Categorized According to Type of Newspapers, in Sweden (1994)

Type of Newspaper	Number of Newspaper Companies	Amount of Operation Subsidies Delivery (in millions of Swedish crowns)	Amount of Subsidies for Joint Home Delivery (in millions of Swedish crowns)
Low-frequency papers with operation subsidies	35	77	0.2
Countryside newspapers with operation subsidies	13	162	5
Countryside newspapers without operation subsidies	70	10	43
Metropolitan newspapers with operation subsidies	3	203	7
Metropolitan newspapers without operation subsidies	4	0	16
Single-copy sale tabloids	4	0	0
Total	129	452	72

Note: Countryside and metropolitan newspapers are by definition high-frequency papers (four issues a week or more).
Source: Hadenius and Weibull (2002: 99).

amount charged for metropolitan papers. The average support for individual papers is 17 million Swedish crowns for the conservative press, 9 million Swedish crowns for the social democratic press, and 3.5 million Swedish crowns for the Center Party press.

Even though the amounts have increased and it might seem that the subsidy system is maintaining the supported papers, this is not the case, especially for the main receivers. For *Arbetet,* whose two editions were granted almost 90 million Swedish crowns a year, these meant an income share of less than 30 percent; and for *Svenska Dagbladet,* the share was only about 5 percent, which was only a tenth of its advertising income. But for some of the small Center Party papers the subsidy exceeded 50 percent of their income. And, of course, even for subsidy receivers, whose support share is small, tax support is in most cases the decisive factor in the paper's survival.

ESTABLISHMENT SUPPORT AND DEVELOPMENT AID

To stimulate the establishment of new newspapers, the 1972 press commission proposed a special support system. These were its terms: If a company presented a solid calculation for a new paper, money could be granted up to a little more than 1 million Swedish crowns; and if the paper survived its first year, the grant could be kept as newspaper support. The support was aimed at weeklies "of newspaper character." However, the establishment support was not successful. Few applications were submitted, and most of them concerned new editions of existing papers. The support was abolished in 1987.

The development aid also initiated by the 1972 commission was aimed at newspapers, which, despite the fact that there were primary papers on the market, met with economic problems. Support was given after application. In 1990 this support form was changed to general development aid, which could be granted to secondary papers as well, especially for expensive investments in new technology. In the beginning this aid played only a minor role, given the small number of potential receivers. After 1990, however, the situation was totally different. The subsidy went from 5 million Swedish crowns a year in 1989 to 24.6 million in 1990 and 34.4 million in 1991. Now the receivers were secondary papers, and these needed to invest in digital technology. This amounted to a temporary extension of the selective subsidies, and in 1997 the support form was abolished.

SUPPORT TO STIMULATE COOPERATION

One of the totally new principles introduced by the 1972 commission was the support of cooperation. In the background was the success with the joint delivery system, which, the commission hoped, could be extended to administration, subscription handling, and advertising (among other things). As with the joint delivery system, the primary papers could be given grants if they wanted to cooperate with the secondary ones.

However, despite the success of distribution cooperation, the new model met with little interest. Support was granted some projects concerning common marketing of newspapers, but no substantial cooperation started. One probable reason was that the amount that could be granted was very small in relation to the value of the area of cooperation for the primary paper (e.g., a well-functioning subscription or advertising department), which could be opened to the competitor. In contrast to the distribution system, the changes needed here were more of a fundamental company character and therefore of no interest to the dominant papers.

Swedish Press Subsidies in Perspective

Looking back on three decades of Swedish press subsidies, we can conclude that the core parts of the system have been the selective subsidies and the subsidies to joint home delivery. But have those systems been effective in terms of their goals to maintain newspaper pluralism in Sweden? This, of course, is the decisive question, and it can be answered in terms of two major factors: structural maintenance and political importance.

STRUCTURAL MAINTENANCE

The goal of the selective subsidies was to maintain pluralism in the newspaper market and, ideally, to give the citizens freedom of party political newspaper choice. From the perspective of party press tradition, it was natural for the Swedish politicians of the 1960s and 1970s to propose a model that would preserve a political newspaper structure. The metaphor used was the importance of having many voices; thus the press was viewed as a party political choir. The basic goals of the press—information, comments, surveillance, and group communication—are related to the role of newspapers in the political process (namely, current affairs reporting), thus indicating that press policy was a matter of party political pluralism.

In terms of structure, the model functioned relatively well for a long time. If the subsidy had not been introduced, most of the secondary, high-frequency papers—in 1971, about 25 total—would probably have had to close down. But to a large extent they survived the 1980s, even though the holding company of the social democratic press went into bankruptcy in the early 1990s. Even if most of the local newspapers survived, with help from development aid (among other things), the social democratic press was significantly weakened. The main paper of the group, *Arbetet*, never did totally recover; and in spite of its annual subsidy of 90 million Swedish crowns, it suffered great losses during the second half of the 1990s and had to close down in the fall of 2000 (Gustafsson, 2002). Three decades later, fewer than half of the secondary, high-frequency papers of 1971 are alive as independent companies, whereas most of the low-frequency papers remain.

One reason for the erosion of secondary papers, despite the selective subsidies, is that the state support was not large enough and couldn't balance out their problems on the advertising market. Behind this circumstance, and probably behind the declining value of the total press support, was the same debate that had started as early as the mid-1960s. Critics saw the subsidies as a government intrusion into the economic market: The task of the state money was to compensate weak papers for their problems in the advertising market, which also resulted in problems attracting readers (SOU, 1975, no. 78). The argument mainly addressed the Freedom of the Press Act, which states that the right for everybody to establish a newspaper is guaranteed—not only as a political right but also as an economic right.[3] It is reasonable to believe that the selective subsidies were meant to be just subsidies, and that the money allocated did not in any way change the structure of the newspaper market.

POLITICAL IMPORTANCE

When they stressed the importance of many voices, the early press commissions were thinking of a press where not only editorial pages but also news of important political matters were biased by the party political affiliation of an individual paper (i.e., by the notion of a party political press). However, during the 1970s and 1980s, the conditions changed. Increasing professionalism among journalists, the transformation of the newspaper market in the 1960s, and the expansion of television news in the early 1970s gradually forced the dominant papers to offer balanced news reporting, covering all types of events and all parties (cf. Asp, 1986; Svedberg, 1995). Paradoxically, the press subsidies helped the secondary papers to go in the same direction, since the state money included no conditions for reporting, whereas the earlier party subsidies had made the papers conscious of who was supporting them and why.

The transition phase can also be observed in relation to the 1972 press commission. The functions formulated for the press include elements of the traditional party press (e.g., group communication) as well as one new perspective for Sweden, which in a way was the opposite of the party press tradition: critical surveillance. The 1972 commission clearly followed the party press tradition, but changes were under way. It is illustrative that a press commission in the mid-1990s, whose task was to review the total subsidy system, changed the goals of the press to *information*, *surveillance*, and *forum for debate*, thus accepting the disappearance of the party press (SOU, 1995, no. 37: 11).

Consequently, newspaper pluralism was increasingly regarded as a questionable outcome for the individual papers, as it already was for public service television news. This pluralism was referred to as "internal pluralism" as opposed to external pluralism (the latter entailed the total press structure) (Cavallin, 1998). However, internal pluralism has never been an issue for the selective press subsidy system, since a measure in this area would offend the Freedom of the Press Act. Instead, the selective subsidy system has developed in the direction of a general industry subsidy, even though it still focuses on the secondary papers. The basic idea now is that competition for the quality of news reporting is important, and that the selective support should be abolished (which, as sometimes discussed, should mean less competition). The problem here, however, is that subsidies nowadays go to relatively few local markets.

A System at an End?

The selective press subsidies in Sweden have been debated for more than three decades. The press commissions have argued in terms of democracy, which would enable all groups to have newspaper platforms, whereas critics have viewed the subsidies as an illegitimate intrusion into free press or as a matter of "vested interests" (cf. Borden, 1995: 203).

On the basis of this overview it is fair to say not only that the subsidies were introduced to keep a broad political debate but also that they have stimulated pluralism in the press. Even though the original basis eroded when the old party press lost its role, the subsidies have given society a clear signal of the importance of newspapers to political debate. This is probably one reason why there has been some basic consensus in spite of all the controversies.

The problem with the selective subsidies is that they could not change the circumstances of the newspaper market, and probably were not even aimed at it. In most cases the distance in market position between primary and secondary papers was too big, and the subsidies were too small to make a difference. However, in some markets, such as Malmö and Östersund, the subsidies resulted in increased competition, which, for a period of time, created problems for the primary papers.[4]

A final aspect of the press subsidy system is that it has focused on competition between independent newspaper companies in local markets. However, in the last decade at least two changes have challenged the traditional subsidy model. Firstly, the expansion of other media in Sweden, the most important being the introduction of commercial television in 1991 and private radio in 1993, has presented newspapers with increasing competition. Secondly, as a consequence of this competition, Sweden has seen an increasing number of mergers between primary and secondary papers, as well as between primary papers on neighboring markets. Most of these mergers have meant that nonsocialist, primary papers have taken over socialist papers and integrated administration, technology, and advertising departments, but kept the smaller paper as an edition. For this edition, which in most cases has a content profile of its own, the primary paper receives the press subsidy. These subsidies to primary papers have been criticized and might even open up a new debate on the role of the subsidy system in the new media era. Thus, subsidies, although important for many years, seem to have lost much of their significance in terms of the pluralism of the Swedish newspaper market.

Notes

1. The reason given was the establishment of television, regarded as the new important medium, in 1956 (Hadenius and Weibull, 2002).

2. It is interesting to note that some of the liberal newspaper critics of the direct subsidies also rejected the indirect ones (e.g., the reduction of the value-added tax). The implication is that such a measure was an intrusion in the free press, which might make newspapers dependent on the political power.

3. The right for everybody to establish newspapers is a basic requirement: No censorship shall take place, and individual sources to newspapers are strongly protected. The center of the law is the newspaper owner, not the citizens if they do not themselves own a newspaper—or publish books—to influence public opinion. The law presupposes a situation in which it is very easy to start a newspaper, thus reflecting the origins of the press in the late eighteenth and early nineteenth centuries (Hadenius and Weibull, 2002).

4. As has been noted, a consequence of the subsidy rules is that when a secondary paper increases its household coverage by more than 40 percent, it loses its support.

References

Alström, Börje, and Nord, Lars (2002). *Expedition Mångfald. Båda tidningarna kvar på ön.* Stockholm: Carlssons.

Axberger, Hans-Gunnar (1984). *Tryckfrihetens gränser.* Stockholm: Liber.

Asp, Kent (1986). *Mäktiga massmedier.* Göteborg: Akademilitteratur.

Borden, William (1995). *Power Plays. A Comparison Between Swedish and American Press Policies.* Göteborg: Department of Journalism and Mass Communication, Göteborg University.

Cavallin, Jens (1995). *Vad är mediekoncentration?* Arbetsdokument från rådet för mångfald inom massmedierna. Stockholm: Kulturdepartementet.

Furhoff, Lars (1986). *Makten över journalistiken.* Stockholm: Natur och Kultur.

Gustafsson, Karl Erik (ed.) (1995). *Media Structure and the State: Concepts, Issues, Measures.* Göteborg: School of Business Economics, Göteborg University.

Gustafsson, Karl Erik (2002). "Arbetet 1887–2000," in Ingela Wadbring, Lennart Weibull, and Annika Bergström (eds.), *Efter Arbetet. Synen påring; nedläggningen och dess konsekvenser.* Göteborg: Department of Journalism and Mass Communication/The SOM Institute, Göteborg University.

Gustafsson, Karl Erik, and Hadenius, Stig (1977). *Swedish Press Policy.* Stockholm: Sweden Books

Gustafsson, Karl Erik, and Weibull, Lennart (1997). "Newspaper Readership—Structure and Development," *European Journal of Communication Research* 3.

Hadenius, Stig, Seveborg, Jan-Olof, and Weibull, Lennart (1968). *Socialdemokratisk press och presspolitik 1899–1909*. Stockholm: Tiden.

———— (1969). "Social Democratic Press and Newspaper Policy 1899–1909," *Scandinavian Political Studies* 3.

———— (1970). *Partipress. Socialdemokratisk press 1910–1920*. Stockholm: Raben&Sjögren.

Hadenius, Stig, and Weibull, Lennart (1973). *Press radio TV. En bok om massmedier*. Stockholm: Aldus.

———— (1978). *Massmedier. En bok om press radio och TV*. Stockholm: Aldus

———— (2002). *Massmedier. En bok om press radio TV i förvandling*. Stockholm: Albert Bonniers Förlag.

SOU [Government Commission Report] (1965). no. 22. *Dagstidningarnas ekonomiska villkor. Betänkande av pressutredningen*. Stockholm.

———— (1968). no. 48. *Dagspressens situation. Betänkande av 1967 års pressutredning*. Stockholm.

———— (1975). no. 78. *Pressens funktioner. En forskningsrapport till 1972 års pressutredning*. Stockholm.

———— (1975). no. 79. *Statlig presspolitik. Betänkande av 1972 års pressutredning*. Stockholm.

———— (1994). no. 94. *Dagspressen i 1990-talets medielandskap. En expertrapport från Pressutredningen—94*. Stockholm.

———— (1995). no. 37. *Vårt dagliga blad—stöd till svensk dagspress. Betänkande av pressutredningen—94*. Stockholm.

Svedberg, Helene (1995). *Massmediernas partiskhet*. In Ronny Severinsson (ed.), *Studier i medielandskapet*. Göteborg University, Department of Journalism and Mass Communication.

Weibull, Lennart (1982). Det politiska tidningsvalet. In Asp, K. et al. *Väljare Parier Massmedia. Empiriska studier i svensk demokrati*. Stockholm: Publica.

———— (1983a). "Political Factors in Newspaper Readership," *Communication Research* 10: 311–331.

———— (1983b). ""Newspaper Readership in Sweden,"" *Newspaper Research Journal* (Fall issue).

———— (1993). "The Status of the Daily Newspaper," *Poetics* 21: 4.

———— (1995). "Media Diversity and Choice," in Gustafsson K. E. (ed.), *Media Structure and the State: Concepts, Issues, Measures*. Göteborg: School of Business Economics, Göteborg University.

Westerståhl, Jörgen (1964). *Dagspressen och den politiska opinionsbildningen*. Department of Political Science, Göteborg University.

Westerståhl, Jörgen, and Janson, Carl-Gunnar (1958). *Politisk press*. Göteborg: Akademiförlaget.

Part III

IN THE SHADOW
OF THE MARKET

CHAPTER 7

Commercialism and Critique
CALIFORNIA'S ALTERNATIVE WEEKLIES

Rodney Benson

Critique and commercialization need not be mutually exclusive, as the Comedia (1984) research group long ago conceded. But alternative media researchers who have followed in this vein (e.g., Khiabany, 2000; Pimlott, 2000) seem to prefer commercialism in small doses—in other words, just enough to survive. Two assumptions generally follow from this formulation. Advertising is seen as the bogeyman to be avoided, whether at the national or local level. Indeed, local television and daily newspapers are often far more sensationalistic and de-politicized than their national mainstream counterparts (Underwood, 1995; McManus, 1994). Thus, paying audiences are viewed as the preferred form of commercial support (Bagdikian, 1992; Baker, 1994), a philosophy that guides such venerable alternative publications as *The Nation*, *Mother Jones*, and *Le Monde Diplomatique*.

America's urban "alternative" weeklies challenge both of these assumptions, with a vengeance. All are distributed in a single metropolitan area, all of them receive nearly 100 percent of their funding from advertising. Most surprisingly, many (if not all) of these weeklies offer genuine critical alternatives to both local and national mainstream media. Yet, with the exception of a few excellent social histories (e.g., Armstrong, 1981; Peck, 1991), this paradoxical blend of a commercially successful yet politically and culturally radical press has largely escaped scholarly notice.

The earliest and most famous example is the *Village Voice*, founded by a collective of Greenwich Village writers and cultural critics in 1955 (Frankfort, 1976; McAuliffe, 1978). The *Voice*'s outsider image and style influenced the first revolutionary "underground" papers of the 1960s, such as the *Los Angeles Free Press* founded in 1964 and the *Berkeley Barb* started in 1965, as well as the urban consumer (non-revolutionary, but generally left-reformist) weeklies from San Francisco to Boston that took hold shortly thereafter. At the end of the 1960s, according to D. Armstrong (1981: 60), 400 American underground and alternative publications had a combined *paid* circulation of 5 million.

Currently, the 118 member-publications of the Association of Alternative Newsweeklies (AAN) have a combined *free* circulation of 8 million and annual revenues of about $500 million (AAN, 2002).[1] Some of these "alternatives" have long used free distribution, others have only recently shifted—the *Village Voice* went "free"

in 1996—but the "paid" status of the old underground papers is somewhat of a mis-
nomer, since many of these also relied heavily on advertising. Fifty-three percent of the
AAN weeklies belong to chains, defined broadly as "companies that own at least one
other media property," although the average size of these alternative chains is only
about three papers.[2] During the 1990s, while U.S. daily newspaper circulation declined 10 percent, alternative weeklies more than doubled theirs and the largest of
these, such as the *Voice* and the *LA Weekly*, now routinely approach profit margins of
15 to 20 percent (Barringer, 2000).

Today, no one disputes alternative newsweeklies' commercial appeal: their ability
to efficiently reach the affluent, college-educated, 18- to 34-year-old urban single with
plenty of disposable income and the propensity to spend it (AAN, 2002). "Alternatives" are the place to be seen for advertisers cultivating an edgy, hip attitude, and both
readers and advertisers are ostensibly attracted by editorial copy that is culturally and
stylistically "radical" (Schnuer, 1998). Rather, what remains puzzling, to rephrase
David Hesmondhalgh's problematic (2000), is why alternative weeklies actually offer
alternative *political* content. Why do some alternatives even bother to go after City
Hall? Why do they *ever* cover the local environmental protest? And why do they attack
the corporate world that pays their bills? Or do they?

California's Alternative Weeklies: General Features and Hypotheses

To answer these questions, I take a closer look at the leading alternative newsweeklies in
two of California's major media markets—the *LA Weekly* and *New Times LA* in Los Angeles, and the *Bay Guardian* and *SF Weekly* in San Francisco. California was the birthplace
of much of the underground and alternative press, and it continues to be a trendsetter in
the cultural and media realm. Another reason for the comparison is that these four publications offer a microcosm of the contemporary American alternative weekly industry.

The *Bay Guardian*, circulation 150,000, was founded in 1966 as a politically committed (though pointedly non-underground) urban weekly joining investigative and
consumer "service" journalism. It is still independently owned by founder Bruce Brugmann. In Los Angeles, the *LA Weekly* has been the dominant alternative newspaper
since the late 1970s and currently has a circulation of 220,000. The *Weekly* was purchased in 1995 by Stern Publishing, which had also bought New York's *Village Voice*
in 1986. Stern's alternative media properties, in turn, were sold in 2000 for an estimated $150 million to Village Voice Media, a newly founded corporation headed by
Voice publisher David Schneidermann though effectively owned by the private equity
firm of Weiss, Peck & Greer, associated with the Canadian Imperial Bank of Commerce (Moses, 2000a; Smith, 2002; Cotts, 2002).

Originally titled the *San Francisco Music Calendar*, the *SF Weekly*, circulation
110,000, has been the *Bay Guardian*'s major alternative competitor since the early
1980s (Alternet, 1995). In 1995, local owner Scott Price sold the paper for a reported
$1.3 million to New Times, Inc. Likewise, *New Times LA*, also circulation 110,000,

was created in 1996 after the New Times corporation bought and closed two other alternative papers in Los Angeles (Adelson, 1996). From its founding in 1970 as a university antiwar paper in Tempe, Arizona, New Times has expanded to 11 papers with a total weekly circulation of 1.1 million, making it the largest alternative chain (Iwan, 2001; AAN News, 2002). In 1999, an undisclosed portion of New Times (now officially NT Media) was sold to the venture capital group Alta Communications, in order to underwrite the continued expansion plans of founders Jim Larkin and Michael Lacey (Cotts, 2002). In October 2002, as this chapter was being finalized for publication, *New Times LA* was closed as part of a deal with Village Voice Media (VVM). In addition to paying NT Media several million dollars to effectively leave Los Angeles, VVM also agreed to shut down its competing Cleveland weekly, leaving New Times with a monopoly in that market (Carr, 2002; Moses, 2002).

Data on individual papers' advertising bases are difficult to obtain, since alternative weekly companies are not publicly traded and thus are not subject to financial disclosure laws. However, a 2001 AAN survey found that, on average, 65 percent of newsweekly revenues come from local display advertisements and inserts, 24 percent from classifieds, 7 percent from national advertising, and 2 percent from personals.[3] Since 2000, national advertising in alternative weeklies has dropped sharply—especially from tobacco companies, which provided more than 60 percent of all national advertising during the late 1990s. The other major national advertisers are alcohol and pharmaceutical companies and, varying according to the local market, telecommunications, clothing brands, and automobiles (Bates, 1999; Smith, 2002; AAN, 2002). Sex-related advertising, both display and classified, provides an estimated 10 percent of total alternative weekly revenues (Neuwirth, 1998). Some publishers, such as the owners of the *Chicago Reader* and *San Diego Reader*, refuse such ads, but they are the exceptions.

A page space analysis of a sub-sample of three California alternative weeklies (see table 7.1)[4] shows that "local display" (chiefly for retail shops) is by far the dominant type of advertising. Sex ads take up relatively more space in the two Los Angeles newsweeklies.[5] Classifieds are most important for *New Times LA*. National advertising—for cigarettes,

Table 7.1.   Types of Advertising in California Alternative Weeklies (proportions of total ad pages)

	SF Bay Guardian 9 January and 24 April 2002	LA Weekly 11 January and 26 April 2002	New Times LA 10 January and 25 April 2001
Local display	.73	.64	.50
Sex	.09	.23	.20
Personals	.03	.05	.00
Classifieds	.12	.06	.26
National	.03	.03	.04
Total ad pages	161	226	133
Total pages	228	344	192
Ads as proportion of total pages	.71	.66	.69

Source: Author's content analysis.

Table 7.2. Audience Demographics of California Alternative Weeklies

	Age 18–34 (%)	Female (%)	Graduated University (%)	Attended University (%)	Professional/ Managerial (%)	Median Household Income
SF Bay Guardian	43.7	37.4	43.1	90.4	45.4	$80,537
LA Weekly	42.3	59.2	26.0	86.0	39.5	$56,700
SF Weekly	42.4	36.5	48.4	91.5	56	$53,000
New Times LA	32.8	30.1	55.9	86.3	54.2	$52,100

Source: www.aan.org. Last accessed in September 2002.

liquor, and portable telephones—takes up only 3 to 4 percent of the advertising page space at all three weeklies.

Turning to demographic statistics, we see that the *Bay Guardian's* readers are the youngest, with about 44 percent of its audience in the 18–34 age group,[6] and the most prosperous, with an average household income of more than $80,000 (see table 7.2). Readers of the two New Times publications are more educated and more likely to hold professional or managerial jobs. The *LA Weekly's* audience is the most female, the least educated, and the least likely to include professional or managerial workers. Nevertheless, the overall impression of these data is not of marked differences, but of the weeklies' shared success in reaching their target audience of young, affluent professionals.[7]

In sum, there seems little in the basic funding and audience features to sharply distinguish these four papers from one another, or to suggest that any of them might publish politically radical or truly "alternative" editorial content. The political economy tradition of media research predicts that an advertising-dependent press, such as America's urban alternative weeklies, would emphasize culture over politics, disdain social protest, and ignore economic injustice and corporate malfeasance (Bagdikian, 1992; Baker, 1994; Lemert, 1984; Collins, 1992; Underwood, 1995). This study takes five randomly selected weeks from the first half of 2002 (the weeks beginning 6 January, 20 January, 27 January, 3 March, and 21 April) and puts these hypotheses to a (preliminary) test: First, how often and in what manner is culture versus government news treated? Second, how often and in what manner is civic activism facilitated and encouraged? And, third, how often and in what manner are corporate abuse and economic injustice covered? We will compare the alternative newsweeklies with each other and, implicitly, with daily newspapers, which, though also primarily advertising supported, are somewhat less so than the alternatives.[8]

How Alternative Are the Alternatives?

CULTURE VERSUS INSTITUTIONAL POLITICS

Within the news and commentary pages (also labeled "news & culture" at some of the papers), government stories outnumber cultural stories at all four weeklies[9] (see table 7.3).[10] Culture, of course, is not necessarily the opposite of politics. While culture stories are often light and humorous (e.g., the *SF Weekly's* "Clear Window: The 13th annual International Window Cleaners Association Convention is transparently entertaining," 30 January), the genre allows room for political critique and reflection. In a *Bay Guardian* cover story titled "The apotheosis of cute: How fluffy bunnies, bouncy kittens, and the Clinton era brought cuteness to an awful climax" (23 January), culture editor Annalee Newitz offers a wide-ranging critical assessment of contemporary American culture, the kind that wouldn't seem out of place in a hip academic journal (indeed, Newitz is a former Berkeley graduate student in English and a founding editor of the Berkeley online cultural studies journal *Bad Subjects*). This passage gives the article's flavor:

> Cultural amnesia, according to [the late Berkeley culture critic] Michael Rogin, is all about using appealing images to wipe out our memories of painful

Table 7.3.   News Article Topics in California Alternative Weeklies (Spring 2002)

	SF Bay Guardian (n = 68)	LA Weekly (n = 87)	SF Weekly (n = 23)	New Times LA (n = 17)
Culture/lifestyle	7 (.10)	15 (.17)	7 (.30)	1 (.06)
Culture/political	8 (.12)	13 (.15)	0 (.00)	5 (.29)
Total culture	15 (.22)	28 (.32)	7 (.30)	6 (.35)
Media	11 (.16)	18 (.21)	2 (.09)	8 (.47)
Government	51 (.75)	34 (.39)	9 (.39)	8 (.47)
Citizen activism	21 (.31)	17 (.20)	4 (.17)	2 (.12)
Economic inequalities	12 (.18)	6 (.07)	1 (.04)	1 (.06)
Business	13 (.19)	6 (.07)	6 (.26)	1 (.06)

Source: Author's content analysis of all news and opinion articles appearing in five randomly selected issues from Spring 2002. Arts and restaurant reviews/listings not included.

historical and political realities. Looked at from this perspective, cuteness is a kind of cultural decoy. . . . It's no coincidence that the recent run on U.S. flag fashions dovetails nicely with cuteness. You can get weensy teddy bears waving American flags and neato sparkly tops and bell-bottoms in red, white, and blue. There's no contradiction, in other words, in the partnership of retrograde nationalist spectacle and mainstream raver chic. Ultimately, the danger of cuteness is that it's a style that plays into the most conservative American tendencies. It vaunts a frivolous, impotent femininity, cartoonish racial representations, and a passive, apolitical view of the world.

Another political, if not strictly government-oriented, aspect of alternative weeklies' news coverage (partly overlapping with the cultural category in table 7.3) is criticism of mainstream media organizations. At the *LA Weekly*, for instance, John Powers' 11 January "On" column laments the virtual absence of any mainstream media investigation of the Enron bankruptcy scandal and its potential connections to the Bush administration. *New Times LA*'s Rick Barrs is widely credited with exposing the *Los Angeles Times*' secret "Staples Center" deal, a blatant editorial conflict of interest, which in turn provoked a national debate over the excesses of marketing-driven journalism.[11]

In its heavy coverage of government institutions, the *Bay Guardian* is clearly the most political of the four weeklies examined. Typical government stories focus on insider gossip (who is up, who is down in local city politics), investigations (e.g., the police cover-up after the shooting of a local black man), and the paper's own political causes. One of the paper's favorite campaigns is on behalf of "public power" (and thus against the private Pacific Gas and Electric company), evident in such stories as "Utility stonewall: PG&E won't give records to CPUC" (9 January), "Following up on public power" (6 March), and "Volt revolt: PG&E faces increased criticism from investors and activists alike" (24 April).

The *LA Weekly* also takes politics seriously, although the emphasis is often national or statewide as well as local. Harold Meyerson (the paper's former executive editor, who recently moved to Washington, D.C., to edit the left-liberal opinion magazine *American Prospect*) contributes a column primarily on national politics in which he consistently takes a pro-labor Democrat position. What most differentiates the *LA Weekly* from the mainstream press is its ability to go in-depth and offer multiple perspectives, such as in its "Dissent Now" issue (1 February) and, even more impressively, in an issue (26 April) commemorating the tenth anniversary of the 1992 L.A. race riots. Readers were unlikely to find anywhere else not only riot posters created by local schoolchildren but the first-person account of a man who participated in the looting, as well as thoughtful postmortems. The journalistic "voice" at the *Weekly* is often highly personal, even impassioned (e.g., Sara Catania's "A Killer Job: How a lousy lawyer landed Stephen Wayne Anderson on Death Row," 25 January), but also intellectually honest, acknowledging that there are other sides to the story.

Journalists at the two New Times papers cover government aggressively, ever on the lookout for corruption, dishonesty, or hypocrisy from politicians. In his column "The Finger," *New Times LA* editor Rick Barrs regularly skewered local and national political figures. Vintage sarcastic Barrs from the 24 January 2002 issue:

> You Go, Girls! Right-wingers were squealing like a **gaggle of little girls** last week about how they'd bitch-slapped a bill in the Legislature that would've brought **Vermont-style civil unions for gays** to California. "We thank **God** for this tremendous victory!" gushed . . . [the] head of the **Campaign for California Families**. "Enough is enough!" shrieked . . . [the] president of **Focus on the Family**, a *Christian* outfit out of Colorado. But hold the phone, ladies! You may have stirred up all your *Bible*-thumpin,' **homo-hatin' bi-atches** with catty howling about how civilization's gonna end if gays get the same legal benefits as married straight couples. But you ain't even reduced by an inch the hard-on that The Finger's favorite WeHo assemblyman . . . is sportin' to reintroduce his civil-union bill, probably next year. (original emphasis)

If the tone is harsh, the reporting is usually solid. One critic notes that New Times muckrakers "prefer exposing individuals to illuminating the systems and institutions that perpetuate inequality and injustice" (Bates, 1998). But it would be unfair to characterize the New Times approach as cynical or apolitical. Barrs and his New Times colleagues clearly care about making government more honest and effective.

CITIZEN ACTIVISM

Advertising funding has been said to promote a consumerist vision of the world, encouraging readers to seek answers to their problems in the shopping mall rather than at city hall. But the *San Francisco Bay Guardian* somehow bridges this consumer/citizen divide, consistently addressing its articles to activist-citizens, with such headlines as "The drive for a minimum-wage hike should put poor people's needs first, advocates say" (6 March) and "Nuke the nukes: Need for radioactive storage gives activists a new weapon" (23 January). Articles often close with exactly the kind of "mobilizing information" (Lemert, 1984) that is said to be missing from the mainstream press. For instance, the "Nuke the nukes" story ends with the suggestion, "To get involved or to send a donation, contact San Luis Obispo Mothers for Peace, P.O. Box 164 [etc.]."

Similarly, an article on a government proposal to tear down affordable housing to build a parking garage ("A lot of problems: Hastings College plans monster garage," 6 March) offers this notice: "A public hearing on the draft environmental impact report will be held Wed/6, 2 p.m., State Building [etc.]." Of the newsweeklies in this sample, only the *Bay Guardian* publishes an editorial page, on which it features an op/ed article by a local activist as well as one or more editorials representing the official view of the newspaper, usually linked to news stories appearing in the same edition. Each issue also prominently features a half-page of "news alerts," essentially a bulletin board of protests, lectures, and meetings sponsored by local activists and political officials.

Compared with the *Bay Guardian*, the *LA Weekly* is more ambivalent about political activism. The *LA Weekly* also lists local "political events," but they are buried inside the regular Calendar at the back of the issue. The "Dissent Now" cover stories in the *LA Weekly*'s 1 February issue are aimed less at activists than at interested, even skeptical, bystanders. The special issue includes an extensive, and largely sympathetic, article on antiglobalization protesters and a backgrounder explaining their chief policy demands. But a third, perhaps intentionally balancing, first-person testimony by columnist Judith Lewis offers a rationalization for not getting involved. Activists and protest movements are often covered more for their curiosity and sensational value than for any real political significance. Typical *LA Weekly* headlines include "Review this Book or Else: The latest gripes from the 'gun-toting lesbians'" (8 March) and "Three Guys and a Megaphone: The JDL's shrinking role in Jewish extremism" (11 January).

The New Times papers are the most consistently antiprotest. Activists appearing in their pages always play comic roles. For instance, the *SF Weekly* delights in exposing what it calls "only in San Francisco" protests. In "Horse Senseless" (23 January), staff writer Matt Smith ridicules a group of horse owners who refused to relocate their horses from city-owned stables in Golden Gate Park, including one woman who threatened to "kill her 18-year-old Jo Jo on the steps of City Hall unless supervisors decreed the horse could remain at the stables." Smith concludes, "In San Francisco, it's possible to spin a struggle for private privilege into a fight for social justice, and the public won't have the horse sense to know the difference."

CRITICISM OF CAPITALISM

Critical stories about businesses and economic inequalities appear most frequently in the *San Francisco Bay Guardian*. As noted, one particular target, the California Pacific Gas and Electric utility company, reappears in several issues. Other articles examine a proposed bill to raise the local minimum wage, report a study on understaffing at low-income nursing homes, and investigate possibly illegal, backroom deals between developers and city officials. The *Bay Guardian* doesn't just report the news, it takes sides and often leads readers by the hand to the "correct" conclusion. If the tone is sometimes simplistic or preachy, the paper is nevertheless sensitive to the contradictions of movement politics. In "Home Creepo" (23 January), Cassi Feldman presents the clash between antigrowth activists opposing the construction of a new Home Depot and black activists supporting the chain retailer for its ability to create jobs. As the title not so subtly hints, the *Bay Guardian* ultimately sides with the antigrowth forces, while urging additional efforts to expand employment.

While generally ignoring poor people, the *SF Weekly* often writes about big business, sometimes even critically. In a story about America On-Line ("Serfing the Web," 9 January), Matt Smith doesn't shrink from broad criticisms of American capitalism:

> Sometime during the last two decades of the Technology Age—perhaps it was after the publication of the 250th touchy-feely management best seller, or after the broadcast of public television's 100th Sesame Street–like investment tips show—Americans came to fully accept the idea that profitable companies are like churches. Successful companies emphasize Love: "At firms with strong cultures, employees care about the company, each other, and customers," writes Whitney Tilson, a management analyst. . . . But this can be a corrupt faith. A class-action lawsuit against the world's most successful online company suggests that profitable corporations still make money the old-fashioned way: They exploit, manipulate, and underpay employees; they usurp Americans' common patrimony; they flout the law. They're certainly not churches.

In contrast to the tenets of mainstream journalism, Smith concludes the article with his own policy recommendations, such as greater scrutiny of "technology age companies" by the U.S. Securities and Exchange Commission and the Labor Department.

But more typical of the New Times approach to business and economic issues is a focus on the colorful, controversial entrepreneur or the off-beat enterprise. Sometimes this approach can include a critical element, as in Jill Stewart's "Master of Disaster: How L.A.'s super-rich Gary Winnick is trying to wash blood from the Global Crossing implosion off his hands—and make more money in the bargain" (*New Times LA*, 25 April). Just as often, business stories are stripped entirely of politics, focusing instead on the amusing and bizarre, as illustrated by these *SF Weekly* headlines: "The Garden East of Eden: Is it a dream—or an obsession—when someone pours a $75 million fortune into an amusement park, based on trees, located in Gilroy?" (6 March); and "Death of a Death School: The 72-year-old San Francisco College of Mortuary Science—perhaps the country's premiere institution of funeral service education—has its last graduation and moves (gulp) into the great beyond" (24 April).

The typical *LA Weekly* story is not likely to dwell on corporate misbehavior or economic injustice. But via the occasional special issue (e.g., "The LA Riots," "Dissent Now") and the regular columns of Meyerson, Powers, and Marc Cooper (also a contributing editor for *The Nation*), the *Weekly* often raises questions that transcend the usual mainstream (promarket) political consensus. As Cooper writes in the 26 April issue:

> In the park-sized back yard of a well-known producer's Mandeville Canyon mansion, under a massive rented circus tent, every table perfectly adorned with fresh flowers and gleaming press kits, liberal [i.e., left] Hollywood reached deep into its pockets to fight the Bush administration's opposition to expanded stem-cell research. No problem with that in itself. But try to organize a similar benefit for the 30 percent in L.A. who live in poverty, or the 11 percent who try to get by on the minimum wage, and

see what kind of turnout you get. Better cancel the valet service and scrub the caterers. . . . And these are the liberals!

What Makes Alternative Weeklies "Alternative"?

This quantitative and qualitative analysis of alternative weeklies finds the *San Francisco Bay Guardian* consistently more "alternative" than the other three newspapers in the sample, at least by measures of political versus cultural emphasis, citizen mobilization, and capitalist critique. While not traditionally leftist, the New Times–owned weeklies still offer important alternatives in their impassioned, provocative writing style and muckraking investigative journalism. In this sense, New Times papers also contribute significantly to engaging (if not mobilizing) the public in debate, rather than just providing it with basic information (Baker, 1994: 43). The *LA Weekly* emphasizes serious commentary and analysis, approaching complex events like the 1992 L.A. riots from a broad range of perspectives. And all four publications are far more politically oriented than predicted. How do we account for these findings? Type of advertising cannot be discounted entirely as a broad background factor distinguishing alternative weeklies from the more "mainstream" press. However, before analyzing the role of advertising, I discuss three other factors that vary more sharply among the alternative weeklies and may also shape editorial content: ownership and professional identity, audience composition and motivation, and competition in the local journalistic field.

OWNERSHIP AND PROFESSIONAL IDENTITY

The *San Francisco Bay Guardian* is the sole independent, non-chain-owned newspaper in this study. Independent ownership, combined with the continued defense of a political mission by its founder-publisher, clearly makes a difference. *Bay Guardian* cultural editor Annalee Newitz[12] portrays the weekly's identity in both personal and historical terms: "A lot of the *Bay Guardian*'s activist stance comes from [founder] Bruce [Brugmann] and the fact that he started it as an explicitly political project. But also at the time he founded the *Guardian*, there was a much stronger sense [than today] that alternative newsweeklies had more of a political mission." Newitz hesitates to call the *Bay Guardian* itself a "social movement," instead labeling it a "socially-conscious business" or even "like a non-profit association": "The money we make is totally in the service of the cause." At the same time, Newitz reports that Brugmann, far more than his editors, is also passionate about the paper's "Best of the Bay" issue, pure "service journalism" in support of urban consumerism. It is this seemingly incompatible mix that has allowed the *Bay Guardian* to survive and thrive.

The New Times chain, despite being vilified as the "Gannett of the alternatives," also is driven by a cause, if a different one from that of the *Bay Guardian*. Shortly after purchasing the *SF Weekly*, co-publisher Lacey was quoted as saying, "If it is political, we are against it, meaning that we are skeptical of political movements and politicians" (Alternet, 1995). At the same time, many New Times staffers appreciate the freedom the chain has given them to dispense with traditional, cautious "objectivity" in order to "tell the truth," as former *Los Angeles Times* reporter Jill Stewart argues. Stewart[13] recalls how she joined New Times:

> [After leaving the LA *Times*] I had been doing this power brokers column for *Buzz* magazine. It was kind of edgy, a little bit snotty. . . . They [the New Times owners] said, we want you to keep doing something along those lines. Anything goes as long as you can prove it. That's the first time I had ever heard that as a journalist. Especially at the LA *Times* where that is absolutely not the rule, where there were so many sacred cows. . . . I thought, my God, that's what I'd come to journalism for. That's like, back from 1976 when I was in college.

Before the recent change in ownership at the *LA Weekly*, former staff writer Ruben Martinez[14] defined his relationship to politics in a way quite distinct from most daily newspaper reporters: "I came from alternative journalistic circles [where] the relationship between alternative journalists and activists, they're one and the same. We all hang out together." Another *LA Weekly* writer, Sandra Hernandez,[15] described her vision of journalism in clearly alternative terms (though in sharp opposition to that of New Times): "I think a journalist's responsibility certainly goes beyond . . . ranting and raving simply to sell more papers. I think my responsibility as a journalist . . . is to bring forth some of the voices and some of the interests of those people who generally have been left out of the debate."

After having been passed on to its third owner in less than ten years, the *LA Weekly*'s "alternative" identity today is less certain. While *New Times LA* was staffed with several ex–*LA Times* editors and reporters (and proud to be "ex"), *LA Weekly* journalists tend to be more closely allied with the mainstream press. Long-time editor Sue Horton is now Sunday opinion pages editor of the *Los Angeles Times*. The current editor, Laurie Ochoa, was most recently at *Gourmet* magazine. Most important, Village Voice Media CEO David Schneidermann has said he wants to remake the *LA Weekly* so that it will compete "on the level of all the major media in L.A. . . . not just . . . alternative media" (Burk, 2002).

In sum, alternative weekly journalists distinguish themselves, albeit in diverse ways, from their mainstream colleagues. But, as elsewhere, publishers have the last word.

AUDIENCE COMPOSITION AND MOTIVATION

Alternative journalists propose two theories about how audiences affect their work. One is that readers, most of them, only pick up the paper to read the non-news sections at the "back of the book"—arts and entertainment listings, restaurant reviews, and the like—and that this, ironically, gives them more freedom to do what they want with the "front of the book." As the founder of the *Chicago Reader* once said, "If they read the articles, fine. If they don't, fine" (Armstrong, 1981: 283).

But alternative journalists also invoke their readers' engagement with what they do. The *Bay Guardian*'s Newitz sees "progressives" as constituting the "core" of the paper's readership. If the *Bay Guardian* is not exactly a case of radical media being supported by radical social movements (Downing, 1995, 2001), its success does demonstrate the importance of organized activist associations and independent alternative businesses, many of which are extremely loyal to the paper.

Assuming that political indifference on the part of "commuters" looking for weekend entertainment is relatively constant, then the size and visibility of local activist networks are probably the more crucial factors in shaping each weekly's particular form of political engagement. Nevertheless, the importance of the "indifference factor" should not be entirely discounted: it is the economic base that gives publishers maneuvering room to risk offering some form of alternative political content, even if only in small doses.

COMPETITION IN THE LOCAL JOURNALISTIC FIELD

If the *Bay Guardian*'s activist orientation is partly due to the strength of the San Francisco/Berkeley/Oakland progressive political community, how then do we account for the *SF Weekly*'s disdain for what it views as "only in SF" political extremism? Here, Bourdieu's notion of a cultural field (1980; see also Benson, 1999) is a useful concept. Cultural discourses, whether literary, political, or journalistic, are produced in discursive and social fields marked by the struggle for distinction. In order to exist in a field, one must mark one's difference. The *SF Weekly* and other papers, such as Seattle's *The Stranger*, have competed by positioning themselves slightly to the right, or rather toward the neo-populist center, of the surviving activist-era weeklies.

Yet in those markets where the only paper is center or center-right, it is important to acknowledge that few papers are emerging now to take up the vast unoccupied space on the left. In other words, the left-orientation of many older alternative weeklies is not due to contemporary struggles for distinction but, rather, is a residual feature of the field's constitution during the relatively radical 1960s and early 1970s. Unless there is a revived left mobilization (not impossible, given the impetus provided by the overreaching of an antiterrorist, national security–oriented U.S. administration), we should probably expect a continued centering or even rightward shift in local alternative weekly fields.

Vigorous local competition itself may also have been a temporary condition, facilitated by a growing economy and rising advertising expenditures. The Village Voice Media/NT Media deal may indicate an increasing trend toward local monopolies, as happened long ago with most U.S. daily newspapers.[16] As a result, surviving weeklies will be in a better position to compete with daily newspapers. Indeed, immediately after the folding of *New Times LA*, Schneidermann remarked: "To me, this is all about making us more competitive, particularly with the *LA Times*. Like most daily newspapers, they have an aging readership and they want our readers. We're not going to sit around and let them have them" (Blume, 2002). Indeed, mainstream media corporations such as the Tribune Company (owner of the *Chicago Tribune, Los Angeles Times,* and a host of other television and print properties) and Gannett (the largest U.S. newspaper chain) are starting to buy up alternative weeklies and to create their own weeklies aimed at younger readers.[17] With mainstream daily ownership, one of the first editorial elements to disappear from the alternatives, not surprisingly, is the media criticism columns.

In sum, I do not share the optimism of some that the market is simply "self-correcting" when it comes to restoring marginal or iconoclastic political voices. Nevertheless, local cultural entrepreneurs, with links to activist networks and a willingness to accept less than phenomenal profit margins, could conceivably move into the audience and advertiser "spaces" left vacant by either mainstreaming alternative chains or their major corporate competitors.

"OUTLAW" ADVERTISING

Many of the most radical underground weeklies of the 1960s were funded by advertisers who paid a premium because no one else would take them: the sex industry. This advertising was "of a sort unlikely to impose pressure on the paper to become traditional," wryly concedes media scholar Edwin Baker, otherwise a staunch critic of advertising funding (1994: 154, fn138). One can go farther than that, positing that certain kinds of advertising may be better than others in facilitating critique. In a sense, this is the flip side of Thomas Frank's (1998) argument that American dissent has been almost completely commodified. To the extent that '60s-era radicalism spawned new kinds of enterprises and professional activist organizations (head shops, eastern religion bookstores, environmentally friendly ice-cream manufacturers, and Greenpeace, to name just a few), a sector of the economy thus arose with a need for consumers, contributors, and low-paid workers sharing these alternative ideas and lifestyles.[18] This alternative business sector has been particularly important and extensive in California.

As we have seen, a higher proportion of sex-related advertising in the *LA Weekly* and *New Times LA* does not correlate with a more radical political posture for these weeklies vis-à-vis the *Bay Guardian*. But there does seem to be a correlation between the journalists' attitudes toward sex-related or other "outlaw" advertising and the extent of the weeklies' radical editorial posture. At one extreme, the *Bay Guardian*'s Annalee Newitz sees sex advertising as "part of our political mission," that is, helping sex workers make it on their own "rather than rely on pimps," and in general, promoting a "sex-positive" attitude. For Sandra Hernandez of the *LA Weekly*, however, back-of-the-book quasi-pornography is an embarrassment or at best a necessary evil:

> Look at the paper. I mean, it's kind of funny. We're supposed to be a left paper yet, if you look at the advertising in terms of women, it's completely demeaning to women. . . . I think there's a sense among the reporters and editors that we wish we had a different advertising base, sure. But you know, I've never been in an editorial meeting where I've heard somebody say, "I've had it! You know, I don't want to see any more 900 number "call Trixie for a good time" ads! That's just not, that's not part of it.

Whatever the effects of particular kinds, mixes, or amounts of advertising, their impact is clearly indirect and diffuse. Just as with the mainstream American press, alternative journalists speak of a "church/state" wall that strictly limits interaction between business-side and editorial-side employees. Yet it would also be wrong to dismiss any "elective affinity" between type of advertising and editorial content. Despite their different approaches to mainstream and movement politics, all four weeklies in this study cover sexuality and alternative lifestyles to a far greater extent and far more sympathetically than the typical daily newspaper. Conversely, in seeming repetition of earlier American press history (see, for example, Schudson, 1978), publishers of alternative weeklies that want to be less partisan, professionalize, broaden their reach, etc., speak in the same breath of "expanding their advertising base." Village Voice Media's Schneidermann has indicated his desire to attract more national and mainstream business advertising while supposedly "downplay[ing] the body-part ads that fill the *Weekly*—plugs for breast enhancements, face-lifts and the like" (Smith, 2002). The private equity group behind Village Voice Media has been described as operating according to the following modus operandi: [They] "typically look for a return on their investment of about 35 percent compounded annually over five to seven years. . . . At the end of that period, the company—Village Voice Media, in this case—often is sold or taken public" (Moses, 2000b). If such rumors are true, one might expect a "centering" or "mainstreaming" of the *Weekly* to make it more attractive to mainstream advertisers, and thus more palatable for such a sale. And this, according to recent reports, is exactly what is happening (Smith, 2002).

Conclusion: Small (But Not Too) Is Beautiful?

This study has called into question the common research assumption that commercialism, especially advertising, *necessarily* undermines the critical, oppositional stance of the press. Although relying on advertising to a greater extent than U.S. daily newspapers, many urban newsweeklies offer news and views ignored by the mainstream media, as well as encouraging passionate democratic debate and, in some cases, active political involvement. This study does not prove that advertiser-supported media are more critical and oppositional than audience-supported media, all other factors being equal. But the foregoing discussion certainly establishes that the *most* advertising-reliant media are not necessarily the most conservative and can even be quite progressive in all senses of the term.

Explaining these findings is a more difficult matter. It appears that critique is facilitated by a complex interaction of multiple factors: publisher commitment, audience involvement, local journalistic competition, and type of advertising. All four factors distinguish alternative weeklies from their mainstream competitors. However, since the *Bay Guardian* is the most politically radical of the newsweeklies examined and differs most from the others in ownership and audience involvement, we may conclude that these factors are particularly crucial. This is not to deny the positive features of the other weeklies profiled here. Ideally, audiences should have access to a broad range of alternative papers.

Urban newsweeklies cannot replace more experimental and intellectual "small journals," but they do offer one key advantage over these types of publications—their potential not only to "preach to the converted" but to broaden the worldviews of ordinary citizens who were literally just looking for a movie on Saturday night.

Notes

1. According to AAN executive director Richard Karpel (telephone interview with author, 4 October 2002), an additional 100 general-interest urban weeklies could potentially join the AAN but have either not applied or not been accepted for membership. The AAN's bylaws (available online at www.aan.org) stipulate that newsweeklies admitted to the association "should exhibit sufficient public service through journalism and editorial distinction and excellence to merit designation as a positive editorial alternative to mainstream journalism."

2. "Chain Ownership in the Alternative Newspaper Business," internal AAN document e-mailed to the author by Richard Karpel.

3. Author interview with AAN director Karpel. The figures do not add up to 100 percent because of rounding and the exclusion of small miscellaneous revenue sources, such as website advertising and out-of-area subscriptions. Of the association's 118 member papers, 75 chose to participate in the survey, but some of the largest papers, such as the *Village Voice*, did not. Papers in the survey averaged $3.8 million in annual revenues, versus Karpel's estimate of $20 million at the *LA Weekly* and the *Chicago Reader* and $35 million at the *Village Voice*.

4. Given that the data are from just two editions, the figures are suggestive only, but a less systematic survey of other editions showed no significant variation in advertising proportions within papers. The *SF Weekly* would not ship back issues of its papers, thus its non-inclusion in this table.

5. In the AAN survey, sex advertisements were categorized as local display or classifieds and not reported separately.

6. Figures for the *Bay Guardian* are provided for only the 21–34 age range. One can reasonably assume that if 43.7 percent of its readers are 21–34, even more would be in the 18–34 range.

7. Demographic statistics are self-reported by publishers and then posted on AAN website newsweekly profile pages. According to the website, sources for the demographic data are as follows: R2 2001 San Francisco Scarborough Report (*San Francisco Bay Guardian*); MRI and Media Audit, undated (*LA Weekly*); and Mediamark Research Inc., fall 2000 (*SF Weekly* and *New Times LA*). Selective presentation of these data, produced by private marketing firms using different methodologies, makes any hard and fast comparisons difficult.

8. Most American daily newspapers earn from 75 to 80 percent of their revenues from advertising, with the rest provided by subscriptions and daily street sales (Baker, 1994).

9. If we take into account all editorial and quasi-editorial copy—arts and entertainment (including restaurant) reviews and events listings as well as news and opinion columns—culture/lifestyle is the dominant focus of all four alternative weeklies. In the same editions analyzed in table 7.1, arts and entertainment reviews/listings as a proportion of all editorial pages ranged from 61 percent at *New Times LA* to 67 percent at the *San Francisco Bay Guardian* and 68 percent at the *LA Weekly*. But this aspect of alternative weekly content is already well known.

10. For the *LA Weekly*, *SF Bay Guardian,* and *New Times LA*, content analyses are of actual print copies. Stories for the *SF Weekly* were taken from its website, the contents of which are supposed to match the print version (confirmed, at least, by a comparison of partner newspaper *New Times LA*'s print version and website). Since many stories were coded for multiple topics, topic *N*'s exceed story *N*'s.

11. An unwritten rule of American journalism is that a metaphorical "wall" ought to separate the domains of news and advertising (Benson, 2000). Dramatically violating this ethical principle, in 1999 the *Los Angeles Times* created a special news supplement about the Staples Center—a new sports and entertainment complex in which the *Times* was also a "founding partner"—and then privately split the advertising revenues from the supplement with the Center.

12. Telephone interview with author, 14 September 2002.

13. Interview with author, Sherman Oaks, California, 14 March 1998.

14. Interview with author, Los Angeles, 6 March 1998.

15. Interview with author, Los Angeles, 4 March 1998.

16. Note, however, that the damage caused by temporary losses in national advertising revenues was exacerbated—in NT Media's case, by heavy borrowing in service of corporate expansion, and in Village Voice Media's case, by its need to maximize short-term profits for its outside investors in anticipation of an eventual sale. In other words, reliance on advertising per se need not ultimately lead to local monopolies.

17. The Tribune Company founded its own weekly in 1991, *City Link*, to compete with a New Times paper in south Florida, and now owns the New England–based Advocate chain of alternative newsweeklies. Recently, the *Chicago Tribune* announced plans to launch a paid-circulation weekly with the working title of *Red Eye* in the Chicago region. The *Chicago Sun-Times*, owned by Hollinger International Inc., quickly announced plans to start its own competing weekly tabloid. Gannett Corp. is in the process of launching weeklies in Lansing, Michigan (reportedly to be titled *Noise*), as well as in Boise, Idaho. Daily newspaper company-owned weeklies possess at least one powerful weapon in their battle against existing alternatives: economic deep pockets that allow them to charge significantly lower ad rates. See Gilyard (2002), Kirk (2002), and Mullman (2002).

18. For example, in the 24 April 2002 *Bay Guardian*, a display ad for the women-owned store Good Vibrations is headlined "Think Globally, Masturbate Locally," and a half-page classified ad titled "Progressive Opportunities" lists job openings at the activist organizations Clean Water Action, Swords to Plowshares, and the Sierra Club.

References

AAN (Association of Alternative Newsweeklies) (2002). Available online at www.aan.org. Last accessed in August 2002.

AAN News (2002). Press Release: Village Voice Media and NT Media Announce Agreement. Available online at www.aan.org. Last accessed in October 2002.

Adelson, A. (1996). "Weeklies Warring in the City of Angels," *New York Times* (16 September).

Alternet (Alternative News Agency) (1995). "SF Weekly Sold."

Ardito, S. C. (1999). "The Alternative Press: Newsweeklies and Zines," *Database* 22(3): 14–22.

Armstrong, D. (1981). *A Trumpet to Arms*. Boston: South End Press.

Bagdikian, B. (1992). *The Media Monopoly*. Boston: Beacon Press.

Baker, C. E. (1994). *Advertising and a Democratic Press*. Princeton: Princeton University Press.

Barringer, F. (2000). "Alternative Press Takes on a New Gloss," *The New York Times* (10 January), p. C-13.

Bates, E. (1998). "Chaining the Alternatives," *The Nation* (June 29), pp. 12–18.

Benson, R. (1999). "Field theory in Comparative Context: A New Paradigm for Media Studies," *Theory and Society* 28: 463–98.

——— (2000). "La logique du profit dans les médias americains," *Actes de la recherche en sciences sociales* 131–32 (March): 107–15.

Blume, H. (2002). "The End of New Times," *LA Weekly* (4–10 October).

Bourdieu, P. (1980) "The Production of Belief: Contribution to an Economy of Symbolic Goods," *Media, Culture & Society* 2: 261–93.

Burk, G. (2002). "Weekly Publisher Departs," *LA Weekly* 24(10, 25–31 January): 16–17.

Carr, D. (2002). "Alternative Weeklies Divide Turf," *New York Times*, 7 October.

Collins, R. K. L. (1992). *Dictating Content: How Advertising Pressure Can Corrupt a Free Press*. Washington, D.C.: Center for the Study of Commercialism.

Comedia (1984). "The Alternative Press: The Development of Underdevelopment," *Media, Culture & Society* 6: 95–102.

Cotts, C. (2002). "Green and Greener: Village Voice Media Shows Its Colors," *Village Voice* (9–15 October).

Downing, J. D. H. (1995) "Alternative Media and the Boston Tea Party," in J. Downing, A. Mohammadi, and A. Sreberny-Mohammadi (eds.), *Questioning the Media*, 2nd ed. London: Sage.

—— (2001). *Radical Media: Rebellious Communication and Social Movements*. London: Sage.

Frank, T. (1998). *The Conquest of Cool: Business Culture, Counterculture, and the Rise of Hip Consumerism*. Chicago: University of Chicago Press.

Frankfort, E. (1976). *The Voice: Life at the Village Voice*. New York: William Morrow.

Gilyard, B. (2002). "McPaper Co. Wants Smallfries with That," *American Journalism Review* (October).

Hesmondhalgh, D. (2000). "Alternative Media, Alternative Texts?" in J. Curran (ed.), *Media Organisations in Society*. London: Arnold.

Iwan, C. (2001). "Two SF Bay Area Alternative Weeklies Sold: East Bay Express goes to New Times, and Urbanview sold to Metro Newspapers," AAN News. Available online at www.aan.org. Posted on 9 January 2001.

Khiabany, G. (2000). "Red Pepper: A new model for the alternative press?" *Media, Culture & Society* 22: 447–63.

Kirk, J. (2002). "Media and Marketing: Tribune offshoot close to launch," Available online at www.Chicagotribune.com. Posted on 4 October 2002.

Lemert, J. (1984). "News Context and the Elimination of Mobilizing Information: An Experiment," *Journalism Quarterly*: 243–59.

McAuliffe, K. M. (1978). *The Great American Newspaper: The Rise and Fall of the Village Voice*. New York: Scribner.

—— (1999). "No Longer Just Sex, Drugs and Rock 'n' Roll: The alternative weeklies go mainstream—and thrive," *Columbia Journalism Review* (March/April), pp. 40–46.

McManus, J. M. (1994). *Market-Driven Journalism*. Thousand Oaks, CA: Sage.

Moses, L. (2000a). "VV Group; Going Once, Going Twice, It's Gone!" *Editor & Publisher* 133(2, 10 January): 4–5.

—— (2000b). "Nashville Scene a Bit Blurry over Move to Chain Ownership," *Editor & Publisher* 13(3, 17 January): 12.

—— (2002). "The Business Side of Alternative Weeklies," *Editor & Publisher* (8 October).

Mullman, J. (2002). "Sun-Times Seeks Young Readers." Available online at www.chicagobusiness.com. Posted on 8 October 2002.

Neuwirth, R. (1998). "Newspapers Reap Big Bucks from Sex Trade," *Editor & Publisher* 131(14): 16–17.

Peck, A. (1991). *Uncovering the Sixties: The Life and Times of the Underground Press*. New York: Citadel Press.

Pimlott, H. F. (2000). "Mainstreaming the Margins: The Transformation of *Marxism Today*," in J. Curran (ed.), *Media Organisations in Society*. London: Arnold.

Schnuer, J. (1998). "Older Generations Just Don't Get Alternative Lure: Papers linking up to sell power of guides that reach youth," *Advertising Age* (April 20), p. S20.

Schudson, M. (1978). *Discovering the News: A Social History of American Newspapers*. New York: Basic Books.

Smith, R. J. (2002). "Ping-Pong Diplomacy," *Los Angeles Magazine* 47(4): 36–40.

Underwood, D. (1995). *When MBAs Rule the Newsroom*. New York: Columbia University Press.

Wizda, S. (1998). "Consider the Alternative," *American Journalism Review* (November), pp. 44–49.

CHAPTER 8

Has Feminism Caused a Wrinkle on the Face of Hollywood Cinema?

A TENTATIVE APPRAISAL OF THE '90s

Andrea L. Press and Tamar Liebes

The short answer to whether feminist ideas have infiltrated into mainstream Hollywood film is—"somewhat, perhaps." The longer answer has to rely on recognizing the constraints of the industry and agreeing on some idea of what feminism is, on what would be considered a feminist representation, and on how to assess influence. This is not an easy task considering the harsh market reality of Hollywood, the indeterminate meanings of art, and the difficulties we as feminists have had in defining unified goals of the movement.

One of the key problems blocking women's visibility in Hollywood cinema arises from the economic constraints particular to the movie industry since the ascendance of television—making any feminist expectations more difficult to achieve in cinema than on television. TV series play in and for the domestic scene, using their potential for close-up psychological realism that thrives on continuity and no closure (Newcomb, 2000), experimenting with forms of everyday life in various genres, and gradually building up viewers' constituencies. Hollywood blockbusters, on the other hand, have to drag people out of their houses, away from the everyday screen, and to sell seats around the globe, often to viewers who would rather watch a chase or a shoot-out than listen to words or, worse, read the subtitles (McChesney, 1999). Trapped into producing grand, panoramic, larger-than-life action movies—at the forefront of crime, war, and science—since television made its way into American homes, Hollywood has eschewed traditionally female forms such as family melodrama or simply dramatic films in favor of those that showcase film's ability to create spectacles through its ever-developing technological capacities. Partly because of these financial realities, and partly because of the mindset of film executives, which biases them against imagining the female film audience or recognizing women's decision-making power as consumers, film roles for women and storylines centering around women are still limited in today's Hollywood.

Looking back over Hollywood history, we see three moments during which roles for women underwent significant change and development. The first can be dated to the strong women stars of the '30s and '40s, bankable enough to inspire many woman-centered films in those decades. The second traces back to the rise of television, when there was increasing interest within Hollywood in the panoramic blockbuster film and a declining incidence of domestic storylines that showcased women stars. This phase was coterminous with the setbacks women experienced in the overwhelmingly domestic culture of the '50s, when women began to be barred from entering the professions of medicine and law, and marriage ages dropped. Third, with the rise of the feminist movement in the '70s, a brief flowering of feminism occurred in Hollywood, with notable woman-centered films such as *Girlfriend* (1978), *An Unmarried Woman* (1977), and *Julia* (1977). Unfortunately, this very brief moment did not lead to a permanent feminist transformation in Hollywood film.

Other changes in Hollywood's economic logic affected roles for women. Many attribute the most recent change to the enormous success of Spielberg's *Jaws* in 1975. The type of money this new kind of special-effects blockbuster pulled in led producers to develop in that direction and to eschew domestic drama once again. Yet, the '90s witnessed some notable changes in feminist directions even when compared with films of the late '70s and '80s. This trend is what we examine here.

First, we want to acknowledge that defining a feminist perspective on film is not a simple task. The feminist movement is diffuse, its ideas often contradictory. Particularly today, in the wake of widespread criticism of feminists, and of the feminist movement itself for lacking diversity and encompassing only white, middle-class women (a category both of the present authors fall into), there is no agreement on what "feminism" is. In fact, there is some question as to whether it's relevant to speak of "feminism" at all, given the current emphasis on cultural, economic, and other differences *between* women. Any attempt to pin down what "feminism" is will necessarily be inadequate. However, there are three key issues that most would agree are central to feminism: (1) the need to increase the presence of women in central roles in a variety of genres; the need to broaden the acceptability, on screen, of women of various ages, sizes, sexualities, races, and appearances; and (3) the need to allow women to assume roles of a status equal to those held by men. Our discussion seeks to focus on these issues, and to highlight how women have been treated in the most popular mainstream films. Of course, over the last several decades, there has been a proliferation of feminist films, most of them made independently or outside the United States. But here we confine our concern to the way feminist ideas appear or don't appear in Hollywood films; we feel this is an important question, given the enormous impact of these films worldwide.

Next, as sociologists, we worried about method: how to address an issue as broad as films of the '90s, or of any era, and whether to make any generalizations about film at all. How to determine which years were most important to treat? How to decide which films were most salient vis-à-vis feminism and its issues? How to avoid the common practice in film criticism of extreme in-depth discussion of only one or two films, which one can always find to illustrate a particular theoretical point? How to refrain from falling into the scientist trap of superficially addressing hundreds of films with a mere content analysis, thereby saying nothing interpretively interesting at all? We felt that assessing feminism's meanings is so complex that neither a focus on a few films nor a broad superficial analysis of a large sample would be effective for addressing our initial question.

We decided to narrow our focus by concentrating on films of the most recent past decade. Once this decision was made, we had to confront the formidable problem of selecting films from the many that had been produced throughout the decade. We decided on a list of the ten most popular films made each year from 1990 to 2000 (see Appendix) and then broadened our list to include 2001, covering 120 films in all. This scheme allowed us to treat a variety of genres, and to include films seen by the widest possible number of people. Rather than discuss the entire list of films, we decided to take a more in-depth approach to those films in which women play a central role, those that highlight either a particularly new, or particularly stereotyped, treatment of women; and those that deal with issues of interest to women, either physically, narratively, or generically. Since films in which women play a major role are few and far between on the highest-grossing list, we occasionally discuss a film that is of particular interest from a feminist perspective but is not on that list. And, finally, we've divided our discussion roughly according to genre, even though the genre boundaries are fluid and have changed with the times. Throughout, feminist influence may be seen in three contexts: through the inclusion of women in roles (narrative and professional) from which they've previously been excluded, through the endowment of these roles with new qualities, and through changes in stereotypical endings or other defining aspects of genres that thereby transform the meanings of the genre texts.

Police/Legal Dramas

The decade began with the Academy Award–winning, seventh-highest grossing film of the year: *Silence of the Lambs* (1991), a film that we consider innovative in a number of ways.[1] *Silence of the Lambs* (hereafter *Silence*) is primarily an investigative police thriller, though it has elements of horror given the ways in which the killer kills his victims. Normally in a police thriller, crimes are investigated and solved by strong, tough, determined men, who at the end of the day save the killer's female victims from horrible, cruel fates. In many horror films, however (in contrast to the detective genre), there is a young girl—Carol Clover's "final girl" (1992)—who remains to destroy the killer even when all the police and other men and women trying to do this have failed and/or been killed themselves. Often extremely young, almost virginal, and somewhat androgynous in appearance and action, this final girl (Jamie Lee Curtis's character of Laurie Strode in *Halloween* is the prototype) has high moral fiber and consistently refuses to employ the sexual wiles shown to characterize her peers' behavior. This kind of sexualized image for women is rare outside of the traditional horror film (which generally has a more specialized teen audience and rarely makes the top-ten lists; on horror and its audience, see Freeland [2000], Pinedo [1997], and Tropp [1981]). *Silence* is actually a blend of the police and horror genres in that the female lead is herself a police officer, but also one who single-handedly struggles with the killer, and defeats him, even when the entire (male) police force has failed to do so.

Other police dramas of the '90s, such as *In the Line of Fire* (1993) and *Seven* (1995), feature demented serial killers who really get under the skin of the detectives or secret service agents investigating their case. But again, what's different about *Silence* is the gender of the police detective. Jodie Foster plays Agent Clarice Starling, just out of the academy and, for her training case, given the assignment of extracting information from a serial killer in prison (Dr. Hannibal Lector, played by Anthony Hopkins), whom the police believe knows either the details about or the psychology of a current serial killer who imprisons large women, kills them, and skins them.

Clarice and Dr. Lector have several meetings in which he trades information about the killer in exchange for intimate information about Clarice's personal life. Beyond revealing her background to the audience, his tactics change the balance of the relationship between the two. Clarice was born to a coal miner and orphaned by the age of ten. She ran away from her cousin's sheep farm, where she could not take their slaughtering of the lambs; she then grew up in an orphanage, and worked hard to get through the police academy and raise her social-class status. In many horror films, the revelation of secrets is extorted by force. Here, it becomes a part of Clarice's professional tactics, but at the same time it makes her vulnerable, putting her into the prisoner's hands psychologically. The reason for reluctance to expose one's secrets is that knowledge of one's intimate secrets gives another person power over oneself. Therefore, revealing what no one else knows about oneself is part of a professional relationship with a doctor, a therapist, or a lover.

In the film, Clarice is depicted as a woman alone in a sea of men, who seem to resent her as a competitor and reject her status as one of the team. They keep making her uncomfortable with stares and sexual propositions. What is unusual about her character is that she consistently refuses to be sexualized in any traditional fashion, following the more androgynous tradition of Clover's final girl. Clarice responds to her superiors and colleagues with professional remarks and resists all sexual advances. This establishes her seriousness about developing her career, and gradually cements her status as "one of the boys." With Lector, however, she chooses to make use of her gender identity. Here, she is vulnerable, anything but one of the boys. His offering to exchange information about the killer for the most painful, traumatic information about herself is a device for restoring some form of equality to their relationship. By showing his skills in "reading" her, and understanding her psychological makeup, he makes her indebted to him. For her, opening up the wounds is a form of liberation and, at the same time, creates a strong bond with him.

It's interesting to compare Clarice's role here with that of, say, Clint Eastwood in *In the Line of Fire*, a similar genre film in which the self-doubts of the protagonist (in this case, a male) are central. The killer taunts Hollywood macho hero Clint Eastwood with what he knows are Eastwood's own doubts about his performance as a secret service agent at the time President Kennedy was shot. Did he really do everything he could to protect the president, or was he a bit cowardly? Clarice's self-doubts have nothing to do with anxiety about her past performance; rather, they arise out of her uncertainty about her move as a working-class woman into a nontraditional profession. One interesting difference between the films is that while Eastwood is not permitted to respond to the killer's sexual overtures, Clarice does respond to Lector's sexual innuendoes. By the end of the film, they have forged a special relationship. She is unafraid of him, having developed confidence in his respect for her. She has respect for him too, in contrast to the relationships between male cops and criminals in *In the Line of Fire* or *Seven*. In another deviation from the typical Clint Eastwood finale, Clarice trembles with fear as she triumphantly yells to the victim, "It's FBI! You're safe!" Clarice continues to sweat and shake in terror as she tries to find the killer in a darkened room.

Clarice's role as triumphant detective redefines the persona: Without losing her vulnerability, she effectively counters both the macho Hannibal and the effeminate, crazed killer. This persona contrasts, for example, with the Renee Russo character in *In the Line of Fire*. Russo acts as tough as the boys on the job, is sexy as hell (at a reception for the president, Eastwood jives her about where she can hide her gun under such a body-hugging gown), and becomes the romantic love interest for Clint Eastwood. In fact, Jodie Foster's generally desexualized character is almost unique on our list, which makes us wonder why, in the ten years of Hollywood films we've examined, this kind of image is so rare for women. Foster's almost unique position in Hollywood as a powerful actress and female director, and her well-known feminist convictions, raises the question of whether it was Foster's interpretation rather than the director's concept that accounts for the film's feminist statement. In more typical films, women's sexuality is almost always highlighted as a major part of their character and, thus, as a driving force behind the narrative.

One such film is 1992's *Basic Instinct*, another top-grossing film of the decade, starring Michael Douglas as the San Francisco detective Nick Curran, and Sharon Stone as the wealthy, beautiful Catherine Tramel, a murder suspect he is investigating. We call this film an example of "Hollywood feminism." Hollywood feminism plays on the ambiguity of women's desire to see stronger roles for actresses in Hollywood films (mirroring women's growing role in public life); yet, instead of being just unambiguously strong, she is evil as well, in a throwback to the femme fatale of film noir—one of the strongest images for women in earlier Hollywood. Unlike the film noir heroines, whose power completely resided in their sexuality, '90s Hollywood paid lip service to feminism by granting "Hollywood feminists" successful careers, almost as a sideline to their sexual power. *Basic Instinct*'s Catherine Tramel is a successful mystery writer, often shown working out plot details or surrounded by drafts of her latest novel. Thomas Austin's (2002) study of the audience for this film shows that she was much admired by young women, many of whom saw her as a role model for themselves, admiring her "cool" image, her wealth, her glamour, and her confidence, and ignoring the clues that suggest she's a serial murderer (to be fair, the film leaves this ambiguous). Note, too, that the mousy girlfriend (played by the also gorgeous and petite Jeanne Trippelhorn), who was *not* a murderer, was less admired.

Another convention, which began in the '80s in the wake of feminist reforms but became overwhelmingly common in the '90s, is the plethora of women professionals in top-grossing films; examples include Susan Sarandon as an attorney in *The Client*, Demi Moore as an attorney in *A Few Good Men*, and Helen Hunt as a meteorologist in *Twister*. Sarandon's character, Reggie Love, is a lawyer who defends a young boy in grave danger of being murdered by those who stand to be convicted through his testimony. Sarandon, while not an enormously powerful attorney, succeeds in protecting her child-client because she is sensitive to his fears, and to the needs of his working-class mother, whereas the male professionals are not. Predictably, Hollywood displays an essentialist view of human nature by representing female lawyers as "intuitive" and "sensitive." Alternatively, they are cast as evil, like the insensitive "user" Carolyn Polhemous played by Greta Scacci in *Presumed Innocent* (1990). Of course, some women professionals *are* sensitive; but some men are as well, and some women are not. A systematic bias toward this type of representation promotes stereotyping of professional women in the culture.

Another instance of Hollywood stereotyping of professional women can be seen in the character of Lieutenant Commander JoAnne Galloway, played by Demi Moore in *A Few Good Men*. She is initially contrasted to Tom Cruise's Lieutenant Daniel Alistair Kaffee, who, since *he* is the brilliant lawyer, has been given the role of leading investigator in the court-martial of Colonel Nathan Jessep, played by Jack Nicholson. Initially portrayed as a by-the-book weenie in contrast to Cruise's unbelievably instinctive mode of operation and the charisma that justifies it, Demi Moore's character develops into a true partner, helping him to strategize and ultimately win his difficult case. Notably, however, Cruise is the one who has the insight into what really happened during the night in question, and he is the one who risks being court-martialed by daringly confronting Colonel Jessep in the courtroom—this after being warned by Moore to act more timid, and not to try it, marking her as lacking the presumably masculine nerve and creativity that are necessary for a brilliant, rather than merely competent, law career. It's interesting that women lawyers can lead when the plot demands sensitivity and empathy, but "women's intuition" is not the same as the brilliance demanded by other plots, usually displayed by men.

Thrillers

The cutting-edge cyber-tech thriller *Disclosure* is a candidate for one of the decade's lowest moments for women. An adaptation of the Michael Crichton novel of the same title, *Disclosure* wins the prize for backlash film of the '90s. The film features Michael Douglas as Tom Sanders, a computer executive in the firm DigiCom, and Demi Moore as Meredith Johnson, the young, sexy woman hired to be his boss. It's interesting that, in the novel, the characters are the same age, whereas in the film there's a twenty-year age gap between Moore and Douglas—another example of Hollywood's preference for pairing older men with younger women, and of the widespread reluctance to cast women older than thirty-five. Douglas plays a middle-aged project head expecting to hear about his promotion when confronted with the news that he has been passed over for Moore, who has been brought in from the outside and, incidentally (and unluckily, as it turns out), is a former girlfriend. When, at her invitation, he stays after work to brief her on his project, she comes on to him sexually, invoking their past relationship to try to rekindle his interest. Tom, now married with two children, rebuffs her advances despite his initial reluctance to overtly rebuff his boss, trapped in a reversal of the classic dilemma of sexual harassment. Meredith becomes angry and screamingly throws him out.

Tom learns the next day that Meredith is suing *him* for sexual harassment. Tom procures a feminist lawyer to defend himself, even though the technical definition of sexual harassment would make it impossible for him to be the harasser. The lawyer's character is quite transparently modeled after real-life feminist attorney/author

Catharine MacKinnon (who is frequently quoted in the news when cases of sexual harassment, such as the Anita Hill/Clarence Thomas controversy, come up). Ironically, unlike petite, blond, glamorous, fashionably dressed MacKinnon (who could pass for a movie star herself), Roma Maffia, the actress cast for this role in *Disclosure*, is an unconventional-looking woman: not a petite size 4, not blond, and so on. Rather, in line with the Hollywood stereotype of "feminist," she is relatively tall and large, with untinted "natural" gray hair, little or no makeup, loose, flowing, slightly ethnic-looking rather than tailored clothing, and loud, blunt speech peppered with curse words.

Meredith gets fired for her actions, but even this satisfaction is tempered by her announcing that she is already being recruited by another high-powered firm, passing on the message that there is no end of interest in compensating young, beautiful women at enormously high salaries for occupying positions that are far above their competence and knowledge. More important, *Disclosure* portrays sexual harassment, a crime normally perpetrated by the most senior bosses against junior women, as something evil that women perpetrate upon their innocent male underlings while claiming "rape!" when the men complain. At a time when acknowledgment of sexual harassment is still precarious, this film tells us that feminism has put all honest, competent, and hard-working white men in danger, and should thus be feared and distrusted.

It should also be noted that the film version transforms Crichton's narrative into an antifeminist story that it is not. True, in the novel Meredith is a "bitch," but the source of her power is her unrelenting promotion by the firm's CEO, who adopts her as the daughter he never had. Thus, the character is the traditional figure of a young star brought to power by an elderly male sponsor. The other women characters (such as Stephanie, Tom's supporter within the firm) are independent, self-made women, defined not by their sexuality but by their spirit and human warmth. In spite of the novel's tremendous success, the film producers must have felt the need to push the narrative in a more stereotypical direction. The casting of the older Michael Douglas opposite a much younger, tougher, and more successful Demi Moore is a change in the direction of "Hollywood feminism": Instead of a weaker character pushed by a stronger older man, in the film Moore's Meredith is herself a huge success, as well as a source of evil. Given this, the film chronicles the triumph of the white male antagonist over the evil woman (though it's important that she is not destroyed but simply moves on to stalk other men in another firm).

A similarly offensive, totally age-inappropriate role was played by Nicole Kidman in the 1997 thriller *The Peacemaker*. In a not-to-be-believed bit of casting, she portrays a scientist who, at the age of twenty-nine (Kidman's actual age at the time), is in charge of a team of about fifteen military officers, all male and over fifty years of age. Her ordering one sixty-year-old general to assemble a staff that "don't mind taking orders from a woman" may please feminists, but the incongruity involves the question of age and experience rather than of gender, indicating that the scriptwriters understand feminist issues only in the most superficial ways.

This type of casting is an example of the basic Hollywood ensemble common to many adventure and thriller films, consisting of several middle-aged men and one young, sexy woman. (She is almost certainly under thirty-five, or has had enough plastic surgery to appear so, while the men's ages can range from early thirties onward; some are in their seventies.) Virtually the only exceptions to this rule are Susan Sarandon, Meryl Streep, and Diane Keaton, who continue to be cast in leading roles in their fifties.[2] A recent documentary produced by Hollywood actress Rosanna Arquette, titled *Searching for Debra Winger* (2002), documents the problem of middle-aged Hollywood actresses who find themselves out of work.

Science-Fiction/Action

In the sci-fi/action films of the middle to late '90s, we find some strong, even central roles for women, in a genre that would not have included women a decade earlier (recall *Bladerunner*, for example, or Schwarzenegger's *Total Recall* from the beginning of the '90s). One example is the role played by Julianne Moore in Spielberg's successful sequel to *Jurassic Park*, titled *The Lost World: Jurassic Park* (the second highest-grossing film of 1997). In this film, Moore plays Dr. Sarah Harding, a scientist cast alongside the men. Somewhat surprisingly, Moore's role is complex, and central to the action of the film. Extremely skillful at establishing rapport with extinct reptiles (as a good woman scientist should be), she travels to Jurassic Park out of a genuine interest in learning more about dinosaurs.

Another turn for the better is Linda Hamilton's role as Sarah Connor in *Terminator 2*, where, in reprising her role from the original *Terminator* (1984), she again stars opposite Arnold Schwarzenegger, who plays T-800 (The Terminator). However, in the newer film (a result of feminist criticism of the former?) Hamilton is less the victim and more the strong, fierce, fighting mother willing to lay down her life in defense of her son John Connor, in the tradition pioneered by Sigourney Weaver in the *Alien* films. (These also featured a fierce mother protecting her child.) Hamilton has put in her time in the weight room, bulking up to achieve the female equivalent of Schwarzenegger's unbelievably muscular physique. Nevertheless, in line with the iron law of Hollywood producers, she's still a petite size 4, reminding us yet again that "normal" women—that is, anyone taking size 10 or, worse, 12–14, the average size of American women—are banished from the screen. Yet, Hamilton is no pushover in this film—we see her breaking out of a mental hospital, wielding huge machine guns to fight cyborgs alongside Schwarzenegger, and generally playing a key role in saving humankind from takeover (though in the end, of course, Schwarzenegger plays the bigger role, and he does have to save her on more than one occasion).

It's worth mentioning that the year 2001 witnessed two films within this general genre: *Lara Croft, Tomb Raider,* featuring Angelina Jolie, and Ang Lee's *Crouching Tiger, Hidden Dragon*, starring Michelle Yeoh and Ziyi Zhang, which offered innovative protagonist roles for heroines, albeit very young ones. In the former case, Jolie, a wealthy heiress, becomes a techno-super hero(ine) in the tradition of Action Man and Superman; in the latter, Zhang simply learns the ancient art of Chinese fighting, but learns it extremely well (and attains semi-superhero powers). These may be the pioneering films in a possible new genre—the genre of female action heroes. If so, the current decade will be an interesting one to observe: Perhaps the feminist legacy of *Terminator 2* and *Silence of the Lambs* that languished in the mid-'90s has finally been continued.

Buddies

Another film that established a feminist statement in 1991—a statement that the decade seemed to drop—was the buddy film *Thelma and Louise*, widely heralded as an example of a traditionally male genre, the "road movie" or the "buddy movie," into which female leads have been inserted. Though the film did not make the top ten that year, the publicity it garnered, and its unusual feminist qualities, justifies including it in this discussion. The film continually surprises us by showing us how different a genre film can be when the gender of the leads is switched. Setting out on a weekend trip, Louise kills a man on the verge of raping Thelma, and the two of them flee the scene since there is only weak evidence that the crime was in self-defense. They drift into more and more criminal activity until they are in too deeply to get out.

The violence against men in this film was widely criticized, yet both violent scenes—Louise shooting the rapist, and the two women setting fire to a harassing trucker's rig—were provoked by sexist violence and harassment against them. This feature was not recognized by most of the film's critics. While we don't want to condone rampant violence in film, what is infuriating about the film's reception is that film critics don't seem bothered by the huge amount of violence, both against men and against women, present in most "male" genre films. The overt feminism of *Thelma and Louise* provoked hostility, proving how little feminism customarily comes from Hollywood, especially in genres that include violence as an accepted part of their formula.

Another film about female bonding that put leading women in roles highlighting their physical skills was the pioneering 1992 film *A League of Their Own*, directed by Penny Marshall, one of the few successful women directors in Hollywood. A historical drama based on the real story of the women's baseball leagues formed during World War II, the film portrays a unique period in which women had the opportunity to play professional baseball. Featuring an array of female stars including Geena Davis, Lori Petty, Madonna, and Rosie O'Donnell, this film delves into the story of the personal lives of several of the women in the All American Girls' Professional Baseball League, which was formed in 1943 in response to the war-caused absence of male baseball players and then disbanded after the war. It chronicles the importance of the sport, and of the opportunity to play it professionally, for each of the women involved. In a touching epigraph the film features the real-life members of the women's team engaged in a game. Though they are quite old now, their athletic grace is obvious, and we are left wondering what might have been had women's sports played a more important role in society than they do.

Romance

Looking at the typically female genre of romance (including romantic comedies and romantic adventures), we find the comic romance *Pretty Woman* (rated third in 1990) setting an alarming tone for the decade. Along with *Disclosure*, this film is arguably part of the backlash against feminist ideas in its adoption of a conventional romantic formula to tell the story of the proverbial prostitute with the heart of gold, who turns into a princess. We think of this film as a cross between Cinderella and Pygmalion's (and *My Fair Lady*'s) Eliza, in that Julia Roberts' Vivian is both saved from poverty and granted fabulous wealth, and educated in the ways of the upper class during the course of the film. It should be noted, though, that Vivian's hilarious cutlery lesson as an illustration of social class difference is only a pale imitation of the British Eliza's diction training—a thin reed on which to base an entire sense of class identity.

Unlike the innovative figure of the prostitute in the feminist film *Klute* (1971), a product of the early '70s feminist period in Hollywood, Julia Roberts' Vivian presents quite a different image.[3] While Jane Fonda's character Bree Daniel was anything but clean-cut, Vivian is supposed to be a prostitute; yet every detail of her personality, words, and behavior actively denies any of the negative attributes of this identity. Unusually optimistic and cheerful for one in her profession, in the first ten minutes of the film Vivian expresses shock that her roommate is spending the rent money on drugs. Vivian herself has only safe sex with her clients and is knowledgeable about cars. She proves her smartness in a feminist way by refusing to have a pimp manage her business, and by maintaining good hygiene in that she worries about her gums and flosses regularly. Finally, she is beautiful in a very healthy way, which we learn as soon as the clothes and makeup come off, along with the wig. (Why would she need a wig with such beautiful hair?) Without the gear, we see a farm girl who has simply ended up in the wrong place, now hired for the week by the wealthy Edward, played by Richard Gere, as his escort since his girlfriend has just left him. In the course of the week, in improbable fairy-tale fashion, Vivian and Edward fall in love; in princely fashion he transforms his Cinderella from a cheaply dressed prostitute, who has never been to the opera, into a Rodeo Drive–clad lady who cries at the opera and manages the art of eating snails in elegant restaurants while making polite conversation. The fantasy ending features Edward riding to her apartment blaring the theme from *Madame Butterfly*, conquering his fear of heights to climb her fire escape and save her. Ironically, what he saves her from is her plan to go back to school, finish her degree, and actually make something of herself. Instead he carries her off, presumably to marriage and the good life of the fabulously wealthy (to which we all aspire, of course).

From a feminist perspective, the film (still making money in video) is full of alarming contradictions. The story's insistence that Vivian is a lower-class heroine remains unconvincing, relying as it does on trivial matters like table manners, the ability to wear a cocktail dress, and inexperience in listening to particular forms of music to make the case. If anything, it highlights our confusion with class identity in this country. While Edward is portrayed as upper class, there isn't much distance in terms of interests, manners, and identity between them. (Do upper-class Americans really spend their time at the horse races?) Social science demonstrates that there is much less class mobility, even in the allegedly egalitarian United States, than most of us believe there is (Wright, 2000). The film draws on stereotypical filmic images of the upper class people: They're rich but unhappy, their lifestyle is constrained by their money (presumably along with money comes the lack of ability to enjoy it, particularly if you are born to it), and they don't have real humanity.

But the film's class confusions are minor relative to its facile equation of gender with class. A lower-class, powerless woman is shown winning over a powerful man with her naturally feminine vulnerability and sensitivity. It is she who teaches him the essential moral truths of the film: that he should focus more on building companies than tearing them apart in his work, and that he should pay attention to the feelings of those with whom he makes business deals. The fantasy of the film lies in the idea that a wealthy man would depend on a prostitute for these lessons, and that he would fall deeply in love with his teacher. Presumably this gives all women viewers the hope that if they develop their "classless," altruistic, empathetic feminine qualities (and if they look like Julia Roberts), they will attract their knight in shining armor, who will take care of them in style. Thirty years of feminist research denying the wisdom of this approach as a life-plan—both because of its inefficacy (given the high divorce rate) and because of the dependency involved—pale in comparison to the strength of this fantasy, reaffirmed by the extraordinary popularity of the film.

Another fantasy romance of the decade is the 1993 film *Sleepless in Seattle*, starring the extremely bankable Tom Hanks and Meg Ryan. Like *Pretty Woman*, *Sleepless* is a storybook romance, except this time it's the Cinderella of the '90s who picks her prince and goes out to seek him. Meg Ryan (a beauty certainly unlikely to be wanting for suitors) plays a career woman who has never found her "Mr. Right." She is engaged to someone who is Mr. Wrong and decides to leave him, despite her friends' allusions to the famous *Newsweek* article of the '80s which reported that unmarried women over thirty have more chance of being hit by lightning than of ever getting married.[4] Sleepless one night, Ryan hears widower Hanks talking about his love for his wife on a radio program. By this time, we are all sobbing. The film situates itself with repeated references to the classic tearjerker melodrama *An Affair to Remember,* remade three times, in which the lovers are supposed to reunite on the top of the Empire State Building. Ryan and Hanks unite in the same place at the end, in a story that claims they are each the "one special love" for each other. From here on, as in all classic romances, they presumably live happily ever after. The film was truly an old-fashioned romance (though in the '90s twist, the couple are set up by Hanks' son—children always know best!).

Another story of a woman rebelling against Mr. Wrong is that of Rose, heroine of the blockbuster film *Titanic* (1997), based on the real-life sinking of the luxury cruise ship in 1912. Featuring teen heart-throb Leonardo DiCaprio and rising star Kate Winslett (of *Sense and Sensibility* fame), the film was both a commercial and critical success, sweeping the 1997 Academy Awards, famous for repeated viewings by teen groups. While most critics found the romance stilted and protracted, audiences warmed to the unlikely love story pairing the boyish DiCaprio (playing poor Jack Dawson, who wins his ticket in a card game and bounds onto the cruise ship with no luggage) and the more staid, mature-seeming Winslett (Rose DeWitt Bukater), a first-class passenger engaged to the domineering character played by Billy Zane (Cal Hockley)—an engagement forced by her mother, who is motivated by her desire to raise the family's waning fortunes.

For our purposes the film's interest lay in the plucky Rose's push toward independence, both from her mother's exploitative interference and from the domineering personality of her fiancee, as she discovers her own desires and moves toward Jack. While Jack perishes in the disaster, Rose is saved and goes on to lead a full and adventurous life, particularly so for a woman of her era. The scenes in which Rose is encouraged by her feelings for Jack to explore her sexuality are particularly appealing. And Winslett maintained her popularity with Hollywood audiences, despite criticism for not having the sylph-like figure of the typical Hollywood actress.

A more realistic romance is the 1996 film *Jerry Maguire*, featuring Tom Cruise in the title role and Renee Zellweger as his love interest.[5] This high-profile, high-grossing film is a mixed bag for feminism. *Jerry Maguire* tells the story of a man who works in a firm representing sports stars who becomes disillusioned with the impersonal way the firm treats their clients. His plea for more personal and humane treatment of the athlete clients gets him fired. Dorothy, a secretarial support worker in the firm, goes off with him to start a new, alternative firm. (Why is she so clearly subordinate to him? And why is the division of labor between men and women in this firm so unquestioningly assumed?) When Jerry is fired, and his current girlfriend leaves him (she refuses to support him and calls him a "loser"), he becomes romantically involved with Dorothy, and as they start their firm together, he marries her and makes friends with her small son. Yet it becomes clear to Dorothy that he is not really emotionally happy with her, and she leaves him.

In a scene that is perhaps the low point for feminism in Hollywood films of the '90s, Maguire comes back to Dorothy during the weekly meeting of the feminist support group for divorced women run by her sister. The women spend much of their time engaging in both general male-bashing and particular criticisms of their own ex-spouses. Dorothy refuses to join this "negative," "man-hating" activity, differentiating herself by the belief that she has had some bad luck but is not giving up the search for Mr. Right. The only visibility for "feminism" in this film (and in many other '90s films) is this extremely caricatured group of women, most of whom, in contrast to Zellweger's movie-star looks, are overweight and ill-kempt. When Jerry returns to her (during the meeting of the group), all the women get up and cheer for romance's "happy end," clearly the victor over the embittered man-bashing sessions they are used to (implying that a little romance would cure any woman of her man-hating tendencies). Relying as it does on a negative stereotype of feminism to highlight the film's own faith in relationships and marriage, *Jerry Maguire,* too, may be considered a backlash film.

Conclusion

As feminists interested in the representation of women, we find that the first thing to point out is their absence in a variety of films. Many of the top-grossing films of the '90s are built around the adventures of a man, or men, with women occupying either minor roles or none at all. A quick glance at these films tells us that an analysis of women's screen time in the films on this list, vis-à-vis that of men, would yield an alarmingly smaller ratio than one might expect given the existence and extent of feminist criticism over the last several decades. Indeed, women are virtually absent from *The Perfect Storm* (2000) and *The Patriot* (2000), to name just two examples from the list of highest-grossing films of the decade. Gaye Tuchman, in one of the first feminist media anthologies published in 1978, noted the "Symbolic Annihilation of Women" wrought by their overwhelming absence from leading roles in prime-time television of the era. Needless to say, their analogous lack of presence in the popular Hollywood films of the '90s is almost as overwhelming.

Now, Hollywood fans might venture a rejoinder to this criticism by saying that it's simply the "male" genres that they represent, and that in these genres[6] one cannot expect to find women in leading or even very interesting roles. Even if we grant this, as Hollywood fans ourselves (Andrea at least has seen every one of the films discussed in this chapter, several times!), what's noteworthy is the absence of a corresponding "female" genre, at least one that is present to anywhere near a similar degree.

Nevertheless, as our chapter attests, there are some high-profile films, even in "male" genres, in which women do appear in leading roles in the '90s. Ironically, in these films, we find that women have made the most progress toward what we would call a "feminist" image or representation. That is, in these films—specifically, *Terminator 2, Crouching Tiger, Hidden Dragon, Lara Croft: Tomb Raider*, and *Silence of the Lambs*—the leading women are shown to have more status, and sometimes even more power, than their male counterparts. Since *Charlie's Angels, Cagney and Lacey, Moonlighting*, and other television shows blazed the trail for women to become central characters in formerly male genres, Hollywood has followed suit, sometimes featuring women in very nontraditional roles. Particularly in fantasy films like *Crouching Tiger, Hidden Dragon* and *Terminator 2*, there are few restraints on the way women appear and perform, perhaps because there are no real-life role models from which these characters are drawn. Once women enter these films, the genres themselves are often transformed—women don't always play by the boys' rules. A notable example of this is the horror/thriller *Silence of the Lambs*, in which the strong, successful detective heroine is also shown as vulnerable and sensitive—and in fact uses these qualities to get vital information about her case. Another example is *The Client*, in which attorney Reggie Love succeeds because of her sensitivity to and empathy with her child-client's needs.

Ironically, films that traditionally feature women and are made for a female audience, dealing as they do with emotions and relationships, seem to stay within traditional genre bonds. Certainly they seem much more regressive when compared with the brief flowering of feminism in Hollywood in the '70s, when films such as *Julia* (1977), *An Unmarried Woman* (1977), and *Girlfriends* (1978) were made featuring friendships among women and challenging traditional family forms. Apparently execs don't think feminism sells anymore; certainly there isn't much evidence of its marketability when you look at the top 100 films of the decade. *Pretty Woman* and *Sleepless in Seattle* do appear on the list, however; and while feminist films seem to have fallen out of favor, Hollywood made a spate of Jane Austen romances during the late '90s, following the phenomenal success of the BBC television version of *Pride and Prejudice* in 1995.

Some argue that romances appeal to women because they fulfill a psychological need for nurturing that is not met in real life (Radway, 1984). This is one possible conclusion from arguments like the one advanced by Nancy Chodorow (1978), who stated that women are raised with a yearning for connection unfulfilled in their relationships with men. Others, like Ien Ang (1985), argue that romance stories allow women to experience strong emotions and happiness vicariously, without paying the price this would require were they to fall in love constantly in real life. Certainly the continued popularity of romance stories requires an explanation; but we also have to believe that executives are loath to abandon a tried-and-tested formula when each new film now requires such enormous capital investment and risk. The increasing success of adventure stories and cyber-tech thrillers featuring women shows that such films can be sold to both men and women. This is fortunate because there has been a push since *Jaws* became such a blockbuster in 1975 toward making movies dependent on enormously costly special effects, rather than films focused on smaller domestic and relationship issues, and many more of the former are being made. Perhaps this is part of the explanation for the drop-off in feminist Hollywood films since the '70s.

The feminism of the '70s has become the Hollywood feminism of the '90s. As we've discussed, in Hollywood feminism the former femme fatale of film noir now appears in a wider variety of genres and holds a more powerful position, giving her power outside of her sexual appeal. The problem, however, is that powerful women are too often portrayed as the source of all evil in the narrative of these films, making Hollywood feminism a trap for women viewers who are faced with the dilemma of either identifying with the power and prestige of these women or hating them for their wrongdoing. We still aren't comfortable in popular film with powerful women as a part of our everyday life.

Despite the gains of the last several decades, women in Hollywood still have a long way to go.

Appendix: Ten Highest-Grossing Films per Year, 1990–2000 (in order from 1 to 10 for each year)

2000
Mission Impossible 2
Gladiator
The Perfect Storm
X-Men
Scary Movie
What Lies Beneath
Dinosaur
Nutty Professor II: The Klumps
Big Momma's House
The Patriot

1999
Star Wars: Episode I, The Phantom Menace
The Matrix
The Mummy
Notting Hill
The Sixth Sense
Austin Powers: The Spy Who Shagged Me

Tarzan
Runaway Bride
Wild Wild West
Big Daddy

1998
Saving Private Ryan
Armageddon
There's Something About Mary
A Bug's Life
The Waterboy
Doctor Doolittle
Rush Hour
Deep Impact
Good Will Hunting
Patch Adams

1997
Men in Black
The Lost World
Liar Liar
Jerry Maguire
Star Wars (reissue)
Ransom
101 Dalmatians
Air Force One
My Best Friend's Wedding
Face/Off

1996
Independence Day
Twister
Mission: Impossible
The Rock
Eraser
The Hunchback of Notre Dame
The Birdcage
The Nutty Professor
Phenomenon
A Time to Kill

1995
Batman Forever
Apollo 13
Toy Story
Pocahontas
Ace Ventura: When Nature Calls

Casper
Die Hard with a Vengeance
Goldeneye
Crimson Tide
Waterworld

1994
The Lion King
Forrest Gump
True Lies
The Santa Clause
The Flintstones
Dumb and Dumber
The Mask
Speed
Clear and Present Danger
The Client

1993
Jurassic Park
Mrs. Doubtfire
The Fugitive
The Firm
Sleepless in Seattle
Indecent Proposal
Maverick
The Pelican Brief
In the Line of Fire
Schindler's List

1992
Aladdin
Batman Returns
Lethal Weapon 3
A Few Good Men
Sister Act
The Bodyguard
Wayne's World
A League of Their Own
Basic Instinct
Bram Stoker's Dracula

1991
Terminator 2
Home Alone 2
Robin Hood: Prince of Thieves
Beauty and the Beast

Hook
City Slickers
The Silence of the Lambs
The Addams Family
Sleeping with the Enemy
The Naked Gun 2-1/2: The Smell of Fear

1990
Home Alone
Ghost
Pretty Woman
Dances with Wolves
Teenage Mutant Ninja Turtles
Die Hard 2
Total Recall
Dick Tracy
The Hunt for Red October
Back to the Future, Part III

Source: Tracey Stevens, Editorial Director, *International Motion Picture Almanac*, 72nd ed. (La Jolla, Calif.: Quigley Publishing Co., 2001), p. 14.

Notes

1. This film has been much discussed; see especially Elsaesser and Buckland (2002) and Staiger (2000).
2. See Durbin (2002: 20).
3. In this discussion we are indebted to Tasker (1998: 43).
4. See Salholz (1986: 55) and Greer (1986: 48).
5. Although technically this film is not a "romance" per se, inasmuch as its plotlines encompass many other issues, we include it here because of the strong romantic subplot.
6. Or *genre*—since we're taking a very loose definition of genre here, which is necessary when looking at current Hollywood; perhaps there really is simply a genre we might call "male," characterized primarily by the absence of women, to which all of these films belong.

References

Ang, Ien (1985). *Watching Dallas: Soap Opera and the Melodramatic Imagination*. New York: Methuen.
—— (1991). *Desperately Seeking the Audience*. London: Routledge.
—— (1996). *Living Room Wars: Rethinking Media Audiences for a Postmodern World*. London: Routledge.
Austin, Thomas (2002). *Hollywood, Hype and Audiences: Selling and Watching Popular Film in the 1990s*. Manchester/New York: Manchester University Press.
Chabron, Michael (2000). *Wonder Boys*. London: Fourth Estate.

Chodorow, Nancy (1978). *The Reproduction of Mothering.* Berkeley: University of California Press.

Clover, Carol (1992). *Men, Women and Chainsaws: Gender in the Modern Horror Film.* London: British Film Institute.

Durbin, Karen (2002). "Breaking the Rule That Actresses Can't Age." *International Herald Tribune*, September 13.

Elsaesser, Thomas, and Buckland, Warren (2002). *Studying Contemporary American Film: A Guide to Movie Analysis.* London: Arnold.

Freeland, Cynthia (2000). *The Naked and the Undead: Evil and the Appeal of Horror.* Boulder, Colo.: Westview.

Greer, William R. (1986). "The Changing Women's Marriage Market," *New York Times*, February 22.

Livingstone, Sonia (1990). *Making Sense of Television: The Psychology of Audience Interpretation.* London: Pergamon.

McChesney, Robert (1999). *Rich Media, Poor Democracy: Communication Politics in Dubious Times.* Urbana: University of Illinois Press.

Newcomb, Horace (ed.) (2000). *Television: The Critical View.* New York: Oxford University Press.

Pinedo, Isabel Cristina (1997). *Recreational Terror: Women and the Pleasures of Horror Film Viewing.* Albany: State University of New York.

Radway, Janice A. (1984). *Reading the Romance: Women, Patriarchy and Popular Literature.* Chapel Hill: University of North Carolina Press.

Salholz, Eloise. (1986). "The Marriage Crunch," *Newsweek*, June 2.

Staiger, Janet (2000). *Perverse Spectators: The Practices of Film Reception.* New York/London: New York University Press.

Stokes, Melvyn, and Maltby, Richard (eds.) (2001). *Hollywood Spectatorship: Changing Perceptions of Cinema Audiences.* London: BFI.

Tasker, Yvonne (1998). *Working Girls: Gender and Sexuality in Popular Cinema.* London: Routledge.

Tropp, Martin (1981). *Images of Fear: How Horror Stories Helped Shape Modern Culture.* Jefferson: McFarland and Co.

Wright, Eric Olin (2000). *Class Counts.* Cambridge, U.K.: Cambridge University Press.

CHAPTER 9

Empire and Communications

CENTRIFUGAL AND CENTRIPETAL MEDIA IN CONTEMPORARY RUSSIA

Terhi Rantanen and Elena Vartanova

Research on globalization has given much attention to the relationship between the global and the local (see, for example, Hall, 1991; Robertson, 1995; Featherstone, 1995, 1996). As a result, academic interest that previously concentrated mainly on the relationship between the global and the national has shifted away from the latter. It has been argued that the national has become much less relevant, and that today the global and the local can interact without the intermediary role of the national.

This research has many merits, but also some faults. First, it has neglected the role of media and communications in globalization. National media and communications have been ignored, although they still act as filters between the global and the local. The national is a much more complex phenomenon than has been acknowledged, consisting of multiple layers that act as mediators between the national and the local. Second, previous research has failed to recognize that there are still countries, such as Russia, with a federal system including several different layers of republics, districts (*okruga*), regions (*krai*), provinces (*oblast*), and areas (*rai'on*). Russia, a former empire consisting of fifteen republics, has lost a considerable part of its territory and people, but it is still a federation with eighty-nine "subjects" (i.e., different administrative units within the state). Accordingly, the Russian media system comprises media outlets with various types of distribution, news coverage, and professional quality, which have different impacts on their audiences. Relationships between district, regional, and national media in different administrative "subjects" are dissimilar: In some areas regional media are a substitute for and supplant the national media, while in other areas they are subordinate to the national media. This is also the case with the hierarchy of technologically different (print and broadcast) media, which form diverse alliances in regional media markets.

The question of the different functions of these media in serving the needs of, or contesting, the "empire" is crucial. As Harold Innis (1950/1972) has shown, media and communications play a crucial role in holding empires together. He distinguishes between two kinds of media: those that emphasize time and those that emphasize space. As he states:

> Large-scale political organizations such as empires must be considered from the standpoint of two dimensions, those of space and time, and persist by

overcoming the bias of media which overemphasize either dimension. They have tended to flourish under conditions in which civilization reflects the influence of more than one medium and in which the bias of one medium toward decentralization is offset by the bias of another medium towards centralization. (Innis, 1950/1972: 7)

One of the key conflicts in present-day Russia is the conflict between centralization and decentralization of political, economic, and cultural actors. Centripetal and centrifugal vectors are present in many areas of social and corporate life, making the Russian situation extremely difficult to comprehend. Many scholars have pointed out the state of flux, chaos, and "mosaic" as important characteristics of modern Russia (Petrov, 2000; Nechayev, 2000). N. Pokrovsky (2001: 40–43) puts it bluntly:

> In Russia we are witnessing a specific symbiosis of proactive global trends with traditional, semi-feudal stratifications. [The] new economic system encompasses very dissimilar and even impertinent "fragments" like technologically advanced post-industrialism and quasi-markets, revived archaic natural exchange of goods, criminal economics, forced labor, industrialization, post-industrialization and de-industrialization. Moreover, the new system is not a transitional multi-faceted way of life, but [a] new stable social and economic structure.

Russia is an interesting case study in several respects. It is a major post-Communist country that has inherited some structures from the past that have turned out to be very enduring, but it has also developed new structures that sometimes coexist with the old structures and at other times contradict them. The marriage between the old and the new media is particularly interesting in Russia, which inherited a media and communications system with relatively developed sections. These originate from different periods: the press from Imperial Russia, broadcasting from the Soviet Union, and the Internet from the post-Soviet period (Rantanen, 2002). The penetration of the different media and communications systems is uneven: Press, TV, and radio achieve a large audience, but the fixed telephone lines needed for Internet access are of poor quality. And satellites are numerous and comparatively advanced, but used by the military.

An additional challenge has emerged from the global environment resulting in a unique situation of "post-Soviet Russian transformation within an exterior framework of globalisation" (Segbers, 1999: 65). Despite its size and former status, post-Communist Russia has experienced globalization in ways similar to other countries, but this has now resulted in increasing nationalism, in terms of both the content and the reception of programs (Rantanen, 2002). The result has been a restructuring of the media and communications system that cannot be observed except with tools that can explore the emerging combinations of the old and the new, penetrated at different levels by processes that go beyond the analysis of the local to the global. Indeed, a detailed analysis of the different levels within the Russian media and communications system helps us to understand the complicated transformations taking place on four different levels: (1) global-national; (2) national-regional; (3) regional-local; and (4) various other combinations such as global-regional, global-local, and national-local. Territorial

Centralization

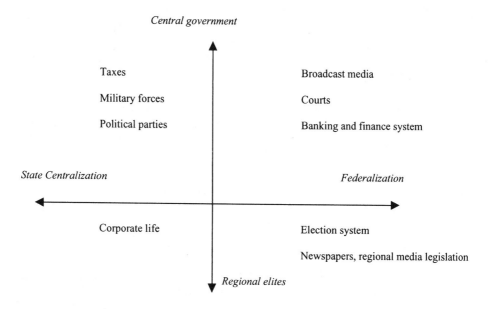

Central government

Taxes   Broadcast media

Military forces   Courts

Political parties   Banking and finance system

State Centralization ←   *Federalization*   →

Corporate life   Election system

                                            Newspapers, regional media legislation

Regional elites

Decentralization

Figure 9.1.   Russian Federalism.
Source: Adapted from Petrov (2000: 10).

and regional diversity, economic unevenness, political uncertainty, multi-ethnicity, and multiculturalism are present in every combination.

In this context, the Russian regional media provide an important dimension for illustrating the interplay between the "global," the "national" (which in Russian conditions is almost equal to the federal), and the "local" (which might be seen as both subfederal [e.g., regional] and communal). Media, being powerful "agents of change," contribute to contradictory processes of both regionalization and federalization, which supplement as well as contradict each other (see figure 9.1 for a diagram representing this scenario); at the same time, however, media inevitably channel global influences. (New formats and new professional standards may also be found in regional and local media.) The media are simultaneously, as part of a changing reality, both dynamic and vulnerable, thus reflecting all the problems of the Russian post-Soviet situation.

Glasnost, which was virtually an unspecified media policy in the Gorbachev period, 1985–1991 (Paasilinna, 1995: 64), gave rise to enormous illusions about the changing role of the media in post-Soviet society. As a result, for a decade Russian people trusted their media more than any other social institution, believing that they would provide solutions to all political and economic problems that existed in the past. Since the establishment of the first Russian print newspaper *Vedomosti* in 1703 by Peter I (the Great), close relations between the country's political elite and the media had been the most important characteristic of the national media system. In both prerevolutionary and Soviet

Russia, the media remained subordinate to the central government/tzars/Communist Party and dependent on the system of censorship that had existed almost continuously since 1796. The paternalistic relationship between the political elite and the media placed the latter in the position of a child more or less obeying the will of an authoritarian father (Vartanova, 2001: 66). This was true at both the national and local levels of the media pyramid existing in the Soviet Union.

Accordingly, Gorbachev's first attempts to introduce openness as a normal media practice immediately placed the media at the center of public debate. The media became the governors of public thought, and journalists enormously influenced public opinion and were effortlessly elected as members of Parliament solely on the basis of their work for leading newspapers or national TV channels. This unique period in Russian history lasted only from 1986 until 1994, but it created the false public impression that the media were a substitute for political parties and able to challenge the established centers of power in Russian society. A liberal ideology, with an emphasis on freedom of the press and free speech as the core of human rights and values, was for some years associated with the activities of the Russian media. However, it became obvious to journalists and media practitioners that only national media could produce such a strong political and public effect. Consequently, the rise of local and regional media as a result of economic liberalization and the dissolution of national communication systems (postal distribution, effective railway transportation, transmission of TV signals) was seen as the most negative effect of postimperial developments. Trivial economic and managerial problems destroyed the revolutionary potential of the *perestroika* media, and the efforts of the new political elite to secure its dominance in parliamentary and presidential elections in 1996 and 2000 finally began to contest the moral and professional independence of most post-Soviet media outlets.

The study of post-Soviet media shows how, at a time of enormous political and economic change, the issue of contesting media power (including alternatives to the established media centers) took the form not of specific "alternative media" practices, as these are conventionally understood, but, rather, of a shifting balance between state and market forces acting on media structures. The different layers played a key role in this process. Hence, we need to redefine the local and ask what the relationship is between the local and other levels, including the different levels of the regional and the national (federal). Eventually, by analyzing these levels, we can better understand not only the relationship between the global and the local but also how centripetal media can contest the power of centrifugal media. In this chapter, we look at a range of different media in terms of their federal and regional operational practices in contemporary Russia. In particular, we consider three contrasting cases: the press, where the result is increased regionalization; broadcasting (TV and radio), where even market forces are pushing toward the federal center; and the Internet, where the level of connectivity is so low that it is almost premature to raise the issue of "alternative media."

The Press

The number of newspapers in the Soviet Union was rather high. Traditionally, the Soviet media were mostly national (all-union): The number of national newspapers was

Table 9.1.   Russian Newspaper Circulation (1990 versus 1998)

	Circulation, in Millions	
Type of Newspaper	1990	1998
National newspapers	80	5
Local newspapers	24	9
National weeklies	33	14
Local weeklies	27	48

Source: *Pechat' Rossiiskoi Federatsii v 2000 godu* (2001): 105–7.

43. This is not to say that there were no regional or local newspapers. On the contrary, in 1990, before the disintegration of the Soviet Union, there were 4,808 national, regional, and local newspapers with a total distribution of 37,848,556,000. There were also 4,765 small newspapers distributed in and around the cities where they were published (*Pechat' Rossiiskoi federatsii v 2000 godu*, 2001: 100). However, the most characteristic feature of the Soviet press was the pyramid hierarchy, which subordinated all levels of daily newspapers to the central (national) newspapers published in Moscow (Richter, 1995; Zassoursky, 1997). Accordingly, the content and layout of regional newspapers often resembled those of national dailies, providing additional items of local news. In this way, the lower-level publications complemented the upper-level dailies, even though they never aspired to the combination of universality and comprehensiveness that the central dailies could offer.

The collapse of the Soviet media pyramid controlled by the Communist Party resulted in a drastic decline in the overall circulation of the print press. After economic liberalization (1994), the total circulation of the Russian press dropped from its 1990 level of 165,546,000 to 85,613,000. The decline was rather uneven: Although total circulation decreased eight times in eight years and the circulation of national newspapers fell fifteen times, their overall number increased from 43 to 333 by 2000 (*Pechat' Rossiiskoi federatsii v 2000 godu*, 2001: 100; *Sredstva massovoi informatsii Rossii, 1997 god*, 1998: 3). Regional and local newspapers survived the economic difficulties of the transitional period better than the national press did (see table 9.1) and have demonstrated much more stability than the national newspapers.

Both Russian and Western scholars have documented the problems of the press industry in Russia, such as the crisis of the national distribution system and the skyrocketing increase in prices of newsprint and printing (Vartanova, 1996; McCormack, 1999; I. Zassoursky, 2001). These developments followed the collapse of many state institutions, including the postal service and the printing industry. During his struggle against the central Soviet leadership in the early 1990s, President Yeltsin quoted a well-known slogan—"Grab as much sovereignty as you can"—in his effort to gain the support of Russian regional leaders. Since December 1993, when the current Russian Constitution came into force, regional elites have gained more legal independence and have been actively pursuing this strategy.

For the print media this circumstance has resulted in new centrifugal trends that have radically changed the Russian print media. The circulation of national newspapers has decreased dramatically in the regions. In the late 1990s the market share of all Moscow dailies in Rostov was only 10 percent of that of the regional daily *Krest'yanin*

("Peasant"); in Vladivostok the distribution of the national daily *Izvestya* was more than thirty times less than that of the local daily *Vladivistok* (Resnyanskaya and Fomicheva, 1999: 3). In 1998, the number of national dailies per 1,000 Russians in central Russia was less than 60, and in Siberia and the Far East it was only 1 per 1,000 (Grabel'nikov, 2002: 11). Another trend has been the change in periodicity of many regional and local newspapers from a daily to a weekly format. This has helped the print media to decrease their distribution costs.

Regional newspapers have experienced the same trends as the central dailies—going from political engagement in the early days of *perestroika* to disillusionment with politics and loss of readers' trust. The regional and local press had to find new ways to survive economically and to attract readers. They experimented with previously unknown tabloid formats, attempting to build a close relationship with their readers. Some scholars (e.g., Tulupov, 2001: 15) have described this process negatively as "boulevardisation," emphasizing that regional newspapers were becoming more sensational and scandalous, less professional, and of poorer quality than national newspapers. Unlike the national political dailies, regional and local newspapers began to concentrate on everyday issues such as gardening, housekeeping, and legal and business advice, using humor, photos, and big headlines. Many editors-in-chief of local newspapers have suggested that the everyday usefulness of their newspapers' content and advertising—in short, their relevance to the practical life of readers—has contributed to their success (*Pressa Rossii,* 1997: 61–69).

An important factor behind the success of the regional press was the change in the political and cultural identities of many Russians. In the past, many Russian and Soviet political leaders made strong efforts to consolidate various regions into one economy and one society. By contrast, Yeltsin, in his attempts to challenge the central Soviet government, put forward the idea of Russia's decentralization in order to gain the support of regional leaders. Indeed, the strengthening of regional independence became the key feature of Russian politics in the 1990s. The formation of regional identities, especially in areas with multinational and multilingual populations and non-Russian minorities, therefore became a vital issue in cultural policies for involving the media, especially newspapers, in the construction of post-Soviet society. Support was also given to new public movements and to the restoration of local traditions, especially in economically and culturally independent regional centers like Niznhyi Novgorod, Samara, Irkutsk, and Stavropol' as well as in the ethnic republics of Tatarstan, Bashkorkostan, and Chyvashiya (Voronova, 2000: 6).

The legitimization of regional independence became an important aim for many regional political elites, who energetically used the regional press to win over and manipulate public opinion during election campaigns (Pietiläinen, 2000). Regional elites actively supported and even inspired the creation of a regional mythology to justify the existence of authoritative regional regimes, and the role of the press was perceived as crucial. By defining a legal and operational framework for the regional press, local elites attempted to reestablish old Soviet means of securing their own positions. The local and regional press contributed to this process by advocating the concept of a *malaya rodina* ("little motherland") to remind their readers of their locality.

Local media regulation in Russian regions became a case that precisely illustrates the centrifugal role assigned to the press by local czars (Richter, 1998/1999: 4). Various regulatory means (i.e., additional subsidies to local newspapers, regulation of access to information and accreditation of journalists, and partial ownership of local publications) are used to incorporate the regional press into the system of local governance. However, this process has not always been a negative one; for the local newspapers of numerous ethnic groups in Ural and Siberia, it became the only way to survive in the new market conditions (Yakimov, 2000: 163).

In contrast to Yeltsin's politics of regionalization, Putin's strategy involves the integration of the federation. This change has resulted in a new wave of deregionalization. Since 1999, Moscow dailies have been trying to expand into regional and local markets. *Komsomolskaya pravda*, *Izvestiya*, and *Moskovskii komsomolets*, published in the capital, have introduced regional inserts with local news and advertising in order to expand their readership outside the big cities. However, the press is not the main factor behind unification. It is TV that has become the key medium for securing Putin's policy of federalization.

Broadcasting

According to the Russian Ministry of Press and Broadcasting, in 2002 the authorities issued 1,276 broadcast licenses for TV broadcasting and 1,002 for radio broadcasting. However, the core of the Russian TV market is composed of nine channels, available to more than 50 percent of population.

- Three all-national federal channels, though of different ownership: ORT (Obshestvennoye Rossiiskoye Televidenie, "Public Russian Television"), with a mixed structure of state and private shareholders; the state-owned RTR (Rossiiskoye Televidenie, "Russian Television"); and the privately owned NTV.
- Four federal TV networks: TVS, broadcasting on the frequency previously allocated to TV-6, Ren-TV, CTC, and TNT.
- Two regional channels with national distribution: the state-owned and financed Kultura ("Culture") and the Moscow municipal TVC (TV Center).

The federal government maintains strong (formal or informal) relations with the nationally distributed state and private TV channels. Many post-Socialist countries experience similar pressures from their central governments, which used to utilize the state broadcasters to promote their own political philosophy and values (Sparks, with Reading, 1998: 174). Jean Chalaby (1998: 446) has also shown similarities in the use of national TV to support the presidential republican regimes in France in the 1960s and Ukraine in the early 1990s. He argues that, although presidential regimes do not resort to overt or violent means of coercion against journalists, in these conditions TV is perceived as a national institution with the obvious duty to present a positive image of the national regime and foster national cohesion. Since the introduction of Yeltsin's policy of political and economic regionalization, the federal government has increasingly used TV to promote Russian integrity and challenge the influence of local authorities (Blinova, 2001). Indeed, TV has become the backbone of the federal media structure in Russia (Vartanova, 2001).

Today, national channels operate as television networks, although three all-national broadcasters—ORT, RTR, and NTV—operate as networks only in terms of signal transmission. Practically all Russians receive two state-controlled channels: ORT is available to 98 percent and RTR to 95 percent of the whole population. The privately owned NTV is available to nearly 75 percent of the population. Three other channels transmitted from Moscow have also achieved firm positions at the federal level: TVS (formerly TV-6) is received by almost 60 percent of all Russians, TVC by 39 percent, and Kultura by 36 percent. However, the technical availability and popularity of channels vary: 41 percent of Russians prefer ORT to other channels; 25 percent, NTV; 13 percent, RTR; and 11 percent, the commercial networks taken together. Six percent of the audience has not consistently voiced any preference (*Telereklamnyi business*, 2001: 83).

The statistics suggest that the number of regional TV companies is still growing; according to the latest estimate there are 700 local stations, under different forms of ownership (*Industriya rossiiskikh sredstv massovoi informatsii*, 2002). Not surprisingly, the development of regional TV has become an indicator of the economic situation in the Russian regions: The most advanced and wealthy parts of the country have the most private TV channels. Of all 89 regions, territories, and republics of the Russian Federation, only 12 economically underdeveloped regions have no nonstate TV channels. In the most developed 15 regions, including Moscow and St. Petersburg, the number of TV programs ranges from a maximum of 58 in the capital and 57 in the Krasnodar region to approximately 15 in the Tver, Vladimir, and Novosibirsk regions and in Bashkortostan. The overall number of available channels in these regions ranges from 20 to 72 (*Freedom of Speech Audit 2000*, 2000).

The factual influence and popularity of regional TV are less significant than those of the national channels. There are two particularly significant reasons for this. First, the state remains the key player in the TV market. In fact, the TV industry is the only segment of the Russian media where the state maintains a controlling position: 50 percent of programming is provided by the state-controlled TV channels. These channels also receive 70 percent of all TV advertising (*Industriya rossiiskikh sredstv massovoi informatsii*, 2002). The unholy alliance of state ownership and private funding is crucial to the competition of state and private channels, especially in the regions. The state control of terrestrial and satellite transmission networks and licensing puts regional companies in very difficult economic conditions. Local news, the most valuable type of local TV content, has had to adopt wholesale the criteria of sensational journalism in order to increase its ratings. With low salaries and underinvestment in TV technology, this essentially decreases the quality of regional production. Surveys demonstrate that the preferred type of local TV news is a "positive model of life," promoting local integrity. However, this often involves positive (noncritical, admiring) attitudes toward regional elites and local businesses as well as a lack of analysis and investigative reporting, resulting in a growing standardization of regional journalism.

Second, there is a question of how local the programs really are. The number of regional and local TV stations does not necessarily mean an increase in local content.

On the contrary, since the stations form TV networks, they often become a means of centralization as their programming schedules and news are becoming synchronized and centralized. For example, in the Perm region, the TV market leader is ORT (with a 40 percent share), but its strongest rival, the private national channel NTV, has reached second position because it collaborates with a number of local stations. In addition, the local station TV-Maxima gained popularity through its partnership with the Moscow-based STS network (Blinova, 2001).

Attempts by the state to establish technical and structural dominance in the TV market inspired the reorganization of the state-owned VGTRK in 1998. The VGTRK holding company now operates two nationally distributed TV channels, RTR and "Kultura," the radio channel "Radio Rossiyi," and part of the radio news channel "Mayak," of which it owns more than a 50 percent share. VGTRK also includes a network of 68 state-controlled regional television stations and 100 centers for the transmission of television and radio signals, which were separated into an independent company in 2001. VGTRK's regionally interconnected structure actually secures a cohesive programming policy aimed at the promotion of a federal (national) identity, thus supporting the policy of the central administration.

The dominance of national channels characterizes the regional TV market. Even the most popular private channels (NTV, TVS) experience heavy informal pressure from the federal political elite, and recent changes in ownership of both channels unquestionably proved this by putting them in the hands of companies loyal to the president. The political concerns of the Russian political elite are obviously one factor in the manipulative role of the national TV channels, but there are also commercial factors, such as advertising, affecting the significant position of TV in the Russian media system. Advertisers represent another strong pressure group vitally interested in the federalization of national TV and the integration of television stations. Commercial TV networks (especially since 1999) form mutually beneficial alliances for central and regional channels. Modes of interaction include the retransmission of programs from Moscow with no changes; partial retransmission of Moscow channels with the addition of regional programs, mostly news and current-affairs programs; and the insertion of some programs from Moscow, mainly entertainment, movies, and news shows, into regional programming on the basis of special agreements. These alliances increased the probability that regional stations will rely on proven program formats such as talk shows, games, and low-cost soap operas mainly imported from abroad.

Paradoxically, commercialization also contributes to the growth of centripetal trends in Russian TV. This is due to two factors. First, advertising in Russian television is increasingly targeted to national instead of local audiences. As a consequence, it is the national television that mainly benefits from advertising revenues. Second, the pressures exerted by regional political elites over regional TV companies are much weaker than the pressures exerted by political elites on national television. Local authorities aim to create favorable economic and regulatory conditions for national TV companies' local affiliates by seeking Muscovite media moguls' support during election campaigns or by lobbying in the capital (Kachkayeva, 1998: 135). Consequently, this attitude partially contributes to the centralization of the TV landscape.

The Internet

Compared with its growth rate in other countries, the Internet began slowly in Russia. However, from 1993 to 1997 the number of Russian Internet users doubled each year. The statistics show that the number of Russian Internet users now stands at close to 12.8 million (8.8 percent of the population). The progress of the Internet initially occurred in big cities, especially Moscow, but in recent years it has also expanded to the regions. The residents of Moscow and St. Petersburg now represent less than 20 percent of Russian users. The share of female users is close to 40 percent. However, the majority of users are still educated and/or high-income urban men between twenty and thirty-five years of age, including state officials, politicians, businessmen, journalists, and students (Rumetrica, 2002).

The Russian media form the core of the Runet, the Russian language content sector of the Internet. There are websites for traditional newspapers as well as for TV and radio companies that offer an online version of their offline content. About 70 percent of Russian online media represent the Internet versions of paper publications (termed "clones" and "hybrids" by Russian scholars), and the rest are Internet-only papers ("originals"). The most popular original online sources are RBK.ru, Gazeta.ru, List.ru, Lenta.ru, and Polit.ru. These have no equivalent in the traditional media or news agencies and successfully compete with them, offering constantly updated news and reviews of other information sources. In contrast to many national newspapers, Internet news services have been promoting objective nonbiased reporting and try to be above politics. Today the Runet contains almost infinite content resources in Russian and the languages of other ethnic groups.

Distances and technical backwardness hamper the all-Russian use of the Internet. These problems arise mostly from the low level of the national telecommunications infrastructure and the crisis in the economy. Only a small number of Russian Internet users have access from home, due to low telephone penetration (no more than 180 lines per 1,000 inhabitants) and the poor quality of telephone lines (ISDN lines are extremely rare even in big cities, and fiberoptics are almost inaccessible). Low living standards also make rapid progress of the Internet unrealistic.

The development of the Internet in Russia can be divided into three main periods. The first one covers the years 1991–1993, when the main users were academic institutions. In the second period, 1993–1996, the Internet spread mainly in Moscow and St. Petersburg among state officials, businessmen, and journalists in large media companies. And in the current period (since 1996), the most rapid growth has taken place in large academic centers (Novosibirsk, Samara, Ekaterinburg, Nizhnyi Novgorod, Irkutsk, Khabarovsk) outside Moscow and St. Petersburg. Although the progress of the Internet in the regions is obvious, its unevenness still characterizes the present situation. Of all Russian Internet users, almost one-third are residents of the Central and Northern regions and one-third are in Siberia and the Far East, whereas the southern areas have a much lower share—8.8 percent (Perfiliev, 2001).

Following the recent creation of seven federal super-regions, several big Internet hubs have been formed around regional administrative centers. And since May 2000,

Russia has been divided into seven federal regions (*okrug*), headed by plenipotentiaries appointed by the president to control the execution of federal laws in the territory of the Russian Federation. In many regions of the North Caucasus, the only users are regional universities (funded by the Soros Foundation). Information and technological wealth directly correlate with the level of economic development of the region and the de-monopolization of the regional telecommunications market. In the competitive telecommunications markets with three or more access providers (Novosibirsk, Nizhnyi Novgorod, Ekaterinburg, and Samara), Internet use is much higher, due to the improving quality of communication and the decreasing costs of access.

The uneven character of the Russian Internet in the regions is characterized by the following features.

- Access is largely limited to big cities; rural areas are completely disconnected.
- Regional content is very limited: The most popular content providers are in Moscow (online "original" media), and the presence of the local media in the Internet is very formal. (Although regional media sites exist, they lack interactivity and are undeveloped, with very limited and outdated content.)
- Local authorities are often noninteractive, and in one-quarter of the regions they had no presence on the Internet (twenty-four regional administrations had no sites in 2000) (Perfiliev, 2001).

The majority of regional access providers, however, are secondary providers and are technically unable to provide access to international networks. (In technical terms, the fact that they are secondary providers means that they are connected to other providers that have direct access to broadband networks. In short, regional access providers are technically dependent upon other companies located in big industrial centers.) Therefore, only in Moscow and St. Petersburg can access providers connect users directly with foreign networks. Another problem is the low number of domains in the regions. The number of domains in the Runet demonstrates the dominance of Moscow (with 35.5 percent of its domains in the net.ru, com.ru, org.ru, and pp.ru zones and 66.5 percent in the .ru zone), St. Petersburg (6.3 percent and 5.8 percent, respectively), and foreign states, that is, domain computers that are located outside Russia (32.9 percent and 6.9 percent, respectively). The presence of other Russian regions is extremely low (Rumetrica, 2002). A similar unevenness is found in the factual use of net resources: Visitors to Runet sites are mostly Muscovites (33.02 percent), residents of St. Petersburg (5.97 percent), and users from abroad (30.92 percent). The residents of other regions are less numerous; for example, Krasnodar region residents comprise 1.46 percent; the Sverdlovskaya region, 1.39 percent; and the Novosibirskaya region, 1.31 percent (Rumetrica, 2002).

Conclusion

By comparison with the cases on which many studies of alternative media focus, the Russian case not only challenges but also expands the concept of alternative media that resist the power of the mainstream media. Alternative media do not necessarily exist outside the conventional media, but conventional media forms can become "alternative media" in the sense of contributing to a dispersal of the power of central media institutions. This process was already present in the Soviet Union, at a time when old media—for example, *samizdat* ("self-publishing") and the Voice of America—served the functions of alternative media. Today in Russia we can distinguish between old and new media, and see how they serve either centrifugal or centripetal purposes.

Innis wrote about ancient empires and largely ignored the role of modern media, such as broadcasting. He considered the difference between time- and space-bound media the most crucial one in relation to various empires. In his view, the media that emphasize time—such as parchment, clay, and stone—are durable in character, whereas those that emphasize space—such as papyrus and paper—are apt to be less so (Innis, 1950/1972: 7). However, his observation about media and communications as centrifugal or centripetal factors is important even to the analysis of modern empires such as Russia, even though the Russian media do not fit his model of materials: those that emphasize time favor decentralization and those that emphasize space favor centralization.

In the former Soviet empire, newspapers favored centralization. In contrast, the present Russian newspaper market has been transformed from a centralized market (neglecting the regional, ideologically dependent, and constructed under state/party guidance) into a variety of independent geographical submarkets. Most Russian newspapers promote decentralization and are more strongly connected to regions and regional identities; these in turn are more dependent on "concrete" local celebrities, myths, symbols, and images. Newspapers are the oldest media in Russia, but there are other factors, too, such as the size of the regions, the unevenness of population in some parts of the country, and the number of regional identities (dailies are economically doomed to be regional), that make them favor decentralization. In the Russian context, newspapers are space-bound, both because they primarily support regionalization and because their frequency is low (dailies have become weeklies) compared with the speed of electronic media.

The media that emphasize centralization have a nonmaterial form (broadcasting waves, digits) and are easily distributed instantaneously across space. Innis's heavy materials (parchment, clay, and stone) have become television signals. For Russia, a country with a vast territory, this has a particular significance. TV is clearly a national medium, but it has some regional elements. It is also the most global given its formats, the dominance of transnational advertising, and news values. Radio, on the other hand, is becoming the most "local of local" in terms of news coverage and transmission, although it also demonstrates the most interesting symbiosis of the global (music formats) and the local (technical availability).

The most recent medium, the Internet, can be defined by its ability to overcome both time *and* space. There is evidence that the Internet follows the same lines as TV broadcasting in an even broader sense, but this observation may apply only to a rather limited part of Russia. The Internet, surprisingly, is mainly a national medium, although the number of regional sites and the volume of regional content are rapidly increasing. It potentially has an increasing role in forming regional identities, but it is still under central control. Paradoxically, the Internet plays an integrating role, providing simultaneous news coverage for the Russian elite (at least among those who have access) nationwide.

It would be simplistic to conclude that the Russian media can be categorized as either centrifugal or centripetal on the basis of media technology. As we have seen, all forms of technology can potentially be both. However, the important point here is that, in different periods and by means of different political or cultural agents, they can be used for different purposes. In the context of this book, particularly where complex, quickly transforming territories such as Russia are concerned, the distinction between centrifugal and centripetal media is crucial to an understanding of the construction of alternatives to older concentrations of media power. In this sense, "alternative media" may be old media as well as new media.

References

Blinova, O. (2001). "Federal'nye mediastruktury: regional'noye izmerenye" (Federal Media Structures: Regional Dimension), in *Regiony Rossii v 1999 godu*. Available online at pubs.carnegie.ru/books/2001/01np/19ob.asp.

Chalaby, J. (1998). "Political Communication in Presidential Regimes in Non-Consolidated Democracies," *Gazette* 5(60): 433–49.

Featherstone, M. (1995). "Global and Local Cultures," in M. Featherstone, S. Lash, and R. Robertson (eds.), *Global Modernities,* pp. 170–85. London: Sage.

——— (1996). "Localism, Globalism and Cultural Identity," in R. Wilson and W. Dissanayake (eds.), *Global/Local: Cultural Production and the Transnational Imaginary,* pp. 47–77. Durham: Duke University Press.

Freedom of Speech Audit 2000 (2000). Moscow: Proekt Obshetvennaya ekspertiza.

Grabel'nikov, A. (2002). *Russkaya zhurnalistika na rubezhe tysyacheletii* (Russian Journalism on the Eve of the Millennium). Moscow: RIP-Holding.

Hall, S. (1991). "The Local and the Global: Globalization and Ethnicity," in A. King (ed.), *Culture, Globalization and the World-System,* pp. 19–40. London: Macmillan.

Industriya rossiiskikh sredstv massovoi informatsii (Russian Mass Media Industry) (2002). Proekt doklada. Available online at www.smi.rusmedia.ru/industrial.

Innis, H. A. (1950/1972). *Empire and Communications.* Toronto: University of Toronto Press.

Kachkayeva, A. (1998). "Rossiiskiye imperii SMI" (Russian Media Empires), in *Televisionnaya mosaika* (Television Mosaics), pp. 125–37. Moskva: IISPTV.

McCormack, J. (ed.) (1999). *Sredstva massovoi informatsii v stranakh SNG. Analiz politicheskoi, zakonodatelnoi i sotsialno-ekonomicheskoi struktur* (Mass Media in CIS. Analysis of Political, Legislative and Socio-Economic Structures), 2nd ed. Düsseldorf: European Institute of Mass Media.

Nechayev, V. (2000). "Regional'nye politicheskiye sistemy v postsovetskoi Rossii" (Regional Political Systems in Post-Soviet Russia), *Pro et Contra* 1(5): 80–95.

Paasilinna, R. (1995). "Glasnost and Soviet Television. A Study of the Soviet Mass Media and Its Role in Society from 1985–1991." *Finnish Broadcasting Company Research Report 5.* Helsinki: Ekholmin kirjapaino.

Pechat' Rossiiskoi federatsii v 2000 godu (Russian Press in 2000) (2001). Moskva: Rossiiskaya knizhnaya palata.

Perfiliev, Y. (2001). "Internet v regionakh Rossii" (Internet in Russian Regions), in *Regiony Rossii v 1999 godu*. Available online at pubs.carnegie.ru/books/2001/01np/25yp.asp.

Petrov N. (2000). "Federalism po-russki" (Federalism in the Russian style), *Pro et Contra*, 1(5): 7–33.

Pietiläinen, J. (2000). "Biased, Political and Unedited: Journalism and Elections in the Russian Regional Press," *Idäntutkimus* 1(7): 4–20.

Pokrovsky, N. (2001). "Transit rossiiskikh tsennostei: nerealisovannaya alternativa, anomiya, globalizatsiya" (Transition of Russian Values: Nonrealized Alternative, Anomia, Globalization), in A. Sogomonov and S. Kukhterin (eds.), *Globalizatsiya i postsovetskoye obshsestvo*, pp. 39–59 (Globalization and Post-Soviet Society). Moskva: Stovi.

Pressa Rossii (Press in Russia) (1997). Moskva: Soyuz zhurnalistov Rossii.

Rantanen, T. (2002). *The Global and the National. Media and Communications in Post-Communist Russia*. Lanham: Rowman & Littlefield.

Resnyanskaya, L., and Fomicheva, I. (1999). *Gazeta dlya vsei Rossii* (Newspaper for the Whole Russia). Moskva: Fakul'tet zhurnalistiki/IKAR.

Richter, A. (1995). "The Russian Press after Perestroika," *Canadian Journal of Communication* 1(20): 7–24.

——— (1998/1999). "Local Media Legislation in Russian Provinces: An Old and Winding Road," *International Journal of Communications Law and Policy*, 2: 1–7.

Robertson, R. (1995). "Glocalization: Time-Space and Homogeneity-Heterogeneity," in M. Featherstone, S. Lash, and R. Robertson (eds.), *Global Modernities*, pp. 25–44. London: Sage.

Rumetrica (2002). Available online at www.rambler.ru/db/rumetrica.

Segbers, K. (1999). "Shivaya loskutnoye odeyalo" (Sewing Together the Patchwork Quilt), *Pro et Contra* 4(4): 65–83.

Sparks, C., with Reading, A. (1998). *Communism, Capitalism and the Mass Media*. London: Sage.

Sredstva massovoi informatsii Rossiii: auditoriya i reklama (Mass Media in Russia: Audiences and Advertising) (2000). Moskva: NISPI.

Sredstva massovoi informatsii Rossiii, 1997 god. Analiz, tendentsii, prognoz (Russian Mass Media in 1997: Analysis, Tendencies, Prognosis) (1998). Moskva: Soyuz zhurnalistov Rossii.

Telereklamnyi business. Informatsionno-analiticheskoye obespecheniye (TV and Advertising Business. Information and Analysis) (2000). Moscow: Mezhdunarodnyi institut reklami.

Tulupov, V. (2001). *Gazeta: marketing, dizain, reklama* (Newspaper: Marketing, Design, Advertising). Voronezh: Kvarta.

Vartanova, E. (1996). "Inside the New Triangle. The State, Market and Society Influences over the Modern Russian Media," in M. Andersen. (ed.), *Media and Democracy*, pp. 103–22. Oslo: University of Oslo.

——— (2001). "Media Structures: Changed and Unchanged," in K. Nordenstreng, E. Vartanova, and Y. Zassoursky (eds.), *Russian Media Challenge*, pp. 21–72. Helsinki: Kikimora.

Voronova, O. (2000). "Dynamika typologicheskoi structury regional'noi pressy" (Dynamics of the Typological Structure of the Russian Press), *Vestnik Moskovskogo Universiteta, Series Zhurnalistika* 5: 3–25.

Yakimov, O. (2000). *Pechat' natsionalnykh regionov Sibiri i Dal'nego Vostoka* (Press of Indigenous Regions of Siberia and Far East). Novosibirsk: Nauka.

Zassoursky, I. (2001). *Rekonstruktsiya Rossii. Mass-media i politika v 90-e* (Reconstruction of Russia. Mass Media and Politics in the 1990s). Moskva: Izdatel'stvo Moskovskogo Universiteta.

Zassoursky, Y. (1997). "Media in Transition and Politics in Russia," in J. Servaes and R. Lie (eds.), *Media and Politics in Transition: Cultural Identity in the Age of Globalization*, pp. 213–21. Leuven, Amersfoort: Acco.

Part IV

IN THE SHADOW OF CIVIL SOCIETY AND RELIGION

CHAPTER 10

Liberalization without Full Democracy
GUERRILLA MEDIA AND POLITICAL MOVEMENTS IN TAIWAN

Chin-Chuan Lee

> It turns out that an eerie type of chaos can lurk just behind a
> façade of order—and, yet, deep inside the chaos lurks an even
> eerier type of order.
>
> —Douglas Hofstadter (quoted in Gleick, 1987)

Taiwan has been undergoing momentous transformation from authoritarian rule to a formal democracy, with all its precious achievements and vast problems. Straddling the process of democratizing the authoritarian regime have been three major revolts of the "guerrilla media": the *Dangwai* political magazines (1976–1986), the illegal cable channels collectively known as Channel Four (1990–1993), and the underground radio stations (1992–1995).[1] Over the years these outlawed, resource-poor, low-cost, small-scale, and technologically crude channels of communication—run by a small group of political activists rather than by professional journalists—rose from the margin to wage "hit and run" battles with state censors and the mainstream media by constructing counter-hegemonic realities. The guerrilla media provided chief sites of contestation for the dissenting voices and protest groups to launch ideological campaigns against domination of the power center. They took aim at the legitimacy of the authoritarian party-state, challenging its patron-client system, its rigid control, and its hegemonic myths-cum-consensus intended to make such practices seem more acceptable (Lee, 2000). Instead of existing in a social vacuum, they were integrated into political movements as powerful organizational and ideological instruments. They galvanized mass support, articulated the grievances and interests of the oppressed, and questioned the party-state's exclusiveness and favoritism that contradicted its lip service to democratic principles. The periphery thus threatens the center, as guerrilla struggles undermine power domination.

The early development literature (such as Lerner and Schramm, 1967) doled out advice to Third World planners to adopt the big media, whereas activists on the left ranging from Hans Enzensberger (1977) to Paulo Freire (1970) seem more sensitive to the unique potential of small insurgent media. The guerrilla media are "weapons of the weak" with which to struggle from a position of marginality, whereas the mainstream media tend to ally with state power and cater to middle-class tastes. As John Downing (2001:15–16) argues, the radical media produce counter-hegemony "to disrupt the silence, to counter the lies, and to provide the truth," while offering "fresh ways of developing a questioning perspective on the hegemonic process." The unanticipated and shockingly potent power of the small media (leaflets, cassette tapes, *samizdat*) in defining new political situations vis-à-vis formidable state repressive and ideological apparatuses during the Iranian and Philippine revolutions (Sreberny-Mohammadi and Mohammadi, 1994; Dionisio, 1986), as well as in contributing to the dissolution of the former Soviet bloc (Downing, 1996; Sparks, 1997), has been most instructive. In Taiwan, the story of the guerrilla media may not be as dramatic, but it is still extraordinarily significant in terms of their role in opening up media spaces and ushering in the process of political democratization. As Karol Jakubowicz (1993: 42) notes, small media arise out of "a coincidence of political turmoil." Once the guerrilla media accomplished their historical role, they faded from the larger landscape of democratization when a more liberal order obtained in Taiwan. I characterize the mixed legacy of the guerrilla media as "liberalization without full democracy."

Dangwai Political Magazines

In the wake of defeat by the Communists on mainland China, Chiang Kai-shek compressed his continental-scale quasi-Leninist Nationalist regime (Kuomintang, or the KMT) into the island of Taiwan, where he took refuge in 1949 (Cheng, 1989). His harsh authoritarian regime controlled the "triple alliance" of party organs, state machinery, and military apparatuses. Though never renouncing the progressive constitution that promulgated liberal political rights and Fabian economic equality, Chiang insisted that democracy must wait until after recovery of the mainland. He declared martial law in the name of anticommunism, which not only justified the suspension of constitutional rights and political participation but also exempted him from term restrictions. His police and spies routinely detained, jailed, or executed whoever dared to challenge the KMT's legitimacy, to express doubts about its ability to recover the lost China, or to advocate Taiwan's secession from China.

Minority mainland elites who followed Chiang to Taiwan dominated the centers of power, whereas the local majority (descendants of earlier Chinese settlers who made up 85 percent of the population) was so marginalized as to occupy less than 5 percent of the seats in a three-house parliament purportedly symbolizing the whole of China. While at liberty to dictate the terms of "national" power structure, the KMT had never established any significant linkages with grassroots people and organizations in Taiwan, and thus decided to allow local elections at the county, township, and village levels as a legitimacy-bolstering measure. Even if the KMT incorporated local elites into its power orbit through reward-and-punishment mechanisms and divide-and-rule tactics, such elections provided essential political schooling for would-be opposition leaders and their followers. Because of the regime's policy of "internal colonialism," Taiwan's identity politics has, from the outset, been defined in terms of ethnic cleavages between mainlanders and Taiwanese who speak different dialects and construct divergent historical memories. In the ensuing decades, ethnic conflict gave force to what amounted to democratic rebellion against the KMT (Lee, 1993), on the one hand, and fostered exclusionary media discourses not conducive to democratic citizenship, on the other.

To manipulate public opinion, the KMT declared a press ban policy in 1951, refusing to grant more newspaper licenses to any aspiring competitors. The existing thirty-one licenses, mostly owned by the party-state and Chiang's mainland loyalists, were not to fall into the hands of potential adversaries. To that end, the KMT siphoned off substantial funds from the national treasury to amass a newspaper empire (owning more than half of the thirty-one papers) while subsidizing its financially weak fellow travelers (Lee, 1987). Mystified by the illusive power of high technology, the regime put up with small media (political magazines and, later, crude cable service) on account of their presumed insignificance. Denied access to influential mainstream media, a group of liberal intellectuals (many of them western-educated), intent on deriving a valuable lesson from the mainland debacle, managed to raise meager funds to publish the *Free China Monthly* in the 1950s. They courageously urged that the KMT abandon its autocratic past; implement democracy, press freedom, and the rule of law; restrain the secret police; and share power with the local populace. Arguing that only democracy could defeat communism, they envisioned Taiwan as a beacon of democracy for the future post-Communist China. But their criticisms fell on deaf ears and instead earned harassment from the secret police. They concluded that no significant change would be forthcoming without the checks and balances of a viable opposition party consisting of mainlander-local reformists. In 1960, no sooner had they undertaken the first party-organizing activities than the regime crushed their lives and organization without mercy.

Growing economic affluence was outrageously incongruous with power discrimination and deprivation; at the same time, Taiwan's expulsion from the United Nations in 1972 and ensuing diplomatic setbacks, the KMT's failure to fulfill the promise of recovering the mainland, and Chiang Kai-shek's somewhat shaky transfer of power to his son, Chiang Ching-kuo, all presented vast challenges to the regime's legitimacy claims. Ending a fifteen-year interlude of silence, the emerging local politicians reassembled to chart their electoral contours. The first order of business, in 1976, was to publish the *Taiwan Political Review*, explicitly as a political project to mobilize grassroots support rather than as an intellectual vocation of the 1950s liberal elites. Wasting little time, the magazine broke strict taboos by denouncing what it called the "permanent parliament," which, after more than two decades, the regime still steadfastly upheld despite its increasing difficulty in finding qualified loyalists to replenish that body's mainlander seats lost to natural deaths. To ease his power transition, Chiang Ching-kuo had to widen the representation for Taiwan province by opening up a limited number of parliamentary seats for election, while keeping the whole structure unscathed. Now the political movement rekindled around this magazine began to attack the "one China" myth that gave the mainlanders their power privileges. Ordered to close down after five issues, the publication was significant enough to set the tone for other journals to follow.

The next year, in 1977, marked the first major surprise victory for opposition candidates when they captured important seats and won 30 percent of the popular vote. This initial taste of conquest, amid a popular protest against the KMT's election irregularities, further emboldened anti-KMT politicians to bring forth a loosely organized *Dangwai* ("outside the party"), a name adopted to avoid clampdown as an unauthorized political party and to distance itself from the autocratic regime. *Dangwai*'s chief organizational and ideological apparatus came to fall on the increasingly bolder and critical *Formosa*, which enabled the newly energized movement leaders and elected legislators to coordinate political rallies and promote anti-KMT ideologies under the auspices of the magazine's twenty-one island service branches. The decided shift of emphasis in names from *Free China* of the 1950s to *Formosa* of the late 1970s suggested that anti-KMT and internal power redistribution took precedence as the movement's primary themes in the larger background of anticommunism.

As if to coincide with and to display its deep-seated insecurity about Washington's switch of recognition from Taipei to Beijing in 1979, the KMT arrested almost all *Dangwai* leaders after they clashed with the police in an International Human Rights Day rally. This watershed event garnered international attention and caused censure from the Carter administration. It killed the *Formosa* magazine itself but did not deter the movement as public sympathies sent more of the victims' spouses and defense lawyers (one of them being Taiwan's current president, Chen Shuibian) back to offices in subsequent elections. *Dangwai* magazines sprouted like grass in its wake, all risking themselves to condemn the KMT. Their subversive and organizational roles became increasingly central to the opposition's need to rally electoral support. They heightened public consciousness of counter-ideologies, legitimized them, raised funds, coordinated political activities, and cemented an in-group identity within the movement and with its supporters—an identity that was vital to sustain a sense of camaraderie and common purpose in the face of external threats. In short, they formed a political united front, forcing the regime and pro-KMT mainstream media to answer inconvenient questions. Since the KMT never formally renounced constitutional democracy, it was no accident that a considerable number of leaders in the *Dangwai* movement came from the rank of lawyers, all at the forefront of exposing the glaring gulf between the KMT's nice words and bad deeds. They developed a powerful motif for their campaign appeal and for their political journals: "Return to Constitutional Rule!" The other slogan was "Why pay 100% taxes for 5% representation?" Press freedom was hard fought, with appeal to such empowering western ideologies as "the public's right to know" and "checks and balances" (Lee, 1987).

By this time the rigid state press organs had lost their influence, and two privately owned newspaper groups had risen to define the center of editorial gravity. With their publishers both co-opted into the KMT's inner circle, the *United Daily News* sided with its conservative wing and the *China Times* endorsed its liberal wing. They were generally unsympathetic to the *Dangwai*'s "unruly" practical politics and found themselves constantly disparaged by the *Dangwai* publications for a display of timidity and hypocrisy. But they nonetheless were active in reaffirming abstract concepts of democracy, press freedom, and the rule of law by inviting major Chinese scholars, home and abroad, to write daily columns expounding such principles. Given their audience reach and certified status, the mainstream media's role in disseminating, educating, and legitimizing democratic values against the backdrop of authoritarian rule could not be underestimated. Moreover, reform-minded reporters from these and other newspapers were found to have contributed—under pseudonyms and behind the back of their bosses—to understaffed *Dangwai* magazines the bulk of trenchant critiques of the KMT's bad behavior (Lee, 1993).

In the 1980s, ideological rifts and competition grew more intense between the fractured *Dangwai* camps: A moderate faction advocated reform through electoral triumph, and a more radical faction was prone to take its grievances to the street. Each faction ran several organs, sniping at each other in addition to attacking the KMT as the common enemy. The confused KMT censors hardened their repression by imprisoning more *Dangwai* publishers, acting on tip-offs to impound their publications at the printers and producing far-right magazines as countervailing forces—but all gradually proved futile. This round of repression turned out to be the last hurrah before democratic change set in. In what Max Weber (1958) describes as a process of "disenchantment of the world," state repressive power suddenly lost its magic, for *Dangwai* figures regarded going to jail as a litmus test of loyalty and a badge of honor, without which they would have no political credential.

The *Dangwai* magazines grew adept at playing "hide and seek" games. Though censorship was increasingly rampant, random, and erratic,[2] a total of twenty-one *Dangwai* magazines remained in circulation. Each faction learned to acquire multiple "reserve" licenses for a weekly, a biweekly, and a monthly so that in case one publication was banned, others could fill the void (Feng, 1995: 130). They even wrote passages deliberately intended to provoke the wrath of the by-now overworked censors, and when a particular issue was confiscated they could immediately have it reprinted somewhere else for underground circulation, often en masse and at a higher price. Unfortunately, rough competition for a niche in the saturated *Dangwai* publishing market, voracious demand for attention-grabbing materials, infighting, and hostility toward the KMT all contributed to the gradual process of succumbing to market pressure, thus repetitively manufacturing sensational and even unethical exposés, inside stories, and gossip (Lee, 1993; Feng, 1995: 133). When idealism caved in to market imperatives, the *Dangwai* magazines undermined their own credibility and, indeed, even their *raison d'être* for the lifting of martial law.

Channel Four

Having controlled most newspapers and radio stations, the party-state further monopolized all television channels (with the KMT, the state, and the military each owning a channel) in the 1960s and 1970s. Television exhibited a bad combination of ideological rigidity and shameless commercialization, reaping a windfall profit averaging 20 to 30 percent per year compared with a gross national product growth of 9 percent. The vulgarity and poor taste of television content (which was the source of its huge profit) came under sharp criticism by both presidents Chiang, but even the paramount leaders could not change the stations' mode of operation and programming as necessitated by market competition. In 1976 some enterprising merchants started accidentally to provide, for a small fee, the semblance of a primitive but illegal cable service—in fact, by simply showing pirated movie tapes from rental stores on the newly available VCRs via cheap coaxial cable and basic retransmission equipment hooked to common antennas. Other stations soon sprang up. Keeping themselves in a low profile to shun official attention, they came to be informally known as Channel Four (thus euphemistically distinct from the three primary television channels). Despite sporadic and intermittent campaigns to confiscate their facilities, the state looked the other way insofar as these urban-based, low-cost, illegal operators were not perceived as a challenge to the KMT's power. By 1985, 1.2 million people in Taiwan (including 40 percent of Taipei residents) had watched Channel Four.

The end of the thirty-seven-year-old martial law in 1987 meant abolition of the long-standing press ban policy. This development thrust the KMT into more fierce electoral contests with the newly legalized, self-confident opposition Democratic Progressive Party (DPP). Intent upon not losing further electoral ground, the ruling KMT regime held on tightly to its monopoly over television, which continued to denigrate the DPP and protest movements. A DPP leader finally obtained a license to start a daily newspaper, only to fold it within eighteen months after discovering how difficult it was to crack into the duopolistic market in a capital-intensive enterprise. It thereupon dawned on the DPP leaders that owning a radio station would be more cost-effective than running a press outlet to launch their campaigns or to promote their ideologies. At this time, even though the KMT granted press licenses to new applicants, it continued to deny public applications for a radio license. The frustrated DPP leaders decided to wage guerrilla warfare again and, in 1990, created the first "democracy television station" by resorting to the use of crude microwave technology and cheap portable transmitters smuggled in from the Philippines. (Shortly after, they also launched an illegal radio station.) They defiantly interfered with state television signals. Within a year, twenty-one stations had mushroomed. They joined hands to form an island-wide, loosely federated Democracy Television Network, vowing to "send state television monopoly to the grave." What started out as harmless, minuscule commercial operations now acquired political import that was both reminiscent of the *Dangwai* publications and wedded to protest movements (Zheng, 1993). Anti-KMT rhetoric on Channel Four was vociferous and unrestrained, but streams of long-winded speeches and monotonous rallies did not make best friends with what essentially was a visual medium—one that demanded more capital and cultural labor than the DPP figures had assumed. The power of Channel Four was exaggerated. In fact, bad programming prevailed.

The authoritarian KMT regime was generally more concerned with power preservation, whereas its Communist counterpart on the mainland (at least until the late 1970s) was determined to maintain wholesale ideological brainwashing. Having tolerated illegal merchants insofar as they presented no challenge to the power, the KMT government now ordered a full-scale crackdown in 1991 to prevent Channel Four from becoming an anti-KMT platform.[3] This and other crackdowns provoked many hostile skirmishes with DPP supporters. To avoid crackdown by distancing themselves from democracy station activists, about 100 operators pledged to the authorities that they would maintain neutrality in the upcoming elections. But the crackdowns eventually proved ineffective. In the post–martial law milieu, the DPP lashed out at the moral bankruptcy of the KMT for monopolizing the avowedly public airwaves and channels, not to mention that there was no legal ordinance to empower bureaucratic crackdowns on new media. Cable operators were too many for censors to contend with. And, besides, cheap mobile cable equipment could be easily disguised, hidden away in high-rise apartments or stored in separate locales to escape the censors' attention. It took one day for the censors to disrupt the service, but just one hour for the operator to revive it. Many cable operators also made friends with the local police and legislators—and in some cases, with gangsters—who would eventually provide advance tips about crackdown attempts and plead clemency with the authorities on the operators' behalf.

Meanwhile, two events coincided. First, even though cross-border satellite communication was still at an early stage, spillover signals from abroad unexpectedly gave each of the 600 illegal stations in Taiwan fifteen free channels. In particular, the Hong Kong–based Star TV, owned by Rupert Murdoch, penetrated 46 percent of Taiwan's households in the early 1990s—the highest rate in Asia before being overtaken by China and India (Chan, 1994). Given cable's increasing popularity, an official crackdown that would disturb the public's viewing pleasure did not seem politically advisable. Second, the United States was beginning to exert increased pressure on Taiwan to prevent local cable operators from infringing on the copyrights of American films. Awakened to the imminent threat by its U.S. patron of trade sanctions, the KMT government that had resisted the opposition's challenge now became eager to pass the Cable TV Act before the imposed deadline (the end of 1992). The proposed draft divided Taiwan into fifty-two cable regions (allowing one system per region), setting a formidable capital threshold for market entry that was vehemently resisted by many current cable operators with modest financial assets. Failure to pass the ordinance before the deadline elicited a strong U.S. reaction by putting Taiwan on the watchlist for trade sanctions. This, as well as increasing reluctance to push cable operators farther to the side of its DPP adversaries, forced the KMT government to change its mind by expediently allowing five channels per region, thus in actuality legalizing many illegal operations and bringing the total to 260 systems (Lee, 1999).

The law was finally ratified in 1993—twenty-four years after cable had existed in Taiwan. With the guerrilla media fighters now enlisted as regular media armies, the lack of scale economy could not sustain 260 cable channels in a small geography. As a result, two conglomerates soon came along to quickly gobble up these small operators; one conglomerate alone ate up 75 percent of Taipei's cable systems. In addition, the new ordinance lowered the "indigenous content" requirement from 75 percent for television to 20 percent for cable—a huge cable channel capacity serving as a conduit of Hollywood products. The "national" is thus being integrated into the global and transnational capital. Moreover, the state tried to protect its television monopoly by yielding a coveted fourth television license to DPP leaders, who were preferred over other applicants who were better financed and professionally more experienced.

Underground Radio

In 1992, the DPP general secretary launched the first illegal underground radio station, which was cheaper than running a cable station, against the backdrop of the

KMT's continued media monopoly. The more radical Voice of Taiwan came along in the following year. Others soon followed suit. Underground radio arose all of a sudden, like a prairie fire, in a mayoral election that was considered ethnically and ideologically the most divisive, rancorous, and explosive confrontation to date. The end of martial law ushered in an uncertain period of momentous power redistribution amid oscillating contests between various forces over the future of Taiwan. Intense power struggles erupted within the KMT hierarchy, in which a conservative and primarily mainlander faction (including the old guard and young Turks) rebelled against the first local-born president, Lee Tenghui, who succeeded Chiang Ching-kuo. The New Party grew out of a split KMT faction, nurturing the resentment of an ardent mainlander minority who felt threatened by the rise in power of the local majority and suspected Lee of colluding with the DPP to move Taiwan away from ultimate Chinese reunification. By the end of 1994, at the height of the mayoral election, nearly half (twenty-four) of the radio stations in metro Taipei were broadcasting underground, all divided by political allegiance (Feng, 1995). The DPP and the New Party berated each other as well as the KMT. The situation was so anarchic that the authorities' clampdown efforts could hardly keep pace with the appearance of new underground stations.

Underground radio seemed to empower marginal and forgotten members of the society (especially taxi drivers and other working-class people) and to bring partisan and ethnic division to the fore. Using call-in programs around the clock as the most popular format, the hosts urged their partisan listeners to vent their discontent, presumably "with the opportunity only a phone call away." Politically charged taxi drivers not only carried partisan flags around the city but also listened intently on their car radios to partisan propaganda emanating from their favorite talk shows; they even rudely screened the political correctness of their customers. At the pinnacle of the conflict, the radio hosts mobilized taxi drivers to attend their partisan rallies at announced dates and locations, creating havoc for public transportation. They even launched a harassment campaign by publicizing some officials' phone numbers on the air. The DPP-leaning taxi drivers once encircled the Ministry of Finance on account of a minor levy issue. The wrestling matches with the police caused unrest, and violent clashes among different taxi-driver factions resulted in casualties.

Catering to self-selective and one-sidedly opinionated audiences, the call-in programs stimulated immediate and contagious arousal of emotion while polarizing ethnic hatred. These programs cost little to produce. The anonymous called-in remarks tended to be inflammatory, repetitive, and verbally abusive. Underground radio, like other guerrilla media, highlighted the structural inequity of media resources. But it was definitely not the best forum for Jeffersonian democracy, in which contending groups rationally resolve their differences of opinion through arguments and persuasion; rather, it was a crude and demagogic instrument intended to inflame ethnic animosity, discharge pent-up frustration, and demonize "the other." Most of these stations received no advertising support, and their reliance on volunteer workers and financial donations could not sustain them beyond the election fever.

In fact, the government, under pressure, had started to grant radio licenses at the end of 1993, but the effort was too late and too small to stem the growth of underground radio. The disorganization created by underground radio consumed so much social capital as to invite public resentment. After the election, the KMT sought to re-lease other batches of radio licenses while preserving its own existing advantages. The DPP, as the largest bloc of owners in underground radio, stood to profit the most from a liberalizing policy. The anti-Lee New Party was weakened after the defeat of its may-oral candidate, who was subsequently granted a radio license but transformed it into a profitable commercial operation, to the chagrin of his partisan supporters. Because of the KMT regime's acquiescent policy, most underground radio stations emerged above-ground to win a legal status. With the political taboos rescinded, more than 100 new radio stations have rushed into the market since the enactment of the new Telecommunications Act in 1997, all peddling drug commercials (Feng, 1998).

Liberalization without Full Democracy

The guerrilla media have to be included in the treacherous story of democratic transi-tion in Taiwan. They not only reflected the larger political and economic contexts but also acted as an agent of political change. The Cold War context legitimized the Nationalist-Communist struggle, which in turn justified the KMT's authoritarian con-trol in the name of anticommunism, thus stifling political dissent and depriving the local majority of media voices. The guerrilla media would have been epiphenomenal, however, had they not been integrated into the larger struggles of political movements. The resource-poor and disadvantaged movements, for want of better alternatives, re-sorted to the resource-poor guerrilla media as their "organized intelligence." These me-dia gave voice to the opposition in challenging structural inequities and in subverting the dominant ideologies over the long haul, all in ways that were largely unanticipated by the powers that be. Political magazines were instrumental in rendering the press ban policy ineffective. The haphazard opening up of cable channels was an unintended consequence of U.S. pressure and domestic challenges, while underground radio de-fied the authorities in a volatile political climate. The guerrilla media's low dependence on capital, technology, and personnel maintenance offered the opposition its necessary operational flexibility and mobilizing power. This condition also imposed paradoxical constraints on long-term growth and credibility of the guerrilla media: Editorial ex-cesses in the last leg of political magazines' life, certain chaotic aspects of Channel Four, and particularly the anarchic underground radio movement were not something to be vacuously romanticized.

In retrospect, the KMT had maintained power and ideological advantages in the context of a remarkably successful dependent-development capitalist economy (Gold, 1986). In the face of challenges to its legitimacy, the KMT's first instinct had always been to crack down; but when crackdown efforts failed, it tended to move abruptly to preserve whatever interests it had enjoyed, even if this meant having to cut deals with major power contenders cum counter-elites or to acquiesce to the fait accompli of the guerrilla media—all the while without developing overall planning or requisite fore-sight. Since the end of the press ban, more than 100 newspapers have rushed into the market—but only one of the new entrants has gained a foothold (Lee, 2000). The

KMT's policy of legalizing Channel Four operators was so indiscriminate as to be irresponsible, whereas opening up radio frequencies primarily benefited counter-elites and commercial operators. Market logic has taken over the already distorted and fractured media order, paving the way for domestic conglomerate control and transnational capital.

The opposition leaders, having moved into the political center, no longer depend on the guerrilla media and are grudgingly content with their new-found media bonanza (Feng, 1998). Most dramatically, in what marked the first watershed change of power in Taiwan's history, the DPP defeated the KMT to become the ruling party in 2000. What has become of it since then? The DPP turns out to be a dutiful student of its former oppressor in terms of paying homage to privatization in a distorted neoliberal market. The DPP *in opposition* had allied with progressive intellectuals in advocating the restructuring of state-owned television into a public-oriented system, and it was at least rhetorically sympathetic to progressive agendas akin to what James Curran (2000) proposed as a democratic media system incorporating the civic sector, the professional sector, the social market sector, and the private enterprise sector. The DPP *in power* has been aggressive in forcing the KMT to retreat from media control, but has so far done little to honor its campaign promise to safeguard the broadcasting media from undue political and market pressure. Public television continues to exist marginally in the thicket of a widely despised commercial system. The pro-DPP People's Television (*minshi*) is as vulgarly commercialized as its three older siblings. Both the KMT and DPP governments, in their mirror images, have failed to act responsibly as a guardian of what John Thompson (1990) calls "regulated pluralism."

Media liberalization is thus a prerequisite to, though by no means synonymous with, full democratization. There are multiple structures of domination and subordination, and democracy is not a finished product but an ongoing project that addresses emerging issues and agendas in an effort to achieve the never fully achievable aims of human liberation. In Taiwan, media liberalization means abolition of state stricture more than it means construction of a fully democratic media order. During the martial law era, market forces did counteract state media control, but in its aftermath they have replaced the state as a main source of media constraints (Lee, 2000, 2001). While the media are virtually free from state censorship (a major achievement not to be dismissed lightly), market forces are exercising a more insidious but no less consequential form of control on them. The glut of media outlets competing in a disorderly market has caused financial losses to almost all players. Lost in their midst has been the vaunted "public sphere."

Instead of conducting democratically enlightening discourses, the media have been so desperate to survive in intensified market competition as to mimic the former guerrilla media's forms, formats, and content—not in terms of challenging the authoritarian order but in terms of creating populist, demagogic, and bombastic narratives that are not necessarily liberating or conducive to the formation of political citizenship. Mobilizing insurgent partisan followers against the martial law, the guerrilla media showed little inhibition against exposing the dirty linens of their ideological foes with sensationalized material or even with falsehood. More than fifteen years after the end of martial law, we are now witnessing a nightly spectacle of six to seven talk shows, call-in shows, and studio shouting matches packed one after another into television and cable schedules—all boisterously self-referential and focusing principally on political scandals, mudslinging, and manufactured controversies. As a microcosm of Taiwan's vibrant and restless yet flawed democratizing process, the media symbolize the more extreme case of tabloidization and trivialization that characterizes most developed capitalist economics (Sparks and Tulloch, 2000; Gunther and Mughan, 2000). People living in stable democracies are said to be turning their attention away from the tired and formulaic staple of formal politics and to be caring more about media fares that are pertinent to their lifestyle concerns (Dahlgren, 2000). Since pent-up energies for nascent democratic change are far from exhausted, Taiwan has, in contrast, found itself mired in a perpetual state of political mobilization. Not only do activists invest their energies and egos in various camps of manufactured controversies, but the larger bystander public, too, finds televised political drama a cheap form of commodified satisfaction.

Of particular concern is the inflamed ethnic division amid recurring and unresolved questions about national identity. Since power inequity under the KMT was primarily demarcated by "primordial ties" (Geertz, 1973) of ethnic differences, the opposition's ideological struggles appealed to such "civil ties" as fair representation, constitutional democracy, and human rights. When the KMT's grandiose pan-Chinese state ideology suppressed local Taiwanese identity, the opposition's struggles for fairer rights on behalf of local constituencies coincided with democratic ethos. Appeals to more universalistic values were profoundly liberating vis-à-vis the regime's autocratic domination based on particularistic claims. As Clifford Geertz (1973: 269) observes, however, political modernization tends initially not to quiet primordial ties but to quicken them. The *Dangwai* magazines were as emancipatory in the late 1970s and first half of the 1980s as the underground radio movement was regressive in the mid-1990s. In the process of democratization, continued overstress by the media on distinctive, essentialized, and reductive local identity has been transformed into something pernicious, revengeful, and exclusivist to the mainlander ethnic group. This is a classic case of Marxist alienation.

Present-day fluffy political and media gossip accentuates the "givens" of being born into a particular linguistic and ethnic community rather than trying to transform primordial sentiments into civil order. Virtually all manufactured media controversies focus on partisan and ethnic conflicts, and the regular proffers of wisdom comprise a small circle of sharp-tongued politicians, loquacious and one-view-fits-all scholars, and journalists cum self-styled experts. The public is nowhere to be seen or heard. And the media have neither tackled difficult but crucial agendas of democratic citizenship nor paid serious attention to other profound social, economic, or cultural issues beyond the narrow box of partisan rifts. Crude media discourses pit Taiwanese against mainlanders. Ethnic conflict has been so absorbing and consuming that the media show little appetite for either international or mainland Chinese news that should bear central relevance for the livelihood of a small trading island-nation under the siege of a giant opponent. The media have not contributed much to arriving at a broad democratic consensus over such key issues as justice, quality of life, and Taiwan's self-identity in relation to China. Vulgarization is in some respects a ghostly shadow of the guerrilla media anachronistically reincarnated. The result has been, in sum, media liberalization without full democracy.

Notes

1. For fuller accounts, see Lee (1993) regarding the life cycle of political magazines and Lee (1999) regarding the politics of cable television, in relation to the larger issues of political economy (Lee, 2000, 2001).

2. From 1979 to 1985, a total of 340 issues were published. But almost 60 percent of them were confiscated.

3. The authorities impounded 44 transmitters from 1987 to 1989, but 222 transmitters from 1990 to 1993.

References

Chan, Joseph Man (1994). "National Responses and Accessibility to Star TV in Asia," *Journal of Communication* 44(3): 112–31.

Cheng, Tun-jen (1989). "Democratizing the Quasi-Leninist Regime in Taiwan," *World Politics* 42: 471–99.

Curran, James (2000). "Rethinking Media and Democracy," in James Curran and Michael Gurevitch (eds.), *Mass Media and Society*, pp. 120–54. London: Arnold.

Dahlgren, Peter (2000). "Media, Citizenship and Civic Culture," in James Curran and Michael Gurevitch (eds.), *Mass Media and Society*, pp. 310–28. London: Arnold.

Dionisio, Eleanor R. (1986). "Small Media, Big Victory," *Media Development* 22(4): 6–8.

Downing, John (1996). *Internationalizing Media Theory*. London: Sage.

—— (2001). *Radical Media*. Thousand Oaks, Calif.: Sage.

Enzensberger, Hans Magnus (1977). "Television and the Politics of Liberation," in Douglas Davis (ed.), *The New Television: A Public/Private Art*. Cambridge, Mass.: MIT Press.

Feng, Jiansan (1995). *Taiwan guangbo ziben yundong de zhengzhi jingji* (The Political Economy of the Broadcast Capital Movement). Taipei: Tangshan.

—— (1998). *Da meiti* (Big Media). Taipei: Yuanzun.

Freire, Paulo (1970). *Pedagogy of the Oppressed*. New York: Seabury.

Geertz, Clifford (1973). *The Interpretation of Culture*. New York: Basic.

Gleick, James (1987). *Chaos: Making a New Science*. New York: Viking.

Gold, Thomas (1986). *State and Society in the Taiwan Miracle*. Armonk, N.Y.: Sharp.

Gunther, Richard, and Mughan, Anthony (eds.) (2000). *Democracy and the Media: A Comparative Perspective*. New York: Cambridge University Press.

Jakubowicz, Karol (1993). "Stuck in a Groove: Why the 1960s Approach to Communication Democratization Will No Longer Do," in Slavko Spilichal and Janet Wasko (eds.), *Communication and Democracy*, pp. 33–54. Norwood, N.J.: Ablex.

Lee, Chin-Chuan (1987). *Xinwen de zhengzhi, zhengzhi de xinwen* (The News of Politics, the Politics of News). Taipei: Yuansheng.

—— (1993). "Sparking a Fire: The Press and the Ferment of Democratic Change in Taiwan," *Journalism Monographs*, No. 138, pp. 1–39.

—— (1999). "State Control, Technology, and Cultural Concerns: The Politics of Cable Television in Taiwan," *Studies of Broadcasting* [Tokyo: NHK], No. 34, pp. 127–51.

——— (2000). "State, Capital, and Media: The Case of Taiwan," in James Curran and Myung-Jin Park (eds.), *De-westernizing Media Studies*, pp. 124–38. London: Routlege.

——— (2001). "Rethinking Political Economy: Implications for Media and Democracy in Greater China," *Javnost—The Public*, 8(4): 81–102.

Lerner, Daniel, and Schramm, Wilbur (eds.) (1967). *Communication and Change in the Developing Countries*. Honolulu: East-West Center Press.

Sparks, Colin (1997). *Communism, Capitalism, and the Mass Media*. London: Sage.

Sparks, Colin, and Tulloch, John (eds.) (2000). *Tabloid Tales: Global Debates over Media Studies*. Lanham, Md.: Rowman and Littlefield.

Sreberny-Mohammadi, Annabelle, and Mohammadi, Ali (1994). *Small Media, Big Revolution: Communication, Culture, and the Iranian Revolution*. Minneapolis: University of Minnesota Press.

Thompson, John B. (1990). *Ideology and Modern Culture*. Stanford: Stanford University Press.

Weber, Max (1958). *The Protestant Ethic and the Spirit of Capitalism*, translated by Talcott Parsons. New York: Scribners.

Zheng, Ruicheng (ed.) (1993). *Jiegou guangdian jiegou* (Deconstructing Broadcasting Structure). Taipei: Yunchen.

CHAPTER 11

The Bishop and His Star

CITIZENS' COMMUNICATION IN SOUTHERN CHILE

Clemencia Rodriguez

> Wherever you look you find Monsignor Ysern.
>
> —Cristina Barría (Quemchi, Chiloé, 2002)

Citizens' Media and the Latin American Catholic Church[1]

The Second Vatican Council—a gathering of all Catholic bishops convened by Pope John XXIII—took place from 1962 to 1965. The next twenty years brought the most significant changes the Latin American Catholic church has ever experienced (Cleary, 1985; Puntel, 1992). *Gaudium et Spes*, one of the concluding documents of the Council, stated that "social justice and peace were requirements of the church's mission" (Puntel, 1992: 38); this and other Council statements[2] would become the foundation for Latin America's liberation theology, a progressive social movement that engaged Catholics, both lay and clerical, in popular struggles for social justice, fairness, and democracy.

This chapter is intended to shed light on the connection between liberation theology and the emergence of hundreds of citizens' media, community media, radical media, and alternative media projects throughout the region. The following pages focus on the case of Bishop Juan Luis Ysern and Radio Estrella del Mar ("Radio Star of the Ocean"), a network of community radio stations in southern Chile. Yet, Bishop Ysern's case should be understood not as an exception but, rather, as an example of what hundreds of Latin American Catholic bishops, priests, nuns, and believers have made possible. If the presence of citizens' media is more robust in Latin America than in other underdeveloped regions (Gumucio Dagron, 2001), it is partly thanks to these progressive Catholics.[3]

After the Second Vatican Council, under the leadership of Chilean Bishop Manuel Larraín, the Latin American Catholic church took even further the commitment to social justice and popular resistance against domination. In 1968, the Latin American

Episcopal Council (CELAM) met in Medellín, Colombia, with the mission of applying Vatican II to Latin American realities. The Medellín document concluded that "Latin America is a region suffering from two evils: external dominance and internal colonialism" (Cleary, 1985: 42). The church called for change and committed itself to join the struggle toward social justice. Finally, "the bishops at the Medellín conference agreed that the church had to choose sides. They chose the side of the poor and oppressed" (Cleary, 1985: 42).[4]

In 1979, the Latin American bishops met again in Puebla, Mexico. Their concluding statements further cemented the church's commitment to the struggles of the oppressed. The Puebla final document blamed economic systems that do not regard the human being as the center of society; the presence of multinational corporations; economic, technological, political, and cultural dependence; the arms race; and peasants' lack of access to land and resources for "preventing or undermining communion with God" (Puebla final document, cited in Cleary, 1985: 48–49).

Liberation theology assumes that the mission of all Catholics is to make the world a better place by repudiating poverty, which implies struggling against the evils of external domination and internal colonialism. Liberation theology understands that this mission can be completed only through strong political activism, which can go as far as revolutionary activity and violent conflict. Finally, the ultimate goal of this struggle is human redemption, which "involves not only a cleansing from individual sin but liberation from oppressive structures of the world of today" (Cleary, 1985: 92).[5]

Vatican II also originated a shift in how the Latin American Catholic church understood its communication actions. Traditionally, the church used the media as tools for evangelization and missionization. That is, the media were seen as tools to transmit a message to the laity. However, in 1971 *Communio et Progressio*, a post–Vatican II document, laid the ground for a wholly new understanding; here, the mission of all Catholic communication endeavors is interpreted as the quest for "communion," an ideal state of togetherness of all humans modeled after the eternal communion of the Father, the Spirit, and the Holy Ghost (Ysern, 1993: 137). On this basis, the document concludes, Catholic communication and media should strive to break the barriers that separate humans, such as denial of access to information (both to be informed *and* to inform) and marginalization from shaping public opinion.

On the basis of *Communio et Progressio*, the Latin American Catholic church advanced its own reflection on communication and media. Several meetings and documents subsequent to the Medellín bishops' conference spell out these novel ideas. Initially a meeting in Melgar, Colombia, in 1970 denounced the monopoly of information in the hands of a few transnational corporations and the mass media as instigators of consumerism and massification. Next, a seminar in Mexico in 1971 appealed to the church to denounce the media as structures of domination and recommended that the church become the voice of the voiceless. Further, three regional seminars in Guatemala, Argentina, and Ecuador in 1972 questioned the church's internal communication structure as vertical and recommended a more participatory model (Puntel, 1992: 113–118). Finally, in 1979, the Puebla final document denounced the big media as sustaining a status quo of domination through ideological manipulation and prompted the church to develop its own media structures (Puntel, 1992: 122–26).

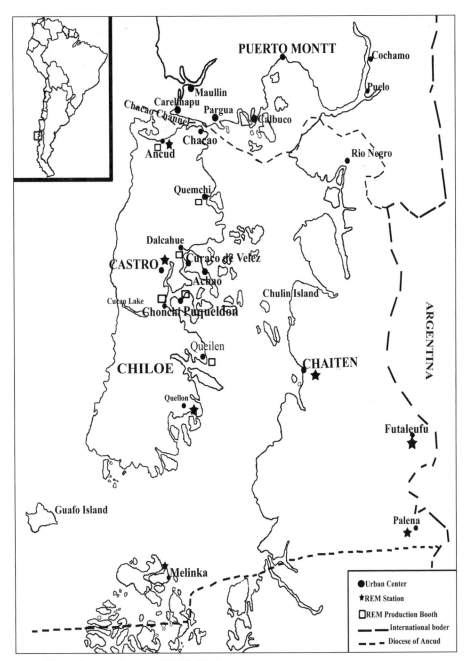

Figure 11.1.   Archipelago of Chiloé, Chile.

Source: Author.

Two important elements emerged: first, a new awareness of the need for a different model of communication for liberation and, second, a belief in small, participatory, horizontal media as alternatives to the exclusionary nature of commercial media.

The model of communication for liberation was grounded in the Brazilian philosopher Paulo Freire's theory of "concientization." According to him:

> An interminable chain of economic, political, and cultural dependence has submerged the Latin American people (*el pueblo*) in a state of "permanent objectification" whereby oppression had stripped them of their humanity and pushed them into a "culture of silence" (Freire 1972). To Freire, historical oppression transforms active human agents (conscious human beings) into passive acritical masses; these masses have lost what makes human beings subjects: their ability to establish an active, intentional, conscious relationship with social reality. . . . The core of Freire's work consists of an attempt to comprehend an historically "damaged" epistemological relationship between the Latin American subject and her/his reality. (Rodríguez and Murphy, 1997: 31–32)

Freire believed that certain communication strategies based on democratic interaction, human dignity, solidarity, and empathy could liberate communities from their state of alienation, passivity, and silence; he called this process *conscientizacao* ("concientization").

During the 1960s and 1970s, hundreds of Catholic collectives developed their own citizens' media projects from Patagonia to the Rio Grande. Using technologies as diverse as theater, dance, puppets, murals, print, video, radio, cassettes, and loudspeakers, they embarked on a myriad of alternative communication projects. They explored participatory and horizontal communication, concientization and action-research methodologies, all aimed toward one goal: the transformation of passive, voiceless, dominated communities into active shapers of their own destiny. In the following pages I document one of these projects inspired by Catholic Bishop Juan Luis Ysern: Radio Estrella del Mar (REM), located on the archipelago of Chiloé in southern Chile (see figure 11.1).

The Bishop

Bishop Juan Luis Ysern has three nationalities: He is a Spaniard by birth, a citizen of Chile since 1959, and a Huilliche by adoption.[6] As a young priest, Ysern moved from Valencia (Spain) to Chillán, in central Chile. In 1972, he was ordained bishop and sent north, to the desert-like mining area of Tacama, a stronghold of labor organizations. During the following two years, one year before and one year after Pinochet's military coup in 1973, Ysern became strongly involved in the struggle for human rights.[7] In 1974, he was sent to Chiloé in the south of Chile as bishop of the diocese of San Carlos de Ancud.[8] Owing to Chiloé's isolation from the rest of the country and the world in general, some speculate that this move was an attempt by the Catholic church to remove Ysern from his involvement in the defense of Pinochet's victims.

In 1978, Ysern learned of a plan to implement a major development project in Chiloé: the Proyecto Astillas ("Wood-Chip Project"). The architects of the project were the Chilean Development Agency (Corporación de Fomento, or CORFO) and two Japanese transnational corporations; the idea was to log immense areas of Chiloé's native forests and to transform all the wood into woodchips for export. Fitting Pinochet's authoritarian regime, the project's design was conducted without any type of consultation among Chiloé's communities. Most *Chilotes* were not even informed about the project, partly because the media self-censored any information about it.[9]

Ysern was greatly concerned about the mysterious nature of the project and its potential impact on the islands. In what I learned to recognize as his ability to detect even the slightest opening within the monolithic dictatorial regime, Ysern took advantage of a declaration to the media in which CORFO's director invited any constructive criticism. Using his power as bishop, he invited national and international academics and CORFO dignitaries to a symposium about the impact of the Proyecto Astillas, and "it became clear that they hadn't done any type of study on the environmental impact, and they didn't even understand the concept of cultural encroachment"[10] (Ysern, personal communication, June 18, 2002). Several international participants spread their concerns regarding what was about to happen in Chiloé, and due to bad publicity and pressure from Japanese religious congregations, the two transnationals withdrew and—to Pinochet's chagrin—the Proyecto Astillas was shelved (Ysern, personal communication, June 18, 2002).

The experience made Ysern realize that Chiloé's prolonged isolation was coming to an end. During colonial times, Chiloé had strategic importance, as all ships going from the Pacific to the Atlantic had to pass between the archipelago and the continent. Traffic and commerce through the archipelago's ports were intense. However, since the opening of the Panamá canal, Chiloé remained greatly isolated from Chile and from the rest of the world. Upon his arrival on the main island in 1974, Ysern found a region without roads, electricity, or schools. Ysern remembers that "the main island itself was like an archipelago; the communities were not connected by land; people went from one to the other by sea" (Ysern, personal communication, June 18, 2002). Chiloé had remained in a quasi-premodern state. It was a land of small farmers; a self-sufficient economy based on agriculture, dairy, and fishing; a community enclosed in itself, where everything revolved around family and communal life (see figure 11.2).[11] However, by the late 1970s, television had arrived[12] and roads began to criss-cross the archipelago. Large national and transnational corporations had begun to detect Chiloé's riches: salmon, shellfish, and timber. Ysern talks about his reflection at the time in terms that clearly express a Freirean inspiration:

> How should we be prepared? First, I thought, somehow the people of Chiloé need to gain awareness of their own values; and second, they need to develop a strong critical consciousness to be able to decide what they want to accept and reject among all that was coming from the outside. (Ysern, personal communication, June 18, 2002)

> From the beginning that was the idea behind the radio stations. The radios were conceived as an instrument that could help in the process toward con-

Figure 11.2.   Achao, Chiloé, Chile.
Source: Author's photo.

cientization. The idea was that if the people of Chiloé could express themselves, communicate with each other, and participate in the making of public opinion, they would develop critical attitudes[13] toward a dialogue of cultures and avoid their transformation into simple masses. (Ysern, quoted in
Radio Estrella del Mar, 2002b)

Again, making use of his ability to find hidden sudden openings within the ranks
of the powers that be, Ysern decided to ask Pinochet for a broadcast license. A territorial dispute around the Beagle Channel had escalated between Argentina and Chile in
1978. Pinochet could not afford an international conflict and, for this reason, welcomed the successful mediation of Cardinal Samoré, sent directly by Pope John Paul
II. Because Pinochet was grateful to the church at that moment, Bishop Ysern decided
it was the right time to ask the dictator for a radio. Radio Estrella del Mar began broadcasting on December 24, 1981.

The Bishop's Communication Project

Bishop Ysern's ideas about communication, culture, and identity have materialized in
complex communication processes that involve interpersonal communication, mass
communication, grassroots organizing, and educational practices. In this section, I attempt to spell out this complexity, although I have to warn my readers of the
labyrinthine nature of Ysern's project.

RADIO ESTRELLA DEL MAR

Radio Estrella del Mar is not really a radio; rather, it is a network of one AM plus six FM radio stations spread throughout the region. Four of the stations are located on the archipelago of Chiloé (Ancud, Castro, Quellón, and Melinca) and three operate on the continent (Futaleufú, Palena, and Chaitén) (see figure 11.1). REM broadcasts twenty-four hours a day, and its programming combines locally produced features with regional and national programming. Each station broadcasts some programs produced by local groups and organizations, some programs produced by other REM stations, and a daily national news feature produced in Santiago.

From its beginning, REM has been regarded as a medium at the service of the communities of Chiloé. In a letter to the then-director of REM, Ysern insisted: "I ask you to take into consideration what I have said many times: what matters is not the radio, but the people, the human beings" (Ysern, 1985).[14] In the words of Miguel Millar, the current director of REM, the ultimate goal of the project is to ensure that both the administration of the radio and most of the programming stay under the control of the community (Millar, personal communication, June 14, 2002). However, this is a complex and difficult task. Communities are not "naturally" able to take over the administration or to become producers. In the period since its inception in 1981 until 2002, REM has secured seven hours a week of programming entirely produced and controlled by the community; that is, almost twenty years of hard work were necessary to reach a level of 9 percent of community-produced programming. Among REM's leaders it is very clear that training community members in the technological aspects of production is only half their task; the other half, and the most challenging, is to involve members of the community in designing their own communication philosophy, the framework that will shape how the technology will be used. The challenge is difficult, because the only model of communication and media known by the communities revolves around commercial media and information transmission. A different model in which media are tools for cultural awareness, dialogue, and critical thinking has the texture of an intangible, fantastic utopia: "We'll probably see a couple of generations of *Chilotes* participating in our projects before we can see the re-appropriation of the radios by the community" (Millar, personal communication, June 14, 2002).[15]

These seven hours are clearly the pride of everybody at REM. Again and again, during my conversations and interviews with Bishop Ysern, with the directors of REM and Servicio de Comunicación (SERCOM), with professional journalists, and even with members of the audience, they emphasized that what made REM different from other radios was the fact that anyone in the community could have their own program. While observing production routines at the stations, I could corroborate the special place of community-produced programs.

For example, one Saturday at around 4:00 in the afternoon, sixteen-year-old Egon, eighteen-year-old Pedro, and sixteen-year-old Janet arrived at the Ancud station, as they do every week. The building was partially deserted; neither the journalists nor the directors were present. Only one radio controller was working. The kids came in early; Egon went into a production studio to cue his tapes and records. He worked entirely on his own; as I observed him coming in and out of the studio, the control room, and other offices in the station, I could see that he felt entirely at home. There was no hesitation; his feeling of entitlement was obvious. This *is* his station. At 4:45 Egon went into the control room and handed the controller the tapes, CDs, and a few vinyl records, all cued; he also turned in a torn sheet of paper with the script for the day's installment of *Rompelatas*, a weekly program about rock 'n' roll and hip-hop. After a few instructions to the controller, Egon joined Janet and Pedro in the recording studio, and the live production began.

The day's show was dedicated to fathers, as the next day was Father's Day. During the following hour, the controller played the songs selected by the kids; the music fare combined classic rock ("Another Brick on the Wall" by Pink Floyd) with heavy ("Daddy" and "Hey Daddy" by Korn and "Father" by Pillar) and *rock en español* ("Amigo" by Attaque 77). Between songs, the three young producers talked about their own fathers and the fathers of the featured musicians. They teased each other frequently and made jokes about themselves and their fathers. On the other side of the dividing glass, I sat with the controller, who laughed at their jokes, played their music, and seemed to genuinely enjoy working with the kids.

Throughout the show and until the kids left, no one told them what to do; no one suggested a different way to do things; no one redirected their ideas, their talk about themselves and their fathers, or their music. I left thinking how ironic it was that in this place, so far from the centers of technology, three kids have such access to media, while so many youngsters in New York or Hollywood are not even allowed in a radio station, much less permitted to produce their own programs. How many conversations among kids about their fathers and their favorite music have been silenced? (See figure 11.3.)

Figure 11.3.   Producers of *Rompelatas*, Ancud, Chiloé, Chile.
Source: Author's photo.

The seven hours of community-produced programming also include *El Werken* ("The Wise One"), produced by the indigenous community of the Huilliches; *Sin andarte por las ramas* ("Not beating around the bush"), by Quemchi's popular communicators; *A la salud de la vida* ("To life's health"), by a group of recovered alcoholics; *Ancud conversa* ("Ancud talks"), by a women's group; *Semillita misionera* ("Little missionary seed"), by a group of Catholic children; and other programs by agricultural technicians, fishermen, and religious groups.

In order to make the radio still more accessible to the community, Radio Estrella del Mar sets up small "production booths" in towns or communities where it does not have a station. A group that maintains a strong and constant commitment to producing its program is provided with its own self-sufficient production booth. No bigger than a small closet, this booth allows the group to gain more control over the production process. Connected via telephone to the closest station, production booths enable groups to produce from their own sites. At the time of this writing, REM had six production booths—one each in Ancud, Quemchi, Dalcahue, Chonchi, Pulquedón, and Queilen (see figure 11.1).

SERVICIO DE COMUNICACIÓN[16]

In the words of Angélica Rosas, the director of Servicio de Comunicación, "SERCOM is what gives meaning to the radios; it is the neurological center of the whole project" (Rosas, personal communication, July 4, 2002). Under Bishop Ysern's leadership, SERCOM was created in 1990 as a nonprofit communication organization parallel to REM. The goal of SERCOM is to design and implement different communication projects as tools for liberation and concientization; Rosas explains: "The idea was to go beyond a project about media; the idea was that here, in Radio Estrella del Mar, our work could encompass a whole series of processes of communication understood as the construction of meaning, not as transmission of information" (Rosas, personal communication, July 4, 2002).

SERCOM consists of a team of fewer than ten communicators working in different directions. SERCOM's staff members spend most of their time with Chiloé's organized civil society; they interact with all women's groups, indigenous organizations, labor organizations, youth groups, religious groups, and cultural organizations, as well as with the agro-tourism network (this last is explained below). SERCOM's responsibility is to stir dialogue within these organizations about the importance of communication to their work—in Rosas's words, "to open spaces for expression within the community" (Rosas, personal communication, July 4, 2002).

Periodically, SERCOM offers communication workshops in which members of grassroots organizations learn the technological aspects of radio production and discuss issues such as culture, identity, communication, empowerment, and democracy. Most of REM's community producers have "graduated" from SERCOM's training workshops. After graduation, a participant becomes a "popular communicator." Popular communicators are members of grassroots organizations who carry out different communication processes, including—but not restricted to—radio production for REM to further their organization's goals. SERCOM graduates approximately fifty popular communicators every year (Millar, personal communication, June 14, 2002).

José Paillaleve,[17] a popular communicator in the community of Quemchi, remembers his own experience:

> In 1990 I went to check out one of those communication workshops and I really liked it. Apart from being fun, the idea that we, as a small and isolated community, could have our own voice on the radio . . . because so many things happen in this community but they never have a place on the radio. . . . No one thinks about coming all the way here to rescue a news-story. So after our training we[18] began producing stories about the activities and accomplishments of every local community organization; we kept doing better and better until today we have our own production booth, where we do everything, interviews, scripts, and production. (Paillaleve, personal communication, June 20, 2002)

Training the community is only half of SERCOM's mission. Under the assumption that "a radio cannot broadcast sounds to an unknown interlocutor, because that can lead to a situation where we are talking about things that have no meaning for them" (Rosas, personal communication, July 4, 2002), SERCOM operates as a facilitator of intense interactions between REM and Chiloé's communities. Although on paper REM and SERCOM appear as two separate organizations, the articulation of the media project (REM) and all other interpersonal and group communication processes (SERCOM) is tight due to the overlap of responsibilities and the closeness of the two teams. REM Director Miguel Millar and SERCOM Director Angélica Rosas are like a couple raising a family. Also, with few exceptions, such as the technicians, most members of REM's staff work in SERCOM's projects. For example, most of REM's reporters and journalists have participated in SERCOM's workshops as trainers.

SERCOM also works closely with the region's educational institutions in an effort to uphold what I believe is the most inspiring and revolutionary of Bishop Ysern's ideas: the Cultural Encyclopedia of Chiloé. The encyclopedia project began in 1995 with the following basic design: SERCOM enlists an interested schoolteacher to develop a booklet of the Cultural Encyclopedia of Chiloé, and the topic is completely open, as long as it deals with local culture and history. Together with her or his class, the teacher selects the topic. Current topics include the forest, local uses of wood, Chiloé's churches,[19] the history of a local high school,[20] and agro-tourism. With the help of SERCOM, the teacher produces questionnaires and other materials designed to collect information about the topic—for instance, local native forests. Using these materials, students interview their parents, grandparents, and other members of their community about their complex interactions with the forest. For example, the students might ask how they used the forest in the past and how it is used now, how the forest has changed and why, what the forest means for the community, and how the community should interact with the forest.

All the information collected is then edited and circulated back to the community in several forms. First, a draft of a booklet on the subject is produced by SERCOM; the draft is taken back to the community, discussed, and approved in public readings. All booklets on a single topic are edited together and 1,000 copies of the approved versions are printed. Each one of these editions becomes a volume of the Cultural Encyclopedia of Chiloé. The encyclopedia's volumes are used as class materials and are also distributed by SERCOM to other schools and organizations in the area. Second, in addition to the printed volume, teacher and students, working with a popular communicator, produce several radio programs for REM about the subject. Each volume of the Cultural Encyclopedia takes about one year to complete and costs approximately US$12,000.00.[21]

Ysern's ideas on culture and identity deeply permeate the Cultural Encyclopedia. According to Rosas:

> The bishop is really the engine behind all this; we hang on to a light he seems to emit. The most urgent aspect we decided to address is the question of cultural identity; that is, who we believe we are, as *Chilotes*, and what we see our role here in Chiloé to be. . . . We wanted to work toward each person feeling that he or she is protagonist of Chiloé's history . . . if he built a bridge, or nailed a board on a school building, the idea is that everyone can feel the importance of his/her participation in the making of the community. (Rosas, personal communication, July 4, 2002)

Ysern, a strong believer in processes over products, sees the strength of the Cultural Encyclopedia not in the production of printed volumes but, rather, in all those almost invisible interpersonal communication processes provoked by the encyclopedia: children and teens interviewing their elders around the stove;[22] community members getting together to discuss drafts of booklets; a child, while doing homework, reading a paragraph of the encyclopedia to her grandmother, who remembers her own version of things and voices her disagreement; a family hearing one of REM's programs about local uses of the forest and engaging in conversation about their own uses. Millar, a witness of these processes, attests: "It's so beautiful how all this activates memory; especially among the elders; when they listen to someone talking about one of these topics and then they start remembering things that happened fifty or sixty years ago. . . . The idea is to generate processes of dialogue to reestablish all those cross-generational communication bridges that have been fractured by modernity" (Millar, personal communication, June 14, 2002). According to Ysern, it is in these dialogues that a community raises its awareness of who it is, of its cultural identity. Ysern's preoccupation with ongoing processes of communication and dialogue is so intense that he encloses a hand-signed letter in every volume of the encyclopedia, inviting readers to respond, to express their views, and to participate—thus "opening" every closed text.

These interpersonal communication processes are just the first step of the encyclopedia's mission. In the words of Rosas, "To remain trapped looking at one's belly-button is not the point. So the next step is to begin a process of reflection about where the community wants to go, about the future" (Rosas, personal communication, July 4, 2002). Accordingly, SERCOM and REM organize series of events in which each volume of the encyclopedia can be critically analyzed by young *Chilotes*. Ysern further elaborates:

> Here the main goal is to work toward critical skills and creativity. [In these sessions] a kid says, "well, here my grandfather is saying that this is the way things are, but television is telling me something different," or "the elders are saying this, but the factory is saying something different." Here the idea is that the kids have to reflect on what their own ideas are, making very clear that they should not equate what's old with backwardness and what's new with progress. So the question for each kid is: what do *you* believe? (Ysern, personal communication, June 18, 2002)

Bishop Ysern's efforts to stir dialogue and critical thinking are also reflected in his agro-tourism project, consisting of farming families that welcome tourists into their homes. For a small fee, tourists receive basic services such as meals, a bed, and use of a bathroom; but the main goal is to experience life as lived by Chiloé's farmers. Thus, tourists are encouraged to join farmers in all activities, such as planting and harvesting, milking cows, making butter and jams, and fishing. Ysern believes that awareness of self and critical assessment of the outside can emerge from processes of dialogue with a different other—the tourist. Maria Luisa Maldonado, one of the ago-tourism farmers, recounts her own experience: "We tell our visitors about using the leaves, or the roots, or the bark to make dyes, for the wool . . . that is, we become their professors, we teach them about our life little by little, and in that process we realize that we, too, have our own wisdom, and at that moment we begin valuing who we are as a people" (Maldonado, personal communication, June 19, 2002). In the words of Millar, "The idea is to force globalization into a dialogue . . . so that globalization doesn't end up rushing in like a huge tractor, flattening everything" (Millar, personal communication, June 14, 2002).

AN ISLAND LOOKING AT ITSELF

Forming the foundation for SERCOM, and especially for the cultural encyclopedia, are Ysern's interesting theories about cultural identity, difference, and community. According to Ysern the human person can understand the world, others, and even God, only from within his or her own culture. Thus, to respect a human person as a subject means to respect his or her culture, because the human person and the culture are the same thing. "To abuse his/her culture is to abuse the human subject" (Ysern, 1993: 116). In this sense, to contribute to the realization and fulfillment of a community is to strengthen its cultural identity. However, Ysern understands cultural identity as a process in permanent flux; culture, for him, is more a process whereby "the active subject, the free and autonomous protagonist finds his/her own meaning for his/her own path toward his/her genuine realization" (Ysern, 1991: 2). On this basis, Ysern strongly disagrees with an understanding of culture as a static essence: "The identity of a community cannot be defended by locking it in the immobility of repeating always the same. This static attitude denies growth, life; it means death for a community" (Ysern, 1991: 2).

When interacting with an other, the human subject experiences different types of changes in cultural identity. First, while cultivating one's own cultural identity, one should never lose sight of the presence of the other:

> I strengthen my own identity, my own culture, and my own history, but the point is not just to look at oneself in a chauvinistic act, but to recognize my contribution to the community; which means that I recognize myself as one able to contribute to the knowledge of the other; if someone in a distant community learns something from what I said in the encyclopedia or the radio, it means that what I am can make others better, that my contribution can help them do what they do better; ultimately I recognize my identity as a contribution to others. (Millar, personal communication, June 14, 2002)

Second, the human subject's possibilities of growth and change are conditioned on his or her interactions with others different from him- or herself. Citing an important document of the Latin American bishops, Ysern writes: "Each person and each human group develops their own identity in their encounters with others (otherness[23])" (Santo Domingo Document No. 270, cited by Ysern, 1993: 120). This moment where identity and otherness meet and learn from each other is what Ysern identifies as communication.[24]

Finally, Ysern's ideas about culture and communication are tightly connected to liberation theology via the concept of "community." To follow God's desire is to become a community, understood as "to live with-others, or to-live-together. This togetherness does not mean to exist side by side as a bunch of rocks would, each one enclosed in itself; what it means is an encounter with the other, sharing with the other, to have a say in a life together, or better yet, to build a life together" (Ysern, 1993: 120).

During my fieldwork in Chiloé, I witnessed a complex mesh of communication and cultural processes that, despite the profound differences among them, share an important outcome: inciting, encouraging Chiloé to look at itself. Included among these processes were youth groups, women's collectives, and indigenous organizations expressing themselves through Radio Estrella del Mar; farming families examining and reflecting on their environment and their lifestyles; a collective of women entrepreneurs figuring out how their "domestic" knowledge could have commercial value; a Huilliche day-care center designed to cultivate Huilliche culture and language among indigenous toddlers and preschoolers; an exhibit by local painters in Ancud's city museum; several volumes of the Cultural Encyclopedia of Chiloé; and teams of popular communicators gathering information to produce news about events in their communities.

Systematic evidence and/or longitudinal studies would be necessary to assess the strength of these processes to resist unwanted attempts to "develop" Chiloé or to integrate it into globalization. However, one questionable development project, a plan to build a bridge over the Channel of Chacao, which would connect Chiloé to the continent by road, has been met with strong resistance as expressed in numerous *No al Puente!* ["No to the bridge!"] graffiti (see figure 11.4).

Figure 11.4.   "No to the bridge!" Chiloé, Chile.
Source: Author's photo.

Conclusion: Three Lessons

In *Fissures in the Mediascape* (C. Rodriguez, 2001), I coined the term "citizens' media" as a more appropriate way to refer to community media, radical media, participatory media, and/or alternative media. My idea was to render visible the metamorphic transformation of alternative-media (or community-media, or participatory-media, or radical-media) participants into active citizens. In other words, "citizens' media" is a concept that accounts for the processes of empowerment, concientization, and fragmentation of power that result when men, women, and children gain access to and reclaim their own media. As they disrupt established power relationships and cultural codes, citizens' media participants exercise their own agency in reshaping their own lives, futures, and cultures.

Fieldwork in Chiloé has allowed me to further my theorizing about citizens' media in several different directions. First and foremost, as scholars interested in the role of media in processes of democratization and social change, we should, in the words of Jesus Martín Barbero (1993), move on from the media to the mediations. I came to Chiloé to examine Radio Estrella del Mar as a case of media in the hands of a community. Had I limited my study to REM, I would have missed seeing how these seven radio stations are tightly connected with a myriad of other processes of interpersonal and group communication for social change. In some instances, the radio stations generate other processes; in others, they voice already-existing processes; and in still others, they allow for previously nonexisting connections—among people, organizations, efforts—to happen. However, the radio stations are only one piece of the puzzle.

Second, we should move from the buzz-phrase of "putting the media in the hands of the community" to what Rosa María Alfaro has called a "cultural project, understood as the need to re-think the meaning, styles, and forms, of communication, [all this] toward a new culture where the protagonists are the social subjects themselves, involved in processes of knowledges in dialogue" (Alfaro, 2002a, 2002b). Clearly, during the 1960s and 1970s, the progressive Latin American Catholic church played a crucial role in the construction of this new vision, in which social change emerges from processes of knowledges in dialogue.

Frequently we reduce the needs of what we call "voiceless communities" to the simple question of their lack of access to technologies for media production. But I believe that, as expressed by Sergio Rodríguez (2002), all communities already have a voice; what is often missing within organized civil society is a holistic program that spells out the role of communication in processes of social change and democratization. Also, too often our discussions revolve again and again around issues of access and control of media technologies. However, Chiloé shows that if the communication, expression, networking, and information needs of specific collectives are intelligible, issues of access, control, and ownership become clear.

Third, citizens' media are valuable only insofar as they are connected to local progressive social movements. Radio Estrella del Mar means nothing without the roles it plays for the Huilliche indigenous organizations, for Chiloé's women's movements, for local youth groups, for fishing and agricultural labor organizations, and for all other community organizations working toward social change. Zooming in on the case of Maria Luisa Maldonado sheds light on the role of REM in her participation in diverse local social movements. Maria Luisa received training through REM; every Saturday she listens to *Palabra de Mujer* ["Word of women"] as a way to stay in touch with local women's groups; she listens to *El Werken* as a way to support her friends and local Huilliche leaders; and she has participated in the production of several encyclopedia volumes, so she follows REM's programs about every new volume. Clearly, Maria Luisa's interactions with REM are multifaceted, inasmuch as she is a producer, a student, and a listener. At the same time, her relationship with the medium is deeply embedded in her participation with social movements. In this sense, REM plays a crucial role in Maria Luisa's agency as an active citizen of her community. This is what makes REM a citizens' medium.

Evaluation studies of citizens' media need to be carried out from this perspective, taking into consideration the role of such media as catalysts of processes, as connectors of people and collectives, and as enhancers of low-volume expressions.[25] Replicating audience surveys designed for commercial media does nothing more than label citizens' media as unsuccessful due to their low ratings. In the words of Angélica Rosas, "It's more important to get five new people to participate in Radio Estrella del Mar than to get a thousand new listeners" (Rosas, personal communication, July 4, 2002).

Notes

1. Although I grew up in a predominantly Catholic country, I consider myself entirely non-religious. However, since the early 1980s, on several occasions, I have worked closely with projects and organizations inspired by liberation theology. The Colombian Cinep is one example (see C. Rodriguez, 2001: ch. 5).

2. Other influential Vatican II documents include *Pacem in Terris, Mater et Magistra, Populorum Progressio,* and *Octogesima Adveniens* (Cleary, 1985: 59–63). The most salient liberation theologians include Gustavo Gutierrez (Peru), Leonardo Boff (Brazil), Hugo Assmann (Brazil), Enrique Dussel (Argentina), and Juan Luis Segundo (Argentina).

3. The Catholic church has three organizations dedicated to communication: the International Catholic Organization for Cinema (OCIC), the International Catholic Organization for Radio and Television (UNDA), and the International Catholic Press Union (UCIP). In Latin America, the regional offices of these three entities decided to merge and have formed the Servicio Conjunto de Comunicación (SCC), which translates as "Joint Communication Service." The SCC works with more than 200 citizens' media projects. Twice, Bishop Ysern has been president of UNDA.

4. "From its foundation the Catholic Church has been structured basically into dioceses. These 'local churches' are geographical units centered around a bishop; [the bishops] relate directly to Rome" (Cleary, 1985: 11).

5. For more on liberation theology, see Cleary and Stewart-Gambino (1992), Gutierrez (1988), and Levine (1986).

6. Huilliche is the main indigenous community in Chiloé. In 1995, two of the highest Huilliche organizations—the Consejo de Lonkos and the Federation of Indigenous Communities of Chiloé—approved the bishop's request to become a Huilliche, based on the bishop's "commitment to Huilliche struggles" (Radio Estrella del Mar, 2002a).

7. In 1995, the Chilean Commission for Human Rights honored Bishop Juan Luis Ysern with its National Award for his commitment to the defense of human rights.

8. The diocese of San Carlos de Ancud includes all of Chiloé, Chaitén, Palena, Futaleufú, and Guaitecas (see figure 11.1).

9. *Chilotes* is the self-designation of the people of Chiloé.

10. *Atropello cultural* in the Spanish original. All interviews were conducted in Spanish by the author.

11. Chiloé was so isolated that it became the destination for many of Pinochet's internal exiles.

12. In most Latin American countries, television began during the 1950s.

13. *Aptitudes de discernimiento* in the Spanish original.

14. Bishop Ysern frequently writes letters to those involved with his projects. These letters, archived in SERCOM, follow the progression of his thinking on communication, culture, media, and theology.

15. John Downing confirms that evaluations of alternative media have to be carried out through longitudinal studies (see Downing, 2001).

16. In English: Communication Service.

17. José Paillaleve works as Quemchi's only medical practitioner; he and his son and wife, Cristina Barría, participate in the agro-tourism network. Along with friends, José and Cristina participate in other cultural activities as well, such as playing folk music and caring for Aucar, a tiny island with an ancient chapel, a cemetery, and an important role in local history. José, Cristina, and their friends have developed trails and gardens with native trees and plants around the island. Bishop Ysern oversees this project because the island belongs to the diocese of Ancud; in the words of Cristina, "Wherever you look you find Monsignor Ysern" (Barría, 2002).

18. Generally, popular communicators work as teams. The production team in Quemchi consists of five adults and a child.

19. The United Nations declared fourteen colonial chapels in Chiloé to be a cultural legacy of humanity.

20. The school was established by the Catholic church during colonial times; therefore, recovering the history of the school implies recovering some of the local history of missionization.

21. The total annual budget of SERCOM plus that of REM is US$220,000.00.

22. In all Chiloé's households, the stove forms the nexus for gathering during the nine months of winter. Family members, friends, and visitors congregate around these low-combustion wood-burning stoves located in the center of the kitchen. Typically, the stove is surrounded by two long benches where everyone spends most of their time before and after work or school.

23. *Alteridad* in the Spanish original.

24. Ysern's ideas have clearly been influenced by Latin American communication scholars such as Jesús Martín Barbero, Antonio Pasquali, and Rafael Roncagliolo (Rodríguez and Murphy, 1997). Since the 1970s, progressive Latin American clerics involved with communication and Latin American critical scholars have established close relationships; they have attended each other's events and have read each other's work. In the late 1970s and early 1980s, they actively joined efforts toward the New Information and Communication Order.

25. See S. Rodriguez (2002) for a discussion of citizens' media as catalysts of the unsaid.

References

Alfaro, R. M. (2002a). Comments at the Preconference: Our Media Not Theirs. Annual Convention of the International Association for Mass Communication Research. Barcelona, Spain.

——— (2002b). Personal communication with author (e-mail). Lima, Peru.

Barría, Cristina (Popular Communicator) (2002). Personal interview, June 20.

Cleary, E. L. (1985). *Crisis and Change: The Church in Latin America Today*. New York: Orbis Books.

Cleary, E. L., and Stewart-Gambino, H. (eds.) (1992). *Conflict and Competition*. Boulder/London: Lynne Rienner Publishers.

Downing, J. (2001, October 12). Feature presentation at the Conference on Global Fusion. Saint Louis, Missouri.

——— (2002, July 24). "Audiences and Readers of Radical Media: The Absent Lure of the Virtually Unknown." Paper presented at the Division of Community Communication, Annual Convention of the International Association for Mass Communication Research. Barcelona, Spain.

Freire, Paulo (1972). *Pedagogy of the Oppressed*. Trans. M. Ramos. Harmondsworth: Penguin.

Gumucio Dagron, A. (2001). *Breaking Waves: Stories of Participatory Communication for Social Change*. New York: Rockefeller Foundation

Gutierrez, G. (1988). *A Theology of Liberation*. New York: Orbis Books.

Levine, D. H. (ed.). (1986). *Religion and Political Conflict in Latin America*. Chapel Hill/London: University of North Carolina Press.

Martín Barbero, J. (1993). *Communication, Culture and Hegemony. From the Media to the Mediations*. Newbury Park, Calif.: Sage.

Puntel, J. T. (1992). "The Catholic Church Searching for Democratization of Communication in Latin America." Unpublished Ph.D. dissertation, Simon Fraser University, Vancouver.

Radio Estrella del Mar (2002a). "Premio por trayectoria en la defensa de la identidad cultural" (document). Ancud, Chile: Radio Estrella del Mar.

—— (2002b, June 16). *Sobremesa* (radio broadcasting). Ancud, Chile: Radio Estrella del Mar.

Rodriguez, C. (2001). *Fissures in the Mediascape. An International Study of Citizens' Media*. Newbury Park, N.J.: Hampton Press.

—— (2002). "Citizens' Media and the Voice of the Angel/Poet," *Media International Australia* 103: 78–87.

Rodríguez, C., and Murphy, P. (1997). "The Study of Communication and Culture in Latin America: From Laggards and the Oppressed to Resistance and Hybrid Cultures," *Journal of International Communication* 4(2): 24–45.

Rodriguez, S. (2002, July 20). "Alternative Media Scholars: What Role Can They Play?" Paper presented at the Preconference: Our Media Not Theirs. Annual Convention of the International Association for Mass Communication Research. Barcelona, Spain. Available online at faculty.menlo.edu/~jhiggins/ourmedia/index.html. Last accessed in September 2002.

Rosas, A. (2002, July 4). Personal communication with author (e-mail). Ancud, Chile.

Ysern, J. L. (1985). "El director de la radio" (photocopy). Ancud, Chile.

—— (1991). "Carta al equipo responsable de la cabina de Quellon" (photocopy). Quellon, Chile.

—— (1993). *La comunicacion social en Santo Domingo*. Bogotá, Colombia: CELAM.

CHAPTER 12

New Nation

ANACHRONISTIC CATHOLICISM
AND LIBERATION THEOLOGY

Keyan G. Tomaselli and Ruth Teer-Tomaselli

The South African press of the 1980s exhibited many of the schizophrenic aspects of the society in general. Deeply divided, strongly allied to particular interests of language, politics, and sociocultural associations, the press mirrored the conflicts of living under apartheid at every level. The complexity of the press in South Africa during the last decade of apartheid is evident in the eleven categories identified by Keyan Tomaselli and P. Eric Louw (1991: 5–6). Four strong press companies, two English-language and two Afrikaans-language, dominated the mainstream commercial press almost entirely. Almost without exception, the English-language newspapers could be characterized as liberal, capitalist-supporting, white-owned, and white-oriented. Afrikaans newspapers, on the contrary, supported the apartheid National Party and were relatively conservative; but they, too, were aimed predominantly at a white readership (Tomaselli, Tomaselli, and Muller, 1987). Black readers were poorly served: *The Sowetan,* owned by white capital in the form of the Argus Group and published in English, was the only mainstream newspaper specifically aimed at an urban black audience. During this period, many black journalists were in detention or on the run, and most were dissatisfied with the way the English press was dealing with the situation (Mpofu, 1995: 60). Into this vacuum, a layer of titles loosely known as the "alternative press" came into being (Tomaselli and Louw, 1991). The growth of this sector was entirely politically driven, with the bulk of the money required for the establishment and sustenance of these publications coming from anti-apartheid organizations abroad. These publications were at odds with the corporate press; seeing the latter as a servant of apartheid, they were under constant attack by the state, which characterized them as subversive and correctly saw them as a point of mobilization against the tyranny of enforced segregation and political oppression.

One such publication was *New Nation.* Based in Johannesburg, *New Nation* was published between 16 January 1986 and 30 May 1997, fortnightly at first and, later, as a weekly. Most of the "alternative press," characterized by Tomaselli and Louw as a progressive-alternative community press, was to be found at the local level and was precariously balanced on the knife edge of survival and dissolution. In contrast, *New Nation,* identified as part of the left-alternative commercial press (Tomaselli and Louw,

1991: 5–6) was situated at the national level, well funded, widely distributed, and hugely influential. It was the only South African paper to provide a systematic vehicle for expression of the social-democratic aspirations of the black urban working class.

New Nation survived two related, and opportunistically allied, state-sponsored assaults during its heyday. The Brazilian lay Catholic movement known as Tradition, Family, Property (TFP) mounted a high-profile theological campaign to discredit the South African Catholic Bishops' Conference (SACBC), the paper's major funder. The right-wing movement also made an appeal to the pope to ban the newspaper; however, this proved to be unsuccessful. What Rome refused to do was happily carried out by the South African state, working within an ideological framework of "Total Onslaught, Total Strategy." Three issues of the newspaper were banned in February and August 1987, and the paper closed for three months later in the same year. The editor, Zwelake Sisulu, was imprisoned without trial for nearly two years. Advertisers were intimidated by state agencies and warned against "sponsoring a newspaper promoting revolution" (Boyle, 1988: 14). The 1987 banning was justified by the state on the basis of TFP's (1987) glossy booklet, *The "New Nation" and Liberation Theology*. TFP claimed that the government had based its decision on the TFP report.

TFP's opportunistic alliance with the Catholic-baiting apartheid government is one of the concerns of this chapter. Our historical analysis of media and Catholicism provides the historical and politico-economic context within which TFP can be understood as an international exporter of repression from its base in Brazil.[1] In the pages that follow we analyze the history of TFP in relation to its attack on *New Nation*, locating both in the broader South African media spectrum.

The Catholic Right and the South African State

Politics, religion, and the media are a heady combination, never more so than in the dying days of the apartheid state, when the battle lines were drawn in blood; but the alliances and discontinuities owed a great deal to pragmatism and opportunism. The apartheid state was characterized in large part as a marriage of the National Party and the Christian-Nationalism of the Afrikaner churches, leading to what has been described as "white patriotic theology" (Villa-Vicencio, 1985: 112). Afrikaner nationalist theology, the theology used to propel the state, always rested on a seeming dichotomy between this patriotic theology and a privatized pietism. When the state-sponsored theological intellectuals faltered in their patriotism, suggests C. Villa-Vicencio (1985: 113), or were "unable to substantiate their position against conflicting political theologies, the secular guardians of the nation, eager for what religious legitimization they [could] muster, opt[ed] for a form of apolitical pietism." These shifting positions were clearly spelled out five years before the establishment of the *New Nation* in the 1981 state-directed Commission of Enquiry into the Mass Media, under the chairmanship of Judge M. T. Steyn (hereafter referred to as the Steyn Commission). Directed toward the media, the Commission Report (1981) also delved into the nature of religion, providing a vision of reformational individualism that was constrained by a patriotic fervor legitimating the conservative state. The essence of religion, it was argued, was "a personal relationship between the individual soul and the Godhead"; but, at the same time, any "social conscience" that may be exercised as a consequence of such a relationship must be of a moderate kind, and never of such an intensity that it distracts from, or negates, the spiritual center (Steyn, 1981: 497). This lack of "moderation," according to the Steyn Commission, was the "essential failure of black and liberation theology" (Steyn, 1981: 498).

The consonance of ideals between TFP and the apartheid government was ironic given that, until at least the 1970s, the Catholic church was barely tolerated by the South African state. Immigration of Catholics to South Africa had been discouraged actively until the fall of the Portuguese colonial regime in Mozambique in 1975. After that year, however, colonial Portuguese-speaking Catholics were welcomed openly to South Africa. This paralleled a growing acceptance of Portuguese ex-patriots through establishment of trade links, visits to Portugal by cabinet ministers, and the brouhaha surrounding the 1988 Bartholomew Diaz centenary celebrations. Portugal was one of the few European countries not to threaten a trade embargo in protest against apartheid, and the 700,000 or so Portuguese speakers who had been relocated to South Africa retained close links with the mother country.

In the context of the Cold War it seemed obvious to the apartheid state that the Soviet machine had triumphed, apparently fulfilling apartheid propaganda about the "communist global domination plot" being in alliance with the *swart gewaar* ("black threat"). At the same time, the state was fearful of growing internal opposition from Black Consciousness intellectuals such as Steve Biko. The more immediate hazard, however, was the revival of black political and union organization after 1973, which resulted in the formation of huge urban labor movements within the decade. The English-language press, and more particularly the alternative press, including those parts sponsored by dissident, nonpatriotic religious organizations, were seen as conduits of black discontent. The Steyn Commission of Enquiry into the Mass Media, referred to above, was preoccupied with the recurring themes of "politicised theology and theologised politics" (Steyn, 1981: 77), which it described as a "particularly significant area of confluence wherein the Marxist, Third World and Western streams of anti–South African action meet, mingle and reinforce each other" (Steyn, 1981: 77).

The influx of Portuguese-speaking refugees presented a conundrum to the apartheid government. In the legitimating doctrine of apartheid—Christian nationalism—the Calvinist original doctrine of Salvation by Election had been reconstituted into a theology of white supremacy. Followers of this predestinarian faith saw Catholicism as a threat, because the latter, like many other religions, makes provision for a *will* to salvation. Thus, Afrikaner nationalist ideology had for many years demonized the Roman Catholic faith as the *Roomse gevaar* ("Roman threat"), on a par with blackness and communism. The matter was not helped by the Catholic church's prosocial stance, which provided solidarity and income to the burgeoning black opposition to apartheid.

Now, however, the state had been presented with large numbers of suitably disaffected, skilled white people who, vanquished in their struggle against "communism," were nevertheless Catholic to the core. These refugees imported a conservative Catholicism, heretofore not evident in South Africa. That a reactionary view of *New Nation* came not from these refugees but via the religious conservative class of another Portuguese-speaking country, Brazil, is the real irony. The belated official approval granted Mozambican Portuguese immigrants, however, could now be easily extended to white Brazilians, the prior demonization notwithstanding.

Sources of TFP Philosophy: Ecclesiastical Conservatism and Class Privilege

The philosophical origins of TFP can be traced to the nineteenth-century papal campaigns to negate the trilogy of the French Revolution: "Liberty, Equality, and Fraternity." Plinio Corrêa de Oliveira, founder of and arch-ideologue for the Brazilian TFP, stresses that the Revolution's final goal was an "anarchic" society in which all inequalities would be abolished. On the other hand, "Rightism affirms ... that in itself, inequality is not unjust." In "a universe in which God created all beings unequal including and especially men, injustice is the imposition of the equality on an order of things which God, for the very highest reasons, made unequal" (de Oliveira, 1980). This starkly dichotomized opposition of left and right enables de Oliveira to argue that *any* political program that pays even lip service to the Republican principles of Liberty, Equality, and Fraternity is necessarily both anti-Christian *and* Communist.

Between the installation of Pius IX as pope in 1846, two years before the tumult of 1848, and the end of the papacy of Leo XIII (1878–1903), the church had to adapt to increasingly powerful secular states. Under Pius IX the church opposed the theological and social tendency of these changes, viewing them as threatening to the authority of the papacy. Leo XIII also opposed democracy and liberalism, and increasingly centralized the Vatican's authority. However, Leo's pontificate marked a turning point, for instead of refusing the modern world, he developed a tactical alliance with it. In social justice politics he was pragmatic: Modern states provided a buffer against anarchy, and therefore cooperation was indicated (cf. the encyclical *Rerum Novarum*, 1891). This was a shift in strategy rather than in fundamental philosophy: The church still refused the legitimacy of the French Revolution. Equally important, Leo XIII revitalized the Catholic intellectual framework and restored the thought of Thomas Aquinas to the center of Catholic theology.

From this Thomist beginning, Catholic rationalism took hold. The intellectual revival encouraged by Leo XIII in his encyclical *Aeternin Patris* (1879) resulted, in part, in the application of a rational, neo-scholastic theology, to be taught in seminaries and university faculties of theology throughout Europe. Neo-Thomism, while influential among the new intellectual circles of the church, was not readily absorbed by the mass of Catholic clergy and laity. Alongside this intellectual thrust, the popular experience of Catholicism was a more sentimental piety, a faith bound up in ritual, often bordering on credulity and superstition. For a large proportion of the Catholic faithful, neo-scholastic rationalism remained outside their experience, external to their thinking and never incorporated into their rituals and traditions or celebration and observance of their religious experience; in other words, it never became part of their religious (and secular) culture. Bernard Connor, Order of Preachers [Ordo Praedicatorum], points out that

> both the rational approach to theology and the sentimental feeling expression of the religion were almost entirely a-social and a-historical. Rational, neo-scholastic theology was concerned with "timeless truths," while religious devotions appealed to each individual's emotions. In their own way, both sought to get away from everyday realities and especially social issues. Neither questioned the status quo in society; it is in this vacuum, especially where Catholics are in the majority and Catholicism is largely identified with the prevailing culture, that a right-wing movement could emerge. (Correspondence with the authors, June 1988)

One such right-wing populist movement was TFP, a moniker that sums up a great deal of its ideological thrust. The organization was founded in South America in the context of the militarism encouraged by the United States' Military Assistance Program of the post–World War II era (Lernoux, 1982: 162–3). According to the Monroe Doctrine, the cornerstone of U.S. policy for Latin America, the former country was befriending right-wing dictators, resulting in what has been referred to as "Creole Fascism" (Lernoux, 1982: 158)—a discourse that increasingly became part of populist politics. Even as fascism retreated from Europe (though it was not stamped out), the ideology survived well into the 1970s in Argentina, in Pinochet's Chile, and in the Brazil of Getúlio Vargas (Lernoux, 1982: 156–59). It was during the regime of Argentina's General Juan Carlos Onganía that TFP, "another throwback to the Middle Ages," first made its political mark (Lernoux, 1982: 161).

Latin American churches, from whence both TFP and Junta Fascism originated, were particularly conservative. Their geographic isolation from the intellectual heartland of Europe caused them to be even slower to react to the influence of nineteenth-century rationalism. Furthermore, the churches of Latin America, well into the twentieth century, were extremely hierarchical, with bishops wielding great temporal power and privilege analogous to the church in prerevolutionary Europe. An example was Archbishop Dom Geraldo Proença Sigaud of Diamantina, "a wealthy landowner, staunch opponent of agrarian reform, and TFP founder. Sigaud belongs to the old school of Latin American bishops who still live in palaces and own huge tracts of land" (Lernoux, 1982: 300).

Meanwhile, at the other end of the ideological spectrum, the condoned conservatism pervasive in parts of the church was to be challenged by the Second Vatican Council (1961–1963). When the theological paradigm did change in the 1960s, it was the Theology of Liberation that challenged the supremacy of the older observations. Since this was a movement that unabashedly opposed the exploitative class structures of capitalism, it was regarded as extremely threatening to the bourgeois elements of the established church. Despite Vatican II and the accompanying Liberation Theology, the sentimentality, superstition, and conservatism of the previous period were never wholly eradicated from the lived experience, the active Catholic culture, of many of the faithful. It was therefore the prerationalistic "tradition" to which TFP paid homage, and which Vatican II opposed. Above all, it was a tradition that felt threatened by critiques of the inequitable distribution of wealth. Not surprisingly, TFP was hostile to *New Nation*, which actively advocated social justice and class restructuring, and a post–Vatican II philosophy (*Evangelii Nuntiandi*, 1975, para. 70). TFP thus offered to the apartheid state

- a repackaged super-conservative viewpoint that struck at the very heart of the legitimate and established Catholic church in South Africa;
- a church-directed (TFP) mobilization against the black labor movement, the most serious threat to the government's security; and
- an attempt from without South Africa to delegitimize *New Nation* and other alternative media.

Anachronistic Church Attitudes toward the Media

Although TFP's notion of Catholic culture differs from the cultural impulses that inform the following extract, on the surface there appears to be something in common with the encyclical *Mirari Vos,* published by Pope Gregory XVI on August 15, 1832, which was a diatribe against the new "popular" media of the time:

> Here belongs that vile and never sufficiently execrated and detestable freedom of the press for the diffusion of all sorts of writings: a freedom which, with so much insistence, they dare to demand and promote. We are horrified, venerable brothers, contemplating what monstrosities of doctrine, or better, what monstrosities of error are everywhere disseminated in a great multitude of books, pamphlets, written documents—small certainly in their size but enormous in their malice—from which goes out over the face of the earth that curse which we lament.

The church's unease with the popular media was widespread in the nineteenth century, and elements of suspicion continued during the early part of the twentieth century. Popular forms of expression were regarded as trivial, degrading, and opposed to romantic classical high culture. A direct influence in discrediting the popular media as a site of evangelism was the "rationalism of neo-scholastic theology and the emphasis on an abstract, metaphysical mode of explanation" (White, 1986: 18). Neo-scholastic theology identified the Word of God with clear, concise, logically defined dogmatic propositions. The resulting abstraction of the language of religious faith discouraged the use of popular media for religious communication.

Vatican II, Communication for Social Justice, and the *New Nation*

The thinking that informed the Second Vatican Council, and the documents that came out of this process, "began the process of breaking the long alliance between Roman Catholicism and socially conservative forces" (Dorr, 1983: 12). As such, they marked a sea change in the relationships between church and state. While it is a feature of papal encyclicals to invoke links with the past in order to demonstrate that they are part of a long tradition of teaching, what marked the documents of Vatican II was an insistence that traditional *issues* were being discussed in the light of changed circumstances, particularly with respect to the role of state in the lives of citizens (Walsh and Davies, 1984: 1). As part of this paradigm shift *Inter Mirifica* (1963), translated as "Decree on the means of social communication," called on the church to use the mass media more effectively, noting that "public opinion exercises enormous influence nowadays over the lives, private or public, of all citizens" (*Inter Mirifia,* 1963, para 8; cited in Flannery, 1975: 286). It follows, then, that

> a responsible press should be encouraged. If, however, one really wants to inform readers in a truly Christian spirit, an authentically Catholic press ought to be established and directed by the ecclesiastical authorities or by individual Catholics, would have for its manifest purpose to form, to consolidate and to promote a public opinion in conformity with the natural law and with Catholic doctrine and directives. (para. 14 in Flannery, 1975: 289)

The Decree was a significant break from the past, since now Catholic culture was reacting vigorously to forms of clerical authoritarian communication that had characterized the church for the previous 150 years. More important, it questioned the principle that "divine knowledge" was above history and cultural contexts (White, 1986: 27). Informed by these understandings, the South African Catholic Bishops' Conference (SACBC) decided on a three-pronged strategy toward fulfilling its media-related mandate. The first aim was to support a specifically Catholic press with the *Southern Cross,* a nationally available weekly distributed through parishes as the flagship. This newspaper was first published in October 1920. While the *Southern Cross* was very supportive of Vatican II, it was politically not an activist newspaper in the 1960s, largely subscribing to the motto that politics and religion don't mix well. An exception would be a bishop's statement concerning apartheid and social justice, or a particular current event that could not be ignored (though many such events were ignored).

A change of editorship in the early 1970s coincided with a greater outspokenness against apartheid within the SACBC, led by Archbishop Dennis Hurley and others. This outspokenness would increasingly be reflected in the *Southern Cross* in the 1970s and 1980s. While the newspaper would not often venture a political opinion, it did cover various stories concerning the anti-apartheid struggle, detentions of activist bishops, statements on issues of social justice, and the like. However, the newspaper was strongly criticized by Catholic anti-apartheid Justice and Peace activists for what was perceived as a lukewarm response to the political situation within the country.

The foundation of *New Nation* coincided with the last few months of this period of the history of the *Southern Cross.* Editorial policy became more haphazard under the editorship of Cardinal Owen McCann (1986–1991). It is apparent that no clear policy or vision existed in terms of political coverage, though "struggle reports" were still published (Simmermacher, 2002).

The second aim regarding the Catholic media mandate was to garner the support of a small number of independently produced newspapers in African languages, among which *UmAfrika* was the most important (see Tomaselli and Louw, 1991). The third aim was to sustain a more secularly oriented press whose main rationale was the promotion of social justice. This is where the SACBC's interest in *New Nation* played a role. The thrust of the newspaper was broadly ecumenical, concerned with other areas of supportive Christian culture—not just with Catholicism.

In 1987 *New Nation* had a circulation of 66,000 and an estimated readership of 260,000. By 1994, at the time of South Africa's first democratic elections, circulation had increased to 100,000. A quarter of its readers comprised students; a second quarter, workers; over a third were white-collar employees; and the remaining 10 percent were unemployed. Readership comprised 13.5 percent whites, 7.5 percent "coloureds," 2.4 percent Asians, and 76.6 percent blacks (Orkin, 1987). *New Nation* focused mainly on the activities of the Congress of South African Trade Unions, United Democratic Front affiliates, church organizations, and other nonaligned bodies adhering to nonracial principles.

Country-wide stringers linked to activist leaders and communities in their respective areas fed the paper with copy. As a national newspaper, *New Nation* could not really serve individuals and organizations at the community level, as did so many other, far less highly capitalized community-based publications, which appeared once every five or six weeks (Tomaselli and Louw, 1991). The newspaper attempted to represent all of South Africa's major geographical regions, but the Pretoria-Witwatersrand-Vaal Triangle—the industrial heartland—tended to dominate its news focus. *New Nation* (Johannesburg), *South* (Western Cape), and *New African* (Durban) established a cooperative news-swapping system by the end of the 1980s.

The paper was run on business principles with funding channelled from the EU and Nordic countries via the SACBC. Consensual editorial practices were developed, together with discriminatory advertising policies. For example, the newspaper refused to accept advertising from the transnational petroleum giant Shell, arguing that despite that company's investment in human rights advertising across a number of papers, the corporation was perceived to be a supporter of apartheid.

Ironically, while opposed to the liberal anti-apartheid but pro-capitalist English-language press, *New Nation* had to rely on this press's distribution company for its national circulation.

The paper covered areas of social and cultural importance, such as education, performance, cultural experiences and expressions of all kinds; it also fostered community awareness and offered community support. Politics was only part of the diet it provided. In short, *New Nation* did not indulge in politics for politics' sake. The church's emphasis on "group media" in the 1980s was incongruent with Paulo Freire's (1970) ideas on consciousness-raising, whereby participants of group discussions were "encouraged to become aware of their unthinking dependency on the cultural environment and to see themselves as active participants in the creation of culture and history" (White, 1986: 31).

As this thumbnail sketch of the newspaper indicates, there was a clear antagonism between the aims of the newspaper and those of the ultra-conservative TFP: Whereas TFP's whole philosophy was to reclaim an anachronistic, authoritarian Catholic culture controlled by the dominant classes in society, making the poor and powerless dependent upon it, *New Nation* wanted to democratize ecumenical Christianity by telling readers that they have agency in contesting oppression. At the same time, TFP's theology, which positioned blacks as passive recipients of an authoritarian culture imposed from above, was totally opposed to the contemporary Catholic church (cf. White, 1986: 34).

TFP preferred to see people as victims of history in terms of prerational Catholic culture. *New Nation* was but one of hundreds of church initiatives around the world engaged in consciousness-raising. Since TFP worked from an inductive position, it was able to single out *New Nation* from the broader contemporary Catholic media culture and thereby generalize anything written in the paper as "communist inspired." Locating the newspaper within the Catholic press in Africa, South America, and other neocolonial countries would have forced them to claim that all Catholic media are "communist." As Robert White (1986: 34) explains:

> The effort to transform the media is part of the broader commitment to build a more just and human society. In Latin America, for example, Christians working in radio started with a traditional instrumentalist version of radio and gradually, with the background of a liberation theology, transformed it into a more participatory communication, the voice of the voiceless.

The above quotes from White describe exactly what *New Nation* was doing: moving away from the rubric of church-as-dogma to church-and-community. One element of this movement was the theology of liberation.

New Nation

New Nation was established to engage not only in a theology of liberation but, more fundamentally, in the post–Vatican II conception of where the church should be going. While the philosophical underpinning was a move away from proselytization through an authoritarian didactical approach toward a small-group, community-oriented approach with a strong emphasis on social and community development, the motivations offered by the paper's staffers were more bluntly mass-political. Post–Vatican II theology goes beyond the traditional confines of doctrine; it moves from being a theology to being a culture of Christianity that permeates all aspects of the lived Catholic (and broadly ecumenically Christian) experience. Liberation theology is only a subsection of the post–Vatican theology. The idiosyncrasies of how the paper's staffers interpreted this mission are not our concern here; however, though the paper was owned by SACBC, one staffer assumed that "the Church eventually ceded ownership to its staffers, who became its 'custodians'" (Mpofu, 1995: 62).

In contrast to TFP's instrumentalist and hierarchical view of communication, *New Nation* fulfilled its mandate for a community-oriented, theologically based people's paper, inspired by gospel values. This approach demanded that resources be redirected from the institutional church (parochial schools, expensive parish hierarchies) into mass-directed but community-oriented channels of information/media. *New Nation* was owned by the church but run by the laity (a movement away from authority-directed instruction). In attempting to build a communication of symbolic gospel witness through free, public, secular mass communications that the church itself did not control, the church entered the public debate, making the paradox of its powerlessness, simplicity, and commitment to the poor the basis of socioethical values in an affluent, consumer-oriented society (White, 1986: 26).

Meanwhile, the international *TFP Newsletter* started life in Brazil in 1980, with the South African edition first appearing in 1987, published by TFP's South African Bureau. Faced with changed political and ideological circumstances that are beyond the scope of this chapter, the newsletter disappeared after 1991. Despite its general position of referring to the potential of all media to "influence the will" (TFP, 1987: 12/13), it was used specifically against *New Nation* to imply that the paper was not "influencing the will" "correctly"—in other words, that *New Nation* was in keeping with prerationalist Catholic doctrine. In choosing to use the late Pope Pius XII's position in their argument for action against *New Nation*, TFP leaders ignored his concern about freedom of thought, as expressed in the following quote concerning his efforts to deal with the task of the Christian press: "Peace is served by true freedom of thought and by man's right to his own judgement, always that is in the light of divine law. Where public opinion ceases to express itself freely, peace is in danger."

Church and State

Ideologically, the church was a more difficult adversary for the apartheid regime than either the labor movement or the press. The church had wide legitimacy among the state's own broad constituency—white, "coloured," and Indian voters. The church was not marginal to the apartheid constituency in the same way as was the labor movement. In fact, labor was the adversary of the state's constituency—that is, big capital and much of the white working class. It would therefore have been extremely unwise to counter the church solely through coercion.[2] The government attempted to delegitimize the church hierarchy in the eyes of its membership. In this case it tried to destroy the popular legitimacy of the bishops, by supporting TFP's attack on the SACBC and thereby negating the authority of the church's resistance to apartheid. The entry of TFP into the arena, with its neatly packaged neo-conservative theology and pseudo-scientific content analysis of *New Nation,* added unexpected support to the state.

Simultaneously, TFP's strategy of focusing on *New Nation* gave further impetus to the wider attack on the alternative press in general (cf. Tomaselli and Louw, 1991). Once government realized how TFP could be co-opted into supporting its onslaught against democratic opposition, the organization received state support and encouragement. In an interview with TFP (Durban), our researcher was shown copies of letters written to TFP by the state president and a cabinet minister in which they commended them for upholding the aims of the National Party government. The end result was that the state's reasons for the three-month prohibition of the *New Nation* during 1987 were couched in terms that TFP had tried to popularize through its publications. Their argument rested, first, on the assumption that the struggle against apartheid was a manifestation of Soviet imperialism; second, on the perception that the alternative press among other forces incited violent revolution; and third, on the belief that a conspiracy allied this press to the forces of communist imperialism.

TFP mobilized anachronistic elements of Catholicism in stating its case against *New Nation*. In his critique of the Republican principle of Liberty, de Oliveira equates the advocacy of freedom with anarchy. Combating this tendency required the adoption of a highly authoritarian stance, in which the support of the strong (preferably military) state was an urgent necessity. Further, his denunciation of those, including some "rightists," who "made concessions to the egalitarian spirit" underscores the centrality of class privilege on which the whole of the TFP movement was based.

The Post-Apartheid Era

The final edition of *New Nation* appeared on May 30, 1997. Battered by falling readership, declining donor support, and a lack of experienced editorial staff, the newspaper barely survived the installation of the democratic dispensation it had fought so hard to help install. Its previously banned editor was now chief executive officer at the South African Broadcasting Corporation. On the verge of liquidation, *New Nation* was bought by New Africa Investments Limited (NAIL) in 1995, owner of the Black Consciousness, Pan African Congress–leaning *Sowetan*. NAIL was owned by African National Congress (ANC)–supporting Dr. Nthato Motlana, and his purchase of the debt-ridden *New Nation* helped NAIL to realign the *Sowetan* politically toward the ANC (Mpofu, 1995: 79a). *Sowetan* editor Aggrey Klaaste told Bheki Mpofu (1995: 78) that "Because *Sowetan* was considered anti-ANC, our new owners were under pressure from the ANC to ensure that they reformed the paper. We were also kind of lagooned into buying *New Nation* because of its obvious connections with the people it supported during the liberation struggle who are now in power."

The *Sowetan* had been sold by Argus to Motlana in late 1993. NAIL's acquisition of *New Nation* two years later also represented a growing consolidation of ANC-led black economic empowerment. Begun with that earlier transaction, this dynamic continued in a deal in 1996 when union-held black-owned capital bought out South Africa's second-largest media conglomerate, Times Media, in the largest cash transaction in South African history (Tomaselli, 2000).

The contraction of the left-alternative and left commercial presses, in the first instance, occurred after 1994 because funding agencies accommodated the shift from activism against the state to a policy of affirmation of the new representative state. The constitutional transformation of 1990–1996 removed the grounds for many organizations' raison d'être. The developmental problems bequeathed by the old state to the new one could be confronted. As a result, funding agencies channeled their support into government initiatives aimed at redress. At the same time, the intellectual and managerial cadres from resistance organizations moved into parliament, government, and the state. *New Nation* survived for only another two years, during which time its socialist content was toned down. TFP disappeared soon after 1992.

TFP had totally misjudged the mood in South Africa. It neither obtained mass support from the local Portuguese-speaking immigrants nor managed to discredit the

SACBC among white South Africans. TFP was most likely a temporary, if useful, flash in the pan as far as the disintegrating apartheid state was concerned.

White offers some germane conclusions regarding two kinds of responses within the Catholic church on the experience of media. The first is that the "Church has feared the popular media as a threat and as a challenge to the rigidities of its past institutional investment" (White, 1986: 35). That this was the position of TFP is absolutely clear. The name of the organization, its revitalization of heraldic symbols, its reference to the words of popes long gone, its autocratic values, and its fear of the modern age are all indicated in its publications. The second kind of response—one in which *New Nation*, for all its own internal religious, theological, and related contradictions and problems, can be located—"is that collectively the Church has wanted to take a longer, more profound look at this [the media] phenomenon in order to understand and appreciate its full significance for human development and development in faith" (White, 1986: 35).[3] One sees in the Catholic media humanism and the great influence of the Second Vatican Council, especially the Pastoral Constitution of the Church in the Modern World (*Gaudium et Spes*). In this sense, the Council has been of great significance for opening the culture of contemporary Catholicism to the new world of mass popular media run by the laity.

Notes

1. This analysis is based on contract research undertaken by the Contemporary Cultural Studies Unit on behalf of *New Nation* (Chetty, 1988; CCSU, 1988).

2. An example of such coercion would be the banning or detaining of church personnel. The church's legitimacy among the state's broad constituency did not prevent the state from placing the Reverend Beyers Naudé, a minister in the quasi-official Dutch Reformed church, under long-term house arrest for his part in leading a theological revolt against apartheid.

3. Neo-scholastic theologies of communication shifted gradually as a result of biblical and historical studies maintaining that the "exact written formulas of doctrine were not in themselves identical with divine knowledge but also reflected the literary genres, historical circumstances and cultural context of the time" (White, 1986: 28). The communicative discourse of the Bible and of religion in general rests on the connotative, evocative power of imagery, symbols, and myth.

References

Boyle, K. (ed.) (1988). *Article 19 World Report 1988: Information, Freedom, Censorship*. London: Times Books.
CCSU (Contemporary Cultural Studies Unit) (1988). *The Sowetan and New Nation–1 January 1987 to 31 December 1987: A Content Analysis and Comparison*. University of Natal, Durban.
Chetty, A., Tomaselli, K. G., Teer-Tomaselli, R. E., and Louw, P. E. (1988). *New Nation: Unmasking Tradition, Family, Property's Media Manoeuvre*. University of Natal, Durban.
de Oliveira, P. C. (1980). "Dissipating the Current Confusion about Just What 'Right' and 'Left' Mean," *TFP Newsletter* 1(5).

Dorr, D. (1983). *Options for the Poor.* Dublin: Gill and MacMillian/New York: Orbis.

Dulles, A. (1983). *Models of Revelation.* New York: Doubleday.

Flannery, A. (ed.) (1975). *Vatican Council II: The Conciliar and Post Conciliar Documents.* Collegeville, Minn.: Liturgical Press.

Freire, P. (1970). *Pedagogy of the Oppressed.* New York: Seabury Press.

Lernoux, P. (1982). *Cry of the People.* Harmondsworth, U.K.: Penguin.

Mpofu, B. (1995). "Corporate Monopoly in the South African Print Media: Implications for the Alternative Press with Particular Reference to New Nation." Unpublished MA Dissertation, University of Natal, Durban.

Orkin, M. (1987). *New Nation Reader Survey.* Johannesburg: Community Agency for Social Enquiry, p. A-18.

Simmermacher, G. (2002). [Editor, *Southern Cross.*] Personal correspondence with the authors, 16 October 2002.

Steyn, M. T. (1981). *Commission of Enquiry into the Mass Media.* Pretoria: Government Printer, RP 89/1981.

TFP (Tradition, Family, Property) (1987). *The "New Nation" and Liberation Theology.* Johannesburg: Young South Africans for a Christian Civilization.

Tomaselli, K. G. (2000). "Ambiguities in Alternative Discourse: New Nation and Sowetan in the 1980s," in L. Switzer and M. Adhikari (eds.), *South Africa's Resistance Press.* Athens: Ohio University Press.

Tomaselli, K. G., Tomaselli, R. E., and Muller, J. (1987). *The Press in South Africa.* London: James Currey.

Tomaselli, K. G., and Louw, P. E. (eds.) (1991). *The Alternative Press in South Africa.* London: James Currey.

Villa-Vicencio, C. (1985). "Theology in Service of the State: The Steyn and Eloff Commissions," in Charles Villa-Vicencio and John de Gruchy (eds.), *Resistance and Hope: South African Essays in Honour of Beyers Naude.* Cape Town: David Phillips.

Walsh, M., and Davies, B. (eds.) (1984). *Proclaiming Justice and Peace: Documents from John XXIII to John Paul II.* London: Collins.

White, R. A. (SJ) (1986). "Mass Media and the Culture of Contemporary Catholicism: The Significance of the Second Vatican Council" (photostat). Centre for the Study of Communication and Culture, London. (Note that this paper builds on White's earlier article, "The New Communications Emerging in the Church," *Way Supplement*, No. 57, 1986.)

CHAPTER 13

Falun Gong, Identity, and the Struggle over Meaning Inside and Outside China

Yuezhi Zhao

During prime time on March 5, 2002, the eight-channel Changchun municipal cable television network in Northeast China was hacked by practitioners of Falun Gong, a quasi-religious movement that has been the target of massive Chinese state repression since July 1999. For nearly one hour, Falun Gong propaganda replaced state propaganda on the television screens of a major Chinese provincial capital. Two videos were successfully broadcast into more than 300,000 households: One glorified Falun Gong and celebrated its global legitimacy and popularity; the other exposed Chinese state brutality against the movement, turning state propaganda on its head. Contrary to state propaganda about the attempted self-immolation of Falun Gong extremists in Tiananmen Square, the Falun Gong–produced video deconstructed CCTV footage frame by frame, concluding that the whole spectacle was conspired by the Chinese state in an effort to discredit the group. The whole city, the birthplace of Falun Gong, was stunned. The result was extensive global media coverage and the Chinese state's intensified prosecution of Falun Gong members in the city.

This is not an isolated incident but, rather, one of many dramatic episodes in a sustained struggle over representation between Falun Gong and the Chinese media. What is Falun Gong? How did it suddenly burst onto the Chinese and global political stage? What explains the intensity of the struggle? What does it say about the politics of representation inside and outside reformed China? Moreover, Falun Gong is not an exclusively Chinese phenomenon. From its nascent Chinese origin, it has been quickly globalized, with Chinese and non-Chinese adherents throughout the world and a transnational network of websites and individual practitioners as local contacts. The Chinese state's outlawing of the movement in July 1999 dramatically intensified the interactions between Falun Gong's overseas networks and its underground elements inside China. The two videos broadcast in the above-mentioned hacking incident, for example, were produced overseas. And the Internet postings put up by overseas Falun Gong members quickly reached underground members inside China. These observations lead us to a final question: In what ways do all of these episodes expose the contradictory nature of "network" communication—as impressively practiced by Falun Gong—which is heralded as liberatory and progressive yet, in this specific case, not only facilitated an unprecedented challenge against a repressive state but also engendered a quasi-religious fundamentalist movement with apparent conservative sensibilities?

Falun Gong presents itself as a virtuous form of self-cultivation and spiritual enlightenment. The Chinese state denounces it as an anti-humanity, anti-science, antisocial evil cult. My purpose in this chapter is to clarify how Falun Gong emerged as an alternative meaning system in China's tightly controlled media environment and to examine its communication patterns from a domestic as well as global perspective. I first address the broad political, social, and cultural context in which Falun Gong exists within China. I then explain the particular ideological and media environment that gave rise to Falun Gong and its contestations over mainstream Chinese media representation, culminating in its famous demonstration in Beijing on April 25, 1999. Finally, I analyze the structural and discursive aspects of Falun Gong's multifaceted media activism and discuss its implications.

Falun Gong and the Dialectic of China's Reforms

Falun Gong's complexity begins with its name. Both its popular name, Falun Gong, and the movement's own preferred name, Falun Dafa, highlight its practical and spiritual dimensions. Falun Gong literally means "Dharma Wheel Practice," which refers to a series of five stretching and meditation exercises aimed at channeling and harmonizing the qi, or vital energy, that supposedly circulates through the body. Theories about the flow and function of qi are basic to traditional Chinese medicine and health-enhancing qigong exercises. At the same time, because traditional Chinese culture assumes "a profound interpenetration of matter and spirit, body and soul" (Madsen, 2000: 244), Falun Gong, as with other forms of qigong, emphasizes the unity of physical and spiritual healing, in contrast to the Western distinction between medicine and religion. To bring about health benefits, the physical exercises must be accompanied by moral cultivation and spiritual exercises as a way of focusing the mind. For Falun Gong, the virtues to cultivate are "truthfulness," "benevolence" and "forbearance."

The religious aspect of Falun Gong is underscored by its integration of folk Buddhist and Taoist discourses in its physical-spiritual exercises. This is the context in which Falun Dafa assumes its meaning. Falun Dafa literally means the "Dharma Wheel Great Dharma," a phrase in which "Dharma" is the Buddhist term for both the cosmic laws and the revelatory doctrines taught by the Buddha. Thus, whereas Falun Gong emphasizes everyday practices, Falun Dafa highlights doctrinal aspects. Following the tradition of Chinese folk Buddhism, Li Hongzhi, the founder of Falun Gong, has written books about cosmic laws. This kind of folk religion, often containing a millenarian element that condemns the corrupt nature of the world and predicts its imminent end, has a long history in China—one that has even inspired massive rebellions.

Falun Gong claims supernatural powers in curing incurable diseases, levitation, and clairvoyance through a "third eye." Drawing upon oriental mysticism and traditional Chinese medicine, it criticizes the limits of modern science, viewing traditional Chinese science as an entirely different, yet equally valid, knowledge system. Concomitantly, it borrows the language of modern science in representing its cosmic laws. Thus, Falun Gong is not conceptualized as a religious faith; on the contrary, its members, which include doctorate holders from prestigious American universities, see it as "a new form of science" (Madsen, 2002: 244).

Falun Gong, then, is a multifaceted and totalizing movement that means different things to different people, ranging from a set of physical exercises and a praxis of transformation to a moral philosophy and a new knowledge system. Its proliferation in China in the 1990s reflected the profound contradictions of the Communist Party's technocratic-oriented modernization drive. Although various forms of qigong had flourished in China in the 1980s, it is no coincidence that Falun Gong, the most influential and extreme form, emerged in 1992. Indeed, it was responding to the deep and widespread ideological and identity crises that followed the 1989 suppression of an elite-led prodemocracy movement. In 1992, Deng called for an end to debates about the political and social meaning of the economic reforms, and urged the entire population to plunge into the sea of commercialism and engage in the pursuit of material wealth and national power. Falun Gong, in contrast, insisted on the search for meaning and called for a radical transcendence of materialism in both the mundane and philosophical senses.

Falun Gong does seem to address the multifaceted concerns of a population undergoing a drastic social transformation. One such concern is physical health, which assumed a new sense of urgency after 1992 when the collapse of the state socialist healthcare system made care increasingly unaffordable to a large proportion of the population. The processes of modernization and urbanization, which accelerated after 1992, have led to drastic social dislocations and created an increasingly atomized society. But Falun Gong's group exercise activities build affinities and provide a sense of community among its participants. On a moral level as well, Falun Gong—with its celebration of the virtues of truthfulness, benevolence, and forbearance, and its condemnation of corruption, moral decay, excessive materialism, and ruthless pursuit of wealth and power— offers a powerful critique of the ideological and moral bankruptcies of the reform program. Contrary to the wholesale condemnation of the state socialist experience by liberal intellectuals, Li Hongzhi's writings display nostalgia for the socialist morality of the 1950s and 1960s and comment on the corrosive impact of commercialization.

Falun Gong is a Chinese manifestation of a worldwide backlash against capitalist modernity and a testimony to the importance of meaning. It underscores the "power of identity" (Castells, 1997). Though Falun Gong is grounded in Chinese cultural traditions and responds to unique post-1989 Chinese realities, it addresses universal concerns, asking humanity to take a "fresh look" at itself and reexamine its dominant value system. It is partly for this reason that Falun Gong appeals to some non-Chinese people in the West. Although the Chinese government condemns Falun Gong as having fallen prey to premodern superstitions, the movement actually articulates a mixture of premodern, modern, and postmodern sensibilities. It has established a "resistance identity"—one that resists prevailing pursuits of wealth, power, scientific rationality, and, indeed, the entire value system associated with the project of modernization. True to the observation that such an identity is generated by "those actors that are in positions/conditions devalued and or/stigmatized by the logic of domination, thus building trenches of resistance and survival on the basis of principles different from, or opposed to, those permeating the institutions of society"(Castells, 1997: 8), Li Hongzhi addresses precisely the actors and aspects of subjectivity bruised by the ruthless march of Chinese modernity—from bicycle riders struck by reckless car drivers to unemployed workers—and provides an alternative meaning system within which individuals can come to terms with their experiences. The multiple unfolding struggles over this resistance identity match, in both speed and intensity, the wider social transformation in China.

In a complete reversal of the events of 1989, which were characterized by an outpouring of desires for political participation, many people turned to Falun Gong precisely because they saw it as an apolitical response to their individual and social concerns. By focusing on self-cultivation and individual moral salvation, and by urging its members to take lightly or give up "attachments" to the desires, ambitions, and sentimentality that ordinarily rule modern human life, Falun Gong is reactive, defensive, and politically conservative. Like many forms of religious fundamentalism, it is not a purveyor of "a social project" (Castells, 1997: 106). Yet, it turns out to be the most politicized and highly mobilized form of social contestation in post-1989 China. No other disenfranchised social group, including overtaxed farmers and laid-off workers, for example, has been able to stage a mass protest near Zhongnanhai, the symbolic heart of Chinese politics since 1989. Similarly, although the post-Mao Chinese state attempted to avert ideological struggles, it ended up having to wage a Maoist-style ideological campaign against the movement. Such is the dialectic of China's "economic" reforms.

Falun Gong, the Chinese State, and Media Politics

If the contradictions of the Chinese reform program provided the broad social and cultural conditions for the rise of Falun Gong, the partial retreat of the Chinese state in social and cultural life and the unique political economy of the Chinese media system made it a reality. Falun Gong was initially legitimated by the Chinese state, which tolerates and sanctions various traditional cultural practices. It was then spread by the highly commercialized and competitive book and audiovisual sectors of the Chinese media system and supported by a massive underground publishing and distribution market. As part of China's rapidly expanding post-Mao quasi-autonomous civil society, various qigong societies, including Li Hongzhi's Falun Dafa Research Society, were established under the umbrella organization, China Qigong Research Society, which is affiliated with the State Sports Commission and thus incorporated into formal state structure. The involvement of a significant number of people from all social strata across the country—as well as the participation and support of officials at the top and middle levels of the Party state hierarchy in Falun Gong, which has its strongest bases in China's industrial and agricultural heartlands and among the late-middle-aged people who have witnessed the most drastic social transformations—increased Falun Gong's legitimacy and popular appeal.

Li Hongzhi, a middle-aged clerk with a high school education, began to introduce Falun Gong in 1992 through public lectures. The practice spread quickly through word of mouth and the demonstrative effect of the spectacle of group exercises in public parks. By 1996, Falun Gong had attracted millions of followers.[1] Reform-era China's unique media and ideological environment provided the necessary communication and cultural infrastructure. On the one hand, the Party state maintained tight control of both media structure and content. On the other hand, the media system underwent a process of rapid commercialization. Both processes were intensified in the years after 1989: A massive post–June 4th media purge aimed at retaining ideological control was followed by the further unleashing of market forces in the media in 1992 (Zhao, 1998, 2000, 2001; Lee, 2000). In contrast to the Maoist approach of politicizing popular culture and waging society-wide ideological struggles, Dengist reformers more narrowly restricted the ideological field to explicitly political doctrines espoused by elite intellectuals and tried to limit ideological campaigns within the Party. The Party state kept a close eye on political and ideological challenges from both the left (i.e., those who opposed further capitalistic developments) and the right (i.e., those who advocated Western-style liberal democracy along with economic liberalization), while leaving considerable leeway for "nonpolitical" content, best symbolized by both Western-inspired entertainment-oriented popular culture *and* traditional Chinese folk culture, including qigong. At the same that the state retained tight control of the news media and suppressed politically oriented alternative media outlets—from elite intellectual journals to newsletters published by disenfranchised workers—it promoted the rapid diffusion of printing, audiovisual, and telecommunication technologies throughout society, and allowed the development of a vibrant private book distribution system and an audiovisual industry of popular educational and entertainment products. Rampant commercialism led state publishing houses, with waning state subsidies, to print whatever would sell.

Several official publishing houses served as first-wave promoters of Li Hongzhi's ideas. Between 1994 and 1996, at least seven official publishing houses were involved in the publication of his books, compiled hastily and sometimes incoherently from his lectures. Most significantly, in late 1994 China Radio and Broadcasting Press, the publishing arm of the State Administration for Radio, Film, and Television, published Li's main book *Zhu Falun,* which contains core Falun Gong doctrines. Meanwhile, two major provincial audiovisual publishing houses in Northeast China released audio- and videotapes of Li's lectures and exercise instructions. The involvement of official publishing houses, like the participation of elites in the practice, ensured the initial legitimacy of Falun Gong. By early 1996, *Zhu Falun* had become a bestseller in Beijing.

The market appeal of Falun Gong publications led to the involvement of China's powerful underground book publishing and distribution network. This unofficial network consists of official publishing houses that have book numbers (that is, book registration numbers or ISBNs, distributed only to state-sanctioned publishing houses) but are unable to find marketable manuscripts and are therefore willing to sell the book numbers for cash; print shops hungry for any business opportunity at all; and underground book distributors and vendors eager to cash in on marketable books. The financially struggling Qinghai People's Publishing House, for example, illegally sold book numbers to book vendors who had been authorized by Li to publish his work. These vendors managed to produce 3.51 million copies of four more books by Li ("Three Major Cases," 1999).

The underground market also supplied numerous pirated versions of the officially published books. These books benefited from the coordinated promotion of Li's Beijing-based Falun Dafa Research Society and Falun Gong's network of local organizers. With the official ban against all Falun Gong publications in mid-1996, the production and distribution of Falun Gong materials went entirely underground through businesses run by agents authorized by Li. For example, between 1996 and April 1999, Falun Gong's Wuhan director, through her husband's business outlet, sold millions of Falun Gong books and audiovisual products, as well as tens of thousands of exercising accessories, badges, pictures, posters, and banners, with a total sale of 91.24 million yuan (US$11 million) and a profit of 27.45 million yuan (US$3.4 million) ("Three Major Cases," 1999).

The Chinese news media, which is more tightly controlled, had a different relationship with Falun Gong. The spectacular rise of Falun Gong received scant journalistic attention. But by mid-1996, articles critical of Falun Gong began to appear, a sign that China's media and ideological establishment were considering Falun Gong's influence on society. On July 24, 1996, the State Press and Publications Administration issued an internal circular banning the further publication and circulation of Falun Gong material ("The April 25 Event," 2001).

A number of factors were involved in the souring relations among Falun Gong and the Chinese state and the news media, including infighting between China's qigong establishment and Falun Gong (Schechter, 2000: 42–43), and possible blackmailing and lobbying efforts on the part of Li's qigong opponents and scientists-cum-ideologues with political motives and affiliations with competing central Party leaders, which caused the shift in the state's position. Between June 1996 and July 1999, there were intense struggles among Falun Gong, the mainstream media, and the Chinese power elite over the status and treatment of this movement. While Falun Gong had some elite support (Liu, 2000) and was implicated in the elite power struggles, given that it was fundamentally at odds with official ideology, there were individuals within the scientific, ideological, and political establishments predisposed to attack Falun Gong in the media. Factional struggles aside, the ruling elite as a whole had three main reasons to be concerned with Falun Gong: There were more Falun Gong believers than Party members; there were Falun Gong members inside the state's military, security, educational, and media establishments; and Falun Gong operated with an organizational structure that was incredibly effective in its ability to penetrate Chinese society.

Elite debates over the Falun Gong were reflected in the Chinese media. Despite sporadic negative articles, many in local and market-oriented papers, there was no systemic and large-scale campaign against Falun Gong in the official media between 1996 and April 1999. In fact, various media outlets offered occasional positive stories. What was significant, however, was Falun Gong's consistent response to any negative media story and its relentless counterattack against the responsible outlets. Falun Gong members were by no means the first victims of the Chinese media's symbolic violence. Nor was Falun Gong the only group that protested against media representation. Nonetheless, it was by far the most mobilized and steadfast in its response to negative media portrayal. Between April 1998 and mid-1999, Falun Gong members initiated more than 300 protests over negative media representation ("Falun Gong," 1999; "The Political Objectives," 1999), with strategies ranging from exercising in front of news organizations to harassing individual editors and reporters. Falun Gong's aggressive tactics had an impact. For example, in May 1998, after a sustained campaign against Beijing Cable Television over a negative documentary, Falun Gong members successfully pressured the station both to broadcast a positive program ("The April 25 Event," 2001) and to discipline a responsible producer. According to a Falun Gong source I interviewed,[2] Beijing propaganda authorities subsequently imposed a blackout against any critical media material about the group. Consequently, He Zhouxin, a member of the Chinese Academy of Sciences and Falun Gong's chief critic in Beijing, had to publish his critique of the group in a small publication in Tianjin in April 1999.

The three-year struggle between Falun Gong and the Chinese media over representation reached its apex in April 1999, with six days of protests by Falun Gong members over He's article in Tianjin, leading to a peaceful demonstration by more than 10,000 Falun Gong members near Zhongnanhai in Beijing on April 25, 1999. In these protests, not only were specific claims disputed, but there was also an insistence on positive reporting of the movement. As the protests would demonstrate repeatedly, at stake is not a matter of evidence and opinion but, rather, a matter of "truth," which is precisely what Falun Gong's revelatory doctrines allowed the group to attain. This decidedly institutional approach to "truth" is underscored by the fact that, unlike an increasing number of Chinese citizens who have taken individual media outlets to the courts in libel cases, Falun Gong did not entertain any notion of separation between media organizations and the Chinese government. Despite its explicit demand that the government lift the publication ban against Falun Gong books, Falun Gong demanded more than the right to reply to media criticism: It demanded the censorship of opponents' views in the first place. Falun Gong, then, may be understood as a movement of resistance, but it is one that offers no resistance to either the theory or the practice of censorship. Indeed, the movement actually urged the Chinese government to use its powers of censorship to muzzle the opponents of Falun Gong. Perhaps the movement's intimacy and comfort with the notion of absolute "truth" and with authoritarian state powers of censorship can be more easily understood if we remember that China's older socialist generation comprises the core Falun Gong membership. From the perspective of this generation, the government is responsible for slanderous content in the media as well as "responsible for preventing their publication through its powers of censorship" (Madsen, 2000: 247). Just as the Party does not allow negative critiques of its doctrines and is averse to ideological pluralism, Falun Gong does not abide any refutation of its claims and negative comments. Thus, although the Party and Falun Gong oppose each other, they have in common their "unitary value orientation" (He, 1999: 24).

Falun Gong and Its Global Media Activism

Though Li Hongzhi began to lecture overseas in 1995 and attracted overseas followers, mostly among Chinese students and new immigrants, Falun Gong's global dimension did not assume significant proportions until July 1999, when the Chinese state outlawed it and began its campaign of repression. This compelled overseas Falun Gong members to assert their presence and mobilize international opinion, pressuring the Chinese government to stop the persecution. If Falun Gong members before July 1999 were audiences of an alternative discourse and the most aggressive negotiators over mainstream media content, state suppression made many of them media activists in an all-out "truth clarification" campaign.

It is with Falun Gong's post-July 1999 media activism that its hybrid and contradictory constitution becomes clear: It is one that combines a "rhizomatic" (Deleuze and Guattari, 1987) global communication network characteristic of information-age "grassrooted networks of communal resistance" (Castells, 1997), with a disciplined and quasi-Leninist organizational structure of local groups linked through cadres of leaders in contact with their counterparts at different levels of the network—a form of organization long used by Chinese peasant rebels and the Chinese Communist Party during its insurgency in the 1920s and 1930s (Madsen, 2000: 246). Falun Gong's interactive network of multilayered media activism encompasses several aims: to sustain the global media spotlight on the Chinese state's ongoing prosecution; to gain direct access to media outlets while at the same time blocking negative views; and, most important, to produce and distribute its own alternative media. Falun Gong's challenge against the Chinese state initially received sympathetic international media coverage, but the story soon lost its freshness. While appeals by Chinese citizens in Tiananmen Square were widely covered by foreign media in the first few months after the July 1999 ban, "day-to-day media coverage dwindled, with interest rekindled only on special holidays or, more recently, during demonstrations by foreigners" (Falun Dafa Information Center, May 9, 2002). To keep the story in the news, Falun Gong members have organized news conferences both inside and outside China, staged demonstrations and exercise spectacles at all kinds of international occasions, and created various news events. And in the United States, Falun Gong members have initiated lawsuits against visiting Chinese officials including Ding Guan'gen, a politburo member and the Party propaganda chief (Falun Dafa Information center, May 17, 2002).

Falun Gong has tried all means to gain direct access to established media outlets outside China. One strategy was to acquire a regular programming slot in public-access cable channels. While Falun Gong has gained limited success in some U.S. cities, one Vancouver activist acknowledged that this has not been an easy route. Vancouver's Shaw Cable, for example, simply responded that Falun Gong material was too controversial. Another strategy was to purchase access on ethnic Chinese media outlets. In addition to paid advertising, one form is to exchange bulk purchase of newspapers for editorial space. In Vancouver, for example, Falun Gong runs a regular Saturday "Falun Gong Special Page" in the *World Journal*, an overseas Chinese-language newspaper with an anticommunist ideological legacy. Falun Gong has also been very aggressive in launching defamation lawsuits and seeking court injunctions to stop the publication of unfavorable material in the overseas ethnic Chinese-language media. Newspapers that have been targeted by the group have included *Les Presses Chinoises* in Montreal and the *China Press* and *Sing Tao Daily* in New York.

Falun Gong produces an extensive range of alternative media content. If books and audiovisual tapes were the main carriers of the Falun Gong message in its early years inside China, the Internet has been instrumental to its more prominent emergence as a transnational global community. This association between Falun Gong and the Internet is indeed "a marriage made in the web heaven" ("Fulan Dafa and the Internet," 1999). Falun Gong has a massive and extremely sophisticated presence on the World Wide Web. Hundreds of websites, maintained by practitioners throughout the world and in multiple languages, promulgate a wide range of content and strategies: Examples include the online teachings of Li Hongzhi, testimonies about Falun Gong's benefits and the personal experience of practitioners, news of government crackdowns in China, counter-propaganda against the Chinese media, and online forums and announcement of all kinds of Falun Gong activities. Falun Gong's ability to develop such a sophisticated virtual communication presence is explained, in part, by the fact that most overseas members are Chinese students and scholars who have both easy access to the Internet and the requisite cultural capital and technical capabilities. If one logs onto the global multilingual network—www.falundafa.org—one ends up at many university addresses. In Canada, Simon Fraser University, University of Toronto, and Concordia University serve as the network's Vancouver, Toronto, and Montreal nodes, respectively.

Falun Gong's interconnected network consists of several major websites and publicity outfits with specialized functions; www.falundafa.org serves as the point of entry and introduces the organization worldwide. Li Hongzhi's books and audiovisual publications, which were banned, shredded, and burned in the millions in China after July 1999, can be freely downloaded. The New York–based Falun Dafa Information Center (www.faluninfo.net), established in 1999, is the equivalent of an official press office. It hosts a sophisticated multilingual network of public relations and Web design experts serving as the movement's spokespersons. The Center provides news releases; feeds a weekly English-language newsletter to governments, news media, and other interested parties; and publishes the journal *Compassion*. The Chinese-language www.minghui.org, or Minghui Net, and its English equivalent, www.clearnet.org, are at the core of Falun Gong's multimedia production and distribution. Minghui Net acts as the official voice of Falun Gong, serving up what in another context might have been called the "Party line." Li Hongzhi issues new teachings exclusively through the Minghui Net. Minghui's editorial department resembles the combined role of the Party's propaganda department and the *People's Daily* in the Chinese media system. It issues calls and instructions on carrying out the "truth clarification" campaign, identifies campaign priorities, releases authoritative editorials that maintain the "correct" Falun Gong line, publishes daily news and webzines, and screens web postings. Among Falun Gong's other major websites, the multilingual Zhengjian Net (www.zhengjian.org in Chinese or www.pureinsight.org in English) is a highbrow site, catering to members with higher education levels and carrying articles ranging from archaeology to new findings in biomedicine and astronomy. Xinsheng Net (www.xinsheng.org), on the other hand, is considered a "lowbrow" site that specializes in the exposure of evil and darkness.

This extensive network of websites not only serves powerful communication, organizational, and community-building functions but also acts as the depository of, and the resource for, other forms of media production and dissemination by Falun Gong members. These include World Falun Dafa Radio, a short-wave radio launched in July 2001 that reaches central and northern China, and Falun Gong's video production arm, Fangguangming TV (FGMTV). Both produce a wide range of news, features, music, and other types of programming and have their own websites. Relying on Falun Gong's global membership as regional producers and local stringers, these operations have expanded their production capacities enormously in the past few years. FMGTV, for example, webcasts a daily news program that shares a name with CCTV's most authoritative prime-time newscast, "Joint News Broadcast" (*Xinwen lianbo*) and features stories related to Falun Gong activities worldwide. FGMTV's most influential production is the video "Self-Immolation or Deception?" This was the aforementioned video successfully broadcast in the Changchun hacking incident. First posted on the Minghui Net in March 2001 and distributed widely on cassettes, the video has been one of the most accessed pieces on the Falun Gong networks. Falun Gong members have also circulated videos on selected current-affairs topics. One such video, for example, critiques Chinese foreign policy and, again, reveals Falun Gong's contradictory affinity with the modern state form. This video claimed that Jiang Zemin made tremendous territorial concessions to Russia over disputed lands behind the back of the Chinese people in undisclosed bilateral agreements between the two countries.

Falun Gong members have also published various newspapers in an effort to carry their "truth clarification" campaign to the general public in a more accessible form. In Canada, for example, the first Chinese-language Falun Gong tabloid was published in Montreal in October 1999. Members in Toronto, Ottawa, and Vancouver quickly followed suit, putting out local papers in Chinese, English, and French. These papers are either print versions of webzines on the Minghui Net or irregular newsprint versions of various Falun Gong fliers and brochures. Regardless, the bulk of their content is downloaded from various Falun Gong websites.

The emergence of New York–based *Epoch Times* in August 2000 marked a significant development in Falun Gong–related media. The Epoch Times website (www.epochtimes.com) and the Epoch Times group of newspapers have grown into one of the largest Chinese-language news websites and newspaper groups outside China in the past two years, with local editions in more than thirty U.S. states, Canada, Australia, New Zealand, Japan, Indonesia, Taiwan, Hong Kong, and major Western European countries. Localized versions of *Epoch Times*, a free weekly newspaper drawing upon content from the Epoch Times website, are distributed worldwide and claimed a weekly circulation of 400,000 to 500,000 copies in August 2002 ("About Epoch Times," July 26, 2002). While mainstream newspapers typically treat Web versions as an extension of the already-existing print version, the Epoch Times website serves as the master for all its worldwide print papers. All a local "franchise" needs to do is choose content from the website and add local material. On August 12, 2002, *Epoch Times* launched its first daily in Washington, D.C.

Although *Epoch Times* displays an indisputable ideological and organizational affinity with Falun Gong, and an editor of an earlier Canadian version of the paper has confirmed that it is both produced and distributed by Falun Gong members or individuals sympathetic with Falun Gong, the *Epoch Times* tries to present itself as a "public interest–oriented comprehensive medium" that is "independent of any political and business groups, free of any country government and regional interests, and objectively and fairly reports facts and truth" ("Epoch Times Publishes," August 12, 2002). In contrast to specialized Falun Gong media, the *Epoch Times* presents itself as a comprehensive journalistic outlet with news, current affairs, and entertainment content. Notwithstanding its claims of objectivity, *Epoch Times* concentrates heavily on negative news of the Chinese government and sympathetic special pages about Falun Gong. Thus *Epoch Times* represents a major step in the evolution of Falun Gong–related alternative media. Instead of focusing on promoting Li's doctrines or the narrow objective of "truth clarification," this paper can be seen as a more Gramscian public organ, articulating the Falun Gong perspective on a wide range of issues. Indeed, through *Epoch Times*, one can discern how Falun Gong is building a de facto media alliance with China's democracy movements in exile, as demonstrated by its frequent printing of articles by prominent overseas Chinese critics of the Chinese government.

The Discursive Strategies of Falun Gong Media

As a networked structure that is constituted by dispersed nodes united under one leader with a common belief system, Falun Gong's media activism displays tremendous efficiency and flexibility. It combines both centralized command and grassroots initiatives. It takes advantage of both Internet-based virtual communication and on-the-ground mobilization. The fact that the community is both virtual and real, both transnational and local, with fixed group-exercise times and locations, makes it extremely resilient and effective. Just as each individual can download material from Falun Gong's websites, so he or she can contribute to Falun Gong's ever-expanding multimedia production and its collective knowledge of media production, distribution, and subversion. This mixture of the Internet and other media forms, regular group-exercise sessions, annual international and regional experience-sharing conferences, and mobilization of individual members as foot soldiers of media activism makes Falun Gong an unprecedented force in contesting and subverting Chinese state media power. Despite the Chinese government's relentless campaign of suppression—from jamming Falun Dafa World Radio to banning, blocking, and hacking Falun Gong websites and arresting any individual caught displaying Falun Gong signs or distributing leaflets—the movement's massive media activism is growing in scope, sophistication, and intensity. The resulting onslaught of Falun Gong material has been overwhelming. Every public space—from cyberspace to Tiananmen Square to the local shopping center and street corner, not to mention China's media system—has become a site of struggle for representation. By late September 2002, Falun Gong had repeatedly hacked not only into China's cable television networks in various cities but also into the Sinosat state satellite, disrupting CCTV programming and many other provincial television channels, and into Sina, China's most popular commercial website. Never before has there been so sustained, pervasive, and costly a challenge against a dominant media regime. Hundreds of activists have been arrested and jailed for distributing Falun Gong literature inside China and for media hacking.

Falun Gong media material shares a number of common discursive strategies. First and foremost is its aforementioned "truth" claim. Falun Gong media conflate two levels

of truth: the truth of Falun Gong—that is, Falun Gong's worldview as absolute truth—
and the truth about Falun Gong, particularly its benign nature and the Chinese government's prosecution of Falun Gong. Since Falun Gong does not make any distinction between "facts" and "values," the statement that "Falun Gong Is Good" is, from this
perspective, as true as the fact that so and so has been beaten by the police. This, against
a background of the Chinese state's brutal prosecution and graphic images of police brutality, gives Falun Gong's "truth clarification" campaign an extraordinary moral power.

Second, Falun Gong material makes extensive use of personal testimonies. These include endless personal testimonies of Falun Gong's magic powers and the Chinese government's persecutions. Since Falun Gong's truth is beyond the normal logic of rational
argumentation, aside from Li Hongzhi's original insights, individual experience of Falun
Gong's physical and spiritual powers becomes the predominant mode of Falun Gong's
truth telling. This general approach is extended to its exposure of Chinese government
prosecution, through both first-person and, more often, third-person accounts.

Third, Falun Gong makes every effort to gain legitimacy from established authorities of all kinds. Countless statements of endorsements by foreign governments and
political and civic leaders, sympathetic news reports by the international media, even
positive news reports by Chinese media before the 1999 crackdown, are frequently
cited as evidence of its legitimacy.

Fourth, Falun Gong makes extensive, though highly selective, use of associations
and historical analogies. While it shuns any comparison to popular religious movements, such as the historical White Lotus movement in China and the contemporary
struggle for religious freedom by China's underground Catholic church (Madsen,
1998), Falun Gong fosters its image as a victim by drawing comparisons between its
members and those who underwent the Cultural Revolution, the 1989 state repression
in China, and even the Holocaust.

Fifth, while Falun Gong has been careful not to foreground its leader, Li Hongzhi, it
has been relentless in demonizing and attacking Chinese leader Jiang Zemin, insisting that
its opposition is directed against him and his operatives, not against the Chinese state or
the Chinese Communist Party. In fact, Falun Gong plays into discourses of Chinese nationalism, presenting itself as patriotic (implicitly distinguishing itself from the Dalai
Lama's Tibetan independence movement) and painting a picture of Jiang Zemin as a trai-
tor (but only in terms of the regime's relationship with Russia, not the United States).

Finally, like many other media discourses associated with social movements, Falun
Gong's media approach is one of activism. Notwithstanding *Epoch Times*'s lip service
to objectivity, Falun Gong makes no pretense to be objective in the conventional sense.
As an editor of the Canadian edition of *Epoch Times* said in an interview, his paper
combines news and commentary, interpreting the world through a specific perspective.
For example, in Falun Gong's view, a natural disaster is always a sign of punishment
for human evil. Almost all natural disasters in China in the past few years have been
reported within this framework.

Though Falun Gong is the antithesis of the Chinese state, and its media structure
differs from the Chinese state's traditional structure, there are considerable structural
and discursive similarities between the two symbolic systems. Like the Party, Falun
Gong maintains a "correct" ideological center and permits neither alternative nor neg-

ative interpretations of its doctrines. Minghui Net, for example, has apologized for failing to be vigilant in its censorship function after posting "articles with gravely mistaken views" ("Statement of Clarification," 2000). Similarly, although Falun Gong has correctly pointed out that the Chinese media use Cultural Revolution language in their propaganda campaign against the movement, Falun Gong's discourse is also not free of the symbolic violence typical of the Chinese official discourse (He, 1999: 24). Minghui editorials, for example, have a discursive style resembling those in the *People's Daily*.

Conclusion

The massive spread of Falun Gong and its sustained global media activism is no doubt the most dramatic episode in the contestation over media power in the Chinese-language symbolic universe. The fastest and most spectacular program of modernization involving the world's largest population over the past two decades has produced an unprecedented, if contradictory, backlash against modernity. In short, one of the most tightly controlled modern media systems in the world has bred one of the most powerful counter-ideological communication networks. Compared with the 1989 prodemocracy discourse, Falun Gong's challenge against the Chinese media system and state power is more profound in its substance, more widespread in its societal reach, more globalized in its structure, and more sustained and militant in its efforts. Whereas the challenge against the dominant media system from intellectuals and students in 1989 was predominantly an ideological contestation from within a modernist paradigm (between authoritarian and liberal democratic versions of capitalistic modernity and between capitalistic and socialistic modernity), Falun Gong challenges the dominant meaning system both from without and within. What is most remarkable about this challenge is Falun Gong members' insistence on the public and collective nature of their practices, their imperative to gain positive representation, their refusal to privatize their dissent, and their willingness to fight for their beliefs at any cost. The Chinese Communist Party once glorified its martyrs for sacrificing their lives for their beliefs; Falun Gong's list of martyrs who refuse to denounce their beliefs to the Chinese Communist Party grows by the day. And yet, though Falun Gong is unquestionably symptomatic of the malaise of Chinese modernity, and though it won the hearts and minds of many followers, its ideological closure and single-mindedness are fundamentally incompatible with any notion of democratic discourse. The fact that Falun Gong is the target of a repressive Chinese state should not lead to knee-jerk reactions about the inherently progressive nature of the movement. As Félix Guattari commented in the context of mass subjective revolutions elsewhere in the world, "large movements of subjectivation don't necessarily develop in the direction of emancipation" and emancipatory aspirations are often intermingled with "retrogressive, conservative, and even fascist, drives of a nationalistic, ethnic, and religious nature" (1995: 2). There are Chinese who genuinely believe that Falun Gong is a problematic belief system and who were critical of many forms of qigong, including Falun Gong, long before the Chinese state singled it out (Rosenthal, 1999).

These individuals are entitled to their views in the Chinese media without harassment. Given Falun Gong's insistence on "positive propaganda" and the impossibility of debating and settling with it, the issue of whether freedom of the press in the context of a liberal media regime is "the only way out" (Zhang, 2002) and satisfactory to Falun Gong's representational demands remains an open question.

Although Falun Gong's accelerated media activism continues to test the limits of media control in China, the sustainability of this movement is by no means guaranteed. Despite both the Chinese state's inability to process the demands of Falun Gong and the existence of a Chinese "media culture" (Couldry, 2000) that fosters "oppositional reading" (Hall, 1980) of official propaganda, the Chinese state remains powerful, with a core constituency that identifies with its modernist and capitalistic reform program. Indeed, despite widespread reluctance and cynicism, many Chinese are either apathetic to Falun Gong or complicit with the Chinese state. Outside China, Falun Gong has won considerable global sympathy, but this is conditional upon a number of factors. Given the global political-economic elite's vested interest in achieving further economic integration with China and the global media conglomerates' own interest in reaching Chinese consumers, it is unlikely that foreign governments and the global media will go beyond sympathetic promulgations and the occasional media story to seriously pressure the Chinese government to legitimate Falun Gong inside China. Nor is Falun Gong as a belief system compatible with dominant Western religious and secular discourses. The escalation of Falun Gong's media tactics is a sign of both determination and exasperation. Whatever the fate of Falun Gong's militant media activism, its implications are profound both inside and outside China.

Notes

1. Falun Gong claimed that a government survey had reported 70–100 million practitioners in China by the end of 1998. The Chinese government, upon the banning of the movement in 1999, claimed only 2 million Falun Gong members.

2. A number of interviews were conducted with Falun Gong activists in Canada between April and August 2002. I have withheld the names of these interviewees.

References

"About Epoch Times" (2002, July 26). Available online at www.epochtimes.com/gb/2/7/26/n207400.htm. Last accessed on 27 March 2003.

Castells, M. (1997). *The Power of Identity*. Malden, Mass.: Blackwell Publishers.

Couldry, N. (2000). *The Place of Media Power: Pilgrims and Witnesses of the Media Age*. London: Routledge.

Deleuze, G., and Guattari, F. (1987). *A Thousand Plateaus*. Minneapolis: University of Minnesota Press.

"Epoch Times Publishes First Daily in Washington, D.C." (2002, August 12). Available online at www.epochtimes.com/gb/2/8/12/n208011.htm. Last accessed on 27 March 2003.

"Falun Dafa and the Internet: A Marriage Made in the Web Heaven" (1999, July). *Virtual China* 30. Available online at www.virtualchina.com/infotech/perspectives/perspective-)073099. html. Last accessed on 22 May 2002.

Falun Dafa Information Center (2002, May 9). "China's State-Run Airwaves: The New Tiananmen Square." Available online at www.fanluninfo.net/DisplayAnArticle.asp?ID=5632. Last accessed on 22 May 2002.

Falun Dafa Information Center (2002, May 17). "China's Propaganda Minister, Politburo Member, Deputy Chief of '6-10' Office Served with U.S. Class-Action Lawsuit for Persecution of Falun Gong." Available online at www.faluninfo.net.DisplayAnArtic;le.asp?ID=5654. Last accessed on 27 March 2003.

"Falun Gong Created Incidents to Disrupt Stability, Attacked Governments and Coerced Media (1999, August 5). *Press Digest*, p.1.

Guattari, F. (1995). *Chaosmosis: An Ethico-Aesthetic Paradigm*. Bloomington: Indiana University Press.

Hall, S. (1980). "Encoding/Decoding," in S. Hall, D. Hobson, A. Lowe, and P. Willis (eds.), *Culture, Media Language*. London: Unwin Hyman.

He, Q. L. (1999). "Identity Crisis in Contemporary Chinese Society: Revelations of the Falun Gong Incident," *Contemporary China Research* 3:16–25.

Lee, C.C. (2000). *Power, Money, and Media: Communication Patterns and Bureaucratic Control in Cultural China*. Evanston, Ill.: Northwestern University Press.

Liu, B. Y. (2000). "Unprecedented Courage in the Face of Cultural-Revolution Style Persecution," in D. Schechter (ed.), *Falun Gong's Challenge to China*, pp. 177–180. New York: Akashic Books.

Madsen, R. (1998). *China's Catholics: Tragedy and Hope in an Emerging Civil Society.* Berkeley: University of California Press.

——— (2000). "Understanding Falun Gong," *Current History* (September): 243–247.

Rosenthal, E. (1999, November 20). "A Star Turn for China's Cult Buster," *New York Times* (Internet edition). Last accessed on 20 November 1999.

Schechter, D. (2000). *Falun Gong's Challenge to China: Spiritual Practice or "Evil Cult"?* New York: Akashic Books.

"Statement of Clarification by the Editorial Department" (2000, July 15). Minghui Net. Available online at http://minghui.org/mh/articles/2000/7/16/6002.html. Last accessed on 27 March 2003.

"'The April 25 Event' Was Not an Incident" (2001, April 28). *The World Journal*, p. B11.

"The Political Objectives of More Than 300 Incidences of Attack" (1999, August 5). *People's Daily* (Overseas Edition), p. 1.

"Three Major Cases of Illegal Falun Gong Publications Uncovered" (1999, October 22). *People's Daily*, p. 1.

Zhang, W. G. (2002, July 12). "Outside Opinion: Freedom of the Press Is the Only Way Out," Minghui net. Available online at http://search.minghui.org/mh/articles/2002/7/12/33221.html. Last accessed on 26 August 2002.

Zhao, Y. Z. (1998). *Media, Market and Democracy in China: Between the Party Line and the Bottom Line*. Urbana: University of Illinois Press.

——— (2000). "From Commercialization to Conglomeration: The Transformation of the Chinese Press within the Orbit of the Party State," *Journal of Communication* 50(2): 3–26.

——— (2001). "Media and Elusive Democracy in China," *Javnost/the Public*, 8(2): 21–44.

Part V

NEW MEDIA SPACES

CHAPTER 14

Global Journalism

A CASE STUDY OF THE INTERNET

James Curran

If Darwinism dominates evolutionary theory, Dawnism presides over the study of alternative media. The literature on alternative media regularly proclaims breakthroughs in which a glad confident morning has dawned. Yet, the new star of the alternative media firmament that it celebrates usually twinkles only for a brief moment before falling to the ground. In a British context, much was promised in relation to *Leeds Other Paper, East End News, News on Sunday, Leveller,* the Rough Trade cooperative, and many other ventures that are now scarcely even remembered (Minority Press Group, 1980; Landry et al., 1985; Sparks, 1985; Chippindale and Horrie, 1988; Hesmondhalgh, 1997). The same is true of a long roll call of alternative media around the world, which were once hailed as momentous developments, and are now forgotten (Downing, 1984; Lewis and Booth, 1989).

The extravagant hopes aroused by alternative media ventures are sometimes based on a fantasy constructed around new communications technology. It is hoped that that the latest communications innovation—whether it be the portable video recorder, citizen band radio, desktop publishing, music synthesizer, or cable television—will place a powerful means of mass communication in the hands of the people and lead to the democratization of the media. This hope has been disappointed, time and time again, for a reason that should no longer come as a surprise: New technology has not fundamentally changed the underlying economic factors that enable large media organizations to maintain their market dominance (Garnham, 1990; Graham and Davies, 1998; Curran and Seaton, 2003).

Yet, the advent of the Internet has once again aroused familiar hopes, this time pitched at a new level of extravagance. The Net, we are told, is bringing into being a cottage industry of small independent producers who are sweeping away "the monolithic empires of mass media" (Negroponte, 1996: 57). It is generating a new culture that is critical, selective, and participatory. People can *pull* from the Web and digital media what they want, rather than settling for what is *pushed* at them (Negroponte, 1996: 84). More generally, the Net is engendering an egalitarian, emancipated, and interconnected world—"cyberspace"—that is reconfiguring the offline world in which we live, and making it a better place (Poster, 1997).

These arguments are so insistent and fashionable that it seems necessary to investigate them further—warily and perhaps a little wearily. Is it just possible that there might be a scintilla of truth somewhere in what is claimed? The reason for pursuing this further is that the Internet does appear to offer an important new means of self and collective expression. Attention, so far, has focused on the way in which organized groups have used the Net for mobilization, as in the antiglobalization protests (Lax, 2000), or have appealed through the Net for international support, as in the case of the premodern Falun Gong in China.[1] It seems worth investigating, therefore, whether the Net makes it easier than before to publish alternative opinions, and also whether Internet technology makes possible new ways of doing journalism. These issues will be examined through a case study of a British-based Internet magazine called open-Democracy.[2] What does this case study reveal about the reality and potentiality of Net "publishing"?

Genesis

OpenDemocracy began as a seemingly typical, rags-to-failure saga of alternative media production. Born as a modest proposal to establish a networking facility between people involved in the constitutional movement in Britain, it was awarded a grant of £40,000 from the Joseph Rowntree Charitable Trust, the offshoot of a Quaker chocolate dynasty. However, its charismatic originator, Anthony Barnett, decided subsequently to develop it into a more ambitious project—an Internet magazine that a Rowntree Trust member hailed, with intuitive insight, as a "virtual *New Statesman.*" This was a reference to a leftish magazine concerned with public affairs and the arts that has been in almost continuous decline since the 1960s. It had employed Barnett as a journalist in the 1980s, and had been a publication on which the related Joseph Rowntree Reform Trust had expended a great deal of money without much credit or satisfaction.

In the event, the Joseph Rowntree Charitable Trust refrained from becoming a major backer of this bigger project—something that was to be a devastating, pre-launch disappointment—although it allowed its original grant to be used as seed money. Barnett gathered together a small group of people: David Hayes, a skilled, intellectual journalist (the first and only one to be paid in the early, pre-launch days); Susan Richards, a gifted film-maker and writer; and Paul Hilder, another writer but the only one of the three to have had some business experience (as the founder of an experimental-theater group), to be in his twenties, and to have strong techie tendencies.

From a garage in North London's Tufnell Park, they planned the new venture—a website that would publish on a fortnightly basis articles on public affairs and culture, to be launched on a pilot basis. The venture went through the usual financial exigencies associated with alternative publishing. Anthony Barnett and his wife remortgaged their house for an additional £15,000 to help fund the project. Two directors lent money when things got tough. OpenDemocracy's current chairman recalls that one of his most pressing concerns in the early days was to limit the magazine's exposure to debt so that it could be wound up, if necessary, in a way that was "clean and quick."[3]

However, two things made openDemocracy different from similar ventures, in addition to its novelty as a Net magazine. Most alternative media are started by marginal groups, and are committed to furthering a political project for which there is only a limited constituency. By contrast, openDemocracy had a bloodline that connected it to the heart of British politics. Barnett had been the founding director of Charter 88, a pressure group that brought together a bundle of issues—devolution, reform of Parliament and the electoral system, a written constitution, and a Freedom of Information Act—packaged together in a demand for a new constitutional settlement. The pressure group brought into being a new public, captured for a time the Labour Opposition, and gave rise to significant legislative reforms. It was one of Britain's most influential pressure groups of the 1990s.

Barnett had also been a leading light in the Town and Country Forum, a small informal organization set up by Roger Scruton that during the 1990s had staged seminars about the relationship between city and country. These had taken the form of debates between left and right, which many of its participants had found refreshing and different.[4] The format of these seminars provided the template for openDemocracy—an open forum in which people could advance opposed views—and many of the people involved in the Forum subsequently wrote for the magazine. OpenDemocracy thus developed an editorial formula that enabled it to appeal potentially to a wider audience than a typical alternative publication would draw.

These two precursors—Charter 88 and Town and Country Forum—provided a network of influential connection. Charter 88 had mobilized reformist but generally centrist people who had been shocked by the authoritarianism of the Thatcher administrations of the 1980s, and had turned to constitutional reform as a form of protection and democratic renewal. The Town and Country Forum was linked to the Countryside Alliance, a formidable lobby that campaigned very effectively in defense of hunting and other issues in the early 2000s. Through these and other networks, a search was made for businesspeople who would give advice and provide a source of reassurance for potential donors. After having first secured the independence of the magazine through the creation of a small trust, a formidable group of establishment figures were brought together, including the heads or former heads of W. H. Smith, Burmah Castrol, Chadwyck-Healey, and the leading city law firm Mishcon de Reya.

This accumulation of social capital was transmuted into financial capital, though only after a prodigious amount of effort had been expended by Anthony Barnett and his shadow team. Most of the money came in relatively small sums from private individuals, and also from miscellaneous charities such as the Andrew Wainwright Reform Trust, David and Elaine Potter Foundation, Esmee Fairbairn Foundation, Atlantic Philanthropies, and Ford Foundation. These grants were threaded like beads on a necklace to constitute openDemocracy's pilot project dowry, amounting to just under £250,000.

This was enough to support a core staff of six people, an office and basic expenses, a group of unpaid external editors recruited from both left and right, and part-time workers, most of whom were young, were paid very little, and worked long hours. However, this amounted to a considerable concentration of writing and subediting talent, supported by a network of goodwill that would generate free articles of quality—probably the magazine's principal asset at this stage. In May 2001, open-Democracy was launched as a pilot project.

Globalization of openDemocracy

It was an immediate failure. Despite being free, the magazine attracted a mere 1,750 visits a week in May–June 2001. Visits rose only marginally to a little over 2,000 by late August and early September.[5] OpenDemocracy lay becalmed in a sea of neglect. Operating on a shoestring, it had no promotional budget and therefore no means of escaping from its cyberspace ghetto. Its hinterland and inclusive approach counted, it seemed, for nothing.

Then, something happened that transformed the magazine—September 11, 2001. The catalyst was Todd Gitlin, who had been a well-known, radical student leader in the United States during the 1960s, and had subsequently become a professor at New York University. Seduced into being a volunteer media, and also North American, editor of openDemocracy while on sabbatical in London, he had returned to New York in time to watch with horrified fascination from his apartment the World Trade Center being engulfed in flames. He wrote the next day in openDemocracy an impassioned, eloquent article that described the numbed horror of New Yorkers and called for restrained retribution. What was needed, he suggested, was "a focused military response—a precise one, not a revenge spasm . . . but an action that distinguishes killers from civilians." Citing Hannah Arendt, he warned that "violence is what happens when politics fails" (Gitlin, 2001). Meanwhile, the small team turned openDemocracy into a daily, commissioning contributions from India to the Lebanon. Gitlin's opening salvo triggered a rolling debate that involved contributors from around the world. Visits to the magazine jumped from around 2,000 to over 8,000 a week in September–October and continued to climb to over 12,000 in the following month. The main reason for this surge was that a significant number of Americans, dissatisfied with their own media, logged onto an alternative media source.

The attention that openDemocracy gained as a consequence of its "After September 11" debate won it a new audience. While visits declined in early 2002, they still remained about four times higher than they had been before September 11. This was followed by a sustained growth of membership as well as a further sharp increase in site visits later in 2002 (see table 14.1).[6]

September 11 also changed the character of the magazine. Before, it had been very much a British publication. Its moving spirits, the garagistes, were all British, as were the paid staff they recruited. Its office was in London. While openDemocracy carried articles about overseas countries, and was conceived from the outset as a global magazine (its five founding values, honed by the "garage team," were to be Global, Open, Quality, Independent, and Participative), its main orientation was originally toward its British base. For example, early issues of openDemocracy carried a regular feature on Worcester Women, key swing voters in the upcoming British general election. And its media strand began in May 2001 with a debate about public-service broadcasting, a very British preoccupation. This debate took the form of a defense written by Oxford economist Andrew Graham (2001) and an attack written by David Elstein (2001), a former head of Britain's channel

Table 14.1.   openDemocracy Audience

Date Membership	Weekly Visits	Monthly Visits
(Pilot Project)		
May–June 2001	1,750	—
800[b]		
Sept.–Oct. 2001	8,550	30,267[a]
—		
Oct.–Nov. 2001	12,900	—
—		
Jan.–Feb. 2002	8,125	36,588
4,284		
May–June 2002	—	37,734
5,825		
Sept.–Oct. 2002	—	60,000
7,500		
(Full Launch)		
Nov.–Dec. 2002	—	195,156
10,194		
Dec.–Jan. 2002/3	—	251,553
14,031		

Sources: openDemocracy Board Meeting Statistics Reports; "openDemocracy Site Statistics since 2001" (January 2003).
[a] Relates to the four-week period up to 6 October (Statistics Reports, 6 October 2001).
[b] Estimated from Statistics Reports (8 August 2001, table 6, p. 7).

5, who focused on the failings of the BBC. It was an insular beginning that typified much of the magazine. Although openDemocracy acquired more of a European focus during its first few months, a watermark of Britishness permeated its content.

After September 11, the magazine became more international. Todd Gitlin's role as North American editor was reinforced by the appointment of Rajeev and Tani Bhargava as South Asia editors. More contributors were recruited from outside the U.K., and the content of the journal became more cosmopolitan. By summer 2002, its most prominent concerns had become a debate about how globalization was changing the world, an argument about how American power should be used (and not abused), and a discussion about Islam.

Above all, the geographical distribution of the magazine's readership changed (see table 14.2). In the early days, the majority of the magazine's readers were British; but

Table 14.2.   Geographical Distribution of openDemocracy Site Visitors (percentages)

Location	May 2001	July 2001	Sept.–Oct. 2001	April 2002
U.K.	57	54	36	28
Continental Europe	12	21	22	20
North America	24	21	33	44
Asia Pacific/rest of world	7	5	9	8

Source: OpenDemocracy Board Meeting Statistics Reports (8 August and 2 October 2001, 4 May 2002).

during the September 11 crisis, an influx of new readers reduced the British contingent to a little more than a third. This shift was not just temporary; it became a permanent feature of the magazine's audience profile. By April 2002, Britain accounted for a mere 28 percent; continental Europe, for 20 percent; and the rest of the world (mostly Asia Pacific), for 8 percent of its readers. The largest plurality (44 percent) was American.[7]

In effect, the magazine was adopted by a wider international community outside Britain, and was lifted into a higher orbit by the whirlwind force of globalizing trends and political developments. However, the key facilitating factor in this process was the Internet, which enabled people living in different parts of the world to log onto a London-generated website. It was the global nature of Internet technology that assisted the transformation of a failing project, hatched in a Tufnell Park garage, into an international magazine of some significance.

OpenDemocracy became a forum of debate for activists, academics, journalists, businesspeople, politicians, and international civil servants from around the world. This made it a more interesting project for charitable sponsors. Whereas more than a year had been required to raise a quarter of a million pounds before the pilot launch, it proved much easier to raise over a million pounds for the magazine to be launched as a nonexperimental project. Its main backers were the Irish-American Atlantic Philanthropies, the Rockefeller Foundation, and, critically, the Ford Foundation.

The magazine acquired a larger office and a staff of seventeen people (many part-time). It was launched in a fully fledged form, with a broader range of content, in November 2002. Its external editors were marginalized, and its left-right debates became less prominent. But it made a major leap forward in terms of quality and presentation, and enrolled an increasingly impressive repertory of good writers and analysts. Boosted by small-scale promotion, the magazine experienced a sharp increase in visits, receiving a quarter of a million in the four-week period between mid-December and mid-January 2003.

What will happen after this initial success cannot be foretold, especially in view of the sorry history of alternative media.[8] However, certain insights can be gleaned from the magazine's short history to date, as well as from other sources, about the way in which new technology affects the economics and practice of Internet journalism.

Political Economy of Cyberspace

Alternative media are usually started by journalists without business experience. They tend to concentrate on editorial content at the expense of marketing and promotion. Through no fault of their own, they often have difficulty securing adequate distribution. Undercapitalization frequently undermines quality, causing alternative ventures to be short-lived.

In some respects, openDemocracy seems to fit this pattern. Most of its energy and resources were devoted to making the website good rather than getting it read. The key time for generating free media publicity was the run-up time to its pilot launch when it was an unknown, innovatory project; however, the team chose to keep the project under wraps during this period in order to avoid negative publicity after its launch. This policy of not raising expectations too high (borne out of defensive perfectionism) succeeded merely in squandering a golden opportunity for promotion. OpenDemocracy received relatively little attention in British media subsequently, save from the BBC. During the pilot phase, the staffing of the magazine was organized overwhelmingly around editorial production, with few resources allocated to marketing. The pilot project was never supported by any kind of paid promotion.

Yet the magazine won for itself—as planned—a second chance. A commercial director, Rob Passmore, was brought in from the advertising industry in the summer of 2002. Management systems were improved, and a modest but effective advertising campaign was initiated.

The magazine was also different from previous comparable ventures in that it basked in the advantages created by Internet technology. First, the Net lowers costs. Online reproduction and distribution costs are transferred directly to the receiver, who pays for the computer and connection charge. Alternative publishers online are thus free from the expensive newsprint and printing costs that tend to account for the small size and poverty-stricken look of alternative, printed newspapers. The nearest thing to installing print machinery online is having a website designed. OpenDemocracy's first design (which did not work properly) cost £40,000; its rushed second one, £80,000; and its third, highly successful, post-pilot one, a further £40,000.

Second, the Net facilitates the recruitment of readers from different countries—a crucial factor, as we have seen, in the way that openDemocracy built up its audience. This has a clear parallel with the art-house movie industry, which survives partly because it is able to aggregate minority audiences from different countries to create a critical mass.

Third, online publishers are able to bypass market gatekeepers. They are not in the position of radical film-makers, who cannot get their films routinely shown in commercial cinemas, or of radical publishers (such as *Tribune*, a radical weekly in Britain) that cannot get their publications routinely stocked in newsagent chains. Alternative websites can be accessed directly on the World Wide Web, without restrictive third-party mediation (at least in nonauthoritarian states).

However, this advantage is only relative. Search engines provide a sign-posting system that influences where people go in cyberspace (Patelis, 2000) One study found that only 42 percent of websites are listed by the totality of major search engines (Introna and Nissenbaum, 2000). Not being listed in the top ten or twenty of a search engine's rankings—broadly reflecting what is already popular and well resourced—also invites neglect since most people do not persevere beyond this point. In effect, there is a distributional system that promotes the mainstreaming of the Web experience. This is why online promotion remains centrally important for alternative websites.

But even if the cost structure, distributional system, and global scale of the online market are relatively favorable to alternative publishing, there remains a major obstacle—namely, the difficulty of generating revenue in cyberspace given the ingrained consumer resistance to paying for online content. This derives from the Internet's pre-market origins, and from the conditioning experience of having access to free websites even during the Internet's commercial phase since 1991. Some users are also concerned about the security of online transactions, particularly in relation to small companies (Office of National Statistics, 2002). Cautionary tales abound concerning attempts by Net ventures to charge, only to see their audiences melt away (McChesney, 1999; Schiller, 2000). A recent example is *Financial Times*'s decision to charge access for its special online features in 2001. Its user base of around 3 million yielded only 17,000 paying customers, in the context of a market with a large number of institutional sub- scribers (Preston, 2002). In general, experience suggests that profits can be made from only two categories of Web content—financial information and pornography.

Consumer resistance to site fees carries over into advertising. Many users instantly press the delete button when they see pop-up ads, while "click-through" rates to adver- tiser sites are generally at or below 1 percent. The time taken to download sophisticated audiovisual ads encourages continued reliance on primitive banner advertising. For all these reasons, Net advertising has grown slowly. In 2002, it accounted for only 1 per- cent of total media advertising expenditure in the U.K. (Advertising Association, 2002).

But while openDemocracy was not managed in a way that was well adapted to the market, it wasn't actually functioning in a market environment. It accepted no adver- tising and derived almost no revenue during its pilot phase. However, openDemocracy is now actively seeking ways of making money. It launched a supporters' scheme in November 2002 designed to extract volunteer subscriptions, and it is exploring meth- ods of generating library subscriptions and selling its back content as e-books. But whether the magazine will be able to buck the general market trend and generate sub- stantial revenue from its online content remains to be seen.

OpenDemocracy's straitened circumstances put into perspective Negroponte's be- lief, cited earlier, that a Net cottage industry will undermine the media giants. In fact, *all* of the most visited websites concerned with public affairs in the U.K. are run by media giants—namely, the BBC, *Guardian, Telegraph, Financial Times*, Times News- papers, and the *Sun* (Curran and Seaton, 2003). Their dominance reflects the enor- mous resources at their disposal. For example, the BBC employs over 20,000 people, compared with openDemocracy's staff of under twenty. In addition, major media or- ganizations enjoy high visibility and use their media to promote their websites, whereas openDemocracy has no cross-promotional resources and remains largely unknown outside a restricted network. Above all, established media have the enormous inbuilt advantage of other sources of revenue for generating content in its original form as ar- ticles and programs. Digitalization makes it very easy to repurpose and supplement this content for Web consumption. Yet, with the exception of *Financial Times*, they are not attempting to defy the market trend by extracting profit from Web content—a strat- egy that openDemocracy is, in effect, now trying to think through.

Redefining Journalism

It is often claimed that the Net offers a new channel of communication that is differ- ent: transnational, interactive, and "postmodern" (e.g., Poster, 1997). Are these alleged qualities leading to a redefinition of journalism on the Net?

Judging from openDemocracy, the answer is, rather surprisingly, a qualified yes. The first key way in which technology changed the magazine was, as we have seen, by enabling it to become a global magazine. Its editorial agenda, its range of contributors, its orientation, and its cultural frame of reference all changed in response to the way an international community adopted the magazine, turning it into something recognizably different from its early British incarnation.

Second, openDemocracy evolved from being a product of print journalism into something that contains elements of a new hybrid cultural form. The magazine's early issues looked like a virtual political weekly such as the U.K.'s *New Statesman* or *Spectator:* heavily text-based with articles rarely running to over 2,800 words. However, as the magazine developed, it began to carry articles of varying length, including essays (6,000 words or more) that took advantage of the magazine's freedom from newsprint costs, and responded to what a significant number of site visitors opted to read. The magazine also began to use visual material in ways that owed more to documentary film-making and fine art than to staid political journalism. In addition, its repertoire expanded to include intellectual finger food, academic essays, journalism, debates, posted messages, fiction, and photo-articles. Although each of these different elements is derivative, they are not found together in any other single genre. OpenDemocracy began to resemble nothing but itself.

An example of its documentary style is the series of articles it offers, based on doctoral research, on "the politics of verticality" (Weizman, 2002). Using maps and photographs, these articles convey a complex picture of the "three-dimensional battle over the West Bank" in the occupied territory of Israel. They show that the dispute is not simply about land but also about transport, sewage disposal, history, collective memory, and, above all, water. These insights, highlighting both the extent and intractability of the conflict, are built up through an extensive use of space and visual detail that no printed publication—even in the 1940s, during the era of photojournalism—could have afforded. Its nearest contemporary counterpart is probably a documentary television program.

An example of openDemocracy's fine-art approach is a photo-journey along a little-seen mural (Roma, 2003). Because the computer lighting comes from behind, it gives the mural a sky-like density and luminosity. However, this is not unlike the visual aids found in some art galleries. More innovative is a series of articles organized around the theme of hair (still continuing at the time of this writing) that combine science, history, anthropology, cultural studies, fiction, journalism, and art to explore the comic, mythic, and symbolic meanings of people's tresses. Through a startling collage of images (drawn from paintings, illustrations, cartoons, photographs, and stills) and juxtaposition of quotations (from poems, drama, fiction, plays, pop songs, and the Bible), the reader is taken on a roller-coaster ride through different significations of hair as a source of beauty and fear, fetish and protest, global universality and local particularity. While these collages are recognizably similar to a certain style of contemporary art exhibition, what makes them different is that they are linked to intelligent insights delivered through analytical essays (the best of which come from anthropologists [Ossman, 2002; Dikotter, 2002]). In terms of both its aesthetic and its orientation, the series is very different from the book–film–live event review format of traditional arts coverage to be found in staid political weeklies.

There are other ways, too, in which the magazine broke free from the anchor of convention. Its early issues had a clear and consistent tone—the modulated sonorities of mandarin English. They were full of examples of "good writing": metaphoric, rich in "shared" allusion, vivacious, and elegant. Enormous effort was expended by the openDemocracy team to, in particular, turn the closed language of academics into a public language that was eloquent and clear. But what resulted was a code that was instantly placeable in a national and educational context: Oxbridge-bred literary English. When a group of mostly overseas postgraduate students were asked in February 2002 why they did not contribute to openDemocracy debates, the main reason they gave was that the quality of the writing, though admirable, was also intimidating, making them feel ineligible to join in.[9] But as the magazine expanded in size and became more international, its style became less homogeneous. Different idioms and accents, some clearly foreign, could be heard. The informality of Internet English began to creep in. Readers' contributions, wearing the equivalent of T-shirts, could be read alongside articles clad in elegant Armani suits or academic tweed jackets. For instance, two posted messages sent by Gary 1970, a U.S. army sergeant, had a natural forcefulness that matched in its own way the eloquence of an anti–Iraq War article by novelist John le Carré, with its practiced declaratory tropes ("This is High Noon for American democracy"), or the sinewy ambivalence of novelist Ian McEwan, writing about the prospects of war (Gary 1970, 2003a, 2003b; le Carré, 2003; McEwan, 2003). The magazine, especially after November 2002, began to speak with different voices in a form that connected to the aspiration of its title, openDemocracy.

As the magazine evolved, its dimensions seemed to change. OpenDemocracy is a views magazine organized mostly around abstract themes. Its articles are not time-bound in the same way as those of conventional journalism because its editorial team is not steeped in a stopwatch culture concerned only with what is immediate. A lot of the magazine's content is also linked to running debates. These different aspects of the magazine, combined with Net technology, had three effects as successive issues of the magazine were published. First, the equivalent of specialist magazines—each accounting for over 100,000 words on discrete topics such as globalization or ecology and place—grew up inside the space constituted by the website (posing questions about how it is used). Second, articles could be read in different ways—either separately when they are published or in batches, retrospectively, since all of them are more or less equally accessible through the touch of a keyboard. Third, a significant number of articles acquired a different meaning when they built up over time. They became rather like that most privileged of academic experiences—a "colloquium," a rolling set of seminars in which different speakers carry forward the same debate while referring to previous papers and contributions. This is different from the journalistic formula that rounds up celebrity views on a current event and invites the reader to make lateral links. OpenDemocracy offers depth of insight through the accumulation of reciprocal debate. In these various ways, it thus provides a different experience—at least potentially—from that offered by traditional print magazines.

The other distinctive feature of openDemocracy is that it enables open participation in debate. Initially, this was something of an illusion. Very few people actually wrote in and joined the formidable debates that the magazine staged. Those who did, however, produced some interesting conjunctions, as in the debate over the politics of globalization that took place between a radical environmentalist in London, a right-wing libertarian in New Zealand, and a social-democratic carpenter in New York State (Belden, Kingsmith, and Watt, 2002). It was only really in late 2002, when the magazine set up and moderated conferences, linked to its debates, that reader participation began to gather momentum. A debate about an imminent invasion of Iraq, for example, attracted over a thousand messages and ran to over forty pages.[10]

Net technology played a part in all these developments. Its interactive nature, its global reach, and the freedom from "normal" space and cost constraints that it conferred—all contributed to a redefinition of journalism that became an increasingly significant feature of the magazine's development. But it was not only new technology that made a difference. Anthony Barnett, now a boyish sixty-year-old, and his team also proved adept at exploring the potential of the Internet as a new medium. Indeed, the most significant thing they attempted was to mediate international debate in a new way.

Global Conversations

The authority of the nation-state in the economic sphere has weakened and been transferred partly to international regulatory agencies, global financial markets, and transnational businesses (Leys, 2001; Held et al., 1999). But these growing centers of power are not held adequately to account because participatory politics is still organized mainly around national governments, and because the world's news media system, apart from a few global news media like CNN, is still constituted primarily by national and local news media. Their news values tend to be inward looking; their scrutiny of global agencies is consequently inadequate; and their linking of groups in political debate is organized within national polities. A void is thus opening up in which the democratic and media systems have not yet adjusted adequately to a shift of political and economic power (Curran, 2002).

OpenDemocracy is significant because it represents an attempt to fill this vacuum. It is one of a number of contemporary initiatives, including new Web ventures, that, in different ways, are seeking to build a new democratic order. Part of the fascination of looking at its pages is to see how it sets about hosting a global conversation and grapples with the problems that stand in the way of meaningful international debate.

At the end of last century, 20 percent of the world's population disposed of an estimated 86 percent of its wealth. This affluent fifth is in general the most technologically advanced, computer-oriented part of the globe. It generates most of the content of the Web and dominates the attention of Net users. In particular, the United States produced almost two-thirds of the top thousand most visited websites and accounted for 83 percent of the total page views of Internet users in 2000 (Castells, 2001: 219). Most people in the developing world are excluded from computer-mediated dialogue because they lacks computer access. North America and Western Europe accounted for 66 percent of the world's Net users in 2000, while the whole of Africa and Latin America accounted for only 5 percent (Castells, 2001: 260).

People are also excluded by language from participating online. An estimated 85 percent of Web content is in English, even though fewer than 10 percent of people around the world speak English as their first language (Kramarae, 1999: 49).

These inequalities and exclusions influence the dialogue mediated by openDemocracy. Africa and Latin America are massively underrepresented in terms of their participation in—and consumption of—the magazine's debates, while America and northern Europe are greatly overrepresented. Japan is another significant absence in openDemocracy's global dialogue, though this outcome arises from linguistic rather than economic barriers.

More generally, much of the discourse of the magazine—despite its staff's best efforts—is clearly a dialogue among elites in different countries: among their intellectuals, politicians, administrators, NGO activists, and businesspeople. The Foreign Ministers of Finland and Bhutan mingle in the pages of openDemocracy with the head of the International Chamber of Commerce and leading antiglobalization activists like Susan George. The likes of Sergeant Gary tend to be confined to openDemocracy conferences, the anterooms of debate.

The debates staged by openDemocracy also reveal something about the dynamics shaping global public dialogue. A significant part of its discussion seems to take the form of a dispute between the United States and the rest of the world. But first appearances can be deceptive. On closer inspection, the forum entails not one part of the globe talking to another but, rather, like-minded groups—such as liberals in the United States and Europe—addressing each other. Alternatively, like-minded people talk to each other about America. For example, a young Iraqi dissident advocates the U.S. invasion of Iraq as a way of toppling Saddam Hussein, prompting an older Iraqi dissident to argue that getting rid of Hussein should be the business of the Iraqi people alone (Alaskary, 2002; Jabar, 2002). Dialogue thus often follows the closed circuits of discourse between those with affinity with each other. Part of the positive function of the magazine is that it has enabled those outside these circuits to eavesdrop, and even to break into the conversation.

However, some people are reluctant to be drawn into a common discourse. Engaging in debate with people holding a different position implies giving them legitimacy, and taking their arguments seriously. People on both left and right have proved at times reluctant to do this. For instance, David Elstein had enormous difficulty in persuading neo-liberals to engage in a debate that put corporate media power in the dock, despite his extensive connections as a senior commercial broadcaster and former Murdoch lieutenant. For defenders of media corporate power to participate in this debate seemed to dignify it, to imply that there was a case to answer, and to take seriously a view emanating from an illegitimate area—academic media studies. The reverse process happened in relation to "antiglobalizers" (a misleading term), even though Anthony Barnett and the magazine's international editor, Rosemary Bechler, had multiple connections with the antiglobalization movement. Here, the problem seemed to be that antiglobalizers were invited to engage in debate with international businesspeople and bureaucrats who were liberals rather than neo-liberals. To participate meant muddying the clear waters of polarized debate and taking seriously a position that was judged to be a fig leaf. In the event, debates were brokered in both cases. But what these difficulties illustrate is an underlying problem. While democratic politicians on the left and right have to engage with each other because at periodic intervals they have to submit themselves to the will of the people, other participants in public debate are under no such compulsion, and can remain contentedly in their separate enclaves.

Global dialogue is not only about conflict. The magazine also highlights points of similarity, as when south talks to south about globalization, when women inside and outside Islamic countries discuss their common concerns, or when lovers of the local connect to each other. To choose two items almost at random, there is a wonderful account by a north London mother about going shopping with her children that describes the experience as an exhilarating adventure, a "street safari" (Baird, 2001), and a Czech describes with equal passion his weekend cottage and allotment, and what its rural setting means to him (Pospisil, 2001). The two articles portray a similar romantic involvement with place, even if the contexts are completely different.

But what emerges above all else is the segregated nature of much global debate. The global public sphere is subdivided into specialist communities, with specific forms of knowledge, organized interests, established NGOs, and well-trodden paths to multilayered power. Much of their debate entails talking to each other in enclosed and almost apolitical ways. One of the merits of the magazine is that it enables their concerns to be communicated to a wider global community, and to be integrated into a political conversation about the future.

In short, openDemocracy belongs to the constituency of alternative media, despite its elite connections, because it is engaged in a marginalized, yet central, project. In its brief and distinguished life to date, it has made a significant contribution toward building a global civil society.

Notes

1. See Yuezhi Zhao's chapter in this book.
2. This study has drawn upon interviews and conversations with people working for open-Democracy, as well as upon its office files. I myself was involved marginally in the project, joining David Elstein and Todd Gitlin as volunteer external editors of its media strand during its pilot phase, though Caspar Melville did most of the work on this strand. In this chapter, I comment in an interim, interpretative way on the wider implications of openDemocracy. A more formal history will be presented in a chapter of my forthcoming book, *Media Political Economy*, due to be published by Routledge in 2005.
3. Conversation with Sir Charles Chadwyck-Healey, December 2002.
4. The debates led to the publication of an interesting book (Barnett and Scruton, 1998). In its introduction is the comment that "from the fertile disagreement of our meetings we have all learned much" (p. xix).
5. OpenDemocracy Board Meeting Statistics Report, 16 October 2001, p. 2, fig. 1.
6. The magazine's internal audit shifted from weekly to monthly figures. Since it was a fortnightly magazine (with weekly updates), its relevant monitoring unit should probably have been fortnightly.
7. It has not been possible to convert the raw data available for the more recent period into a form that would have been consistent with the classification system that was used for the magazine's early development. However, these raw data do confirm the continuing international

character of the magazine's readership. Among other things they also show that, in the four-week period of mid-December 2002 to January 2003, 2,549 visits to the openDemocracy website were logged by the U.S. military and 1,269 by the U.S. government.

8. Alternative media have flourished only when great political and social movements lifted them over the economic hurdles they faced, as in the case of the rise of the radical press linked to the growth of the trade union movement and mass social democracy in western Europe during the early twentieth century, and the rise of alternative media in countries like Korea and Taiwan, linked to their democracy movements in the later twentieth century.

9. MA Media and Communications course seminar, Goldsmiths College, University of London.

10. This was at the time of writing in early February, more than a month before the 2003 Iraq war.

References

Advertising Association (2002). *Advertising Statistics Yearbook 2002*. London, Advertising Association.

Alaskary, Y. (2002). "Iraq After Saddam: Two Generations in Dialogue" (18 December). Available online at www.opendemocracy.net. Last accessed on 1 October 2003.

Baird, N.(2001). "On Street Safari" (29 November). Available online at www.opendemocracy.net. Last accessed on 20 May 2002.

Barnett, A., and Scruton, R. (eds.) (1998). *Town and Country*. London, Jonathan Cape.

Belden, D., Kingsmith, P., and Watt, P. (2002). "Dialogues on Globalisation—Left, Right and In-Between" (2 May). Available online at www.opendemocracy.net. Last accessed on 20 May 2002.

Castells, M. (2001). *The Internet Galaxy*. Oxford: Oxford University Press.

Chippindale, P., and Horrie, C. (1988). *Disaster! The Rise and Fall of News on Sunday*. London: Sphere.

Curran, J. (2002). *Media and Power*. London: Routledge.

Curran, J., and Seaton, J. (2003). *Power without Responsibility*, 6th ed. London: Routledge.

Dikotter, F. (2002). "Bring Out the Beast: Body Hair in China" (4 December). Available online at www.opendmocracy.net. Last accessed on 28 January 2003.

Downing, J. (1984). *Radical Media*. Boston: South End Press.

Elstein, D. (2001). "The BBC No Longer Washes Whiter" (16 May). Available online at www.opendemocracy.net. Last accessed on 20 May 2001.

Garnham, N. (1990). *Capitalism and Communication*. London: Sage.

Gary 1970 (2003a). Posted contribution (1348) (February 4). Available online at www.opendemocracy.net/debates/viewpost. Last accessed on 7 February 2003.

——— (2003b). Posted contribution (1383) (February 5). Available online at www.opendemocracy.net/debates/viewpost. Last accessed on 7 February 2003.

Gitlin, T. (2001). "Is This Our Fate?" (12 September). Available online at www.opendemocracy.net. Last accessed on 6 February 2003.

Graham, A. (2001). "Quality Not Profit" (16 May). Available online at www.opendemocracy.net. Last accessed on 20 May 2002.

Graham, A., and Davies, G (1998). *Broadcasting, Society and Policy in the Multimedia Age*. Luton: John Libbey.

Held, D., McGrew, A., Goldblatt, D., and Perraton, J. (1999). *Global Transformations*. Cambridge, U.K.: Polity.

Hesmondhalgh, D. (1997). "Post-Punk's Attempt to Democratise the Music Industry: The Success and Failure of Rough Trade," *Popular Music* 16(3).

Introna, L., and Nissenbaum, H. (2000). "Shaping the Web: Why the Politics of Search Engines Matters," *The Information Society* 16.

Jabar, F. (2002). "Iraq after Saddam Hussein: Two Generations in Dialogue" (18 December). Available online at www.opendemocracy.net. Last accessed on 10 January 2003.

Kramarae, C. (1999). "The Language and the Nature of the Internet: The Meaning of Global," *New Media and Society* 1(1).

Landry, C., et al. (1985). *What a Way to Run a Railroad*. London: Commedia.

Lax, S. (2000). "The Internet and Democracy," in D. Gauntlet (ed.), *Web Studies*. London: Arnold.

le Carré, J. (2003). "A Predatory and Dishonest War" (12 January). Available online at www.opendemocracy.net. Last accessed on 5 February 2003.

Lewis, P., and Booth, J. (1989). *The Invisible Medium*. Basingstoke: Macmillan.

Leys, C. (2001). *Market-Driven Politics*. London: Verso.

McChesney, R. (1999). *Rich Media, Poor Democracy*. Urbana: University of Illinois Press.

McEwan, I. (2003). "Ambivalence on the Brink of War" (12 January). Available online at www.opendemocracy.net. Last accessed on 5 February 2003.

Minority Press Group (1980). *Here Is the Other News*. London: Minority Press Group.

Negroponte, N. (1996). *Being Digital*. London: Hodder and Stoughton.

Office of National Statistics (2002). *Omnibus Survey* (April). Available online at www.statistics.gov.uk. Last accessed on 20 July 2002.

Ossman, S. (2002). "Hair Goes Global: The View from the Salons of Casablanca, Cairo and Paris" (19 December). Available online at www.opendemocracy.net. Last accessed on 10 January 2003.

Patelis, K. (2000). "The Political Economy of the Internet," in J. Curran (ed.), *Media Organisations in Society*. London: Arnold.

Pospisil, M. (2001). "Holiday Homes: The Czech Enthusiasm for Weekend Cottages and Allotments"(12 December). Available online at www.opendemocracy.net. Last accessed on 20 May 2002.

Poster, M. (1997). "Cyberdemocracy: Internet and the Public Sphere," in D. Porter (ed.), *Internet Culture*. New York: Routledge.

Roma, S. (2003). "The East Is Offering Its Riches to Britannia" (22 January). Available online at www.opendemocracy.net. Last accessed on 28 January 2003.

Schiller, D.(2000). *Digital Capitalism*. Cambridge, Mass.: MIT Press.

Sparks, C. (1985). "The Working Class Press: Radical and Revolutionary Alternatives," *Media, Culture and Society* 7.

Weizman, E. (2002). "The Politics of Verticality" (25 April). Available online at www.opendemocracy.net. Last accessed on 10 January 2003.

CHAPTER 15

The Independent Media Center Movement and the Anarchist Socialist Tradition

John D. H. Downing

> We do not hesitate to say that we want people who will continue
> unceasingly to develop; people who are capable of constantly de-
> stroying and renewing their surroundings and renewing them-
> selves; people whose intellectual independence is their supreme
> power, which they will yield to none; people always disposed for
> things that are better, eager for the triumph of new ideas, anxious
> to crowd many lives into the life they have.
>
> —Francisco Ferrer i Guardia[1]

The Independent Media Centers (Downing, 2002a, 2002b, 2003), numbering over
ninety worldwide at the time of this writing in late summer 2002, sprang into being
with remarkable speed. The first IMC had seen the light of day less than three years
previously, during the momentous WTO confrontations in Seattle in November–December 1999. The others developed subsequently most often in response to (1) a particular meeting of global power circles, such as the World Bank, the International
Monetary Fund, or the G8 countries' political leaders; (2) major world fora on issues
such as racism (Durban, 2000); or (3) party conventions, such as the U.S. presidential
nomination meetings of the Republican and Democratic parties. Having been instituted to help focus nonmainstream media coverage of protests at that particular time
and place, they often continued on afterward, acting as communication nodes for political resistance on both local and international issues.

At their simplest they comprised a connected server, a webpage, and one or
more activists. Some were extremely active, with multiple postings every day; others, much less energetic; still others, somewhere in between. Overwhelmingly they
were nonsectarian, defining their role as a service contribution, not as directive.
Their webpages carried text, still photos, cartoons, sometimes audio and video files,
and all carried hyperlinks to each other. As of 2002 they were initially concentrated
in the United States, Canada, and Western Europe, but were represented in Australia, Aotearoa/New Zealand, and Latin America as well as in a few other non-
"Western" locations.

The IMCs represented a remarkable surge of energy in the application of digital communication technologies to political contestation strategies. In this overview of their operation, or at least certain aspects of it, I locate their significance within the simultaneous predicament and health of movements challenging the transnational corporate order, at the beginning of the twenty-first century CE. In particular, I relate the IMCs to some of the *leitmotifs* of political thought represented by the anarchist socialist tradition. I first characterize the current context as well as the political tradition, though both only in outline, and then proceed to explore certain key dimensions of the "Indymedia" phenomenon as they relate to this context and tradition. My argument is that the IMCs may constitute a very fruitful path to pursue, among the many that are needed to lead out of our present dilemmas.

The Current Context and Its Dilemmas

Since the collapse of the Soviet bloc in 1989–1991, endless toner has been devoted to discussion of the global consequences. The stargazers have solemnly assured us of their own often mutually contradictory certainties: the end of ideology, the final victory of liberal democracy, the imminence of Muslim convulsions against the world order, the assured collapse of U.S. dominance, the merits of the Blair-Schroeder "Third Way" between capitalism and sovietized socialism, the shift of global power to East Asia, and—not least—the conclusive burial of all hopes that a significantly different and more attractive world is *possible*. The newspapers and magazines of quality, read by people of quality, and largely owned by corporations of tremendous wealth and power, have mostly signed on to one or another of these certainties, or have framed our range of options as limited to them.

So what are our options to deal with malnutrition, disease, high infant mortality, environmental disaster, plunder of the weaker nations' resources, racism, sexism, war, unjust laws, corporate and political corruption, and, beyond them, systemic and transnational corporate priorities? Did the socialist alternatives dominating the previous century offer a viable alternative to market-forces fundamentalism?

The answer has to be no.

Had the Soviet bloc survived, it would have done so only as a monument to repression in the name of justice and equality. Admittedly, the scale of repression slowed in a major way following Stalin's death in 1953, and began to tail off substantially in the 1980s, but the structural foundations of the bloc were so deeply flawed, ethically and economically, that true reform of them was inconceivable. True, in the fight against global fascism and militarism in the third to fifth decades of the last century, the myth of the Soviet Union as the homeland of justice and liberation served to embolden countless people who put their lives on the line for the rest of us to defeat those threats. True, that myth also constrained capital to deal with workers' movements and demands more flexibly at times than it would have done without the myth, and thus had much to do with the welfare rights installed in many nations for a number of decades. The very poor lot of Soviet workers enabled a better deal for their western counterparts, just as their sacrifice in tens of millions warring against Hitler was crucial in the collapse of fascism.

All this notwithstanding, the system itself was a step backward from capitalism—a "military-feudal despotism" as Nikolai Bukharin, one of its leaders liquidated in the 1938 show trials, once put it. It was not a step forward, in and of itself.

Social democracy, the constitutional and parliamentary alternative, eschewing the violence of a compulsory revolution ("The bourgeoisie will never give up power willingly, so comrades, let's go for their throats!"), had the corresponding negative virtue of seeking to talk our way into a better world rather than shooting our way into it, and the altogether positive virtue of having organized better living conditions for many ordinary folk in many countries.[2] People in Britain used to laugh about the humdrum meat-and-potatoes character of "municipal socialism," but our lives are made up of humdrum details, and they make an unromantic but worthwhile difference.

If that were as far as it went, parliamentary socialism might indeed be worth settling for. Life is messy, and muddling through may be the only option for many of us much of the time. In practice, the story has been much more complicated and much less reassuring. In order to win the crucial electoral middle ground, social democratic parties have pretty consistently struggled to adopt policies made popular by rightist parties and have pretty consistently avoided a social justice agenda. This was especially the case over the final three decades of the past century, when health care and welfare rights, migrant workers' rights, labor union rights, women's rights, children's rights, the rights of the elderly, and citizens' information and privacy rights were cut back, often savagely, and when bellicose foreign policies favoring war and "Third World" resource exploitation were much in evidence. Corruption among leading politicians has been an equal-opportunity scenario, not at all the preserve of the historical Right. To be in power, to be able to play the game and not skulk forever in opposition, has dominated the process for Social Democratic[3] political aspirants. Successfully spinning the media has been much more important than developing democratic media policies.

It is in this context of continuing issues of global and local injustice and poverty, and the inadequacy of twentieth-century socialism in practice to address them, that we are forced to look around for what else there may be to offer as a starting point, at least, for new reflection on the potential for progress. We need to be ruthlessly honest in this process, and that means, frankly, admitting that as of now, there are no obvious step-by-step solutions to constructing a different world. Our conviction that a different world *is* possible is driven more by contemplation of the one we inhabit than by developed, let alone coordinated, alternative policies. There is no point in pretending this is not the case: Indeed, doing so only slows us down and sets us back. There is no government-in-waiting at this time, no NGO or single political movement, that is about to act as global beacon guiding the way to achieve constructive societal change.

Thus it makes sense to look again at what may be found in the socialist[4] anarchist tradition, largely eclipsed in the twentieth century by communism and social democracy, and associated in the public mind with a love of disorder and of creating chaos, even with sanctifying terroristic actions against public figures. Let us take a risk, though, and peer for a moment beneath these conventional wrappings to try to recover a basic sense of what this tradition actually was about, and to discover whether it still has any clues or questions for us in the dilemmas we face in the search for social justice. In particular, let us ask whether it is reflected in—and suggests fruitful avenues for—current struggles against corporate media hegemony.

The Political Tradition of Socialist Anarchism

It may be helpful to recall how widespread socialist anarchist movements have been (Marshall, 1992; Préposiet, 2002), especially before the Bolshevik Revolution, which had the effect of draining many anarchist activists away, impressed by the early Soviet state—or reports of it—into thinking that perhaps the Marxists had gotten it right after all (Quail, 1978). Though not all, many Chinese anarchists reacted in a similar fashion to the 1949 Communist victory. The most famous example of anarchism in action is of course to be found in Spain, where it had been a tremendously powerful presence for eight decades until the 1939 fascist victory in the Civil War (Hofmann et al., 1995; Rider, 1989). Spanish and Italian anarchist influences spread via migrant workers and political exiles to a number of Latin American nations, especially Argentina, Peru, and Mexico, and also in the Balkans, Switzerland, and France (Levy, 1989: 44). Italian and other migrant workers were equally important in Brazil's anarchist movements (Alves de Seixas, 1992). Anarchism in Russia was one of the major tendencies on the Left up to 1917 (Avrich, 1973), and from 1918 to 1921 it was the dominant political force in Ukraine (Archinov, 2001). Nor should the United States (Goldman, 1970) and Canada (Fetherling, 1998) be left out of this picture. India has had its share of anarchist thinkers and activists (Ostergaard, 1989), in some respects including even Mahatma Gandhi, as did China and Japan (Dirlik, 1991; Pelletier, 2001; Zarrow, 1990) in the earlier decades of the twentieth century.

Moreover, some of the socialist anarchists' core ideas have become commonplace without most people knowing it. Their proposals for "integral" education and the "modern school" movement—science in the curriculum, sex education, coeducation, the importance of continuing adult education, secular education, the need for practicums—are now standard (Smith, 1989). Kropotkin's arguments in favor of decentralizing urban settlements were adopted by early urban planners and have continued to be very influential in those quarters (Crowder, 1991: 166, n. 159).

Tracing the later history of socialist anarchism in the twentieth century is totally beyond my scope here. I would simply point to certain moments of great intensity in which key anarchist principles (though not necessarily language) have been evident—namely, the situationist movement, whose influence was so visible during the 1968 Paris revolt (Viénet, 1992; Marelli, 1998); political movements in Italy and Portugal in the 1970s (Downing, 2001: 237–98); the U.S. civil rights movement (Egerton, 1994; Payne, 1995); and some key aspects of the feminist and ecological movements. The antiglobalization movement that emerged in the 1990s and continues to the present, the Zapatista movement in Mexico, and the World Social Forum meetings in

Porto Alegre are further examples in certain respects—and so not least is the Indymedia phenomenon, as we shall see in more detail below.

A signal difficulty of the task I have set for myself in summarizing socialist anarchist thought has to do with its protean character.[5] Anarchism has been as contentious a political movement as any other; and beyond that, its basic premises have discouraged even the emergence of competing absolute authorities such as Lenin, Trotsky, or Mao. No single person has represented, or been able *credibly* to claim to represent, "true" anarchist philosophy. There are major influential names from the early anarchist period, running approximately from 1860 to 1930, but none of them has sacral status: Pierre-Joseph Proudhon (France), Mikhail Bakunin (Russia), Errico Malatesta (Italy), Piotr Kropotkin (Russia), Francisco Ferrer (Spain), and Emma Goldman (United States). Moreover, contemporary socialist anarchist thought often has a sharply different flavor, as we shall see in a moment.

Even among these classical figures there could be sharp differences. Malatesta, for example, had no time for the assumption made by Kropotkin and some of the other classical anarchists that the historical process would automatically engender a decisive revolution; neither had he anything but contempt for sectarian squabbles,[6] nor any interest in Bakunin's secret societies (Pernicone, 1993: 244–51, 274–75). Malatesta also denounced projects to socialize agriculture that took no account of farmers' wishes to maintain their farms (Levy, 1989: 40). Proudhon argued that violent revolution might indeed be the consequence if the ruling circles dug their heels in against any reform, but that, in principle, violence threatens the very ideals of mutual respect and freedom that are anarchism's political objective (Crowder, 1991: 147). Malatesta and Kropotkin were both against physical attacks on people, while accepting them against physical property. Some anarchists have welcomed Marxist analysis while denouncing Leninist practice (Guérin, 1989); others have fought tooth and nail against both. Some have focused their efforts entirely on labor organizing (anarcho-syndicalists); others, on developing a federated network of democratic, responsive power-centers.

However, there is a dialectic between freedom and organized action in anarchist practice. Given the verbal linkage "anarchism≈anarchy≈chaos," it comes as a surprise to some to discover that *organization* is a central theme in socialist anarchist philosophies. Malatesta preferred the term "association," but saw it as essential and constructive. Proudhon and Kropotkin emphasized the principles of solidarity and mutual support that they argued were evident in many facets of human history that anarchism could build upon. And Goldman (1969: 35) stated that "organization, as we [anarchists] understand it . . . is based, primarily, on freedom. It is a natural and voluntary grouping of energies to secure results beneficial to humanity." She contrasted this "grouping" sharply and unfavorably with governmental and corporate "organization," which she epitomized as "the ceaseless piracy of the rich against the poor" (capitalist industry), "a cruel instrument of blind force" (the military), and "a veritable barracks, where the human mind is drilled and manipulated into submission to various social and moral spooks" (formal education at all levels).

Anarchist organization, in this perspective, was not a constraint on freedom but an expression of the public's actual interdependence, of which the cooperative

movement was one example (Cahill, 1989). It did not preclude variety or conflicting views. As Serge Salaün (1995: 323) puts it in his description of the language of
anarchist publications in Spain:

> To claim to generalize about the totality of Spanish anarchist movements is
> highly hazardous on account of their multifaceted, motile (*sinuosa*), plural
> dimension. Verbal practices give the impression of fluctuating from one pe-
> riod to another, from one region to another, from one group (including one
> individual) to another, from one newspaper to another, and even within a
> single newspaper.

And yet, as Nick Rider (1989) notes, there was nothing primitive, disorganized, or
convulsive in the tactics developed during the organization of a major rent strike in
Barcelona in 1931, when anarchist influence was predominant. The strike was
grounded in popular conditions and grew out of community networks.

Thus for anarchist thought, the following logo, popular in the Spanish anarchist
press, has no contradiction: *The true anarchist will not be chained, even by anarchists
themselves* (cited in Litvak, 1995: 220).

Here we see the heart of the discord between classical Marxism and classical anarchism. For advocates of the latter, it was impossible to see the state as anything other
than a restraint on freedom and, therefore, as entirely antithetical to the practicalities
of achieving a just and free society. The situation was akin to asking an enraged
800-pound gorilla to lie on its back to have its tummy tickled, whereas for Communists and Social Democrats the state could be slewed around in its tracks and pointed
in a just direction, by revolution or legislation, depending on the viewpoint in question. (Evaluating the results of these strategies is entirely another story.)

Today, with the bonus of hindsight, some of these arguments may seem to wear a
different hue, and even to look rather patchy. In the twentieth century many states in
affluent nations undertook welfare and education functions, even if with contradictory
results and for contradictory reasons. The state was no longer simply police, courts, jails,
and the military. By the end of the century there were some 200 nation-states, possess-
ing radically different levels of autonomy in the transnational corporate era, and various
kinds of interstate "regimes" were emerging even as the Soviet bloc disintegrated (with
the EU, NAFTA, and the WTO in the lead). The public's experience of the negatives
of state bureaucracies had provided fertile soil for thatcherite and reaganite antistatism
and the fetishism of market forces, which began in earnest in the 1980s.

It was a different planet. Yet the attempt to hold at the center of one's political vision a marriage of justice, freedom, and organized activism to those ends can hardly be
dismissed as irrelevant. These are not the only features of anarchist thinking worth noting, some of which have certainly moved on from the earlier anarchist period. Nevertheless, let us briefly examine them, recalling that there is no anarchist canon except as
regards the broadest of principles (freedom, justice, activism), and then apply them to
the Indymedia movement as it has developed since 1999.

Three ongoing principles of socialist anarchist thinking that especially deserve attention are the priority given to *movements* over institutions, the attention given to *prefigurative* political activity, and the place allocated to *direct* action.

The first is the logical corollary of anarchism's deep distrust of the state, though as suggested above we also have to ask whether that distrust might not more usefully be conditional than absolute.

Prefigurative politics have been nicely defined by D. T. Wieck and by David Porter, and I will rely on their words to indicate what the term means:

> Anarchism proposes the continuous realization of freedom in the lives of each and all, both for its intrinsic and immediate values and for its more remote effects, the latter unpredictable because they depend on the unpredictable behavior of persons not known and of non-personal historical circumstances. (Wieck, 1979: 144)

> Any liberated areas, however limited, are a challenge to the capitalist order. The challenge lies in their visceral resistance to and struggle against the system, and in their offering time and space for potentially less sublimated behaviors. . . . Such zones sustain the energies of militants. (Porter, 1979: 223–24)

Hakim Bey (1991: 95–141), similarly, has argued for the notion of Temporary Autonomous Zones, places or activities in which for a while people may live and work as though many of capitalism's priorities and the state's restrictions do not apply. Like Jon Purkis (1997: 141–42), who refers to the "fairytale illusion of the nineteenth-century European insurrectionary model," Bey denounces what he sees as the quasi-suicidal strategy of seeking to overthrow the state and the hopelessly compromising tactic of trying to infiltrate it. Alan O'Connor's (2002) account of Who's Emma? (a Toronto queer punk record store) both evocatively describes one such project and addresses the conceptual issues involved.

These zones do not equal political quiescence, however. As Lindsay Hart (1997: 52) proposes in his discussion of direct action,

> An anarchist perspective of civil disobedience goes further than one which merely calls for the powers that be to respond to direct action in a positive way, so that the direct action can ultimately cease. Instead, anarchists believe that political activism goes beyond the instrumentalism of the State and established channels, and that the purpose of direct action is to create organizational and social structures which can and do exist outside of and beyond the State.

Thus these three aspects of socialist anarchist thought—the priority of movements over institutions, prefigurative politics, and direct action—are intimately linked.

Today's anarchists, while no more tightly unified than before, are likely also to have at the center of their thinking such issues as ecology and feminism (Bookchin, 1989), how to operate in relation to popular and mass culture (Davies, 1997; Goaman and Dodson, 1997; Rosen, 1997), how to gain influence over private and government land development initiatives (Ward, 1982), and how to respond to globalization and consumerism (Purkis, 1997). By and large, the expectation of a cataclysmic revolution that will usher in a radically new and constructive world has rightly ebbed away. The long haul is here for good, with no quick fixes.

However, this does not preserve anarchists, or many of them, from continuing negatives: their tendency toward Manichean political thinking; their habit of seeing danger from capitalism and the state, but not from within the public itself in its own collective action (an implicitly perfectionist view of human beings); the weakness, at least until recently, of their international analyses; and not least, their tremendous vagueness about how to sustain levels of economic functioning that would maintain acceptable standards of mass global health care, even in a noncapitalist or postmarket economy.

It is useful at this point to import some of the perspectives in Foucault's work into our discussion. Todd May (1994) has argued that Foucault, along with Deleuze and Guattari, developed a "poststructuralist" anarchism. The core of May's argument appears to be deduced from Foucault's emphases on (1) the potential of power to make things happen, rather than simply stopping them from happening by repressing them, and (2) the diffuseness of power, the error of seeing it as purely located in capital and the state. Foucault's argument about the diffuseness of power has sometimes been caricatured, as though he no longer perceived capital and the state as having any power; but this would hardly explain the work he put in on reforming French higher education in consultation with the Ministry of Education, or the cracked rib he received from a police baton in one of the many militant street demonstrations in which he joined. At the same time, his acknowledgment of the micro-circuits of social and cultural power and the necessity to defy them on that level is one that works well in relation to socialist anarchist thought, helping to expand it beyond some of its traditional positions.

It is at all these points on the compass, positive and negative, that the emergence of the Independent Media Centers suggests, and perhaps provides, a major step forward. Let us see why.

The IMC Movement, Communication, and Strategy-Building

There is always a danger in getting overenthused about a new development, and Independent Media Centers, at the time of this writing, certainly qualified as new. It is possible that just as they sprang up like mushrooms after the 1999 Seattle confrontation, so they might melt away, though the heavy-handedness of transnational corporations and police suppression of peaceful anticorporate street protests were likely to demonstrate without further ado how much they are needed. Nonetheless, even were IMCs to vanish, the experience of their activities would continue to be important to understand.

Systematic studies of anarchist media are relatively few;[7] many accounts of anarchist history refer to them in passing, but often more for evidence of political content than in their own right.[8] Although Lily Litvak (1995) presents an absorbing account of the intricacies of readership practices and of both content and layout in the Spanish anarchist press, there has been a fairly frequent tendency among anarchists, it would seem, to assume that the media communication process is relatively unproblematic. The working public simply needed to hear the message and then it would act, instantaneously. Or governments and mainstream media were perceived as "systematic poisoners, interested stupefiers of the popular masses."[9] This naïve model of the media communication process can hardly survive the scrutiny of a Gramscian-influenced Cultural Studies, or Foucault, and indeed Jude Davies (1997) makes a strong pitch for the relevance of a Cultural Studies perspective and of Situationism for anarchist cultural politics.

The IMCs have not described themselves as anarchist, although some, like Indymedia Nigeria, have been strongly in tune with eco-anarchism. In terms of tight definitions, therefore, they do not fully fit the bill. Nonetheless, they fit it better than any other working model of media activist politics, inasmuch as they typically did not ally themselves with any particular political group with a claim to absolute truth but, rather, sought to be of service to a variety of anticorporate tendencies engaged in direct action and publication. There was no ambition to be any kind of Leninist directing center, any more than there was interest in allying IMC work with any mainstream political party. The IMCs were self-managed, and linked to each other in a voluntary Malatesta-style federation. Their only apparent uniformity was in webpage layout, which was reproduced rather systematically on the Seattle model; but this had to do with the simplicity and speed of taking over an existing design, which would also be compatible in terms of its hyperlinks with the other IMC sites. The Seattle site, as the oldest and with one of the biggest teams, inevitably wielded particular influence in the first few years, but nevertheless shunned functioning as any kind of authoritative Curia.

Building on a long prior experience of grassroots organizing (Kidd, 2002), the Seattle IMC functioned during the WTO protests as a voluntary communications center.[10] Around 100 independent videographers roamed the streets during the confrontations, working inside the demonstrations, not on the other side of the police lines as mainstream journalists mostly do, and so were able to capture the reasons people were there in their own words, as well as the traumas they faced from the police. They got the full story, in other words, not the "violent anti-trade flat-earthers" story that widely circulated in mainstream accounts.[11] Others—still photographers, audio-recordists, print and Web journalists—joined the videographers in these micro-circuits of power by downloading their materials onto the servers in the IMC's temporary site, which could then be immediately transmitted to other machines at a distance. Those who wished could leave their materials for use by documentarians seeking to provide various kinds of records of the event, such as emerged not long after: Seattle Indymedia's *Showdown In Seattle* (2000), Big Noise Films' *This Is What Democracy Looks Like* (2000), and the Paper Tiger Television series.

The Seattle story, like most of the other IMC genesis stories, fused the global and the local, and in the months and years that followed, this constant admixture characterized the daily and weekly postings on the Indymedia site. As such, it represented an important gain in media activism, which all too easily opts for one over the other, admittedly sometimes for lack of resources to cover the international level. Yet the combination of dual-level coverage with hyperlinks to all the other IMCs as well as to numerous other activist groups around the world, provided an extraordinary freeway to users to connect up political, economic, and cultural issues as needed, or simply to explore, and thereby intensify their state of information.

Furthermore, there was an opportunity for constant dialogue on a level much more vital and immediate than that of the relatively stodgy newspaper readers' letters format. This dialogue could also be and frequently was international, and constituted part of the ongoing available analysis of the current global conjuncture, whether related to war in the "Middle East," to exploitative trade and labor practices, or to ongoing crises such as the AIDS pandemic. The discussion in most if not all IMCs was very open, although after much internal debate the Seattle IMC found itself compelled to respond to neo-Nazi attempts to flood its discussions by hiving off those postings to a separate file where they could be examined if users wished.

The Seattle website (seattle.indymedia.org/policy), like others, constantly invited contributions. Here is how it did so, as of fall 2002:

> The IMC newswire is designed to empower individuals to become independent and civic journalists by providing a direct, unmoderated forum for presenting media, including text articles, audio and video recordings, and photographs, to the public via the internet. Within that general framework, we specifically encourage individuals to publish:
>
> - Researched, timely articles;
> - Eyewitness accounts of progressive actions and demonstrations;
> - Coverage of Seattle/Northwest regional issues;
> - Media analysis;
> - Investigative reports exposing injustice;
> - Stories on events affecting underrepresented groups;
> - Media produced from within underrepresented groups;
> - Local stories with national or global significance;
> - Stories on people or projects working towards social justice.

One of the most significant innovations of the Seattle site was the construction of an archive of discussions, labeled Process, about strategy and tactics during the course of both direct-action campaigns against corporate globalization and the development of the IMC's own modus operandi. The term "archive" sounds pretty dry and dusty, but its importance in the contemporary political context is signal.

As I argued above, there is much to learn from twentieth-century experience of contesting power, but much of it is also negative, going in directions that would have been far better not taken. In the meantime, because of the hegemony of the "seemingly practical," much experience that did not fit inside the anti-utopian realisms of Leninism or social democracy, including socialist anarchist, feminist, cooperative, ecological, and—thank goodness!—*unclassifiable* political movement stories, floated away on the tides, and is now accessible only in dusty back numbers of forgotten publications and in oral history interviews with aged political veterans.

Thus having a nonsectarian open archive that can be accessed easily, retaining arguments *over* time in the language *of* the time about how to organize contestation and media activism most effectively, represented a vital forward move. The need perpetually to reinvent the wheel was correspondingly reduced. Corporate and government offices have their memory banks on disciplinary strategies, but the public movements challenging a whole range of negatives rarely, if ever, have generated their own archives.

This is what is particularly valuable now in a webpage format, where a variety of political experiences can be reviewed and shared even across nations and continents—and, moreover, on an ongoing basis. Socialist anarchism does not mean disorganization, as already underlined; rather, it entails organizational development against—and, so far as possible, outside—the hegemony of capital, the state, or organized religion. Historical memory of past campaigns, debates, and decisions is a vital part of that organizational development.

We do not know yet how to build a different world of a kind most of us would want to live in, only that the twentieth century offers more negative than positive illustrations. In the course of continuing to defy the powers that be, global and local, and by discussing our experiences of doing so through "glocal" counter-public spheres such as the Indymedia network, it is possible and even likely that constructive new ideas and perspectives will begin to germinate. It is virtually impossible to imagine their emergence other than through such an open and painstaking process.

Conclusion: The IMC Movement and Socialist Anarchism

Historically, socialist anarchist movements have had their own vices: sectarianism; Manicheism; naïveté concerning the public's universal instinctive addiction to cooperation, or concerning the necessary imminence of a decisive totalizing revolution; sometimes an aggressive economic reductionism (in the case of many anarcho-syndicalists). Even some of their virtues, as set out in this chapter, may seem to be more negative than positive: a necessary skepticism concerning the state, and toward transcendently correct revolutionary parties, thus avoiding the Bolsheviks' disastrous descent into Stalinism; a readiness to acknowledge that "democratic" parties of the Left play not only by the democratic rules but also often *anti*-democratic roles.

Yet certainly, too, there are positive virtues in this political tradition that need holding onto: a genuine interest in the public's interests and cultures; a passionate sense for the public's rightful sovereignty; a ferocious commitment to freedom in conjunction with, inseparably from, social justice; a vision of social units small enough for people to feel and exert a connection with decisions made in them; a vision of the potential for federated political structures; an internationalist commitment; a dedication to forms of learning and mental growth that dissolve traditional boundaries of gender, "race," and class, and are profoundly open to fresh perspectives; and, not least, a continual orientation toward forms of direct action, both to challenge injustice and to create those moments and locales which prefigure the reality that another world is possible.

In the light of these perspectives, the various opportunities brought into play by the Independent Media Center movement are grist to the socialist anarchist mill, and whether the term itself is used does not particularly matter. Systematic thinking about media and communication has not, so far as I know, been energetically pursued within many anarchist circles, although in artistic terms socialist anarchists have often figured prominently (Gustave Courbet, Camille Pissarro, and František Kupka, to mention only three particularly well-known names). But many anarchists have been fascinated by the potential of new technologies, and have embraced them enthusiastically (*pace* Mahatma Gandhi). The upsurge of Independent Media Centers, their openness, their blend of internationalism and localism, their use of hyperlinks, their self-management, represent a development entirely consonant with the best in the socialist anarchist tradition.

The IMCs are not heaven-sent. They are ours, us at work, to act as best we can to make them empowering agencies and fora—not uniquely so, but as part of the tapestry. As the Indymedia Italy site puts it: "Don't Hate the Media! *Become* the Media!"

Notes

1. From Ferrer's *The Origins and Ideals of the Modern School* (London: Watts, 1913), cited in Smith (1989: 222). I have taken the liberty of re-translating *hombres* in the original as "people."

2. Millett (1997) makes a valid observation in his attack on the historical welfare state—namely, that often it did not do much or even anything for the very poorest. But he goes about his case with a bludgeon rather than a scalpel and, in so doing, omits to consider those poor*er* people, very large in number, whose lives were enhanced by welfare measures. Nothing was perfect: The terrible tower blocks used to house them, whose construction greatly enriched building firms, are one of many cases of the contradictions involved. But the situation was contradictory, not just negative.

3. I include here, for brevity's sake, parties such as the Canadian Liberal Party and the U.S. Democratic Party, whose practical policy history has much in common with Social Democratic parties despite the difference in official ideologies. Of course, the specific histories of all these parties are both different and significant, but there is no space to explore those dimensions here.

4. I am aware that anarchists of the Left have long held to various terms to describe themselves, and "socialist" has not usually figured as one of them. But I am writing for a more general readership, for whom the term still has some sense attached to it of a generic concern for global social justice and freedom. Moreover, there is an individualistic anarchism of the Right—quite common in U.S. popular culture, for example—which therefore necessitates some qualifying adjective for the tradition discussed here.

5. For a lucid and fair account, though longer than I can offer here, see the "Introduction" to Goodway (1989: 1–22).

6. Pernicone (1993: 247) writes: "Utopian blueprints, a priori assumptions, abstract and rigid formulas—Malatesta eschewed them all. . . . Theoretical differences should be subordinated to the immediate demands of the common struggle against the state and bourgeois society." Absolutist doctrinal splits had bedeviled the anarchist movement in Italy, Spain, and Argentina.

7. See Atton's (2002: 80–156) study of British anarchist print media and Walter's (1971) study of an earlier phase from 1945–1970; Dickinson's (1997) study of the British local alternative press; the studies by Sakolsky and Dunifer (1997) and Soley (1999) of the U.S. free radio movement, and Kogawa's (1985) study of the Japanese micro-radio movement; and the studies of the Spanish anarchist press up to 1939 by Litvak (1995), López Campillo (1995), Salaün (1995), and Tavera i García (1995).

8. See, for example, Pernicone (1993: 243–46) and Krebs (1998: 117–48).

9. See Bakunin, cited by Davies (1997: 66). It is only fair to note that some anarchist journalists, such as the rather flamboyant Felipe Alaiz in the 1930s, complained bitterly of the "social prose" of publications with "neither vigor nor color . . . pale, plain, drab, without exuberance, without spice (*jugo*)" (Tavera i García, 1995: 389).

10. DeLuca and Peeples (2002) argue that, in fact, at the Seattle confrontation, dramatic violence enabled issues to be ventilated on television, which they suggest we term "the public

screen" (as opposed to Habermas's public sphere); and that the absence of such violence on the Tuesday (the third day), and at some subsequent top-level globalization policy get-togethers in other locations, was reflected in the lack of news coverage of trade policies on those occasions: "[The] emphasis [was] on the new, drama, conflict, objectivity, and compelling visuals, open up the public screen" (p. 136). Their claim for the political potential of telespectacle and the public screen is stimulating, if controversial. They do not make reference to the Seattle Indymedia operation.

11. Rojecki (2002) similarly argues from a study of U.S. op-ed commentaries, *USA Today,* and CBS TV News that major U.S. media were for the most part surprisingly open to the perspectives of the demonstrators, largely distinguishing the majority from "the anarchists" who smashed windows. I have screened some of the movement documentaries to various groups with often no prior interest in or commitment to the issues involved, and, indeed, my own sense is that an image of the events as one in which unruly crazies took over Seattle's streets has become pretty widespread, and that this image has since consistently stuck to movements contesting corporate globalization in the United States and elsewhere in the world. A difficulty in resolving these seeming contradictions comes from our lack of information as to how op-ed commentary in major dailies influences whom.

References

Alves de Seixas, Jacy (1992). *Mémoire et Oubli: anarchisme et syndicalisme révolutionnaire au Brésil.* Paris: Éditions de la Maison des Sciences de l'Homme.

Archinov, Pierre (2001). *La Makhnovchtchina: l'insurrection révolutionnaire en Ukraine de 1918 à 1921.* Paris: Spartacus.

Atton, Chris (2002). *Alternative Media.* London: Sage Publications Co.

Avrich, Paul (1973). *Anarchists in the Russian Revolution.* London: Thames & Hudson.

Bey, Hakim (1991). *T.A.Z.: The Temporary Autonomous Zone, Ontological Anarchy, Poetic Terrorism.* New York: Autonomedia.

Bookchin, Murray (1989). "New Social Movements: The Anarchic Dimension," in David Goodway (ed.), *For Anarchism: History, Theory and Practice,* pp. 259–74. New York: Routledge.

Cahill, Tom (1989). "Cooperatives and Anarchism: A Contemporary Perspective," in David Goodway (ed.), *For Anarchism: History, Theory and Practice,* pp. 235–58. New York: Routledge.

Crowder, George (1991). *Classical Anarchism: The Political Thought of Godwin, Proudhon, Bakunin and Kropotkin.* Oxford: Clarendon Press.

Davies, Jude (1997). "Anarchy in the UK? Anarchism and Popular Culture in 1990s Britain," in Jon Purkis and James Bowen (eds.), *Twenty-First Century Anarchism: Unorthodox Ideas for a New Millennium,* pp. 68–82. London: Cassell.

DeLuca, Kevin M., and Peeples, Jennifer (2002). "From Public Sphere to Public Screen: Democracy, Activism, and the 'Violence' of Seattle," *Critical Studies in Media Communication* 19(2): 125–51.

Dickinson, Robert (1997). *Imprinting the Sticks: The Alternative Press beyond London.* Aldershot, U.K.: Ashgate Publishing Ltd.

Dirlik, Arif (1991). *Anarchism in the Chinese Revolution.* Berkeley: University of California Press.

Downing, John (2001). *Radical Media: Rebellious Communication and Social Movements.* Thousand Oaks, Calif.: Sage Publications Inc.

——— (2002a). "Independent Media Centers: A Multi-Local, Multi-Media Challenge to Global Neo-Liberalism," in Marc Raboy (ed.), *Global Media Policy in the New Millennium,* pp. 215–32. Luton, U.K.: University of Luton Press.

—— (2002b). "The Indymedia Phenomenon: Space-Place-Democracy and the New Independent Media Centers," presented at the BOGUES: Globalisme et Pluralisme conference in the University of Québec, Montréal, April 2002. Available online at www.er.uqam.ca/nobel/gricis/even/bog2001/b2_pr_f.htm. Last accessed in August 2002.

—— (2003). "The IMC Movement beyond the West," in Andy Opel and Donnalyn Pompper (eds.), *Representing Resistance: Media, Civil Disobedience, and the Anti-Globalization Movement.*, pp. 296–317. Greenwood, Conn.: Greenwood Publishing Group.

Egerton, John (1994). *Speak Now Against the Day: The Generation before the Civil Rights Movement in the South.* Chapel Hill: University of North Carolina Press.

Fetherling, George (1998). *The Gentle Anarchist: A Life of George Woodcock.* Seattle/Vancouver: University of Washington Press/Douglas & McIntyre.

Goaman, Karen, and Dodson, Mo (1997). "A Subversive Current? Contemporary Anarchism Considered," in Jon Purkis and James Bowen (eds.), *Twenty-First Century Anarchism: Unorthodox Ideas for a New Millennium,* pp. 83–98. London: Cassell.

Goldman, Emma (1969). *Anarchism and Other Essays.* New York: Dover.

—— (1970). *Living My Life.* New York: Dover.

Goodway, David (ed.) (1989). *For Anarchism: History, Theory and Practice.* New York: Routledge.

Guérin, Daniel (1989). "Marxism and Anarchism," in David Goodway (ed.), *For Anarchism: History, Theory and Practice,* pp. 109–26. New York: Routledge.

Hart, Lindsay (1997). "In Defence of Radical Direct Action: Reflections on Civil Disobedience, Sabotage and Nonviolence," in Jon Purkis and James Bowen (eds.), *Twenty-First Century Anarchism: Unorthodox Ideas for a New Millennium,* pp. 41–59. London: Cassell.

Hofmann, Bert, Joan i Tous, Pere, and Tietz, Manfred (eds.) (1995). *El Anarquismo Español: sus tradiciones culturales.* Frankfurt a.M./Madrid: Vervuert/Iberoamericana.

Kidd, Dorothy (2002). "Which Would You Rather: Seattle or Porto Alegre?" Paper presented at the second Our Media Not Theirs IAMCR Preconference, Barcelona, July 2002. Available online at faculty.menlo.edu/~jhiggins/ourmedia. Last accessed in August 2002.

Kogawa, Tetsuo (1985). "Free Radio in Japan," in Douglas Kahn and Diane Neumaier (eds.), *Cultures in Contention,* pp. 116–21. Seattle: Real Comet Press.

Krebs, Edward S. (1998). *Shifu, Soul of Chinese Anarchism.* Lanham, Md.: Rowman & Littlefield.

Levy, Carl (1989). "Italian Anarchism, 1870–1926," in David Goodway (ed.), *For Anarchism: History, Theory and Practice,* pp. 24–78. New York: Routledge.

Litvak, Lily (1995). "La prensa anarquista 1880–1913," in Bert Hofmann, Pere Joan i Tous, and Manfred Tietz (eds.), *El Anarquismo Español: sus tradiciones culturales,* pp. 215–36. Frankfurt a.M./Madrid: Vervuert/Iberoamericana..

López Campillo, Evelyne (1995). "Vanguardia burguesa y cultura anarquista en la *Revista Blanca* (1923–1936)," in Bert Hofmann, Pere Joan i Tous, and Manfred Tietz (eds.), *El Anarquismo Español: sus tradiciones culturales,* pp. 237–42. Frankfurt a.M./Madrid: Vervuert/Iberoamericana.

Marelli, Gianfranco (1998). *L'Amère Victoire du Situationnisme: pour une histoire critique de l'Internationale Situationniste (1957–1972).* Paris: Éditions Sulliver.

Marshall, Peter (1992). *Demanding the Impossible: A History of Anarchism.* New York: HarperCollins.

May, Todd (1994). *The Political Philosophy of Poststructuralist Anarchism.* University Park: Pennsylvania State University Press.

Millett, Steve (1997). "Neither State nor Market: An Anarchist Perspective on Social Welfare," in Jon Purkis and James Bowen (eds.), *Twenty-First Century Anarchism: Unorthodox Ideas for a New Millennium,* pp. 24–40. London: Cassell.

O'Connor, Alan (2002). *Who's Emma? Autonomous Zones and Social Anarchism.* Toronto: Confused Editions.

Ostergaard, Geoffrey (1989). "Indian Anarchism: The Curious Case of Vinoba Bhave, Anarchist 'Saint of the Government,'" in David Goodway (ed.), *For Anarchism: History, Theory and Practice*, pp. 201–216. New York: Routledge.

Payne, Charles M. (1995). *I've Got the Light of Freedom: The Organizing Tradition and the Mississippi Freedom Struggle*. Berkeley: University of California Press.

Pelletier, Philippe (2001). "Un oublié du consensus: l'anarchosyndicalisme au Japon de 1911 à 1934," in *De l'Histoire du Mouvement Ouvrier Révolutionnaire*. Actes de colloque international "Pour un autre Futur." Paris: Nautilus, CNT. 173–225.

Pernicone, Nunzio (1993). *Italian Anarchism, 1864–1892*. Princeton: Princeton University Press.

Porter, David (1979). "Revolutionary Realization: The Motivational Energy," in W. J. Ehrlich (ed.), *Reinventing Anarchy*, pp. 214–28. London: Routledge & Kegan Paul.

Préposiet, Jean (2002). *Histoire de l'Anarchisme*, 2nd ed. Paris: Tallandier.

Purkis, Jon (1997). "The Responsible Anarchist: Transport, Consumerism and the Future," in Jon Purkis and James Bowen (eds.), *Twenty-First Century Anarchism: Unorthodox Ideas for a New Millennium*, pp. 134–50. London: Cassell.

Purkis, Jon, and Bowen, James (eds.) (1997). *Twenty-First Century Anarchism: Unorthodox Ideas for a New Millennium*. London: Cassell.

Quail, John (1978). *The Slow Burning Fuse*. London: Flamingo.

Rider, Nick (1989). "The Practice of Direct Action: The Barcelona Rent Strike of 1931," in David Goodway (ed.), *For Anarchism: History, Theory and Practice*, pp. 79–105. New York: Routledge.

Rojecki, Andrew (2002). "Modernism, State Sovereignty and Dissent: Media and the New Post–Cold War movements," *Critical Studies in Media Communication* 19(2): 152–72.

Rosen, Paul (1997). "'It Was Easy, It Was Cheap, Go Do It!' Technology and Anarchy in the UK Music Industry," in Jon Purkis and James Bowen (eds.), *Twenty-First Century Anarchism: Unorthodox Ideas for a New Millennium*, pp. 99–116. London: Cassell..

Sakolsky, Ron, and Dunifer, Steve (eds.) (1997). *Seizing the Airwaves: A Free Radio Handbook*. Edinburgh/San Francisco: AK Press.

Salaün, Serge (1995). "Teoría y práctica del lenguaje anarquista o la imposible redención por el verbo," in Bert Hofmann, Pere Joan i Tous, and Manfred Tietz (eds.), *El Anarquismo Español: sus tradiciones culturales*, pp. 323–33. Frankfurt a.M./Madrid: Vervuert/Iberoamericana.

Smith, Michael (1989). "Kropotkin and Technical Education: An Anarchist Voice," in David Goodway (ed.), *For Anarchism: History, Theory and Practice*, pp. 217–34. New York: Routledge..

Soley, Larry (1999). *Free Radio: Electronic Civil Disobedience*. Boulder, Colo.: Westview.

Tavera i García, Susanna (1995). "Revolucionarios, publicistas y bohemios: los periodistas anarquistas (1918–1936)," in Bert Hofmann, Pere Joan i Tous, and Manfred Tietz (eds.), *El Anarquismo Español: sus tradiciones culturales*, pp. 377–92. Frankfurt a.M./Madrid: Vervuert/Iberoamericana.

Viénet, Ren (1992). *Enragés and Situationists in the Occupation Movement, France, May '68*. New York: Autonomedia.

Walter, Nicholas (1971). "Anarchism in Print: Yesterday and Today," in David E. Apter and James Joll (eds.), *Anarchism Today*, pp. 147–68. London: MacMillan Press.

Ward, Colin (1982). *Anarchy in Action*. London: Freedom Press.

Wieck, D. T. (1979). "The Negativity of Anarchism," in W. J. Ehrlich (ed.), *Reinventing Anarchy*, pp. 138–55. London: Routledge & Kegan Paul.

Zarrow, Peter (1990). *Anarchism and Chinese Political Culture*. New York: Columbia University Press.

CHAPTER 16

The Gay Global Village in Cyberspace

Larry Gross

A half-century ago homosexuality was still the love that dared not speak its name: It was a crime throughout the United States (whereas today it is criminalized in eighteen states) and in most countries around the world. Newspapers and magazines referred to homosexuals only in the context of police arrests or political purges, as in a 1953 headline: "State Department Fires 531 Perverts, Security Risks." Hollywood operated under the Motion Picture Production Code, which prohibited the presentation of explicitly lesbian or gay characters and ensured that any implied homosexual characters would be either villains or victims (Gross, 2001).

The emergence of a gay movement in the United States in the 1950s coincided with the societal transformations wrought by television and the increasing centrality of communications technologies in American society. In this post–World War II America, lesbian women and gay men began, with difficulty, to create alternative channels of communication that would foster solidarity and cultivate the emergence of a self-conscious community. Typically, the first alternative channels to appear were those with low entry barriers, minimal technological needs, and relatively low operating costs. Indeed, newspapers and magazines have long been the principal media created and consumed by minority groups. In recent decades, new technologies have made it possible for anyone with a video camera and a computer to produce fictional and nonfiction programs. But the problem of distribution remains a major hurdle, and most independent films rarely break out of the festival ghetto; those that do are likely to be confined to subscription cable channels. The balance of power shifted somewhat with the emergence of the Internet, which utilizes a relatively cheap technology to provide Web-based news and magazine sites, chat lines, bulletin boards, and mail networks. For the first time, it seems, control over the means of reproduction has been placed in the hands of ordinary citizens—the residents of cyberspace.

"Cyberspace" is a term first introduced in 1981 by science-fiction writer William Gibson to describe the newly emerging electronic frontier now widely referred to as the Internet. Cyberspace offers an electronic *agora* that comes close to a level playing field of information and opinion. It also guarantees a cacophony of competing voices in which your message may suffer the fate of the tree falling in the forest with no one to hear it. The scarce commodity in this new world is not information but attention. However, for all the blooming, buzzing confusion of cyberspace, it is possible to navigate as well as surf, to find information, and to make friends and influence people.

New media create opportunities for the formation of new communities, and the Internet is no exception. In contrast to most other modern media the Internet offers opportunities for individual engagement both as senders and receivers, permitting the coalescing of interest-based networks spanning vast distances. The potential for friendship and group formation provided by the Internet is particularly valuable for members of self-identified minorities who are scattered and often besieged in their home surroundings. A brief tour of the Web will reveal countless sites devoted to specialized interests that draw like-minded participants across national and international boundaries. Notable among the interests served by this (so far) uniquely egalitarian and open medium of communication are those represented by sexual minorities.

Queers were among the first to realize the potential of this new technology. As an Associated Press story put it, "It's the unspoken secret of the online world that gay men and lesbians are among the most avid, loyal and plentiful commercial users of the Internet" (24 June 1996). Not surprisingly, it wasn't long before entrepreneurs began to develop this promising tract of electronic real estate. An explanation was offered by Tom Rielly, the founder of *Planet Out,* an electronic media company that began on the Microsoft Network in 1995: "Traditional mass media is very cost-intensive. Gays and lesbians don't have a high level of ownership of mainstream media properties. The Internet is the first medium where we can have equal footing with the big players" (Rielly, quoted in Lewis, 1995: D3). For Rielly and his financial backers, the attractions of marketing to a large and underserved group were obvious. But cyberspace also provides "a gathering point for millions of lesbians, gay men, bisexuals, transvestites and others who may be reluctant to associate in public" (Rielly, quoted in Lewis, 1995: D3). For those who are, with or without good reason, afraid to visit gay establishments or subscribe to gay publications, "gay online services bring the gay community into their homes, where they're shielded from their neighbors and coworkers" (Associated Press, 24 June 1996).

The queer cybernaut who sets sail guided by the many search engines available on the Internet will readily find a wealth of information and organizational resources. The Queer Resources Directory, for example, offers a structured map of topics and areas housing files and links to other sites. Among the national organizations in the United States that can be reached via the Internet are the National Gay and Lesbian Task Force, the Gay and Lesbian Alliance Against Defamation (GLAAD), the Human Rights Campaign, and Parents and Friends of Lesbians and Gays (P-FLAG), as well as several specifically electronic magazines and cyber-versions of print magazines. Beyond the organizations and the electronic magazines lies the vast territory of the "chat rooms" and bulletin-board discussion groups. "On any given evening, one-third of all the member-created chat rooms on America Online are devoted to gay topics" (Associated Press, 24 June 1996).

Queer Teens as Demographic Niche

The changing circumstances of gay people in the 1990s led quite predictably to the emergence of media products not only produced by gay people themselves, which after all had been the case since the start of the gay liberation movement (then called the homophile movement) in the 1950s, but also targeted at segments not previously addressed so directly. Notable among these are gay youth, who have been generally avoided—both as customers and subjects—by media wary of the accusation of "recruiting" or seducing the innocent.

XY, a San Francisco–based magazine for gay male teens, was founded in 1996; by 2002 it boasted: "We sell over 60,000 copies per issue and have more than 200,000 readers from all over the world. Our average reader age is 22, according to our last reader survey, and *XY* is officially targeted toward 12–29 yo [year-old] young gay men." The magazine's twenty-four-year-old editor told the *San Francisco Chronicle,* "I don't think there's a magazine in the country that means more to its readers. I say that because we're dealing specifically with a demographic of gay teenagers who are not living in L.A. or New York, or some place where being gay is accepted. There's really no other forum for them to read about that experience." The magazine's price—$7.95 per issue and $29 for a six-issue subscription, in 2002—might be a deterrent to many in the magazine's target audiences. A competing magazine, *Joey,* was modeled on mainstream teen magazines such as *Seventeen I* (Fisher, 2000). The first issue of *Joey* included a Frequently Asked Questions (FAQ) section including: "I'm not out to my parents, so I don't want to have *Joey* delivered to my house. So how do I get the magazine?" The answer wasn't likely to reassure potential subscribers: "*Joey* is mailed in a very plain business-like envelope. If your parents are violating your privacy and opening your mail for you, then you have our sympathies." *Joey* did not survive long, and left the field to *XY.*

If the success of magazines for lesbian and gay teens is limited by steep prices and prying parents, the Internet offers most young people readier access and greater privacy (those without access to computers and the Internet are also less likely to have the money for a subscription to *XY*). The website for *XY,* in fact, offers much more than enticements to subscribe to the magazine, order back issues, or buy such tempting merchandise as "glamourous laminated cardboard containers to neatly store your *XY* issues ... only $12" or a $5 *XY* bumper sticker. The section called *Bois* contains personal "profiles"—called "peeps"—submitted by young men after they type in their name, e-mail address, and age (the site pledges that complete privacy will be maintained). As of August 2002 there were 13,559 profiles listed on the site, many of them containing photographs. Scanning through the lists—it is possible to specify location and to view only those profiles that contain pictures—one discovers that the listings are far from evenly distributed across the United States and beyond. Still, the numbers are often impressive, as is the geographical dispersion. Alabama listed 132 peeps (35 with photos) and Montana had 60 (17 photos), whereas Chicago boasted 390 (193 photos). Outside the United States the patterns are probably predictable, with Toronto offering 175 peeps (86 photos), London 54 (18 photos), and Australia 104 (24 photos). Once we leave the English-speaking world, the numbers fall off, as would be expected. There are 28 listed in Germany (12 with pictures, and some of these would appear to be older than the target age), 8 in France (3 photos), 7 in Japan (4 photos), and only 1 in China, without a picture.

While there is no lesbian equivalent of *XY,* the most successful lesbian magazine, *Curve,* includes on its website extensive "personals" listings, with and without photographs, that specify ages beginning at eighteen (and going up to ninety, although there seem to be only two listers above seventy). In the section called "community," discussions are posted under many group and topic headings, including, for instance, "Baby Dykes—Youth Hangout."

Sites run by magazines are only the tip of the Internet iceberg, however, when it comes to opportunities to post personal ads and engage in conversation. Despite a slant toward the interests of those old enough to get into bars and spend more money, the major gay websites appear to be accessible to gay teens. *PlanetOut,* the largest commercial gay site, boasting over 350,000 personal ads that seem to range from fifteen to the early sixties, is likely to attract the attention of many teenagers looking for information, connections, and for many, no doubt, sex. There are, in addition, sites specifically developed for gay youth—such as *OutProud, Oasis,* and *Mogenic*—that combine support, counseling, and information with news and links to other youth-oriented sites.

Growing Up Gay in Cyberspace

In today's world, young people grow up reading words and seeing images that previous generations never encountered, and few can remain unaware of the existence of lesbian and gay people. Yet despite the dramatic increase in the public visibility of gay people in nearly all domains of our public culture, most young lesbian, gay, bisexual, and transgendered people still find themselves isolated and vulnerable. Their experiences and concerns are not reflected in the formal curricula of schools or in our society's informal curriculum, the mass media. For these teenagers the Internet is a godsend, and thousands are using computer networks to declare their homosexuality, meet, and seek support from other gay youths.

"Does anyone else feel like you're the only gay guy on the planet, or at least in Arlington, Texas?" When seventeen-year-old Ryan Matthew posted that question on AOL in 1995, he received more than 100 supportive e-mail messages (Gabriel, 1995). The stories that fly through the ether make all too clear that the Internet can literally be a lifesaver for many queer teens trapped in enemy territory:

> JohnTeen Ø (John Erwin's AOL name) is a new kind of gay kid, a 16-year-old not only out, but already at home in the online convergence of activists that Tom Rielly, the co-founder of Digital Queers, calls the "Queer Global Village." Just 10 years ago, most queer teens hid behind a self-imposed don't-ask-don't-tell policy until they shipped out to Oberlin or San Francisco, but the Net has given even closeted kids a place to conspire. Though the Erwins' house is in an unincorporated area of Santa Clara County in California, with goats and llamas foraging in the backyard, John's access to AOL's gay and lesbian forum enables him to follow dispatches from queer activists worldwide, hone his writing, flirt, try on disposable identities, and battle bigots—all from his home screen. (Silberman, 1994: 1)

> Kali is an 18-year-old lesbian at a university in Colorado. Her name means "fierce" in Swahili. Growing up in California, Kali was the leader of a young women's chapter of the Church of Jesus Christ of Latter-day Saints. She was also the "Girl Saved by E-mail," whose story ran last spring on CNN. After

mood swings plummeted her into a profound depression, Kali—like too many gay teens—considered suicide. Her access to GayNet at school gave her a place to air those feelings, and a phone call from someone she knew online saved her life. Kali is now a regular contributor to Sappho, a women's board she most appreciates because there she is accepted as an equal. "They forgive me for being young," Kali laughs, "though women come out later than guys, so there aren't a lot of teen lesbians. But it's a high of connection. We joke that we're posting to 500 of our closest friends." (Silberman, 1994: 1)

Jay won't be going to his senior prom. He doesn't make out in his high school corridor the way other guys do with their girlfriends. He doesn't receive the kind of safe-sex education at school that he feels he should. He can never fully relax when he's speaking. He worries that he'll let something slip, that the kids at his Long Island high school will catch on. He'd rather not spend his days at school being beaten up and called a faggot. It's not like that on the Internet. "It's hard having always to watch what you say," said Jay, which is not his real name. "It's like having a filter that you turn on when you're at school. You have to be real careful you don't say what you're thinking or look at a certain person the wrong way. But when I'm around friends or on the Net, the filter comes off." For many teenagers, the Internet is a fascinating, exciting source of information and communication. For gay teenagers like Jay, 17, it's a lifeline. The moment the modem stops screeching and the connection is made to the Net, the world of a gay teenager on Long Island can change dramatically. The fear of being beaten up and the long roads and intolerant views that separate teens lose their impact. (McAllester, 1997: 84)

Jeffrey knew of no homosexuals in his high school or in his small town in the heart of the South. He prayed that his errant feelings were a phase. But as the truth gradually settled over him, he told me last summer during a phone conversation punctuated by nervous visits to his bedroom door to make sure no family member was listening in, he became suicidal. "I'm a Christian—I'm like, how could God possibly do this to me?" he said. He called a crisis line for gay teenagers, where a counselor suggested he attend a gay support group in a city an hour and a half away. But being 15, he was too young to drive and afraid to enlist his parents' help in what would surely seem a bizarre and suspicious errand. It was around this time that Jeffrey first typed the words "gay" and "teen" into a search engine on the computer he'd gotten a few months before and was staggered to find himself aswirl in a teeming online gay world, replete with resource centers, articles, advice columns, personals, chat rooms, message boards, porn sites and—most crucially—thousands of closeted and anxious kids like himself. That discovery changed his life. (Egan, 2000: 110)

Without unfettered access to the Internet at Multnomah County Public Library, 16-year-old Emmalyn Rood testified Tuesday, she might not have found courage to tell her mother she was gay. "I was able to become so much more comfortable with myself," Rood told a special three-judge panel weighing the constitutionality of the Children's Internet Protection Act. "I basically found people I could talk to. I didn't have anybody I could talk to in real life." In the summer of 1999, Rood was a freshman at Portland's Wilson

High School, confused about her sexual identity but eager to learn. Today, she is attending a Massachusetts college and is a determined plaintiff in a lawsuit aimed at scuttling the new federal law, which she said would have hindered her search. (Barnett, 2002)

Similar accounts abound, not only in the United States but in many other parts of the world. Sometimes, as in the case of Israeli gay teenagers interviewed by Lilach Nir, online discussions offered them contact and confirmation unavailable to them in their "real" environments of smaller cities, rural villages, and kibbutzim. While one of the clichés of computer-mediated communication is that one can hide one's true identity, so "that nobody knows you're 15 and live in Montana and are gay" (Gabriel, 1995), it is also true, as Nir's informants told her, that in their Internet Relay Chat (IRC) conversations they "are unmasking the covers they are forced to wear in their straight daily lives" (Nir, 1998).

Beyond the Anecdotes

In September and October of 2000 an online survey was conducted by two of the largest websites serving lesbian, gay, bisexual, and transgendered youth: (1) OutProud, an arm of the National Coalition for Gay, Lesbian, Bisexual and Transgender Youth, founded in 1993 to provide advocacy, information, resources, and support to in-the-closet and openly queer teens through America Online and the Internet, and (2) Oasis Magazine, which came online in December 1995. The survey, authored by OutProud director Chris Kryzan, was advertised on the two sponsoring sites, as well as on several other youth-oriented websites and, as it turned out, two sites devoted to gay and lesbian erotica. The survey was completed by 7,884 respondents, of whom 6,872, aged twenty-five or under, constituted the primary sample.

The survey permitted respondents of any age to complete the form, thus hopefully discouraging older respondents from presenting themselves as younger in order to participate. Obviously, respondent age, like anything else queried over the Internet, is subject to falsification, but there seems little reason to imagine that many people would be moved to spend an average of thirty-eight minutes pretending to be something they're not. Nearly 60 percent of those beginning the survey completed it. As the researchers discovered mid-way, slightly more than half of the respondents (60 percent of the males) entered the survey site from an erotic stories site targeted at gay males; however, there were no systematic differences in respondents corresponding to the point of entry. This pattern does, however, reveal something about the importance of erotic content sites for gay youth, who aren't likely to find similar erotic material in mainstream media, as well as giving further evidence of the centrality of pornography to the Internet's appeal. For queer youth, of course, pornography is often the only available source of the sort of sexual imagery and information widely available in the media for heterosexual youth.

While the respondents clearly do not constitute a probability sample from which one can generalize about queer youth—and, indeed, no such sample can ever be obtained for gay people, who remain largely hidden from the survey researcher's sampling frames—the size and diversity of the group do offer illuminating insights into the lives of queer youth and their relationships to the new communications technologies that came into the world as they were being born.[1]

The sample of respondents included 5,310 males, 1,412 females, and 150 individuals who identified as transgendered. The median age of the respondents was eighteen (the mode was seventeen), the median age reported for realizing that they were gay was thirteen, and the median age of accepting that they were gay was fifteen.[2] As might be expected, this is a group of young people who are familiar with the Internet: Nearly half of those sixteen and under and two-thirds of those twenty and over had been online for at least three years; fewer than 10 percent had been online less than one year. Over 90 percent of the respondents reported going online at least once a day, nearly half said several times per day. About 50 percent reported spending more than two hours online each day.[3] The most frequent activities online included: looking at specific sites, 28 percent (males more than females cited this—presumably "specific sites" include the erotica site from which so many respondents came to the survey); chatting, 24 percent; and e-mail, 20 percent (these last two were cited by females more than males). Unspecified surfing absorbed 20 percent, reading message boards, 2 percent. Downloading music, the Recording Industry Association of America (RIAA) would be relieved to learn, accounted for only 5 percent of reported time.

Given the makeup of this sample, one would expect the respondents' online experiences to be related to their sexuality. In fact, two-thirds of the respondents said that being online helped them accept their sexual orientation; and 35 percent, that being online was crucial to this acceptance. Not surprisingly, therefore, many said they came out online before doing so in "real life"—although this was much more the case for males (57 percent) than for females (38 percent), and also more the case for those who had spent more time online.

Connections online sometimes lead to real-life meetings: About half of the respondents reported such meetings, and 12 percent of the males (but only 4 percent of the females) said they met someone offline for the purpose of having sex. About a quarter of both males and females met someone "with the hope that we might become more than friends." In general, a quarter of the respondents said that they met the people they've dated online. It is good to know that 83 percent reported having enough knowledge of STDs to follow safer sex practices; nearly a third cited the Internet as their primary source for this information.

Queer youth often feel isolated and rarely have access to a supportive queer community in their vicinity. Sixty percent of the respondents said they did not feel as though they were part of the gay, lesbian, bisexual, and transgendered community; but 52 percent said they felt a sense of community with the people they've met online. Mass media, even minority media, do not necessarily provide a great deal of contact and support for these young people. Only 47 percent have bought a gay or lesbian magazine, and only two of these, the *Advocate*, the largest U.S. gay magazine, and *XY*, for young gay males, were read by as many as a fifth of the sample. Even fewer reported familiarity with *Oasis*, the longest-running online magazine for queer youth.

A frequent concern regarding the isolated and vulnerable situation facing many queer youth is that they are peculiarly vulnerable to suicide, and, indeed, it is commonly reported that the rate of attempted and completed suicides is disproportionately high among this group.[4] Among the online survey respondents, 40 percent of the females and 25 percent of the males reported seriously thinking about suicide sometimes or often; 30 percent of the females and 17 percent of the males said they had in fact tried to kill themselves (the median age for these attempts was fourteen). For queer teens the Internet can often be a lifeline: 32 percent of the females and 23 percent of the males in the sample said they've gone online when feeling suicidal, so that they would have someone understanding to talk to. Among those who reported frequent suicidal thoughts, 53 percent of the females and 57 percent of the males said they've gone online for this reason.

Electronic *Gemeinschaft*

It isn't only teenagers for whom the Internet can provide a lifeline and a bridge. Moving beyond the highly developed and fully furnished gay subcultures found in most western and westernized countries, emerging gay communities in many parts of the world have found the Internet a venue for solidarity and support.

In 1973, Canadian sociologist Benjamin Singer observed the impact of television on African Americans in the United States and suggested that "although mass media may have a conformative potential for majority groups, [television] possesses a transformative function for minority group identities." Singer saw in television a "potential for revolutionizing minority groups" by extending their communication networks beyond the boundaries of their local environment. "TV makes minority groups lose their minority weakness and perceive their strength through numbers in other cities and become bolder as lines of communication are opened up; the black community becomes extended much like McLuhan's 'global village'; a process of electronic *gemeinschaft* has accomplished this." Singer further proposed that "with future developments of multichannel cable vision and other 'individualized' media, an accentuation of this process may occur" (Singer, 1973: 141). The phenomenon Singer identified can readily be seen in the role of the Internet in facilitating the emergence of self-conscious and organized gay communities in many countries—by connecting gay people with others in their own country, in neighboring countries, and around the world.

Polish gays, speaking to an American journalist, noted that unlike neighboring Hungary and the Czech Republic, where gay life flourished after the fall of communism, democratic Poland was influenced by the Catholic church, and there was little tolerance for gay lifestyles. A forty-year-old software engineer credited the Internet revolution, more than anything else, with accelerating the emergence of a gay community in Poland. "The Internet has been a huge force for change. The access to information, to literature, to other gays—this is our real revolution," he said. "The new generation, the ones in their 20s who use the Internet, have a completely different view of themselves. I can see it in the way they think about themselves. Gays from my generation still feel this shame, and we are still afraid to talk openly, but not the new generation" (Hundley, 2002: 8).

In South Africa, one of the few countries in the world to include in its constitution a prohibition against discrimination based on sexual orientation, the editor of that country's first gay and lesbian website, Q-online (www.q.co.za/), sees the Internet "playing a vital role in connecting South African gays and lesbians with their counterparts on the rest of the continent and around the world. . . . Q-online must become an 'umbrella' site for gay and lesbian Africa" (DiGiacomo, 1999).

In India, where gay people aren't accepted by society and, as a result, have been extremely closeted, the gay community has "moved into and flourished on what has probably been the most accepting space they could have ever hoped to find—the Internet. . . . But in India, the Net is still an urban phenomenon, available only to those who can afford to be connected as well as communicate in English. Now, the more affluent meet people online and avoid the dangers associated with cruising the streets to look for partners" (Iyengar, 2001). In 1999, Vinay Chandran started Swabhava, a nonprofit website providing online, telephone, and personal counseling to sexual minorities: "The name originates from the word *svabhaava* which translates into: *sva* meaning self, inner or innate and *bhaava* meaning nature, expression or temperament. Swabhava was set up to provide support services to marginalised populations like lesbian, gay, bisexual, transgender people and others" (www.swabhava.org/weare.htm). Chandran is slowly mobilizing resources and networking with similar organizations in India to repeal the antisodomy statute still included in the Indian Penal Code instituted by the British in 1861. "The Net has helped us bring about some sort of change," he said. "Like when I go to a debate about gay rights, there is so much more information available now that it gives us an idea of the bigger picture—about what groups in the West are lobbying for, and on what they are basing their arguments" (Chandran, quoted in Iyengar, 2001).

China has no national laws forbidding—or even involving—homosexuality. Still, it's hardly congenial territory for sexual minorities. "Gays and lesbians in China aren't so much in closets as in concrete bunkers, inhibited by a traditional family structure and an intolerant Communist government. But social progress—slowly emerging as more Chinese gain in affluence and leisure time—appears to be giving the growing middle class a chance to ponder their sexual identities and explore them on the streets and over the Internet" (Friess, 2001a). The Internet enables them to read gay magazines from the United States such as *The Advocate* and to meet in chat rooms. "It is impossible for the government to control the Internet," Zhen Li, thirty-nine-year-old gay activist in Beijing, told American journalist Steve Friess. "It is a great tool for people to find the gay world in a secret way" (Friess, 2001a). Friess reported estimates of 250 gay-themed websites in China, ranging from local chat rooms to one for gay Buddhists. Even the nation's largest Web portals, Sina.com and Sohu.com, offer gay sections for posting messages and chatting. The number of Internet users continues to skyrocket, too, with an estimated 27 million Chinese having access to the Web. In November 2001 the Chinese gay movement experienced a minor revolution when the owners or operators of some thirty gay and lesbian Chinese websites met in Beijing to discuss how to use the Internet to promote HIV/AIDS awareness and create a more comfortable environment for *tongzhi* (gay) people. "We provided a physical space for website owners to meet face to face and get to know one another," Hong Kong–based gay activist Cheng To told Friess. (Cheng is the founder of the Chi Heng Foundation, which funded the meeting.) "They have the most potential to reach out to gay people in this country. . . . It's still a small number compared with the general population, but it is growing very rapidly and it is usually a younger, better-educated, more socially responsible population," Cheng added. "It's a different crowd than those who hang around toilets and parks looking for sex. That's not to put a value judgment on that, but the Internet population is more likely to do something significant about being gay" (Cheng, quoted in Friess, 2001b).

Will the Circle Be Unbroken?

The involvement of teens, gay or otherwise, in the Internet highlights one of the most controversial aspects of this electronic frontier—its ability to transmit sexually explicit images and words. Every new communications technology has been put to work in the service of humanity's boundless interest in sex. "Sometimes the erotic has been a force driving technological innovation; virtually always, from Stone Age sculpture to computer bulletin boards, it has been one of the first uses for a new medium" (Tierney, 1995: 1E). Thus the Internet quickly attracted the attention of the censorious and, as would be expected, the protection of children was their rallying cry.

When Anthony Comstock secured passage by the U.S. Congress of *An Act for the Suppression of Trade in, and Circulation of, Obscene Literature and Articles of Immoral Use*, which President Grant signed in 1873, he was focused on the distribution of information about abortion, contraception, or sexual activity through the mails, and in his specially created position as Special Agent of the U.S. Post Office he served as America's censor for forty years. "Spread throughout the country, indiscriminately accessible, public and private at once, the postal system had (odd as it may sound) something sexy about it. Left unpoliced, sex bred chaos; uninspected, the mails might do the same" (Kendrick, 1987: 145). If Comstock were alive today he would be even more terrified of the Internet, as it far exceeds the postal system in speed (to put it mildly) and in its potential to reach those he considered susceptible to the traps laid for the young.

U.S. Senator Jim Exon, Democratic Senator from Nebraska, like his predecessors back to Comstock, presented his role as protecting children, not as restricting expression. "I'm not trying to be a super censor. The first thing I was concerned with was kids being able to pull up pornography on their machines" (Exon, quoted in Andrews, 1995: D7). Special Agent Comstock was present in more than spirit, however, as the U.S. Congress enacted Senator Exon's Communications Decency Act (CDA). The CDA prohibited making available to minors online materials that, "in context, depicts or describes in terms patently offensive as measured by contemporary community standards, sexual or excretory activities or organs." The CDA was the target of an immediate lawsuit filed by the ACLU in the name of a group of plaintiffs that included the Critical Path AIDS Project and the queer teen website *YouthArts*. In 1996 Federal Judge Stewart Dalzell wrote that "the Internet may fairly be regarded as a never-ending worldwide conversation. The Government may not, through the CDA, interrupt that conversation. As the most participatory form of mass speech yet developed, the Internet deserves the highest protection from government intrusion" (*ACLU v. Reno*). The following year the U.S. Supreme Court voted 7 to 2 to affirm the lower court's decision.

Having lost the battle of the CDA, congressional censors turned to a technological fix akin to the V-chip mandated for inclusion in TV sets: The Internet School Filtering Act of 1999 required that Internet "filtering software" be used by schools and libraries to block material deemed inappropriate for children.[5] This law, too, was struck down by federal courts, as was the Children's Internet Protection Act of 2001, another attempt to mandate filtering technology in schools and libraries. The court, while sympathetic to the goal of "protecting children," ruled that the technology blocks so much unobjectionable material that it falls afoul of the First Amendment. The author of the opinion, Judge Edward Becker, wrote, "Ultimately this outcome, devoutly to be wished, is not available in this less than best of all possible worlds" (Becker, quoted in Schwartz, 2002: 1).

Web users in many parts of the world have reason to envy citizens of the United States, whose "less than best of all possible worlds" includes constitutional protections of free speech that often restrain the devout wishes of the establishment. Authorities in other countries have more power to block sites and control access to the Internet.[6] The nascent gay community in China is sprouting in the electronic soil of the Internet; yet, according to a Rand report, *You've Got Dissent,* "the government's crackdown on dissidents is succeeding in cyberspace. As a result, while the Internet may ultimately support change, this will more probably occur in an evolutionary manner" (Chase and Mulvenon, 2002). Still, the authors conclude, "as the use of the Internet expands across Chinese society, the government will have a harder time suppressing information, making it easier for dissidents to expand their efforts and perhaps push the country toward gradual pluralization and eventually maybe even democracy" (Chase and Mulvenon, 2002). Democracy is only a faint hope in Saudi Arabia where, according to a Harvard Law School study, the government is censoring public Internet access to a degree that goes "significantly but haphazardly beyond its stated central goal of blocking sexually explicit content that violates the values of Islam. The study's detailed list of blocked sites offers a glimpse into the areas that the Saudi government has deemed most troubling. Among them are sites related to pornography, women's rights, gays and lesbians, non-Islamic religions and criticism of political restrictions" (Lee, 2002).

Government censorship isn't the only threat to the viability of the Internet as fertile soil for emerging grassroots communities. The growing consolidation and commercialization of Internet companies raise concerns that as single companies begin to control both Internet content and systems for gaining access to that content, the Web could resemble a shopping mall with no prime space available for startups with little money. Lesbian author and Internet innovator Patricia Nell Warren, founder of the queer-youth website *YouthArts,* warned:

> Already we see the emergence of gay big business—banking, advertising, investment, media conglomerates, mega-malls, mega-sites. Already it's questionable whether everything GLBT [Gay, Lesbian, Bisexual, Transgendered] on the Net can be found through our own search engines. A publicist tells me that cost of promoting a new GLBT site to the Net is now $5000 minimum. Who can afford this? If the Net is to continue to nurture the "gay community," and keep it inclusive, it's important not to forget the original

reasons why the Net attracted us: low cost, grassroots access, ease in finding each other, inclusiveness, the dignity of the individual. (Warren, 2000)

In 1988 I concluded an essay on the ethics of media representations on a pessimistic note, observing that "history offers too many precedents of new technologies which did not live up to their advance billing; which ended up being part of the problem rather than part of the solution. . . . There surely are opportunities in the new communications order for more equitable and morally justifiable structures and practices, but I am not sure we can get there from here. As Kafka once wrote in his notebooks, 'In the fight between you and the world, bet on the world'" (Gross, 1988: 201). It remains to be seen whether the odds are better in the gay global village of cyberspace.

Notes

1. Most (77 percent) of the respondents were from the United States, with the next largest number from Canada (8 percent), the U.K. (5 percent), and Australia (4 percent); seventy-two other countries contributed fewer than 1 percent each. In general, few differences seemed to follow from geographical origin, suggesting that many of those responding from other countries might not have been of local origin (e.g., children of diplomats or overseas businessmen). A somewhat similar, more qualitative survey was conducted by the Australian Research Centre in Sex, Health and Society (Hillier et al., 2001).

2. There were significant correlations between the respondents' reported position on the Kinsey scale (0 = completely heterosexual, 6 = completely homosexual) and the age of becoming aware of their sexuality [-.06] and the age of accepting their sexuality [-.20]. That is, the more strongly they identified as gay, the earlier they recognized and accepted their sexual orientation. (These correlations are controlling for gender.) Needless to say, causality may run in either direction.

3. The usage figures reported in the survey put these young people well above the average of 9.8 hours per week found in the 2001 UCLA Internet Report, *Surveying the Digital Future* (available online at www.ccp.ucla.edu).

4. A comprehensive list of studies and other materials on queer youth suicide can be found at www.virtualcity.com/youthsuicide/.

5. The Internet School Filtering Act opened a door much wider than that of the local school and public library, as commercial providers have rushed to offer parents a variety of filtering services. In the words of Joan Garry, executive director of the Gay and Lesbian Alliance Against Defamation (GLAAD), "We had gone from the frying pan of active censorship [the CDA] into the fire of censorship by passive omission" (GLAAD, 1997). Commercial filtering software works by blocking access to sites based on keywords presumed to signal sexual content, and these often include the very words "gay," "lesbian," "homosexual," or even "sexual orientation." Parents—or schools and libraries—that install such filtering software thus prevent teenagers (and adults, in many instances) from gaining access to support groups, informational sites, and even the Association of Gay Square Dance Clubs. Indeed, sites offering safer-sex information are routinely excluded by many filtering programs (along with sites focused on breast cancer).

6. U.S.-based Internet providers can even be intimidated by the laws of other countries. In 1995 the online firm CompuServe (later bought by AOL) temporarily blocked access to hundreds of sexually explicit sites in response to a threat from a Munich prosecutor who

cited German antipornography laws. A CompuServe spokesman told the *New York Times,* "It's a huge global market, and in order to play in each country we have to play by their rules" (Meers, 1996).

References

Andrews, Edmund (1995). "Panel Backs Smut Ban on Internet," *New York Times,* March 24.

Associated Press (1996). "Gay and Lesbian Net Surfers: A Dream Market in the Online World," June 24.

Barnett, Jim (2002). "Gay Teen Testifies against Law on Internet," *The Oregonian,* March 27.

Chase, Michael, and Mulvenon, James (2002). *You've Got Dissent.* Santa Monica: Rand Corporation. Available online at www.rand.org/hot/press.02/dissent.html.

DiGiacomo, Robert (1999). "Off-Hours: Gay and Lesbian South Africans Can Now Connect Online." Available online at www.gfn.com (Gay Financial Network). Posted 12 January 1999.

Egan, Jennifer (2000). "Lonely Gay Teen Seeking Same," *New York Times Magazine,* December 10.

Fisher, Cory (2000). "Teens Coming Out: Hip, Trendy Magazine Targets Gay Audience," *Los Angeles Times,* March 24.

Friess, Steve (2001a). "Chinese Gays Slowly Come Out into the Open," *USA Today.* Available online at www.usatoday.com/usafront.htm. Posted 9 March 2001.

—— (2001b). "Beijing's 'Secret' Gay Web Confab," *Wired News.* Available online at www.wired.com/news/culture/0,1284,48545-2,00.html. Posted on 23 November 2001.

Gabriel, Trip (1995). "Some On-Line Discoveries Give Gay Youths a Path to Themselves," *New York Times,* July 2, p. 1.

GLAAD (1997). Access Denied: An Impact of Internet Filtering Software on the Gay and Lesbian Community. Available online at www.glaad.org/access_denied.

Gross, Larry (1988). "The Ethics of (Mis)representation," in L. Gross et al., *Image Ethics: The Moral Rights of Subjects in Photographs, Film, and Television,* pp. 188–202. New York: Oxford University Press.

—— (2001). *Up from Invisibility: Lesbians, Gay Men, and the Media in America,* New York: Columbia University Press.

Hillier, Lynne, Kurdas, Chyloe, and Horsley, Philomena (2001). *'It's Just Easier': The Internet as a Safety-Net for Same Sex Attracted Young People.* Australian Centre for Research in Sex, Health and Society, La Trobe University. Available online at www.Latrobe.edu.au/ssay.

Hundley, Tom (2002). "Gay Life Gains Steam in Warsaw: Catholic Church's Reduced Influence, Internet Play Role," *Chicago Tribune,* August 2.

Iyengar, Swaroopa (2001). "India's Different Gay Divide," *Wired News.* Available online at www.wired.com/news/culture/0,1284,45206,00.html. Posted on 24 July 2001.

Kendrick, Walter (1987). *The Secret Museum: Pornography in Modern Culture.* New York: Viking.

Lee, Jennifer (2002). "Saudi Censorship of Web Ranges Far Beyond Tenets of Islam, Study Finds," *New York Times,* August 29.

Lewis, Peter (1995). "Planet Out's Gay Services on Virtual Horizon," *New York Times,* August 21, p. D3.

McAllester, Matthew (1997). "What a Difference a Modem Makes," *Newsday,* January 28.

Meers, Erik Ashok (1996). "Border Control," *The Advocate,* February 6, pp. 34–36.

Nir, Lilach (1998). "A Site of Their Own: Gay Teenagers' Involvement Patterns in IRC and Newsgroups." Paper presented to the International Communication Association's 48th Annual Meeting, Jerusalem.

Schwartz, John (2002). "Court Overturns Law Mandating Internet Filters for Public Libraries," *New York Times*, June 1.

Silberman, Steve (1994). "We're Teen, We're Queer, and We've Got E-Mail," *Wired*, December, pp. 1–3.

Singer, Benjamin (1973). "Mass Society, Mass Media and the Transformation of Minority Identity," *British Journal of Sociology* 24(2): 140–50.

Tierney, John (1995). "From the Stone Age to the Information Age SEX SELLS," *Baltimore Sun*, July 23, p. 1E.

Warren, Patricia Nell (2000). "Chasing Rainbows: GLBT Identity and the Internet," *Cybersocket*, March. Available online at www.cybersocket.com.

CHAPTER 17

The Internet, Social Networks, and Reform in Indonesia

Merlyna Lim

The Internet is quickly expanding beyond its origins in the United States to the rest of the world. At present, 533 million people in the world are estimated to be active Internet users (Cyber Atlas, 2002). This figure is growing exponentially, and by 2004 a predicted 945 million people will be using the Internet around the world. Due to this rapid growth, the Internet has made a huge impact upon societies everywhere.

Research on this impact is increasing. Among the leading issues being studied is the relationship between the Internet and democracy. For some time prophetic scholars have envisioned the Internet as a source of ideas for a possible transformation toward democratic politics (Barber, 1984; Becker and Slaton, 2000). Moreover, there are politicians and policy experts, notably in the United States, who seem to have faith that the Internet is an appealing force for democracy that will undermine authoritarian regimes around the world (Friedman, 2000; Wright, 2000). However, the population of Internet users is still very much concentrated in higher-income democratic countries. This raises the question of what impact the Internet has made upon political life, especially in terms of advancing democratization in authoritarian states. How might this impact change in the future?

Until recently, Indonesia was still among those countries under authoritarian control. For decades following independence, informational media in Indonesia developed under the strong control of the state. The Suharto regime made use of the media as a means to spread its propaganda over the archipelago to legitimize and maintain its identity as a progressive "developmental state." Communications and media technologies, particularly satellite and television, were deliberately used to build a national identity under the state, thus blockading society from accessing information other than that which the state provided (Kitley, 1994; Shoesmith, 1994).

The Internet, which came to Indonesia during the early phase of the political crisis in the 1990s, has risen both economically and politically to become an alternative medium that has found its way out from under the control of the state (Hill and Sen, 2000; Lim, 2002). However, the Internet was initially just available to a small segment of society. The medium was still very new, immature, and elitist. How, then, could the Internet have had a pervasive impact on Indonesian society? Is it true that it helped Indonesia become a more democratic state? And if so, how was this accomplished?

These questions cannot be resolved just by looking at the Internet and its users. Rather, the answers emerge from a deeper exploration beyond the Internet. The relation between technology and society ranges far beyond the causal relationship between the technology and its immediate users. Rather, the interconnection between technology and society is historically and culturally rooted in a local context, which is the nexus where technology and society meet, and the basis on which technology's impact spreads widely through society.

Using the case of Indonesia, this chapter addresses both democratization of media and democratization in general, with the aim of demonstrating a firm connection between the two. It also describes how the Internet could have wider impacts than those revealed by statistical analysis. These impacts are greatly facilitated by the convivial attributes of the Internet itself, which in turn foster a multiplier effect starting from the small Internet café—the *warnet*—and spreading to people and places throughout Indonesian society.

The Internet: A Convivial Medium for Civil Society

Communication media can be used by different groups for various purposes, but some are more suited to certain purposes than to others. For democratization, these media should have features that are suited to civil society and grassroots citizen action by making it less easy for a small number of groups to control the flow and content of information, knowledge, and ideological or symbolic representations. These features include one-to-one communication, affordable cost, ease of use, broad availability, and technological resistance to surveillance and censorship.

The Internet is a medium that possesses most of these features. E-mail, for example, allows one-to-one communication at a relatively low cost and is easy to use. Through the availability of Internet café and other public-access points, the Internet is now broadly available not only in developed countries but also in developing countries like Indonesia. The anarchic characteristic of this technology, originally designed by the U.S. Department of Defense to facilitate survival of a nuclear war (Abbate, 1999; Cerf et al., 2000), is what hinders efforts to control or censor it. Indeed, the overwhelming volume of information flooding the Internet in open networks rather than in a hierarchically controlled form limits such attempts. The Internet can thus be considered a "convivial medium"—borrowing Ivan Illich's (1973) concept of "convivial technology."

The conviviality of the Internet as an informational and communication medium is more crucial for civil society in authoritarian states than in democratic states. However, when the space for dialogues and exchanging information is limited to Internet users, rather than encompassing larger segments of society, the conviviality of the Internet is less effective than its potential suggests. Information that circulates only among the members of a small "elite" loses its power to mobilize people to challenge the cordons of hegemonic power. No political revolution can happen without involving society on a wider scale. Even those efforts made within cyberspace are fruitless unless they can be extended into real social, political, and economic spaces.

Through a narration of the Indonesian experience, the remaining sections of this chapter explore how the Internet has risen as a medium that, while new, is nonetheless rooted in traditional culture and social networks—thus providing its users with the ability to reach wider strata of civil society and to be engaged in challenging the domination of the state in both private and public life.

May 1998: The Question of the Role of the Internet

When the "father of development" à la New Order, President Suharto, was forced to step down in May 1998, some writers drew a parallel between this event and the Zapatista's Net movement in Chiapas, Mexico—implying that the political revolution in Indonesia was (Inter)Net-driven (Basuki, 1998; Marcus, 1999). However, many Indonesian media and information technologists do not accept this opinion, arguing that it was impossible for the Internet to have such a role in the overthrow of Suharto's New Order government. This dissenting opinion is heavily based on the following argument:

1. According to a statistical analysis, the estimated number of Internet users in Indonesia in 1998 was just less than 1 percent of the population, and this 1 percent was assumed to be an elite group that was unlikely to join in anti-hegemonic actions.
2. In any case, the Internet is only an extension/advancement of old/previous media, and as such—even though it has transformed the mode of communication and the transfer of information—it is considered a neutral technology that could only reflect the existing power structures of society.
3. By inference, the Internet is part of the media and culture of dominant social forces, retaining a rigid connection with existing power holders.

These reasons are sufficient to explain the long domination of the Indonesian state over the use of communication and media technologies. All of these technologies, from the telegraph to the radio, from satellites to television, have been developed to suit the quest of domination by elites (Kitley, 1994; Shoesmith, 1994). It is apparent that the vast majority of people have never been able to exercise power from their marginalized positions. However, by putting the Indonesian experience in the picture, this chapter argues that the Internet is not neutral with respect to power and, further, that power can act in unpredictable nonlinear ways in cyberspace as in other cultural sites. In short, those with limited power can create or continue their own agendas, and their own forms of identity, culture, and community, by using a medium such as the Internet—especially one so new to its users.

To be effective, however, the Internet would have to reach far beyond the computer. To explain how the Internet works in Indonesian cultural sites and how it can serve as a medium that supports those who are dominated as they attempt to challenge the hegemonic power of the dominant (state), the following section describes how in Indonesia the Internet was transformed into a new medium based on a traditional network culture.

Warnet: A New Medium Arising from a Traditional Network

Superficially, the Internet is a "non-Indonesian" technology. Imported from outside, it came to Indonesia in the early 1990s and began to be commercialized only in the mid-1990s. Available to just a small segment of society, the Internet was so limited in terms of social access that it seemingly could have no significant impact on society. For example, data from the International Telecommunications Union (ITU) indicate that in Indonesia in 1999 there were only 21,052 Internet hosts with 900,000 users, while in the United States during the same year there were 53,175,956 hosts with 74.1 million users (ITU, 2001). By 2001, however, the number of hosts in Indonesia (46,000) had increased by 120 percent and the number of users (4 million) by 350 percent, compared with a 100 percent increase in hosts (106,193,339) and users (142.8 million) in the United States (ITU, 2002). These figures suggest an explosive, even chaotic, rate of growth in Indonesia.

Even these figures of rapid expansion tell much less than the full story. The impact of the Internet on Indonesian society cannot be measured simply by counting the number of direct Internet users. It is difficult to see the dynamics of change at the macro level that only tallies numbers of nationwide Internet users. If we step down from the macro-level to the micro-levels of the district, the community, the neighborhood, and the family, where real Indonesian social life is lived, only then can we see that the actual channels of access to the new technologies are much wider than previously appeared, including the real and potential uses by segments of society that are excluded from direct use. Dynamic social mobility in the unstable context of contemporary Indonesia allows usage of the new media to grow in "invisible" ways. But, paradoxically, the Internet may be simultaneously elitist and not elitist. That is, while it is directly accessible to only a very few, the social and cultural linkages that connect others to these select members of civil society create non-elitist—and even counter-elitist—tendencies as well.

To understand the Indonesian Internet is to understand the social dynamics of its smallest but most popular Net-access point: the Internet café, or *warnet* (see figure 17.1). From 1990 to 1994, the only access to the Internet was through universities or research institutions. But in 1995–1996, with the emergence of commercial Internet service providers (ISPs), Indonesians could suddenly have an independent dial-up Internet connection from their homes or offices. At least *some* Indonesians could. What with the economic crisis under way, and the combined costs of a subscription fee, connection fee, and telephone tariff, ISPs were prohibitively expensive for most people. Also, telephone penetration was still low. So, in this context, the *warnet* emerged in the mid-1990s as an alternative point of access for the public (Lim, 2002).

As with Internet cafés in other countries, use of the *warnet* does not necessitate computer ownership or ISP subscription. Access is instead rented by the hour or minute. However, what does differentiate the *warnet* from generic Internet cafés is that the *warnet* is attached to the historic cultural context of Indonesian life. The *warnet* is not only a point of Internet access but also the result of a transformation and localization of Internet technology; in short, the *warnet* is an Indonesian In-

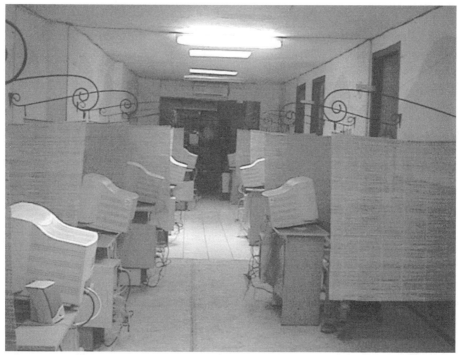

Figure 17.1.   A *warnet* (Internet café) in Bandung, Indonesia
Source: Author's photo.

ternet. The Internet, as embodied in the *warnet*, is a medium that is "continuous with and embedded in other social spaces," within everyday "social structures and relations that they may transform but cannot escape into a self-enclosed cyberian apartness" (Miller and Slater, 2000).

Warnet and the Traditional *Warung*

The term *warnet*, which is an abbreviation of "*warung* Internet," is rooted in the term *warung*, which refers to a very simple place where people from the lower-middle and lower classes buy snacks or meals and congregate with friends or family while eating. A *warung* can be physically located in the front part of a house, usually in an erstwhile guestroom. Alternatively, it can be built as a room extension in the frontyard or on the street. *Warung* usually consist of just one small room with one table. However, sometimes they have a bigger room, allowing for more than one table. In this type of *warung*, people would sit on the floor (*lesehan*) and eat on the short tables. This *lesehan* type is more family-oriented. A common feature of *warung* is the *krepyak*—a bamboo curtain used for covering the front side of the structure (see figure 17.2). The *krepyak* has two functions: By separating the people inside from the public outside, it protects them from the sun and gives them a sense of privacy.

Figure 17.2.   The traditional *warung*
Source: Author's photo.

The physical appearance of traditional *warung* has been substantially adapted by the *warnet*. The physical location of the *warnet* is exactly that of the *warung*: the front part of a house. Wood and bamboo also dominate the materials used to culturally impart a *warung* feeling to many of the *warnet* in Indonesia, particularly in Bandung. The *krepyak* is commonly used either as a window cover (for sun protection) or as a partition separating computers from each other. The *lesehan* type of *warnet* is very popular among teenagers. In a *lesehan* room there can be three or four computers that a single group can reserve for a certain duration. This yields a sense of closeness and group privacy. Even in terms of its physical attributes, then, the *warnet* is attached to local cultural practices.

Yet, such "traditional" adoption can be superficial. The physical elements of the *warung* represent only one attempt, albeit an important one, to anchor the *warnet* in Indonesian culture. To enable its linkages to be truly realized, social networks based on cultural traditions must also flourish in and beyond the built environment of the *warnet*.

Traditional Social Networks

Beyond its physical attributes, the *warnet* is culturally entrenched in a traditional social network formation that has existed for hundreds of years. As a traditional food outlet, the *warung* is an important social and culinary focus for most Indonesians (Rigg, 1996). The presence of a *warung* in the neighborhood is very important, especially to lower-middle and lower-class people. Whether in a city or a village, the *warung* is simultaneously a point of commerce, a meeting place, and an information network for the households in the neighborhood. Not just a place to eat, the *warung* is where people meet to chat and to gain and spread information—although the most popular form of information spreading is gossip. It is a place to talk about various things from the price of meals to business matters, from love life to politics. It is public, yet altogether private. *Warung* and *warung*-like places such as the *pasar*, or "traditional market," take on the role of civic space—that is, as one of "those spaces in which people of different origins and walks of life can co-mingle without overt control by government, commercial or other private interests, or de facto dominance by one group over another" (Douglass et al., 2002). This role is similar to that of the old-fashioned coffee shop in North America and Europe, where people are generally free to linger and can engage in conversation at a reasonable cost and with few commercial nuisances. The *warung* also parallels the public baths of Japan and Korea, where all people in a community gather not only to bathe but to engage in conversation (Douglass, 1993). *Warung* can also serve as micro-civic spaces. The conversations and dialogues created in *warung* are brought to other communities, such that markets, families, working-spaces, and paddy fields all become civic-space nodes for social engagement. Together with these nodes, the *warung* create a network of information flows that reach far beyond the nodal sites themselves.

However, with the influence of globalization, which has trapped people in hyper-real lifestyles, much of the urban middle class no longer has an opportunity to go to *warung* or *warung*-like places. The habit of visiting such places has been replaced by frequent trips to fast-food restaurants and shopping malls, which do not provide spaces for dialogues or the privacy to talk freely for any length of time. Most of the conversations that do happen there are commodified and inhibited.

In this setting, the *warnet* has emerged as a reincarnation or contemporary form of the *warung*. Even though people can access the Internet from other places like home, office, public library, or university, the *warnet* accounts for approximately 60 percent of total Internet users.[1] As an entry point to cyberspace, it provides spaces for dialogue and accessing information that are substantially free from intervention and manipulation by the state and corporate economy. People can make use of this technology without losing or compromising their personal or social identities and without being inhibited by matters of political correctness or commercialism.

As a physical space, the *warnet* is also a kind of civic space. Accessing the Internet from the *warnet*, unlike connecting from home, office, public library, or university, is a direct form of social engagement. While sitting at a computer in the *warnet*, a user interacts physically both with the *warnet*'s physical space and with other users. Those who want to enjoy accessing the Internet together with friends can choose a *warnet* with a private *lesehan* lounge, where they can relax by sitting on the floor and sharing interesting URLs or listening to songs downloaded via MP3 technology. And those who want privacy can sit in the *krepyak*'s partitioned space, where others cannot see the computer screen.

Thus there are social networks as well as physical spaces created by cyberspace. The most common online activity in the *warnet* is chatting. The privacy provided by chat rooms is particularly important to Indonesian youth, especially those trying to gain more autonomy from their parents or the older generation than is possible in offline space, especially in matters of social relations between the sexes (Slama, 2002). Indeed, the Internet offers access to a subculture that is distinct from other spaces and places in society. Just like the *warung*, it is both public and private. *Warnet*, too, facilitate not only online social relationships but also offline ones—as when young people meet in person in a *warnet* as a follow-up to their online chat.

The physical and virtual nodes created within and by the *warnet* are aspects of social network formation, which does not stop in the *warnet* itself. Rather, the *warnet* extends its flows of information outward to other social networks within society. Using the existing cultural foundations of communication, including the traditional network of *warung*-like places, Internet users spread this information beyond the *warnet* and capture spaces where people may not even be familiar with the word "Internet."

As an example of how information flows from cyberspace to the *warnet* and to traditional networks in Indonesia, let us now consider the political revolution that occurred there in May 1998.

From Global Flows to the *Warnet-Warung* and the Political Spaces of Revolution

The flow of information from global to local scales of interaction was facilitated by the existence of virtual and physical nodes of the *warnet* linked to traditional social networks. Both the *warnet* and its *warung*-like linkages to the rest of society were crucial to the rise of civil society in a very short period before the downfall of Suharto in May 1998.

As previously noted, up to the advent of the Internet, all information that came into and spread throughout the country was subject to political cleansing by the state's filtering apparatus, manifested in the creation of the Ministry of Information. All broadcast television and radio channels relayed only that information which did not endanger the harmony and unity of the nation-state. The press was under the strict control of the state, with tight practices of scrutiny, censorship, and banning. In this regard, during the last four to five years of the New Order era, Internet-based information was considered a luxury. The main reason is that the Internet could supply controversial information that was previously unavailable to most Indonesians—for example, details related to the Indonesian Communist Party (PKI) or to Suharto's wrongdoings, or that would undermine the president and *Pancasila*.[2] To be able to access such information was a privilege for Indonesian Internet users.

There were a few major sources of this kind of information. Among the most important were Apakabar,[3] George Aditjondro,[4] SiAR (1998a), Pijar (KdPnet, 1998), Munindo (2000), and CSVI (2002). Of the information classified as "unavailable and controversial," the most popular was the famous *Daftar Kekayaan Suharto,* or "list of Suharto's wealth." This information was originally written by Aditjondro, an Indonesian professor teaching the "Sociology of Corruption" at the University of New Castle in Australia. He called himself "the scent dog of Suharto's wealth."

The original information comprising the "list of Suharto's wealth" was not a list but, rather, a series of four long e-mails under the subject *Kekayaan Suharto* ("Suharto's Wealth"), versions 1 to 4, with *Yayasan-yayasan Suharto: cakupan, dampak, dan pertang-gungjawabannya* ("Suharto's foundations: their coverage, impact, and blameworthiness") as a subtitle. These e-mails revealed how Suharto used his "charity" foundations to cover his corrupt business network, who was involved, and the amount of money spent or gained. On 31 January 1998, Aditjondro sent the e-mails to John MacDouggal—the moderator of *Apakabar*—and to other colleagues and friends. MacDouggal spread these e-mails through the *Apakabar* mailing list on 1 February 1998 (Aditjondro, 1998c).

Among the other earliest recipients besides *Apakabar* were Munindo (Aditjondro, 1998a), Pijar (KdPnet, 1998), and SiaR (1998b). All published the information on their homepages and/or spread the information through mailing lists. By April 1998, many other websites had also published this information. Additional websites, even personal ones, added links to it. Some of the reproductions of Aditjondro's original message used the title he had specified; others used an edited title with a more incendiary vocabulary; still others used a title with a much more provocative, cynical, or hilarious line.[5] The format of this information was also modified—for example, from a long narrative into a shorter version. Some changed it into a summary; others paraphrased the narrative.

Among these changes, the most remarkable was the transformation of a long narrative format into a short list (Luknanto, 1998b). This list captured only the names of foundations and their links to business networks, but it provided a kind of information that was simpler and more readable for ordinary people. Meanwhile, the process of dissemination continued intensively, especially by e-mails corresponding to Indonesian mailing lists. Just a few months after Aditjondro posted his article—especially by March–April 1998—the information about Suharto's wealth had effectively spread throughout cyberspace.

In April 1998, some activists published their online tabloid first edition, called "Indonesia Baru." While publishing this politically related information, they also described five ways to disseminate information in their website. Two of these were as follows: (1) Print out this homepage's contents and fax them to your friends; and (2) photocopy the printout, then give it to non-Internet users (Indonesia Baru, 1998). The latter suggestion was a true breakthrough. Other websites thus published the same request.

From April to May 1998, many mysterious faxes—sent anonymously and carrying various messages, the most popular of which was the "list of Suharto's wealth"—came into private and public offices in major cities in Indonesia. The people in those offices—from directors to janitors—became aware of this information and were willing to spread this information to other people within their networks.

The printout version of this information was also disseminated. Many *warnet* in Bandung put the list on their announcement board, together with other Net-related issues such as the "top-10 hot IRC chat rooms." The *warnet* users then spread the list to other *warnet* users and sent the photocopied materials to nonusers.

The photocopied version of the "list of Suharto's wealth" was commonly found on the streets during March–May 1998. Newspaper sellers and street vendors sold this photocopied version at traffic lights, gas stations, and bus stops and stations. In Bandung, one page of a copy of the list sold for 1,000 rupiahs (approximately US$.10). From here, the information reached ordinary people in cars, motorcycles, buses, and other public transport.

In Jakarta, two social groups had speedy access to political information: (1) taxi drivers, who always knew where the students held or would hold street demos, and who updated their passengers with this information, partly just to avoid traffic jams, and (2) the *warung* owners near universities, where students live and engage in their activities. These ordinary people developed sympathy for the students, listened to their gripes, and occasionally supplied them with food. The cabs and the *warung* thus became small local hubs in the information flow. From these and other hubs, politically charged information reached many people. The traditional style of networking information had been awakened. The end result was the creation of resistance identities that spread from a small segment of society to the mass scale of civil society and, after thirty-two years of Suharto's authoritarian rule, rose up to overthrow his regime.

As the information reached innumerable people from various walks of life, it was finally time to launch a real mass-based anti-hegemonic movement. The accumulation of collective resistances reached its peak in May 1998, when students and ordinary people joined to demand that President Suharto step down. Greatly affected by the impact of the military's violent practices, which resulted in the death of some students during the protests, an intense social movement reverberated through civil society, generating an authentic political revolution that culminated in Suharto's resignation as president on 21 May 1998.

Various actors took key roles in the successful dissemination of information during this process. The informants (e.g., Aditjondro) and the first layer of disseminators (e.g., the owners of Munindo, Pijar, and Indonesian Daily News Online) were mostly based abroad.[6] The second layer consisted of Internet users in Indonesia who, for the most part, had accessed the information from the *warnet*. Comprising the third layer were the mediators (e.g., newspaper sellers, street vendors, taxi drivers, and *warung* owners) who connected the "elite" with ordinary people). And the final layer was made up of average citizens at large. The interconnectedness of all actors from all of these layers created the necessary multiplier effects for information dissemination to result in mass mobilization and political reform.

Indeed, the Indonesia story shows how meaningless the previously mentioned figure of "1 percent" was as an indication of the scope and impact of the Internet's spread of information. As the crisis broke, Indonesian authorities had no geared-up plans for controlling or censoring the Internet and were quite naïve about its political potential—in stark contrast to the methods the regime had used to censor previous forms of communications and media. This situation put the Internet in a unique position to support antiregime social movements. Under such an immense crisis, it was easier for civil society—including cyber- as well as student activists—to make use of the Internet to awaken and tap into traditional networks of information that had been suppressed under the authoritarian regime. Through such nonhierarchical networks, social groups could have multiple horizontal as well as vertical interconnections. Uneducated, elderly, technologically blind, poor, female, and other marginalized segments of society no longer faced a cumulative set of barriers to participation in transforming the spaces of information flows.

The Retreat of the Civil Society Movement and the Rise of the Corporate Economy

Even though it was available to only a small segment of Indonesian society, it is clear, from the events of May 1998, that the Internet has become a novel space for information exchanges. It has enabled political discourse to be carried out without substantial barriers and thus, together with the traditional network that brought information to the public, has accelerated the transformation of Indonesian society into a more democratic one.

Although the new informational web of the Internet intensified the political revolution in Indonesia, since the fall of Suharto it has not supported a continuation of the civil society momentum toward reform. Up to the point when the revolution reached its zenith in May 1998, people had focused on a common agenda, which was confronting the government. However, after the May 1998 political revolution, the society did not know what to do next. Like its predecessor, the new, semidemocratic government lacks a clear political agenda or strategy, placing society in a chaotic political-social-economic situation.

The new post-Suharto democratizing yet unstable regimes have embraced more openly than ever before the world economy of the transnational corporations (TNCs). The International Monetary Fund, acting as an agent of TNC globalization and using loans to cover the Asia finance crisis of 1997 as its leverage, has compelled Indonesia to open its economy to trade and investment and to privatize its government-owned companies and institutions. This circumstance has provided the TNCs with unprecedented opportunities to capture the spaces of information flows and to create another front of accumulation in cyberspace. At the same time, economic reform is worsening the political-social-economic situation by diverting public resources from social funds to subsidize competition for vagabond capital (Douglass, 2002b). The student movement continuously confronts the new government but without a clear vision, adding to the chaos. Currently, individual interest has taken over the political agenda of civil society, while communal interests are pitting elements of civil society against each other around issues of race and religion—thereby undermining the "civil" attributes of civil society (Lim, 2002).

Thus while civil society movements are dissipating, and the state is in a state of chronic instability, a shift is occurring in hegemonic tendencies away from authoritarian regimes toward global capital. As evidence of this shift, *warnet*, which used to belong to the younger generation and students, are being seized by big national corporations and TNCs. A new corporate economy has entered the arena and is steadily capturing this valuable treasure of civil society. One of the most ambitious companies is M-Web Holding Limited, a South African media giant that has also invested in Thailand, China, Namibia, and Zimbabwe (M-Web, 2001). Starting its business by acquiring Cabinet, an Indonesian ISP, in May 2000, M-Web saw the *warnet* as a prospective target for monopolizing the Internet business in Indonesia. Thus, in January 2001, it acquired PT Warnet Gemilang (M-Web, 2002), a company that has linked nine big *warnet* in Jakarta. Subsequently, in collaboration with many universities in major Indonesian cities (e.g., the University of Indonesia in Jakarta, the Institute of Technology Sepuluh November in Surabaya, and the University of Gajah Mada in Yogyakarta), M-Web set up the biggest *warnet*-network in Indonesia (M-Web, 2002). In less than one year M-Web has already established more than 1,500 stations in its network.

The M-web type of *warnet* is nothing like the small, old-generation version with its simple, traditional look. One Internet center—the "Student Internet Centre"—has more than 30 screens; others have more than 200. An appropriate name for it would be "Net-mall," because it resembles a shopping mall much more than a simple *warung*.

M-Web has also killed the individual *warnet* businesses located near its Internet centers, which cannot compete with this giant company (NatnitNet, 2001). By announcing its goal of "making the Internet widely available for everybody, especially students," M-Web has successfully drawn universities into its commercial ground, and with its motto "Everything is provided here," it ties the students to a commodified identity. M-Web and other actors of the corporate economy are increasingly commercializing and controlling the Internet through giant *warnet*, ISPs, and other Internet-related business.

As a result of this shift of ownership from the "people" to the corporate economy, the Internet is on the way to becoming a sanitized medium. While the change in the places where people access the Internet might not by itself lead to such an effect, it is the damage done to the link between Internet use and civil society that is crucial.

Conclusion

The Indonesian political revolution of May 1998 may be considered an Internet-"coincident" revolution, but in fact the Internet was not the only or even the principal source of information for social mobilization leading to the downfall of Suharto. However, it is clear that the Internet emerged in Indonesia at precisely the time when other forms of media were being tightly controlled and traditional networks of information circulation could still be tapped. The most important factor was not cyberspace itself but, rather, the linkages between cyberspace: cyber nodes such as the *warnet* and the physical spaces of cities, towns, and villages.

Manuel Castells (1996: 469) argues that, in the current information age, dominant functions and processes are increasingly being organized around networks. Networks constitute the social morphology of our society, and the diffusion of networking logic has substantially modified the operation and outcomes involved in the processes of production, experience, power, and culture. While the networking form of social organization such as the *warung* has existed in other times and spaces, the *warnet* paradigm has provided the basis for its near-simultaneous expansion throughout the entire social structure. The power of network flows has become more important than the specific interests they represent, so it is vital now to be present in a network and not to be excluded from it. At a certain moment in history, the nodes of cyberspace—*warnet* and *warung*-like settings—joined to create a powerful network that, in the case of Indonesia at the end of the twentieth century, was more dynamic than the collapsing networks of the state-corporate economy. Castells refers to this outcome as "the pre-eminence of social morphology over social action" (1996: 469), a pre-eminence that is the main characteristic of network society.

Today, the Indonesian state is still trying to recover from the crisis. Civil society is no longer so critical of government in terms of democratic reform, though the latter continues to be an issue. More generally, the concern is shifting to the corporate economy. This new juggernaut can potentially depoliticize cyber-exchanges by transforming civil society into little more than a sum of individual consumers having no identity other than the biggest name brands and latest corporate commodities. Thus, as noted earlier, the Internet may potentially become a sanitized, homogeneous medium whose main function is to sell consumerism to people and people to advertisers. Hence the threat to the Internet's role as an ideal public sphere, one that facilitates a rational-critical discourse where everyone is an equal participant and supreme communication skill is the power of argument (Habermas, 1991). This deformation of the public sphere is happening through the growth of culture industries and the penetration of large private interests into the ownership and control of cyberspace. Large companies are devoted to maximizing profit and turning the Internet into an agent of manipulation toward the same end. As summarized by Jürgen Habermas (1991: 185), through the shift from state to corporate hegemony "it [becomes] the gate through which privileged private interest invaded the public sphere."

Cyberspace and the *warnet,* as well as all the traditional social networks attached to them in Indonesia, are now back to their long sleep, hidden under the flood of consumerism and waiting for students or civil society or society at large to wake them up. Like the developmental state of the Suharto government, this global corporate force seeks hegemony over social power and identity while masking state-corporate relations that continue to threaten the rise of an authentic, politically active society. Sustaining an active civil-society presence in the public sphere thus faces formidable challenges related to both state and corporate economic penetration of the virtual and actual physical spheres of power. Technology in general, and use of the Internet in particular, must therefore be seen as comprising a dynamically changing milieu in which political struggles will continue into the future. Whether the new shadow will be the commodified world of economic exchange spreading over local communities and culture is a question for further research to answer as globalization continues to weaken government as a source of regulation over the economy and submerges nation-states in the turbulence of successive international crises.

Notes

1. Based on the survey done by *Swa and Mark Plus* magazine in November 2000.
2. *Pancasila* is literally translated as "five principles." These principles are fundamental for the society.

3. The e-mail address for Apakabar is Indonesia-l@indopub.com.

4. Aditjondro fled Indonesia a short time after his lecture in Yogyakarta in 1994. This lecture, about the oligarchy of the political regime, was claimed to be insulting the President Suharto. The police interrogated him after the lecture. Knowing that he would not be able to escape from the Indonesian government's hegemonic trap, which could possibly end his career, he decided to fly to Australia before the state took any further actions. When Aditjondro arrived in Australia, the state attempted to bring him to court. But this action was fruitless since Aditjondro had already been outside the geographical boundary of the Indonesian government's authority (Munindo, 1998).

5. One title was *Daftar Isi Kekayaan Eyang Kakung,* or "The List of Grandfather's Wealth" (Luknanto, 1998a). *Eyang kakung* is a family-oriented Javanese term that literally means "grandfather" (or "great-grandfather"). It is generally used to confer respect and thus reflects good manners. In this regard, the positive connotation of this word was intended to humiliate Suharto, a grandfather "not worthy of respect." At the same time, the term implied that Suharto was no longer the "father" of the nation-state but, rather, was outdated and old and should have stepped down long ago.

6. The cyber-activists who operated Munindo, Indonesian Daily News Online, and Pijar were based in Germany.

References

Abbate, J. (1999). *Inventing the Internet.* Cambridge, Mass.: MIT Press.

Aditjondro, G. (1998a, 30 January). *Kekayaan Suharto I,II,III.* Available online at www.munindo.brd.de/george/george_kekayaan_suharto1.html,suharto2.html,suharto3.html. Last accessed on 29 August 2002.

———— (1998b, 30 January). *Kekayaan Suharto: Yayasan-yayasan Suharto: cakupan, dampak, dan pertanggungjawabannya.* Available online at www.geocities.com/CapitolHill/Senate/4427/mpr.htm. Last accessed on 29 August 2002.

———— (1998c, 30 January). *Kekayaan Suharto I,II,III,IV.* Available online at www.hamline.edu/apakabar/basisdata/1998/02/01/0003.html,0004.html,0005.html,0006.html. Last accessed on 29 August 2002.

Barber, B. (1984). *Strong Democracy: Participatory Politics for a New Age.* Berkeley: University of California Press.

Basuki, T. (1998). "Indonesia: The Web as a Weapon," *Development Dialogue 2: The Southeast Asian Media in a Time of Crisis,* pp. 96–103.

Becker, T., and Slaton, C. D. (2000). *The Future of Teledemocracy.* Westport, Conn.: Praeger.

Castells, M. (1996). *The Rise of Network Society.* Oxford/Malden, Mass.: Blackwell Publishers.

Cerf, V. G., Clark, D. D., Kahn, R. E., Kleinrock, L., Leiner, B. M., Lynch, D. C., Postel, J., Roberts, L. G., and Wolff, S. (2000, 4 August). *Brief History of the Internet.* Available online at www.isoc.org/Internet/history/brief.shtml. Last accessed on 29 August 2002.

Cyber Atlas (2002, 21 March). *The World's Online Populations.* Available online at cyberatlas. Internet.com/big_picture/geographics/article/0,1323,5911_151151,00.html. Last accessed on 29 August 2002.

CSVI (2002). *The People's Resistance in Indonesia.* Available online at www.xs4all.nl/~peace/. Last accessed on 29 August 2002.

Douglass, M. (1993). "The "New" Tokyo Story: Restructuring Space and the Struggle for Place in a World City," in K. Fujita and R. C. Hill (eds.), *Japanese Cities in the Global Economy:*

Global Restructuring and Urban-Industrial Change, pp. 83–119. Philadelphia: Temple University Press.

—— (2002b). "From Global Competition to Cooperation for Liveable Cities and Economic Resilience in Pacific Asia," *Environment and Urbanization,* special issue on *Globalization and Cities* 14(1): 53–68.

Douglass, M., Ho, K. C., and Ooi, G. L. (2002). "Civic Spaces, Globalisation and Pacific Asia Cities," *International Development and Planning Review Journal,* special edition, November.

Friedman, T. L. (2000). "Censors Beware," *New York Times,* 25 July.

Habermas, J. (1991). *The Structural Transformation of the Public Sphere: An Inquiry into a Category of Bourgeois Society.* Translated by Thomas Burger, with Frederick Lawrence. Cambridge, Mass.: MIT Press.

Hill, D., and Sen, K. (2000). "The Internet in Indonesia's New Democracy," *Democratization* 7(1): 119–36.

Illich, I. (1973). *Tools for Conviviality.* London: Calder & Boyars.

Indonesia Baru (1998, 8 April). *Langkah Penyebaran Informasi.* Available online at www.geocities.com/CapitolHill/Senate/4427/grafikin.htm. Last accessed on 29 August 2002.

ITU (2001, 26 November). *Information Technology—World 1999.* Available online at www.itu.int/ITU-D/ict/statistics/at_glance/Internet99.pdf. Last accessed on 29 August 2002.

—— (2002, 25 March). *Information Technology—World 2001.* Available online at www.itu.int/ITU-D/ict/statistics/at_glance/Internet01.pdf. Last accessed on 29 August 2002.

KdPnet (1998). *Pijar Indonesia.* Available online at www.uni-stuttgart.de/indonesia/pijar/. Last accessed on 30 July 1999.

Kitley, P. (1994). "Fine Tuning Control: Commercial Television in Indonesia," *Continuum: The Australian Journal of Media and Culture* 8: 103–23.

Lim, M. (2002). "CyberCivic Space in Indonesia: From Panopticon to Pandemonium?" *International Development and Planning Review Journal,* special edition, November.

Luknanto, J. (1998a). *Daftar Isi Kekayaan Eyang Kakung.* Available online at www.isnet.org/~djoko/Reformasi%201998/Kekayaan%20Suharto/00Index.html. Last accessed on 29 August 2002.

—— (1998b). *Daftar Kekayaan Soeharto.* Available online at www.isnet.org/~djoko/Reformasi%201998/Kekayaan%20Suharto/Kaya03.html. Last accessed on 29 August 2002.

Marcus, D. L. (1999). "Indonesia Revolt Was Net Driven," in E. Aspinall, G. Klinken, and H. van Feith (eds.), *The Last Days of President Suharto,* pp. 73–75. Australia: Monash Asia Institute.

Miller, D., and Slater, D. (2000). *The Internet: An Ethnographic Approach.* Oxford: Berg.

Munindo (1998, 5 October). *JP: Aditjondro; sosok dan kiprahnya.* Available online at www.munindo.br.de/george/george_wawancara_george.html. Last accessed on 29 August 2002.

—— (2000, 29 June). *Ruangan George.* Available online at www.munindo.brd.de/george/george.html. Last accessed on 29 August 2002.

M-Web (2001). *Corporate Profile.* Available online at www.id.mweb.com/company_profile.php. Last accessed on 29 August 2002.

—— (2002). *Corporate Profile: Milestones.* Available online at www.id.mweb.com/milestones.php. Last accessed on 29 August 2002.

NatnitNet (2001, 14 August). *Berita: Bisnis Warnet di Yogya Berguguran.* Available online at www.natnit.net/weblog/archives/00000040.htm. Last accessed on 29 August 2002.

Rigg, J. (eds.) (1996). *The Human Environment: Indonesian Heritage Series Vol. 2.* Singapore: Archipelago Press.

Shoesmith, B. (1994). "Asia in Their Shadow: Satellites and Asia," *Southeast Asian Journal of Social Science* 22: 125–141.

SiaR (1998a). *Indonesian Daily News Online*. Available online at www.uni-stuttgart.de/indonesia/news/index.html. Last accessed on 30 July 1999.

——— (1998b, 13 March). *SiaR→GJA: Yayasan-Yayasan Suharto . . . (1,2,3,4)*. Available online at www.geocities.com/CapitolHill/Senate/3005/harta1.html,harta2.html,harta3.html,harta4.html. Last accessed on 29 August 2002.

Slama, M. (2002). "Towards a New Autonomy: Internet Practices of Indonesian Youth—Conditions and Consequences." Paper delivered to the *Third International Symposium of Antropologi Indonesia Journal*, Denpasar, 16–19 July.

Wright, R. (2000). "Gaining Freedom by Modem," *New York Times*, 28 January.

CHAPTER 18

The Alternative Media in Malaysia
THEIR POTENTIAL AND LIMITATIONS

Sharon Ling

The media in Malaysia have grown rapidly in the past twenty years—particularly during the 1990s, when new terrestrial, cable, and satellite television networks and newspapers emerged (Zaharom, 2000). However, state control over the media remains tight and has even been strengthened through ownership by "politicians and politically influential businessmen"[1] as well as through the amendments of laws such as the Official Secrets Act and the Printing Presses and Publications Act

Given this context, it is not surprising that studies of Malaysia's media tend to focus on the mainstream press and broadcast media and how they are influenced, to their detriment, by government control (e.g., Mustafa, 1990; Zaharom, 1994). While these studies are important in pointing to the workings of state control, they overlook a significant section of the media scene—alternative publications whose content is not controlled by the government.

On 2 September 1998, Malaysian deputy prime minister Anwar Ibrahim was sacked, a decision that sent shockwaves throughout the country. After all, Anwar had long been seen as the chosen successor to the prime minister, Mahathir Mohamad. His abrupt sacking on allegations of corruption and sexual impropriety provoked an unprecedented public outcry against Mahathir and the government. The *reformasi* ("Malay for reform") movement, which Anwar set in train following his dismissal—with its strident calls for justice and truth as well as political, social, and judicial reforms—also garnered widespread support among ordinary Malaysians dissatisfied with the government's authoritarian tendencies. In addition, an assortment of Anwar websites sprang up across the Internet, urging support for the deposed deputy premier and serving as channels for the expression of critical viewpoints.

It is within this context that I propose to explore both the potential capabilities and the limitations of the alternative media in Malaysia. How would the alternative media, with their tradition of critical and oppositional coverage, represent the downfall of someone who had once been the second most powerful man in the government? How influential would their coverage be, given that they provide dissenting viewpoints rather than parroting the government in the manner of the mainstream press? How important would the Internet prove to be for the alternative media? And what limitations, if any, do they face?

The Alternative Press: The Dissenting Voices of *Aliran Monthly* and *Harakah*

The alternative press in Malaysia mainly comprises newspapers and magazines published by nongovernmental organizations (NGOs), activists, and opposition political parties. These publications are characterized by low circulations and, in the case of the smaller or more outspoken ones, a short lifespan inasmuch as their permits are often revoked or not renewed by the government.

The Anwar saga proved to be a watershed of sorts for the alternative press, enabling it to become more visible as the alternative nature of its content became more evident in comparison with the sycophantic mainstream media. In fact, the alternative press has traditionally departed from the government's point of view in its content, striving to provide critical or dissenting viewpoints and opinions. As public dissatisfaction and demonstrations grew over Anwar's sacking and arrest, the alternative press became more vocal in criticizing the authorities whereas the mainstream press reverberated a growing chorus of pro-Mahathir and anti-Anwar sentiments. Thus the polarization between the alternative press and the mainstream media became more clearly defined in the wake of Anwar's fall from power. This is best illustrated by reference to two of the most established alternative publications, *Aliran Monthly* and *Harakah*.

ALIRAN MONTHLY

Aliran Monthly is an English-language magazine published once a month by Aliran Kesedaran Negara ("National Consciousness Movement"), an independent NGO that campaigns for social justice and reform in Malaysia. Established in 1977, Aliran has a multi-ethnic membership and is guided by "universal spiritual values" rather than by any one religious or ethnic philosophy (Aliran Online, 2003). Its fifteen executive committee members are mostly middle class and include university lecturers, analysts, and activists, while its president P. Ramakrishnan is a retired schoolteacher (Eng, 1999).

Aliran began publishing *Aliran Monthly* in 1980 and considers the publication of the magazine its main activity, aimed at raising public awareness on current issues in Malaysia (Aliran Online, 2003). The magazine carries no advertisements in order to safeguard its neutrality, and it is financed through donations from supporters (Eng, 1999). Since its inception, it has never shied away from addressing issues ignored by the mainstream media because of their controversial nature, such as the Bakun hydroelectric dam project and government bailouts of crony companies. It is also frequently critical of what it sees as flawed government policies and actions.

It comes as no surprise, then, that the magazine's coverage of the Anwar affair in its September and October 1998 issues was characterized by a critical and at times hostile tone toward the authorities. I would suggest that this tone reflected the "fit" between the events and Aliran's struggle for justice, freedom, and democratic rights, while the *reformasi* movement resonated with its own reform agenda. The magazine's staff was clearly outraged by the manner of Anwar's sacking and arrest. Moreover, they saw justice, truth, and reform as the real issues of the sacking, as indicated by the magazine's cover stories: "Justice must prevail" (September 1998) and "A nation on trial" (October 1998).

While *Aliran Monthly* did not contain traditional news reports in the inverted-pyramid, objective, third-person style, it provided commentaries and analyses, eyewitness accounts of related events, and press statements and letters from readers and various organizations. What distinguished *Aliran Monthly* from the mainstream press was the magazine's perception in contextualizing the dismissal of Anwar within recent economic and political developments in Malaysia and Southeast Asia, something the mainstream press failed to do. The most the mainstream press could offer was a brief chronology of events, without further comment or analysis beyond reasoning that the sacking of Anwar was the prime minister's prerogative and therefore need not be questioned as he was bound to have a good reason for doing so. However, *Aliran Monthly*, in its September 1998 issue, pointed to recent pertinent developments that led to Anwar's dismissal. These included the economic recession, the emergence of a book titled *50 Reasons Why Anwar Cannot Become Prime Minister* in which Anwar was accused of having an illegitimate child, the removal of economic decision-making from Anwar to a trusted Mahathir ally, the forced resignations of senior media personnel aligned with Anwar, and the ousting of Indonesia's President Suharto. The September 1998 issue also reminded readers of the imprisonment of an opposition political leader for alleged sedition and the summary dismissal of three Supreme Court judges, both of which rendered the judiciary's independence questionable. Tellingly, the magazine saw these developments as the "silencing of outspoken voices and potential challengers to the political leadership" (*Aliran Monthly*, September 1998).

Hence, *Aliran Monthly* was able to offer a much greater depth of commentary and analysis on Anwar's dismissal and arrest. Whereas the mainstream media were content to reduce the conflict to a simple "Mahathir-is-right, Anwar-is-wrong" dichotomy, *Aliran Monthly* questioned how someone who had become almost like a son to the prime minister could be disposed of so ruthlessly. It also explored the consequences of Anwar's dismissal for Malaysian society, concluding that it meant "the loss of a potential counter-balance" to Mahathir and that if Anwar planned a political comeback he would have to find a better solution than the one he had offered during his sixteen years in office (*Aliran Monthly*, September 1998). In addition, *Aliran Monthly* focused on the urgent need for political and judicial reforms and stressed the importance of a fair trial for Anwar. Rather than drawing attention to the unpalatable allegations against Anwar, as the mainstream press had done, the magazine condemned the manner of his sacking and criticized Umno politicians as well as the mainstream media for their vilification of Anwar even before he had been tried and found guilty.

Nevertheless, despite its espousal of Anwar's cause, *Aliran Monthly* did not seek to idealize Anwar but recognized his shortcomings as a politician: "Let us not be naïve. Anwar is not your innocent bystander. . . . He is a seasoned political *gajah* [elephant] who played for the highest stakes in the power game, and lost" (*Aliran Monthly*, September 1998). The magazine also ran a commentary that assessed the "competing explanations of Anwar's sacking," pointing out that "Anwar's faction was hungry for power too" and that "the so-called 'Reform Movement,' warts and all, was an initiative from the top, not from the bottom" (*Aliran Monthly*, October 1998).

In addition, *Aliran Monthly's* coverage included several eyewitness accounts of Anwar's rallies, his arrest, and the street demonstrations that followed—accounts that provided a stark contrast to the reports found in the mainstream press. For example, one eyewitness observed tellingly that "one local newspaper reported 'stone-throwing crowds' confronting the FRU [Federal Reserve Unit] and that the crowd was chanting '*bakar, bakar*' (burn, burn); neither of which I saw or heard" (*Aliran Monthly*, October 1998). Another eyewitness reporting on the demonstrations at the National Mosque and Independence Square in Kuala Lumpur recounted how Anwar told the crowd, "You must be orderly and well-behaved. Do not disturb others or cause a commotion," adding that he "never heard anyone tell anyone else to go to the Putra World Trade Centre (the ruling party headquarters) or to Sri Perdana (the Prime Minister's residence)" (*Aliran Monthly*, October 1998). In contrast, one mainstream newspaper told readers in an editorial: "In a clear attempt to incite the people against the Government, Anwar today held two illegal assemblies. . . . In addition to this, encouraging and inciting supporters to march to the Prime Minister Datuk Seri Dr Mahathir Mohamad's residence is definitely a treacherous act" (*New Straits Times*, 21 September 1998).

The mainstream press also exhibited a collective myopia when it came to the police's brutal handling of peaceful demonstrators. *Aliran Monthly*, however, carried an eyewitness account of how the FRU unleashed water cannons and tear gas indiscriminately on protesters and onlookers alike. All its eyewitness accounts of demonstrations, moreover, agreed that at no time had the crowd become violent. Additionally, it printed an excerpt from Australia's *Sydney Morning Herald* detailing Anwar's arrest by balaclava-clad, heavily armed members of a special police squad and their rough handling of foreign journalists. It is a compelling account of an unnecessarily forceful arrest that was heavily played down by the mainstream press.

Aliran Monthly's coverage also represented critical and dissenting viewpoints with regard to the government's actions over the sacking and arrest. It printed, in full, statements from NGOs, opposition political parties, and prominent individuals who voiced their concern over the government's failure to satisfactorily account for Anwar's dismissal. It also printed the translated texts of Anwar's letters to Mahathir dated 25 and 28 August 1998 denying the allegations raised against him in poison-pen letters, as well as the translated text of a speech given by his wife, Dr. Wan Azizah Wan Ismail, at the launching of the People's Movement for Justice, in which she condemned Anwar's arrest under the draconian Internal Security Act (ISA) of 1960. Further, the magazine's letters page provided a forum for concerned individuals to express their opinions. Its October 1998 issue, for example, carried readers' letters that attacked the mainstream media's one-sided coverage of the affair and criticized the actions of the government and the police. The reactions from various NGOs such as the Society for Christian Reflection ("The erosion of fundamental rights and liberties, the manipulation of the media and the blatant undermining of the institutions of state . . . should not go unchallenged!"), Amnesty International ("The timing and nature of statements and actions by the Royal Malaysian Police and the Attorney-General's office have prompted charges of political bias"), and women's groups ("We are appalled at the exercise of excessive use of police force through the use of tear-gas, water-cannons, batons and verbal intimidation on members of the public") were also carried in the issue.

It must be noted that these viewpoints come from diverse voices within Malaysian society that were not represented in the mainstream press.

On the whole, then, *Aliran Monthly* was able to see the bigger picture of Anwar's sacking, and its coverage represented diverse dissenting viewpoints without descending into hysterical rhetoric in blind support of Anwar. It therefore deserves to be taken seriously as a credible source of alternative information.

HARAKAH

Harakah was first published in 1987 by the central information division of the Pan-Islamic Party of Malaysia (PAS), the main opposition party in the country.[2] It is published mainly in Malay but carries an English-language section introduced in 1986 (KAMI, 2001). Originally published twice weekly, on Mondays and Fridays, it has since been directed to reduce its publication to twice a month. *Harakah* started out as a party newsletter with a limited circulation of 35,000 among party members. However, its editors decided in the early 1990s that the paper, while continuing to promote party interests, should serve the interests of the public at the same time (KAMI, 2001).

Inasmuch as *Harakah* aspires to be more than just a party organ, it publishes news and editorial pieces that are largely, but not exclusively, informed by a PAS-cum-Islamic philosophy. However, in the wake of Anwar's sacking, the paper also sees itself as an important alternative channel of information and expression, particularly for the opposition, as its editorial of 7 September 1998 pointed out:

> *Harakah* has to serve not only as a paper for PAS but also the media for the opposition and for the dissenters. Since all the media, both print and electronic, are controlled by the ruling party or its agents, there is no way PAS members would know what are the views of other opposition parties on any issue which is the concern of the people as a whole.

Harakah's coverage of the Anwar affair is particularly interesting in this context. Prior to his dismissal, Anwar had been the second-most powerful individual in both the Barisan Nasional (BN) coalition government and its dominant political party, the United Malays National Organisation (Umno). By virtue of his position, then, Anwar would have been viewed as a leading political opponent by PAS, and one might have expected *Harakah* to gloat over his political demise. Such, however, was not the case. *Harakah*, while not passing up the opportunity to lambast the government, also saw fit to defend Anwar and jump onto the *reformasi* bandwagon. The paper's championing of Anwar was not out of character given that, prior to entering politics with Umno, Anwar was an influential Islamic activist admired even by PAS. Although PAS leaders were aware that he chose Umno over their party, they sympathized with him over the manner of his dismissal and the nature of the allegations against him. This was duly conveyed by *Harakah* in a commentary that told readers "This is not the time for anyone who has a personal or 'political' grudge against [Anwar] from within the party to grind their axe. . . . The current Anwar debacle cannot simply be brushed aside by saying things like 'padan muka engkau!' (you deserve it, Anwar!)" (*Harakah*, 21 September 1998).

In a similar vein, the paper gave prominence to the largely sympathetic response of PAS leaders to Anwar's dismissal and arrest. Then–PAS president Fadzil Mohd Noor was reported as saying that Anwar should be either released or brought to face charges in open court (*Harakah*, 25 September 1998). Another article reported Fadzil's support for the reform movement, quoting him as saying that "it could increase awareness and build the confidence of the people to defy tyranny and uphold the truth" (*Harakah*, 25 September 1998). And another PAS leader, Nik Aziz Nik Mat, was reported as saying that "the right to hold demonstrations cannot be denied because it is a basic human right" but that demonstrators should not damage public property (*Harakah*, 28 September 1998). In contrast, the mainstream *Utusan Malaysia*, covering the same press conference, angled its report to say that Nik Aziz advised Anwar's supporters not to demonstrate as this would disrupt public order.

As did *Aliran Monthly*, *Harakah* focused on issues of justice and political reform, but with a heavy emphasis on Islamic perspectives. For instance, it argued that

> as Muslims, we cannot give any weight to hearsay or blind accusations. Lest we become a party to back-biting or the slandering of innocent people (which is a grave sin in Islam). As Muslims, we must ensure that anyone who is thus accused of grievous sins or "munker" gets a fair chance to prove his or her innocence. (*Harakah*, 21 September 1998)

Inevitably some party propaganda can be found in *Harakah*'s coverage as well, advocating the merits of PAS in contrast to the government and Umno. An example of this is its editorial of 14 September 1998, which stated that the secular BN government could not guarantee justice for citizens and therefore the political system needed to be changed to an Islamic one led by PAS. The paper took the opportunity to point out that the Malay population should stop assuming that Umno alone had the right to govern the country. It also said that "Anwar's sacking incident and harassment could only further prove that the Umno-led BN government have [*sic*] to be changed for a better one. Let us strive to achieve victory through PAS!" (*Harakah*, 21 September 1998).

Harakah also supported the *reformasi* movement but stressed that it must be guided by Islamic principles and that preferably PAS should be leading the movement. It expounded the view that since PAS has always struggled for reform, Anwar's Muslim supporters should "understand that if they are really keen to see an Islamic transformation of the government they should lend their support to PAS and together in the name of Islam strive to save this beleaguered nation of ours" (*Harakah*, 21 September 1998).

In keeping with its role as an alternative medium, *Harakah* also carried the viewpoints of other groups. For example, it printed statements issued by the Malaysian People's Party, a small opposition party, that criticized Mahathir as authoritarian and called for his resignation. It also reported the reactions of NGOs such as Aliran and Amnesty International that demanded justice for Anwar. The paper even carried a Reuters story of France's support for Anwar and an editorial from *The Times* of London condemning Mahathir's regime. Anwar himself received broad coverage from the paper. His detailed press statement denying the allegations against him was reprinted in full as a special report in the 7 September 1998 issue, and his press conferences and rallies were covered in a sympathetic tone.

Although *Harakah* remains primarily a party paper, it tries to be a genuine alternative publication as well. It succeeds in this effort to some extent, but Islamic perspectives and party propaganda tend to drown out other viewpoints.

Limited Impact

John Downing (2001) makes the point that many radical alternative media operate within a framework of challenging the dominant hegemony of those in power and attempting to replace them with alternative visions. Both *Aliran Monthly* and *Harakah* fall into this category of alternative media, but to what extent do they offer alternative visions?

In *Harakah's* case the answer appears quite clear: Replace the present BN government with a PAS government that would rule according to Islamic principles; only then would Malaysians have justice and freedom. However, the paper failed to set out clearly how PAS should go about reforming the existing political system if indeed it does come into power one day. It also failed to address the question of whether or not PAS would set in place a new form of domination rather than reform. As an opposition party whose goal is to come into power and form a new federal government, PAS remains within the power structure and may very well replace BN's dominance with its own. Moreover, *Harakah* neglected to acknowledge that PAS's fundamentalist Islamic ideology and political ambition of setting up an Islamic government would not go down well with Malaysia's non-Muslim minority, particularly the Chinese. As Ahmad Ibrahim (1989) has observed, PAS is not yet capable of replacing BN because it has neither fully thought out the practicalities of establishing an Islamic society based on the Quran nor considered the multi-ethnic nature of Malaysia's society. As such, the alternative vision proposed by *Harakah* does not appear to be viable or tenable.

Nevertheless, *Harakah's* oppositional coverage and alternative content proved popular with a public tired of reading the government's point of view in the mainstream press. According to its editor Zulkifli Sulong, its circulation surged from 75,000 in mid-1998 to 345,000 by the end of the year (Cordingley and Oorjitham, 1998; Safar et al., 2000).

Aliran Monthly, while not making references to an Islamic government, called for political, judicial, and social reforms. It set out its ideals clearly enough—an independent judiciary, a free press, upholding justice and truth—and these seemed to attract reader interest. However, it neglected to spell out what forms these reforms should take and how they could be achieved. As in the case of *Harakah*, though, the magazine's normal circulation of 8,000 copies increased in the months following Anwar's sacking (Eng, 1999).

Significantly, neither publication conducted investigative reporting on the Anwar affair. Thus their claims of a conspiracy to topple Anwar and their implicit suggestions that the authorities found him too hot to handle remained unsubstantiated by evidence. Although their opinions and viewpoints were clearly delineated, they would have carried more weight had they been corroborated with facts. However, investigative journalism is rarely, if ever, done in Malaysia. It is extremely difficult for journalists to get hold of government documents because of the Official Secrets Act (OSA), which prohibits the unauthorized publication of all government information classified as official secrets and carries a mandatory jail sentence upon conviction (Wong, 2000: 121).

Hence, I would argue that these alternative publications find it difficult to have an impact that would lead to changes in Malaysian society. It is not enough merely to point out what the desirable alternative is; there must also be clear and practical solutions as to how this alternative can be achieved.

In addition, there is a powerful factor limiting the impact that the alternative press can have in Malaysia: the legal restrictions imposed by the government in the form of the Printing Presses and Publications Act (PPPA). Under this law, every newspaper and magazine requires from the home minister a publication permit that must be reapplied for every year. It empowers the minister with absolute discretion to reject applications and to suspend or revoke a permit. These decisions are final and cannot be challenged in court.

Both *Aliran Monthly* and *Harakah* have felt the force of this law. Under the terms of its permit, *Aliran Monthly* can be published only in English; its applications to publish a Malay version have been repeatedly turned down without explanation (Chandra, 1990). This significantly limits the magazine's circulation and influence because English-speaking Malaysians constitute a minority of the population and are mainly found in urban areas. It is highly unlikely that the magazine would be able to penetrate the rural Malay population, traditionally the bastion of Umno's support.

In addition, the magazine occasionally faces difficulties in finding printers. In September 1999, Aliran released a statement apologizing for a delay in distributing that month's issue because it was unable to find a printer prepared to print the magazine. According to the statement, *Aliran Monthly* had been printed by four different printers in recent months because each in turn had been pressured to stop printing the magazine (Aliran Online, 1999).

Harakah's permit, on the other hand, allows it to be sold only to PAS members, although the party has frequently flouted this regulation by selling the paper openly from newsstands (Safar et al., 2000). Nevertheless, the authorities have come down hard on the publication following its increased popularity in the wake of Anwar's dismissal. The government decreed that the paper should be labeled "For members only," but this seemed to make it easier for the public, including nonmembers, to spot the paper. Then the authorities issued a directive stating that only those who qualify to be PAS members—meaning Muslim newsagents—could sell the paper, thereby restricting its distribution because non-Muslim Chinese and Indian newsagents were no longer allowed to sell it (KAMI, 2001).

Further, *Harakah* editor Zulkifli Sulong and printer Chia Lim Thye were arrested in January 2000 on charges of sedition with regard to an article concerning Anwar; both pleaded not guilty (World Press Freedom Review, 2000). Two months later, the Home Affairs Ministry issued *Harakah*'s new permit, which stated that it could be published only twice a month instead of twice weekly as before, and warned that the paper could be shut down if it failed to meet the terms of its permit (KAMI, 2001; World Press Freedom Review, 2000).[3]

Internet-Based Alternative Media

Recognizing the restrictions of the PPPA on print publications, many dissenters turned to the Internet to voice their support of Anwar and criticisms of the government. In the wake of the sacking, a large number of websites professing support for Anwar sprang up on the Internet; one observer estimates that at least sixty such websites were created (Zeitlin, 1998). Their intention is clearly indicated by their names, such as *Free Anwar Campaign* (www.freeanwar.com); *Laman Reformasi*, which means "Reform Page" (www.mazalim. net); and *Justice for Anwar and Reformasi* (members.tripod.com/~Anwarite). These websites are characterized by strong pro-Anwar sentiments, outrage at the manner of his dismissal and arrest, and anger toward the authorities. Rage is expressed in a number of ways, including leveling charges of conspiracy at the government, satirizing Mahathir and his cronies, calling for reforms, and exchanging unflattering comments about the authorities. The *Justice for Anwar* website (www.geocities.com/WallStreet/Market/1497) lists a series of developments prior to Anwar's dismissal and asks, "Are we that stupid [that we] cannot put all these thing[s] together[?]. Definitely this is the highest-level conspiracy ever." It goes on to urge viewers to "voice your disgust & show [your] support." Some of the websites express such disillusionment and anger with the authorities as to verge on the slanderous; for instance, *Justice for Anwar and Reformasi* (members.tripod.com/~Anwarite) features a list of what it calls "the 12 most evil persons in Malaysia," headed by none other than Mahathir Mohamad, who is described as "the father of corruption" and "the most dictatorial prime minister ever."

These websites share a number of similar features. Their news items, including coverage of the Anwar affair, are frequently sourced from foreign news agencies and media such as Reuters, the Associated Press, the BBC, and CNN. Very few sites have original coverage, but the ones that do largely consist of eyewitness accounts. The websites' staffs are also aware of the mainstream media's subservience to the government and recognize the possibilities of the Internet for disseminating alternative viewpoints and information. The *freeMalaysia* website (www.freemalaysia.com) offers a typical example of this, telling viewers: "With the poor quality and obvious bias of the 'official' media, the need for such alternative sources of quality information is clear."

One significant feature of these websites is that they urge readers to print and distribute their pages—an acknowledgment that the majority of Malaysia's population do not have access to the Internet. *Justice for Anwar and Reformasi* (members.tripod. com/~Anwarite), for instance, tells readers: "Please print and distribute freely. Not all people have access to Internet, u know!" Another website (www.anwar/freeservers.com/) consists merely of a leaflet announcing a nationwide demonstration on 28 September 1998 and urging readers to print, photocopy, and distribute it.

Other websites go beyond supporting Anwar and his cause, and seek to be channels of alternative information not only on the Anwar issue but on other injustices in

Malaysia. One such site, titled *Free Anwar Campaign* (www.freeanwar.com), as noted earlier, started out as a website campaigning for Anwar's release but has now expanded into a site that channels alternative news and information on Malaysia largely sourced from foreign news media. In addition to campaigning for Anwar, it currently campaigns on behalf of activists detained under the ISA in April 2001 and advocates the abolishing of the ISA. The *freeMalaysia* site (www.freemalaysia.com) is steadfastly not "pro-anybody": "We consider reform inevitable and the lack of justice in Malaysia today painfully apparent, but we are not advancing anyone's political agenda. What we espouse is that Malaysians take control of their political destiny," it says.

These websites can be regarded as the forerunners of malaysiakini.com, also known as Malaysia Now, launched in November 1999 as Malaysia's first and so far only independent online newspaper with no print counterpart. This Internet publication, with its taglines of "Only the news that matters" and "Get both sides of the story," has an excellent track record in breaking news stories that reach an estimated 100,000 readers every day.

Malaysiakini.com is an illustration of the possibilities offered by the Internet for the alternative media. The Printing Presses and Publications Act does not apply to the Internet, so news sites such as malaysiakini.com do not require a permit to set up operations. Moreover, there is as yet no official regulation of the Internet. The government has often promised that it will not censor the Internet—specifically, in order to attract foreign investors to the Multimedia Super Corridor, a high-technology park of multimedia and Internet industries. In line with this, both the Multimedia Bill of Guarantees and the Communications and Multimedia Commission Act 1998 stipulate that the Internet will not be censored.

However, there remain limitations as well. First, while it is difficult to determine exact figures, there is no doubt that Internet users constitute a minority of the population in Malaysia. The websites' tactic of urging users to print and distribute messages of protest appears to have been effective, but there are no records of the actual extent of its success.

Second, it is difficult to determine the accuracy and credibility of information posted on the Internet due to its mostly anonymous and uncorroborated nature. For example, the *Justice for Anwar and Reformasi* site (members.tripod.com/~Anwarite) includes a letter e-mailed to the webmaster, and signed "an insider," alleging that Mahathir plotted to have Anwar "mentally tormented and brutalised in order to weaken and subdue his spirit." The letter goes on to say:

> If the injury could be disguised as being self-inflicted, and Anwar's spirit could be tamed and subdued, the plan was to assassinate Anwar in his cell, leaving the body in suicidal posture. Further enquiries would have "proved" that Anwar had committed suicide, with the explanation that an intense sense of guilt and shame might have caused his severe state of mental depression.

This potentially explosive piece of information, however, does not offer any corroboration or evidence to support its claims; it is up to the reader whether to believe it or not. Indeed, very few of these websites are able to provide hard facts or evidence to substantiate their opinions, which in turn damages their credibility and therefore their influence.

Third, despite promises of noncensorship of the Internet, there are no guarantees that the government will not take action against these websites. In fact, an anti-defamation committee has identified forty-eight websites as having made defamatory accusations with a view to bringing lawsuits against their writers, while malaysiakini.com and *Harakah*'s online edition face possible charges of sedition (Lebowitz, 1999; Ranawana, 2001). Also, the webmaster of the *Free Anwar Campaign* website was one of ten people detained under the ISA in April 2001 in a crackdown on dissent. Hence, although alternative websites escape the restrictions of the PPPA, other laws such as the Defamation Act, the Sedition Act, and the ISA can and will be used by the authorities to harass and intimidate them.

Fourth, these websites appear to face difficulties in sustaining their operations over a long period of time. A large number of pro-Anwar websites are no longer in existence as they have not been maintained for some time. Even *freeMalaysia* (www.freemalaysia.com), which started out with high ambitions of becoming a forum of lively, rigorous discussion, has disappeared from cyberspace. Malaysiakini.com, meanwhile, told readers in an editorial on 16 August 2002 that it faced a Hobson's choice: "Lock up the website [for subscription purposes] and stand to lose our readers—and there is no guarantee we can still survive—or continue to keep malaysiakini.com free until we bite the dust in the coming months" (malaysiakini.com, 2002). In the case of malaysiakini.com, then, the difficulty of sustaining its publications can be attributed to the different economics involved in online newspapers as opposed to print media. As for the pro-Anwar websites that have ceased to exist, it is difficult to say whether their absence is due to official intimidation, lack of resources, or loss of interest.

Conclusion

The alternative media came into their own in the aftermath of Anwar's sacking and arrest. In particular, the new phenomenon of pro-Anwar websites and online news sites multiplied the number of channels through which Malaysians could express dissenting viewpoints and obtain alternative sources of information. These media, in complete contrast to the mainstream press, spare few punches in criticizing the government.

Thus the media in Malaysia remain polarized between supporting and opposing the government. This polarization, which will continue as long as the authorities maintain their powerful control over the mainstream media to stifle dissent, is clearly detrimental to press freedom in Malaysia. In such a situation, the role of the alternative media in providing critical and dissenting coverage remains vital if Malaysians are to have access to a wide range of viewpoints. Yet the state is also able to repress the alternative media through various laws, while their small audiences and lack of resources also limit their influence on society.

Despite such hardships, the alternative media must continue to exploit the potential of the Internet in disseminating information and facilitating debate. Admittedly, Internet access is mainly confined to young, educated Malaysians in urban areas, and the government has not backed off from cracking down on dissident Internet users. Nevertheless, as one commentator has noted, the Internet remains "the realm where creative experimentation—with technology and democratic space—can, and should, be explored" (Mustafa, 1990, 2000).

Notes

1. For example, the New Straits Times Press—which publishes a number of newspapers, including the leading English-language daily, the *New Straits Times*, and a Malay-language daily, *Berita Harian*—is owned by the Malaysian Resources Corporation Bhd (MRCB), a conglomerate with close ties to senior United Malays National Organisation (Umno) politicians (Gomez, 1990; Gomez and Jomo, 1999: 68–69). Umno is the dominant party in the ruling Barisan Nasional (BN) coalition government.

2. By winning 27 seats in the 1999 general election (its biggest-ever haul), PAS overtook the Democratic Action Party as the opposition party with the most representatives in Parliament. PAS also retained its hold in Kelantan state while capturing neighboring Terengganu state from BN.

3. Although *Harakah* has thus far avoided being closed down, other pro-opposition alternative publications were not so fortunate. In 2000, the Home Affairs Ministry refused to renew the publishing permits of the biweekly *Detik*, its sister publication *Al Wasilah*, and the weekly *Eksklusif*, effectively shutting them down (World Press Freedom Review, 2000). Undeterred, *Detik* promptly launched itself on the Internet with the name *Detik Daily*.

References

Aliran Monthly, September and October 1998.

Aliran Online (1999). "We Apologise." Available online at www.malaysia.net/aliran/ ms 991020.htm.

——— (2003). "About Aliran." Available online at www.malaysia.net/aliran/more.html.

Chandra, Muzaffar (1990). "The Muzzled Media," in K. S. Kua (ed.), *Mediawatch: The Use and Abuse of the Malaysian Press*. Selangor: Selangor Chinese Assembly Hall.

Cordingley, Peter, and Oorjitham, Santha (1998). "How the Media Have Fared: Mainstream Newspapers Take a Beating," in *Asiaweek*, 13 October. Available online at www.asiaweek.com/ Asiaweek/98/1113/cs4.html.

Downing, John (2001). *Radical Media: Rebellious Communication and Social Movements*. Thousand Oaks, Calif.: Sage.

Eng, Peter (1999). "A Small Magazine Defies a Despot," *Columbia Journalism Review*, January/ February. Available online at www.cjr.org/year/99/1/malaysia.asp.

Gomez, Edmund Terence (1990). *Politics in Business: Umno's Corporate Investments*. Kuala Lumpur: Forum.

Gomez, Edmund Terence, and Jomo, K. S. (1999). *Malaysia's Political Economy: Politics, Patronage and Profits*, 2nd ed. Cambridge, U.K.: Cambridge University Press.

Harakah, 7, 11, 14, 18, 21, 25, and 28 September 1998.

Ibrahim, Ahmad (1989). *Konflik Umno-PAS dalam Isu Islamisasi*. Petaling Jaya: IBS Buku Sdn Bhd.

KAMI (2001). "Kebebasan akhbar: pengalaman Harakah," in *Detik Daily*, 27 July. Available online at detik.daily.tripod.com/julaia/27julai_9.htm.

Lebowitz, R. Frank (1999). "Silencing Web Sites in Malaysia," *Digital Freedom Network*. Available online at dfn.org/focus/malaysia/malaysites.htm.

malaysiakini.com (2002). "Online Media Hobson's Choice." Available online at www.malaysiakini.com/editorials/2002081601273.php.

Mustafa, K. Anuar (1990). "The Malaysian 1990 General Election: The Role of the BN Media," *Kajian Malaysia* 8(2): 82–102.

—— (2000). "Malaysian Media and Democracy," *Media Asia* 27(4): 183–89. *New Straits Times*, 21 September 1998.

Ranawana, Arjuna (2001). "A Crackdown on Dissent: The Malaysian Government Targets Web Critics," *Asiaweek*, 20 March. Available online at www.asiaweek.com/asiaweek/daily/foc/0,8773,102638,00.html.

Safar, H. M., Asiah binti Sarji, and Gunaratne, Shelton A. (2000). "Malaysia," in Shelton Gunaratne (ed.), *Handbook of the Media in Asia*. New Delhi: Sage.

Wong, Kean (2000). "Malaysia: In the Grip of the Government," in L. Williams and R. Rich (eds.), *Losing Control: Freedom of the Press in Asia*. Australia National University: Asia Pacific Press.

World Press Freedom Review (2000). "Malaysia: 2000 World Press Freedom Review." Available online at www.freemedia.at/wpfr/malaysia.htm.

Zaharom, Nain (1994). "Commercialization and Control in a 'Caring Society': Malaysian Media 'Towards 2020,'" *Sojourn* 9(2): 178–99.

—— (2000). "Globalized Theories and National Controls: The State, the Market and the Malaysian Media," in J. Curran and M.-J. Park (eds.), *De-Westernizing Media Studies*, pp. 139–153. London: Routledge.

Zeitlin, Arnold (1998). "Web Sites Backing Ousted Malaysian Official Evade Government Control." Available online at www.freedomforum.org/templates/ document/asp?documentID=4965.

Index

Note: Page references in *italic type* refer to illustrations.

303

About the Contributors

Chris Atton is Reader in Journalism in the School of Communication Arts at Napier University, Edinburgh, Scotland. He is the author of *Alternative Literature* (1996) and *Alternative Media* (2002) and has published widely on alternative and radical media. He is currently researching the use of the Internet by far-right political groups in the U.K. His next book, *An Alternative Internet*, will be published in 2004.

W. Lance Bennett is professor of political science, Ruddick C. Lawrence Professor of Communication, and director of the Center for Communication and Civic Engagement at the University of Washington. He is also the author and editor of numerous books including, most recently, *Mediated Politics* (co-edited with Robert Entman, 2001).

Rodney Benson is an assistant professor in the Department of Culture and Communication, New York University.

Nick Couldry is senior lecturer in media and communications at the London School of Economics and Political Science, as well as the author of *The Place of Media Power* (2000), *Inside Culture* (2000), and *Media Rituals: A Critical Approach* (2003).

James Curran is professor of communications at Goldsmiths College, London, and the author and editor of many books including, most recently, *De-Westernizing Media Studies* (co-edited with Myung-Jin Park, 2000), *Media and Power* (2002), and *Power Without Responsibility*, 6th ed. (co-authored with Jean Seaton, 2003).

John D. H. Downing is John T. Jones, Jr., Centennial Professor in the Radio-Film-Television Department of the University of Texas at Austin. Beginning in January 2004, he will be director of a new global media studies center at Southern Illinois University, Carbondale. He is author of *Internationalizing Media Theory: Reflections on Russia, Poland and Hungary, 1980–95* (1996), *Radical Media*, 2nd ed. (2001), and, with co-author Charles Husband, *Representing "Race"* (2003).

Larry Gross is director of the Annenberg School of Communication, University of Southern California. His most recent book is *Up From Invisibility: Lesbians, Gay Men, and the Media in America* (2001), and he is co-editor of *Image Ethics in the Digital Age* (2003).

Chin-Chuan Lee is professor of journalism and mass communication at the University of Minnesota, professor of communication at the City University of Hong Kong, and the author of numerous books including, most recently, *Power, Media and Money* (2000), *Global Media Spectacle: News War over Hong Kong* (with J. Chan, Z. Pan, and C. So, 2002), and *Chinese Media, Global Contexts* (2003).

Tamar Liebes is chair of the Department of Communication and Journalism at the Hebrew University of Jerusalem. Her recent books include *American Dreams, Hebrew Subtitles: Globalization from the Receiving End* (2002), *Reporting the Arab-Israeli Conflict: How Hegemony Works* (1997), *Media Ritual and Identity* (co-edited with James Curran, 1998), and *The Export of Meaning* (co-authored with Elihu Katz, 1993).

Merlyna Lim has a degree in architecture, is a doctoral candidate in technology and society studies at the University of Twente, Enschede, the Netherlands, and is a research fellow with the Social Construction of Technology Research Group in Bandung, Indonesia. Her doctoral research explores the sociopolitical dimensions of Internet technology in the Indonesian-global context, with a focus on relationships among the Internet, identity politics, and democratization.

Sharon Ling is a journalist working in Malaysia.

Michael Meadows is associate professor of journalism at Griffith University in Brisbane, having previously worked for ten years as a print and broadcast journalist. He is the author of *Voices in the Wilderness* (2001), which deals with images of Aboriginal people in the Australian media, and *Songlines to Satellites*, co-authored with Helen Molnar, which concerns Indigenous media in Australia, the South Pacific, and Canada (2002).

Christine Morris is Indigenous Research Fellow at the Australian Key Centre for Cultural and Media Policy, Griffith University, Brisbane, Australia.

Andrea L. Press is research professor in and director of media studies at the University of Illinois at Urbana/Champaign. She is the author of *Women Watching Television* (1991) and (with Elizabeth Cole) *Speaking of Abortion* (1999), and editor (with Bruce Williams) of *The Communication Review*. She is currently doing ethnographic research on issues of adolescence and media use.

Terhi Rantanen is director of the MSc Global Media and Communications Programme at the London School of Economics and Political Science. She is also the author of *The Global and the National: Media and Communications in Post-Communist*

Russia (2002, with a Russian edition forthcoming) and *The Globalization of News* (co-edited with O. Boyd-Barrett, 1998, with a Chinese edition published in 2002).

Clemencia Rodriguez is associate professor of communications at Oklahoma University as well as the author of *Fissures in the Mediascape: An International Study of Citizens Media* (2001).

Keyan G. Tomaselli and **Ruth Teer-Tomaselli** are both professors in culture, communication, and media studies at the University of Natal, Durban. They are editors of the book series Critical Studies on African Culture and Media and of *Critical Arts: A Journal of South-North Cultural and Media Studies*. Both worked with *New Nation* during the 1980s while opposing the attack on it analyzed in their chapter.

Elena Vartanova is professor in the Faculty of Journalism at Moscow State University and Deputy Dean for Research. She is the author and editor of many books including *The Finnish Model at the Turn of the Century: Finnish Information Society and Mass Media in a European Perspective* (in Russian 1999) and *Russian Media Challenge,* 2nd ed. (co-edited with K. Nordenstreng and Y. Zassoursky, 2002).

Lennart Weibull is professor of mass media research at the Department of Journalism and Mass Communication, Göteborg University, and co-director of the SOM-Institute, Göteborg University, which is carrying out annual surveys on media and public opinion in Sweden. He is also the author of numerous books and articles on Swedish media history, media structure, and media audience.

Yuezhi Zhao is assistant professor in the School of Communication at Simon Fraser University, Canada, and the author of *Media, Market, and Democracy in China* (1998) and *Sustaining Democracy?* (with Robert A. Hackett, 1998).